BLACK OVER BILL'S MOTHER'S

BY MICHAEL LAYTON & STEPHEN BURROWS

Copyright © 2016 by Michael Layton and Stephen Burrows.

All rights reserved. This book or any portion thereof may not be reproduced or used in any manner whatsoever without the express written permission of the author(s) except for the use of brief quotations in a book review.

This is a work of fiction. Names, characters, businesses, places, events and incidents are either the product of the author's imagination or used in a fictitious manner. Any resemblance to actual persons, living or dead, or actual events is purely coincidental.
(See author's note below)

DEDICATIONS

Michael Layton - To my wife Andry and our families here and in Cyprus. To the police officers and staff in the United Kingdom, who, as part of the 'thin blue line', maintain law and order within our society, and in so doing protect us from anarchy.

Stephen Burrows – To my wife Sue, who suffered the tapping of computer keys at bedtime and when she awoke with admirable stoicism, and my daughters, Hayley and Victoria, for just being wonderful. Finally, to all my colleagues in the Police Service who constantly put themselves at risk to protect the vulnerable and our society.

Published by 'Bostin Books'

First Published: June 2016

Revised: February 2017

Other books by Michael Layton and Stephen Burrows

Joint:

Fiction:

Keep Right On

Non-Fiction:

The Noble Cause.

Walsall's Front Line. (Spring 2017)

By Michael Layton Non-Fiction:

Hunting the Hooligans

Tracking the Hooligans

Police Dog Heroes

Birmingham's Front Line

Violence in the Sun

The Hooligans Are Still Among Us

Author's Note:

'Black Over Bill's Mother's' is a complete story in its own right. It also has a sequel, 'Keep Right On,' which is set within the timeline of 'Black Over Bill's Mother's'. A number of characters appear in both books, and for those reading 'Keep Right On' first, previous events relating to joint characters are only alluded to, so as not to spoil the enjoyment of 'Black Over Bill's Mother's' by revealing the plot.

'Black Over Bill's Mother's' contains a number of true historical events, Real persons are mentioned, and every effort has been made to relate events and their part in them impartially and with accuracy. All of the plot characters are fictional.

Chapter List

Prologue: The Funeral

Chapter One: 'Tonight We Love'

Chapter Two: 'No Love, No Nothin'

Chapter Three: 'Prisoner Of Love'

Chapter Four: 'An Apple Blossom Wedding'

Chapter Five: 'I Love You So Much It Hurts'

Chapter Six: 'Blowing Wild'

Chapter Seven: 'Crazy Man Crazy'

Chapter Eight: 'Shake A Hand'

Chapter Nine: 'Wild Horses'

Chapter Ten: 'Money Honey'

Chapter Eleven: 'Rags To Riches'

Chapter Twelve: 'Shake, Rattle & Roll'

Chapter Thirteen: 'Tutti Frutti'

Chapter Fourteen: 'Mack The Knife'

Chapter Fifteen: 'Love Is A Many Splendoured Thing'

Chapter Sixteen: 'All Shook Up'

Chapter Seventeen: 'Remember You're Mine'

Chapter Eighteen: 'He's Got The Whole World In His Hands'

Chapter Nineteen: 'Who's Sorry Now?'

Chapter Twenty: 'You Are My Destiny'

Chapter Twenty One: 'Rumble'

Chapter Twenty Two: 'Broken Hearted Melody'

Chapter Twenty Three: 'Cradle Of Love'

Chapter Twenty Four: 'Working For The Man'

Chapter Twenty Five: 'Leader Of The Pack'

Chapter Twenty Six: 'From A Jack To A King'

Chapter Twenty Seven: 'All You Need Is Love'

Chapter Twenty Eight: 'The Mighty Quinn'

Chapter Twenty Nine: 'With A Little Help From My Friends'

Chapter Thirty: 'Street Fighting Man'

Chapter Thirty One" 'Proud Mary'

Chapter Thirty Two: 'Come Together'

Chapter Thirty Three: 'He's Gonna Step On You Again'

Chapter Thirty Four: 'Back Stabbers'

Chapter Thirty Five: 'I Gotcha'

Chapter Thirty Six: 'The First Time Ever I Saw Your Face'

Chapter Thirty Seven: 'For The Love Of Money'

Chapter Thirty Eight. 'Behind Closed Doors'

Chapter Thirty Nine: 'This Town Ain't Big Enough For The Both Of Us'

Chapter Forty: 'Waterloo'

Chapter Forty One: 'Takin Care Of Business'

Chapter Forty Two: 'Only Women Bleed'

Chapter Forty Three: 'Pick Up The Pieces'

Epilogue

Prologue: The Funeral

2004

His pupils flickered in the darkness, as the effects of the heroin started to wear off and he hovered in and out of consciousness. He struggled to breathe and his head throbbed as he tried in vain to wake up from one hell, knowing instinctively that another one waited for him. *'Just where the fuck am I?'* His brain demanded to know as his body suddenly became tense and alert.

Drenched in cold sweat and alone he tried to find a way through the claustrophobic mists consuming his mind and body.

'Hands and feet tied tightly, with a gag in his dry mouth, he struggled vainly to loosen his bonds, in the confined space which had become his prison, and he knew would become his final resting place.

The space had no specific shape to it; sometimes it was a cell, sometimes a locked cupboard, sometimes it could even be a small cabin on a ship, or simply a hood placed over his head which denied him light and oxygen. Lately, increasingly, this time, it was a coffin - the lid closed and screwed down just inches from his face. He could hear the clods of earth landing on the lid as they began to fill the grave in. He swore 'When I get out of this I am going to burn them all. I am The President and no-one messes with me.'

No-one could hear him. He could shout and bang on the inside of the lid, but the result was always the same.

He always took time to die – plenty of time for him to reflect before he lapsed into delirium and coma - plenty of time for his mood to change from anger to absolute terror. Over the centuries many 'martyrs' had been buried alive as a consequence of their determination to stay true to their religion and values. He was no martyr, had no true values, nothing now to mark him out as belonging to anything - as once belonging to something important.

His mind roved to another plac,e and in the darkness stood the Cop holding a cell door open and waving him in. He didn't want to go in, knew the terror that awaited him in there, but it was a dream and there was no escape.

Banging on the door, punching the walls, banging on the door again. No-one came. He was buried alive and no-one would come.

Another shift of focus, and now he was looking into the muzzle of a gun held by a black hand. He watched fascinated as the finger tightened on the trigger.

He jerked upright, and was violently sick into the bowl that lay conveniently by his bedside, as he scratched compulsively and picked at the sores on his arms.

The dreams would return, they came most nights these days. There would not be an end to his agony whilst he lived. He laughed to himself – at himself, '*a martyr with a cross to bear,*' he thought, '*the fucking 'General' would have loved to see me now*'.

Today however, he needed to focus as he dragged his body out of bed and to the toilet.

Today there was something he must do, something to finish. Perhaps it would help and there would be no dream tonight.

He was not a great fan of funerals but this was a moment that he felt he had to share with a man whom he had come to know well, a man he had hated. The suit was ill-fitting, and the black tie uncomfortably tight, but he could hardly wear his old uniform. An untidy beard and glasses completed a false image of normality.

Driving a car today - no point in drawing attention. He left it some distance from the crematorium and walked along the narrow winding road between the headstones and trappings of death. The cortege arrived just as he reached the chapel where a lone officer in full uniform, and wearing white gloves, saluted the coffin as it was carried inside. On top of the coffin was draped the flag, together with his enemy's cap, silver braid signifying his rank, and brown gloves.

Directly behind walked the lonely figure of the mourning wife dressed in black and supported by another female that he knew, who stood proud and composed. Sandra had determined that for this day only she would be there for the woman who had occupied the position that she might well have taken herself in another life. She was suntanned from her years abroad and still attractive.

Sandra's presence unsettled him. He had not anticipated this scenario. Despite his change in appearance he would need to be careful. Today was not a day to be rising from the dead – even if it was an apt location.

Dutiful to the end, the wife played her part with the skills of a classic actor. She shed just enough tears, and felt safe in the knowledge that within six months she would be able to move in with the neighbour with whom she had been having an affair for more than thirty years. At least she would be able to find some warmth in her last few years.

Whilst the man in the coffin had lived, and loved the job, he had never been able to find the real love of a woman. His widow by contrast had found hope and happiness just ten doors away.

The onlooker reflected that the ceremony was not much different in style to some of the paramilitary funerals he had witnessed in Northern Ireland; the only difference being that for this one there would be no volley of pistol shots at the end.

It was a good turn out, with a great deal of hand-shaking and warm greetings from old comrades, presided over by some shiny young boss who had been sent to represent the organisation and looked anxious to get to his next appointment.

The onlooker deliberately stood at the back, the last thing that he wanted to do was to attract attention. Some specially chosen hymns filled the room with the sadness that only music can bring. The man shook his head. There was no hymn that could do justice to the bastard in the coffin. There was only one direction for him, and if it existed, the onlooker knew he was going there too - after all he was already in a personal hell whilst still alive.

One of the old colleagues read the eulogy and the vicar concluded with some pointless trivia whilst watching the clock to make sure that they didn't run over the allotted thirty minutes.

At the end of the service, to the tune of 'Amazing Grace,' the dead hero's coffin was carried from the chapel to the plot where others awaited him in the soil. The procession followed on foot whilst the onlooker remained firmly at the rear.

He stood at the back, watching men who for the most part had been his opponents for many years, filing slowly past the grave. Some stopped to throw a handful of soil onto the coffin; whilst others simply paused for a moment. Comrades- in-arms, they had stood together and sorted some 'nasty bastards' during their time.

As people started to melt away, to make their way to the wake, the man approached the open grave and took the signet ring from his pocket. The engraved letters 'BS' still remained and for a moment in time the man was alone with his thoughts as he reflected on what he had done in the name of those initials and the pain that this circlet represented.

He picked up a piece of clay from the mound of soil, pressed the ring into it, and threw it down into the hole. He could only hope that tonight's dream would be less painful.

He walked slowly away – his nose running constantly. He could do with another fix, a drink, or both. Maybe he would decide what to do with the rest of his life after today, now that the last full stop had been added to the events that had caused his sorry condition. It was time to clean himself up.

In the distance Sandra turned for one last look, as she was about to enter one of the waiting black limousines. She saw a solitary figure bent over the grave and for a fleeting moment something familiar about the man's build registered in her brain and for some inexplicable reason the tune to 'Zorbas Dance.'

'Not a day for Greek music,' she mused, *'time to get back to the sun.'*

Chapter One: 'Tonight We Love'

(Freddy Martin)

1942

Mary Docker had decided that she was going to die - and she was not going to waste the time she had left. From the moment she could walk and talk she had been precocious and rebellious, straining at the standards imposed by her parents - decent, working people whose front step was always clean and buffed.

Now those parents were gone, leaving their nineteen-year-old daughter alone to look after her fourteen-year-old brother Charlie.

The German bombers had done for them both - pounding Birmingham on an endless November night of bombing. An incendiary had landed near to their Anderson Shelter, blowing the doorway in where they were sat playing cards.

Mary had been at a friend's house in the next street when the sirens sounded and hadn't had time to get home. Whilst she sheltered with her friend, fate had decided that the bombs would miss Lily's house and make Mary an orphan instead.

Charlie had survived by a miracle; he had heard the whistle of the bomb growing louder and had been small, and athletic enough to launch himself under the metal bunk bed. It had saved his life and the blast left him unscathed bar some temporary deafness.

That had been two years ago, and the Battle of Britain, as they were calling it, had been won that year. Mary was an intelligent and capable girl and had got on with it, as everyone had to. Everyone knew someone who had lost a loved-one, either to bombs, or fighting in the air, on the sea, or in foreign lands. The British had been backed against the wall on their little island but Hitler had got a bloody nose from the RAF and no invasion had come.Matters were not going well elsewhere though, hence her pessimism.

The Japs had taken Singapore earlier in the year, taking thousands of men and women prisoners. The Germans had stormed across Russia, although it looked as if they had been temporarily halted at Stalingrad. Locals were saying that The Allies were taking 'a good bell oiling' everywhere and it was only a matter a time before Hitler's attention returned to invading Britain. Mary, with her youthful zeal, had already decided that she would die a heroine's death by killing some Nazis rather than be enslaved by them. She had seen the newsreels; she knew what that would mean.

Along with her parents, she had also lost another love to the war, her first and only love.

His name was Richard Burns. They had met at school. He was three years older and those extra years made him dazzling in her eyes. They had been inseparable until war came and Richard had joined up and gone to fight. The odd letter had got through, heavily censored.

She thought he was somewhere in the Far East, but there was never enough detail to know what he was doing. There hadn't been a letter for a while now though, and the news from Singapore had only served to diminish her hopes.

She was not sure if he was dead, captured and unable to write, or still fighting somewhere. The biggest worry though, was the insidious worm of doubt that whispered in her ear, '*he has moved on from you, there will have been other women, exotic women, and you are just too ordinary.*' Had his eyes been opened to wider possibilities? Had he decided that an eighteen-year-old school sweetheart from Birmingham was just a beginning, not an end?

His parents had no news either - besides they disapproved of her, not good enough for their precious boy. Her family was much poorer, her father had been a manual worker, whereas Richard's was a manager, His mother had pretensions and an unwavering belief that her only son was destined for greatness of some kind.

They hadn't had sex before he went. He wanted to of course, but she had been sixteen when he left, swayed by the influence and attitudes of her parents, and a little bit scared too. 1940 seemed a lifetime away now though, and her thoughts had turned more and more to what she wanted to do before she died, and in her young mind her planning horizon ended at age twenty-one.

Losing her virginity was top of the list and her memory of, and belief in Richard had faded, to the point where he had dropped down the order of suitable men. Actually, she didn't want a suitable man. All around her civilisation seemed to be crumbling, and she intended to make a statement - do something reckless, and with complete abandonment – she wanted to make love to a stranger.

So here she was with Lily at this dance in the church hall, all made up in the latest 'fashion', - cooked beetroot juice for lipstick, soot for eye make-up, and stocking seams painted on slim long legs with gravy browning.

Mary was a looker, 5'6" tall and slim with a petite waist. She had shoulder-length dark hair that was sometimes tied up, but tonight it hung free – as free as she intended to be. When Mary smiled she conveyed warmth and openness. With a combination of green 'come to bed' eyes she simply radiated. The figure- hugging blouse and knee-length skirt completed the picture.

She scanned the hall, assessing the likely candidates. All the younger men were in uniform, RAF, Navy, Army. The RAF ones looked smart but they were all cast into the shadows by the dazzling Yanks.

They had started to arrive that year. At first in dribs and drabs from Ireland, but as America responded to Pearl Harbour the trickle had become a flow and now there were thousands billeted around the country with their flashy uniforms, sprawling accents, and endless supplies of gum and stockings.

There was something else though, something new, something fascinating. Some of them were Negroes. They were attractive, thrilling, a novelty – and as the local band played 'We'll Meet Again', she caught glimpses of one in particular through the smoky haze of the crowded dance-floor.

Virgil Halloran loved to fight. He would fight anyone, anywhere, and he knew that he was going to enjoy this war – the perfect opportunity in which to engage in his favourite sport.

As a kid in 'The South' he had stood up to the bullies and racists and won. He learnt to enjoy it. He definitely was an 'uppity nigger' who didn't know his place and had the knocks to prove it. One night a group of whites had beaten the crap out of him to put him in his place. He had been twelve-years-old and had never forgotten his anger and helplessness as he lay on the ground being kicked.

He had vowed never to let a white man do that to him again. He had learnt to fight. Firstly with his peers, and then he had been drawn towards boxing. Nature had helped. He had grown big quickly and worked hard to maximise the gifts of his physique. As a teenager he had boxed and trained, trained and boxed, and by eighteen years of age he had a good reputation. He could have had a future in the ring but wanted more than boxing could offer.

Virgil had found that he enjoyed violence. He enjoyed the feeling of power as he inflicted pain, the feeling of mastery and the submission of another. He had looked around and found the Army. He liked the thought of taking his trade to another level and had joined up.

Now, at twenty-three-years of age, he was Sergeant Halloran of the US Marines, a 6'2" athlete, with a square jaw that could absorb a good punch, and fists that could deal out a better one. He was proud of who he was, and what he had done, and no-one gave him any shit anymore.

Soon he was going to fight the Germans, and this time he was allowed to follow his aggression to its ultimate conclusion, taking a life – and even better, a Nazi or a Jap one.

He had watched and waited in frustration as the war started

and America stood by. Now, after the yellow bastard's cowardly attack at Pearl Harbour he wanted to kill something real bad.

1942, and here he was in England, billeted just outside Birmingham. The English had been through the mill and the Yanks had found to their delight that they were an irresistible lure to British women, starved of food, love, and men.

When the end of the world was happening, and death lurked nearby, boundaries were crossed and morals flung aside by both sexes. Virgil couldn't believe his luck.

A good example was this dance. There were lots of broads here, lots of pretty ones too, and more than one of them trying to catch his eye. *'Look at that one over there'*, pretty, great figure, looking at him in a very direct way. Her friend was rattling away to her but not sending out the same signals.

He started to make his way around the dance floor. He could feel her gaze and she was still there when he reached the other side.

"Hey there beautiful, how come you're not dancing?" he asked casually. She seemed to look at him for a long time before replying, as if weighing something up in her mind.

The Birmingham accent twanged out, "Well, firstly no-one's asked me, and secondly I don't just dance with anyone, what do you think I am?"

Her friend giggled, "He thinks you're from round the back of Rackham's Mary." She laughed too, knowing that the Yank wouldn't have a clue that the saying related to an ancient red light area in

Birmingham. He liked the way her head tilted up, her confidence, her freshness. "Get you a drink?" he asked. "Definitely, I'll have half of beer," responded Mary, dropping both the 'h's' as Brummies do.

Virgil hadn't got a clue what that meant either apart from beer, but he understood the physical language she was talking. She said something about him having a *'bob on hisself'* to her friend, who giggled and walked off to talk with some other girls, whilst she went and sat at a nearby table. There was plenty of liquor at these dances if you had money and he quickly returned to her with a beer.

They were soon deep in conversation, attraction bridging the difficulties of accent. His Southern drawl fascinated her. His physical presence attracted her. She could feel the eyes of others on her, a white girl with a Negro – and that thrilled her, appealed to the wayward streak within her.

Virgil quietly breathed thanks for the circumstances that allowed these wartime dance-hall games to breach all the barriers of his old life.

They danced, and danced again. The night wore on and they were not alone. Around them others met and danced, sometimes disappearing for a while from the hall.

"Do you want to go somewhere more private honey?" he finally asked.

She considered the options whilst they danced. She knew that the moment of truth had been reached. Adulthood lay a daring walk across the dance-floor and through those battered church hall doors.

She glanced across at Lily and saw that she was deep in conversation with a good looking RAF man, hanging onto his every word. Anyway they had agreed, with much giggling, that tonight might be the one for both of them. They had agreed to watch out for each other but not get in the way if fate, in the form of a suitable man, manifested itself.

Her decision was easy really. She had already reached it over the previous months and years of privation and struggle. She wanted some fun, some experiences, some adventure; the war had shattered the old conventions and restrictions along with taking her family and boyfriend.

Mary looked him in the eyes, "Yea, I'm sick of everyone watching us. Let's go."

They actually left separately - they would have been pushing their luck to walk out hand in hand.

They met outside. The November air was bitter cold and their hot breath created small clouds of steam. She had retrieved her coat on the way out but still shivered. He seemed impervious and produced an Army greatcoat that he draped around her shoulders.

In the dark, behind the hall, there were a few other couples in clinches. They found a dark doorway. He suddenly seemed unsure.

"Are you okay with this?" he asked tentatively. "Just kiss me and I'll let you know," Mary replied.

The first one was gentle and reassuring. Soon the air did not seem so cold. He was pressed against her with the greatcoat around both of them, her back against the wall. She could feel his hardness pressed against her now. Their breath grew hotter as his hands ran down her back and pulled her pelvis against him.

Suddenly she started to feel that this was going far, too fast, but he was so strong and his urgency increased. His right hand was on her breast now and he was teasing the nipple erect through her dress. He began to fumble with the buttons on the front and then he had her breast cupped inside her bra and was rubbing. His other hand began to stroke the inside of her thigh, gradually climbing and lifting her dress with it.

He reached between her legs and began to rub the damp patch there. She gasped and couldn't stop her body moving against his hand. His other hand left her breast and then he pulled her knickers down. She stepped out of them and his fingers were inside her.

Now that it was happening she was suddenly conscious that it was madness. He was fumbling with his trousers now,

"No, I ain't ready, stop!" Mary insisted.

Virgil had passed the point of no return, "It's too late for that sister." He held her firmly.

He pulled her thighs apart. She felt a moment of pain then he was inside her thrusting, ramming her back against the wall. She beat her hands weakly against his back but he was unstoppable now. The pace of his lunges into her increased and she felt the warmth as he spurted his lust.

"There now, wasn't so bad eh?" said a satisfied Virgil, looking to recover the situation.

Mary said nothing – just hung between him and the wall. She could feel his seed running down her leg, She was a fool to have done this - a young fool with stupid romantic notions of adventure and rebellion. She felt soiled, dirty and diminished - used. She needed to get away.

Virgil was out of her now and buttoning his trousers up. She hurriedly pulled her knickers up and put her dress straight. She could feel emotions welling up inside her and then she was crying. She broke free of him and ran, leaving him in the dark doorway with a look of surprise on his face.

Back home there was no-one to either comfort or reprimand her. She washed whilst tears turned her eyes red until she could cry no more. She began to think. *'Who had seen her?'* A few had seen her go outside, but apart from Lily they were strangers. The other couples in the darkness had their own secrets and none of them would have taken any notice of what had happened in that doorway.

She knew that she would never see the soldier again, to him she was just a golden memory of England and he would soon be sent to do his killing, or be killed. She would erase this episode and start again. She would wait for Richard and he would never know.

Lily arrived early the next morning as usual. They walked through the bomb- shattered streets to the stop where they caught the bus to the munitions factory. She was avid for every detail and jealous, her evening had ended in disappointment. Mary wished now that she hadn't been so lucky.

As they got off the bus she tugged at Lily and nodded at the lowering sky, "Come on, we need to leg it - its bloody black over Bill's Mother's."

There was a big storm on its way.

Chapter Two: 'No Love, No Nothin'

(Johnny Long)

1943

August 1943, and the tide of war had changed. The German Army had wilted and dissolved at Stalingrad. The Russians were rampaging forward. Italy was on the verge of defeat. Mussolini had been deposed. British troops had landed on Sicily. In the Far East the Japanese were fighting a bloody retreat, but retreat it was.

Now her impetuous act of last year seemed so foolish. Still no word from Richard though and, even if she had known where he was, she would not have been able to bring herself to write.

She knew from the midwife's face that there was something wrong. Barely conscious, and sweating from the exertions of birth, she had still been able to register a flicker of something pass across that matronly face, followed by the comment, "Well I'll go to the foot of our stairs," as she exchanged glances with her equally matronly colleague.

Mary had been confined and given birth at home with two midwives in attendance. Charlie was hovering about downstairs being busily useless. She could hear infant cries so it was alive at least, but what if it was defective in some way, how could she cope with that on top of everything else?

"What's up?" She almost whispered. "There's nothing actually wrong bab," came the response. Mary persevered, "I saw you look surprised, or shocked. What's wrong? I bet you've seen it all, so what is it?"The midwife gave her a long and searching look while Mary's heart beat a little tattoo.

"I'm just concerned for you. You're a young girl alone and you ain't going to have an easy time of it," said the midwife.

"I know people will judge me but I can live with it, sod them." Mary fired back.

"Yes, well that's the first reason. This is your first time but you must have felt the second kid come?" The midwife moved in closer to grasp Mary's hand.

Mary went into shock."All I felt was the unbelievable pain. I didn't really know what was going on." "You've had twins, but the second one was much smaller than the first." The midwife was inching the conversation towards the truth.Mary's mind raced, *'Two babies, how was she going to cope?'*

She had left the armaments factory when she became too big to continue and had been relying on Charlie, who had been bringing in some money, working for a shady local character who she suspected of being part of the black market. They had managed to keep the house running between them but she couldn't expect a young lad to keep her and two kids.

The midwife hesitantly began again, "That ain't all. Can I ask you, was the father coloured?"

Mary's heart sank. Here it came, the moment she had been dreading, the final damnation. The irony was exquisite. Her wish for freedom and adventure – to have a life before life ended, had chained her via a grubby five-minute act in a doorway.

She was not going to go through the rest of her life shamed and apologising. She lifted her head defiantly and looked the midwife in the eye, "Yea, Yank serviceman."

"Well you're certainly not the first, and you won't be the last, but it's just such a shame. You're going to have to live with this every minute of every day for the rest of your life." She began to busy herself putting her instruments; such as they were, away.

"I suppose the babbies are half-caste"? Mary enquired.

"Not exactly, in fact bab it's a small miracle, something I've heard about but never seen before," came the response.

Hope suddenly sprang in Mary's beating breast, "Are they white - but no, that can't be right or you wouldn't have asked – what miracle?"

It was time for the midwife to tell it how it was, "The first baby, the big one, is black, not half-caste; the second is as white as they come. That's what surprised me."

Mary shook her head in disbelief, "How can that happen?"

"I don't know, way beyond me knowledge bab, but as I said I've heard of it. But they're both healthy and perfect, the second one is small but a fighter, and I think they'll both be okay, they're a couple of bostin babbies," the midwife said soothingly.

She could hear the babies mewling now, and then there was a lustier cry.

"That's the big one, he's a strong one, would you like to hold them dear?" enquired the other midwife, keen to get the bonding process underway, and ever conscious that they had other visits to make.

Mary nodded, her mind still whirling with the implications of the midwife's revelations.

The babies lay on her chest. They both stopped crying the moment they felt the warmth of her body. She looked down at their perfect faces, *'I'll protect you.'* she thought, *'I had despaired, felt dirty and lost, but you are so beautiful and innocent.'* She marveled that the grubby thrustings in that doorway had been transformed into this wonder of life.

***

It had been a desperate time since the birth. She had experienced the full range of human reaction. She had been shunned and abused, but had also received unexpected kindness from others.

They had survived for three reasons: Her parent's house still stood and it belonged to Charlie and Mary. No rent to pay.

Charlie, annealed by the war and loss - street wise beyond his years, had scraped together the materials to repair the bomb damage. His 'connections' meant he had been able to acquire necessities beyond the ration books, often in lieu of any money for himself.

Finally Lily Rossiter, and her family had been unbelievable, especially Lily's mother Alice, who had embraced the twins as if they were her own. Her unstinting help had enabled Mary to work part-time and bring in some money. The Government had introduced compulsory part-time working for women to assist the war effort so there was no shortage of employment.

She hadn't dared approach Richard's parents. She had seen them one day whilst out with the children in a pram. They had made clear their contempt for her, with hard stares, shaking of heads, and then crossed the street to avoid speaking to her.

Mary was under no illusions that her delicate structure of support could not continue for the long term. The war would end. People would stop pulling together. The old order would re-assert itself and she would be beyond the pale with her black and white babies born out of wedlock. 'Aunty' Alice was getting older and there was no telling how her husband would react when, and if, he returned from the war, but Mary could hazard a pretty good guess. Her memory of Lily's father Fred was of a rather stern, straight-laced character who was unlikely to embrace bastard children - and coloured ones at that.

Then there was Charlie. He had done far more than she deserved, but he was growing up fast. She couldn't expect him to carry on caring for her and her mistakes. It just wasn't fair. He would have his own life to lead and if the war lasted he would be off to join it when he reached eighteen. She could tell that he was already beginning to yearn to go and fight but she hoped it would all end before then.

No, she had to have a plan. She had briefly considered prostitution but had clinically dismissed it. Fate had punished her for that one night of madness and she had no wish to tempt it, or sell what was left of her pride and self-belief. She still wanted some sort of a life for herself and the twins.

It was a bitter position that she found herself in. She loved her boys but they had trapped her. All her hopes and ambitions were now subjugated to their needs. She could see no freedom or self-fulfillment until she was old. She had put such fancies out of her mind but they lurked deep inside, mocking her for that stupid juvenile night of madness.

Richard was on her mind though, *'was he alive or dead? If alive, did he occasionally think of the girl he had left behind? If he came back what could she say to him? How could she possibly hope he might still want her with another man's children in tow?'* She couldn't even begin to hope that her salvation lay in that direction.

There would be other men though, and she was still pretty and had managed to get her figure back to its previous petite state. She had seen the older ones looking at her appraisingly sometimes. She had no illusions, she was a 'spoilt' woman but that clearly made her attractive to some. They were all old, and mostly married, but the boys would come home sometime, *'Surely there would be someone who would want me?'*

It wasn't much of a plan, or much of a future, but it was the only one she had, provided she survived the war.

Chapter Three: 'Prisoner Of Love'

(Perry Como)

1946

1946 dawned cold and bleak. The war had begun to recede into memory. Hitler was dead and moldering. The Nazis were destroyed along with Germany. VE Day had come and gone and Churchill had proclaimed that an Iron Curtain had come down, but here she was, still alone in the house with her boys.

Mr. Rossiter had come home, and as predicted Alice's help had been removed by degrees. Lots of soldiers had returned and taken the jobs, including hers. Some men had shown an interest but they were offering to look after her for sex, or for her to act as a servant, and she had drawn away from each of them as their terms became clearer.

The boys were growing fast. Joe, the black one, was large-boned and bodied. She recognised the father in him, although her memory was becoming clouded by time and her mind's gradual erasure of that night. Rob was much smaller and lighter with blue eyes and straw-coloured hair. He was a happy-go-lucky little boy with a ready smile and chuckle. Joe by contrast seemed dour and serious as if he already knew what life had in store for him. There was no doubt though that Joe adored his pale sibling, following him everywhere. Already the bond between them was strong and Rob seemed to instinctively know that the lottery of birth had dealt him a loyal protector and comrade in mischief.

By the time summer arrived her situation was becoming desperate. Charlie was still helping but he had a girl now and she knew that she was losing him. He was also a living embodiment of her guilt, he too was being punished for her sins and though he never complained, his presence, and her reliance upon him, was a constant reminder and reproach. She knew that he wanted to sell the house and move on but he didn't dare raise the issue.

Then one day there was a rap on the doorknocker and there stood a ghost. He was still thin and emaciated, but that wasn't it. He had a hideous scar across his face from temple to chin with a deep cleft where his nose looked as if it had been cut in half and healed badly, but even that wasn't it. It was his eyes, stranger's eyes. She could only imagine what those eyes had seen, but whatever it was they were now disquieting where once they had twinkled merrily. There was no innocence left in that face, those eyes,

"Hello Mary, how you doing, you can take that shocked look off your fizzog, I know I ain't no oil painting?" Richard said quietly.

Richard's voice was deeper than she remembered and caught every so often, as if holding back emotion.

"Richard, my God, what happened to you? You stopped writing and I thought you was dead. When you didn't come back with the other soldiers I was sure."

A bitter laugh escaped his mouth, "You've got a face as long as Livery Street – look like you've seen a ghost. Not a pretty sight am I?" He rubbed the scar, "Jap officer's sword did this - I dared answer him back, the bastard. Nearly killed me. I didn't forget you though, in fact I thought about you all the time when I was in the camp being tortured and starved, and in the military hospital afterwards. Plenty of time to think and plan, but now I hear you forgot me pretty quick. It took mom and dad a few months to decide to write me in case it finished me off in the hospital."

She didn't know what to say, how to respond. Her needs and frustrations of four years previously were petty and irrelevant in the shadow of that face. She quaked before its accusing stare and began to babble inanely,"I...I thought you wasn't coming back. I thought you'd forgotten me. I thought I was going to die after me mom and dad got bombed and I wanted to be loved by at least one person before I did." The words came out of Mary's mouth lamely.

"So you fucked the first nigger you could find," snapped Richard, flecks of spit coming from his mouth as his fury mounted.

She had no answer and the tears began to well up. Mary persisted, "Why are you here if you hate me so much?'Richard gathered himself, "There ain't much distance between love and hate Mary. I had you on a pedestal for three years in that camp and now I find that you couldn't wait to jump off it! Betrayed me, and with a coon of all people. That's hard to take. The Japs treated us like vermin, but the thought of you kept me going. How do you think I felt when me mom wrote me about you? I needed to see for myself, see if there was anything left of the girl I once loved."

So here it was. The final act of punishment for her transgression, the man she had loved, and who had loved her, stood before her, maimed and hating her, and he had the best of reasons.

"I need to go and check the twins are okay. I suppose its goodbye then?" Mary tried to end the pain of the situation.

"I ain't going yet, I ain't finished. I'll come in and we can sort it out inside rather than on the doorstep. I think I deserve that much at least."

Richard brushed past her into the hallway without waiting for a response, "I hear Charlie is still about?"

"Yes, he's been wonderful, without him I dunno what we'd have done." Mary tried to gather herself but she had been rocked, and the situation was moving faster than her startled wits could match.

"But he won't want to keep you, and your two bastards, for the rest of his life will he?" Richard retorted.

God, he had so much anger inside him, he was spitting the words out at her – she could almost feel the impact of them physically, "No, Charlie has a girl now and I think it's serious."

"Where is he today?" Richard asked innocuously.

"He's had to go into town to work, then he's going out with his girl. He won't be back till late."

The sound of the boys came from the front room. As she walked towards the room he followed her, shutting the front door behind him.

They had been colouring pictures, but a squabble had resulted in a wrestling match and Joe was sat on top of Rob. He always won, but she admired the fact that Rob never gave up trying to beat his bigger sibling. There was never any real anger in their fighting though. Already she knew they shared a bond that was somehow beyond her, one that she would never be able to penetrate.

They stopped wrestling as she entered the room and looked at Richard quizzically.

Mary chided, "Rob, Joe, stop that argy-bargy now. This is Richard, a friend of mommy's. He's been away fighting the war but now he's come home."

Joe, always the confident one, got straight to the heart of the matter from his point of view, "What's that on your face, it scares me?"

For a second she saw emotion flash across Richard's face then it was gone, "A bad man did it to me."

"Why, were you naughty?" enquired Rob.

"Oh yeah very, and this is what happens to naughty boys." He pointed to the scar. "So you two are gonna be good now and play quietly while I go and have a nice cup of tea with your mom."

They looked at Mary doubtfully.

"Yeah that's right, you stay here and play nicely while Mummy as a chat with Richard. If you're good I'll bring you back a jam piece each," soothed Mary. The twins resumed their game, Richard already forgotten for the bribe of a jam sandwich.

Mary turned to Richard, "Let's go in the kitchen and I'll pop the kettle on. They'll be okay for a bit and we can talk if that's what you want to do."

They left the boys and she closed the door to the room so that they wouldn't wander out. She didn't want them hearing or seeing the next conversation.

The kitchen was at the other end of the hallway. It was a big terraced house with a 'best' front room, a middle room they used for living, and big kitchen where they ate. The kitchen led into a washroom with a Belfast sink and a mangle.

She entered the kitchen and turned to ask him how he wanted his tea. She was sent reeling as he backhanded her across the face. His face was contorted with anger, twisting the scar into a new horror, "that's for fucking cheating on me!"

She was too shocked to react. Before she could say anything he was on her, forcing her backwards onto the kitchen table. For some reason the first thought in her mind was relief that the table was empty so nothing would be broken.

He held her down with body weight, his hand across her mouth.

"Now I'm gonna have what you should've kept for me. You ain't going to scream are you because if you do I'll hit you again and you won't want to upset them brats will you?" Richard spat the words out.

She nodded and he slowly removed his hand. She was broken and spoiled anyway so what did this matter? Anyway, she had always known in her heart that punishment was due and she had been waiting for it. Perhaps it would bring some closure so she could get on with loving her boys without guilt.

"Once we're done I'm going to make an honest woman of you. On my terms - but I don't think you have a choice any how." Richard stated in a matter-of-fact tone.

She shut her eyes and closed her mind while he fucked her. He didn't kiss her; it wasn't an act of love. It was retribution, an outpouring of bitterness and anger.

He finished, "Right, clean yourself up and I'll have that cuppa now."

Numb, she went into the washroom, performed a perfunctory toilet, and rearranged her clothing.

They sat in the kitchen over cups of tea like a married couple. It was so tragic it was almost funny, *'What a great life I'm having'* she pondered.

All her dreams, her romantic notions had come to this. Two acts of 'love', one just minutes against a wall that had ruined her, the second a rape that had broken her.

Now he was talking again and his words began to penetrate her thoughts. "....I learnt a lot in that camp about human nature, about survival, about the cheapness of life. I lost any chance of a woman wanting me to a little yellow bastard with a sword. He did it for fun - enjoyed it. I coped and survived by realising what the world is really like. I grew up. I suppose in your own way you did too, so

I'm gonna make you a business proposition."

She could see something of the old Richard in there, buried, but this was another person speaking.

He went on, "I'm a realist now as I said. No woman is going to want to have this face near her, at least none that I would want. You on the other hand are a good looking woman, but no man is ever going to want you with them two bastards, specially the sambo one, he'll be your badge of shame, for all to see, forever. No, the best you can expect is to sell yourself, or be a kept woman, or you'll starve, and your kids with you."

She wondered how he could so unerringly pinpoint her weaknesses and dilemma, but realized he had been brooding and planning for weeks, maybe months, *'When had his mother written to him in that hospital?'* They had been so close in those innocent days - so recent, yet a lifetime away for both of them.

"Here it is then," he continued, "I'll marry you and take in those brats. I'll provide for you and them though fuck knows why I should. The Japs used to bayonet the babbies, they didn't want anyone coming after them for revenge years later, maybe they were right," he mused, then continued.

"In return you'll look after me and love me as best you can. That's the deal. Up to you, but I don't really think you've much choice and I think you owe it to Charlie to let him get on with his life. On the subject of Charlie, you'll sell this house and give him half the money so he can go and marry his girl if that's what he wants. That's fair and I fought for fairness although life hasn't been fair to me. I get the other half of the money when we marry. I'll use it for a house for us, and it gets Charlie out of the way so it suits me. Take a minute to think it over while I drink my tea."

Before he had drained his cup she took the deal - there really was no choice.

Chapter Four: 'An Apple Blossom Wedding'

(Sammy Kaye)

1947

To the outside world it must have looked like a fairy-tale come true. The return of the wounded war-hero. A beautiful bride waiting faithfully to marry and care for him. The rehabilitation of the fallen girl into a respectable woman – perfect.

Whilst the twins were still the subjects of unwanted stares in the street, it seemed that many began to accept her collapse from grace as a product of the war; it's collective madness, and the death of her parents.

1947 witnessed record divorce rates as marriages made in haste were repented at leisure, and thousands of women left to join their GI husbands in America. She was not alone in having succumbed to a momentary aberration with disproportionate consequences.

Mary encouraged and built this veneer around her relationship with Richard. Sometimes she allowed herself to be deluded into pretending it was the truth, but those moments of fantasy decreased and eventually tailed off, as the reality of her life with her 'hero' pervaded and eventually encompassed her.

In the beginning it had been better than she expected. Richard was true to his word and had even insisted upon a period of some months 'engagement' to preserve appearances. Of course it suited him to appear magnanimous in accepting the tainted package of Mary and the twins. He was now a hero twice over, once for war, and once for love. A saint who had redeemed his sweetheart and would provide a home and father for her bastards, and one a truly black sheep at that!

After that first rape he had behaved with perfect decorum towards her, as if the act of brutality had drained the pent up anger and hurt from him. He played the part of polite fiancée to perfection, only having the physical contact expected of a young couple awaiting marriage. He had not asked to stay, to sleep with, or to have sex with her. He carried on living with his parents, the prodigal son had returned.

Mary thought that Charlie, who knew her better than anyone, had some intuition that all was not as perfect as it seemed, but he had his girl, Vivian, and a life to lead that had been put on hold by Mary's needs and his brotherly duty to help her.

It was her turn to make sacrifices for him now, to let him follow his own path, so she actively encouraged the 'romantic' view of her situation in Charlie, and anyone else that may have taken her side, such as Lily.

She was building a prison for herself, she knew, as certainly as if the walls were bricks and mortar. In fact these invisible walls of belief in Richard, and prejudice against her past, mortared by the post-war euphoria and hope in a better world, were more unassailable than physical ones could ever have been. As each virtual brick was formed and put into place she realised that no-one would believe Richard could ever do wrong, but she had an atonement to make. Anyway, who listened to even a decent woman's complaints? The men were the masters in their houses and no woman could gainsay that position.

But it had been okay for the first months. The house had been sold with Charlie's, possibly too eager agreement, and the money split. Richard was the personification of honour and decency, insisting on a scrupulous transparency that boosted his standing with Charlie to new heights and bolstered her brother's belief that he was now free to leave her in the wake of the new life that lay ahead of him.

Richard had taken the money of course, that was part of the deal, but he had used it all to buy a terraced house for the new family in Moseley. The house still had some damage from the war but it was basically sound. It was also far enough from her childhood haunts and friends to ensure her isolation, tethered as she was to house, husband, and children.

They had married in January 1947, just one couple amongst the multitude of war-torn relationships consecrated in the new world of hope and light. No church, just a Registry Office with his parents disapproving but proud, Lily, Alice and Charlie approving of her apparent happiness and return from purgatory.

She had taken on the bonds of marriage with open eyes, speaking the vows willingly and confidently. Her heart beat like a frightened bird's wings but she had quietened it by thinking of Joe and Rob, of Charlie - and of Richard as he was before the Japanese got hold of him.

Her hope and gamble was that somewhere in there was the Richard she had loved, and who had loved her. Surely, she had fantasised, there was a chance of unearthing that person, as the war and its memories faded, a chance to re-discover the purity of their teenage love?

This had also been her chance to begin to make amends, tentative first steps towards a redemption she desired greatly. End the regret and anger at the childish and selfish stupidity that had placed her in this situation, and had been gnawing away at her insides whilst Charlie had worked to keep them alive. She liked to think her parents would now approve as her life reset itself upon the path they had no doubt planned for her.

After the vows they had gone to the pub. Richard's friends turned up, his parents left, and Richard got drunk. She drank no alcohol. She remained clear of mind and purpose on this fateful day.

That night there had been no romance. The drink brought out the demon within Richard. He had been so drunk he could barely perform but he seemed determined to exercise his right. It had been easier to accept than the rape in one sense, but it was just a physical coupling with no tenderness - so different to her juvenile imaginations of her wedding night. No kiss, just a series of thrusting's whilst he breathed fetid breath across her face as he lay on top of her. Then he had rolled off her and fallen asleep almost instantly, his back towards her.

She had stoically gone down to the kitchen sink and cleaned herself, then returned to the new marital bed and lain beside him, staring at nothing in the darkness. A sudden rush of grief had roiled inside her but she had forced it away – there could be no tears and no honeymoon for her.

***

Life settled into a parody of domestic normality. At least the outside observer would have thought so. Richard had a job. He had been a driver in the Army before his capture and quickly found employment as a bus driver. The twins were a growing handful of energy and mischief and dominated Mary's waking hours.

They had become a common sight in Moseley Village. She had refused to hide them, and regularly took them out shopping, defying the stares with an uplifted head and unflinching return gaze. The initial curiosity amongst the locals had polarised into those who ignored her, those who felt sorry for her, and those who clearly viewed Joe as some sort of aberration and a challenge to the fibre of normal life. The latter she did her best to avoid as there always seemed to be an underlying aggression in their demeanour.

On the whole she still felt that her existence, her daily life, lay in a nether world outside of society. She had transgressed, broken rules, and been punished by a million to one quirk of fate that trumpeted her guilt whenever Joe could be seen. She did her best to shield the boy, easy at two, but she knew what the future held for him.

She would need to prepare him for it when he was old enough to understand. She also realised that Rob would face a different kind of pressure, but still one that would mark him as different to other lads.

The neighbours mirrored the reactions of the denizens of Moseley Village. The Dawson's, a couple in their thirties, kept themselves to themselves. On the other side were Mr. and Mrs. Terry, both in their sixties. Rita Terry showed interest in the kids, treated them both the same, and showed kindness towards Mary. Her husband, Bill, on the rare occasions they interacted, spoke to her in a tone edged with disapproval and refused to acknowledge Joe's existence. She suspected that the Burns family was a regular topic of debate between them

Mary would have liked to reach out to Rita, but the resolute antipathy of her husband deterred her. So she continued alone in her quest to exorcise her husband's demons when they began to surface. It was worst when he drank, and he drank quite often. After only a few weeks of marriage she came to recognise the warning signs. He would sit and stare into space, his thoughts God knows where. He would withdraw into himself, taciturn and impenetrable at these times and she could do, or say nothing, that seemed to reach him. Sometimes she would catch him staring at her with a look of bitterness on his face.

At first it was just the moods, every few weeks. She tried to work out what prompted them but the trigger was buried deep in his Malayan horrors. Work and the company of his mates seemed to help, but they also provided him with drinking partners and he began to settle into a routine of going to the pub after his shift finished. Initially it was only once or twice a week, and he would be home for tea at a reasonable time and in a manageable mood. She didn't object - it meant less time coping with him, and more with Joe and Rob.

As the months rolled by she witnessed a slide into something far worse. Something inside him crawled out of whatever cave he had buried it in and turned it's malevolent gaze upon her.

He never slept well, often waking sweating and shaking. She tried to help; it was after all in her interests to keep him balanced and functioning. She had conceived a plan of gradually getting him to rely on her, to see some worth in her, in the hope that eventually he would begin to value her as more than a domestic skivvy and repository for his lust.

But in the darkness, as he lay trembling, he rebuffed her attempts at compassion.

"What do you know about what I've been through? You think you've got it bad but you wouldn't have got through. Not many lasted as long as I did. They treated us like animals-we became animals. They tortured us, demeaned us, and far worse. I had to rely on myself and I survived. I don't need you or your help. Keep out of me head."

She tried a number of angles of attack, but he had built a wall in his mind to keep out the Japs and if they hadn't breached it, she had no hope. He was trapped by his demons and he seemed to find solace increasingly in drinking. This hurt her worse than the physical and emotional distance. She was at heart a caring person and had cared for him. She still wanted the chance to have a human relationship and the fact that she could not breach his defences was more of a failure to her than anything. It also meant she couldn't access his emotions, a fount that she desperately needed to tap into on behalf of her children.

As regards Joe and Rob, he had kept to his word so far in terms of providing for them - but it was impersonal. He made no effort to be a father to them. There was no bond at all. They too were kept at a distance and she worried what the future held for them as he gradually slid into his cups and wrestled his terrors.

At first he found his outlet in sex, and she put up with his drunken fumbling, but he began to get rougher, pinching her, then biting and holding her down. She felt like a physical possession, as useful as his favourite chair and nothing more. She hardened herself to this soulless ordeal as it was directed at her, rather than at the children, and she had settled into martyrdom for their sakes long ago. It scared her though. She knew that a possession has no claim on its owner and once its wears out or fashion changes it is easily discarded.

It was a Saturday night in late August 1947 that his violence reached a new level. He had come home unusually morose and drunk. It was a year since Japan had surrendered and the anniversary seemed to awaken more buried memories, he had been in a sullen, brooding mood all week. It was his weekend off and he always drank more when there was no driving to do the next day. She never knew exactly what the catalyst was for his mood and the extra drink but he was aggressive from the moment he flung the door open and demanded his tea.

She had been rushed that day with washing, then shopping, and the boys had been unusually demanding. The bus had been held up in traffic and she had arrived home flustered and sweating and had thrown the food together praying that he wouldn't notice. The fates had conspired against her though. He sat and looked at it for a while.

"You dare to serve me this shit, I lived on crap before and I ain't standing for it again!" Richard shouted at the top of his voice – loud enough for the neighbours to hear. Not that this would have made any difference.

He picked the plate up and deliberately tipped the food onto the kitchen floor.

"Now get your arse down there and clean it up," he barked at her.

Richards's voice was full of menace and drink. She could sense the anger building and fetched a cloth and dustpan from the sink. As she knelt he stood up and loomed over her, swaying slightly. She was fixated on his feet, still wearing his black work shoes, right in front of her. She quickly scraped the food into the dustpan and wiped the floor. She began to stand but he put his foot on her left hand – he was smart enough to remember she was right–handed. He bore down and a small cry escaped her lips.

"No, you stay right where you are you bitch," some part of him seemed to be elsewhere, reliving some past experience.

She looked up and he ground her hand harder into the lino, forcing another involuntary gasp of pain from her. His breath came faster and she realised that it wasn't just anger, he had become aroused. Looking up from the floor she could see the bulge in his trousers.

"You need punishment; I've been too soft so far." Richard

continued the pressure on her hand and undid his fly buttons,

"You know what to do," he hissed.

She didn't know, never had, and she shook her head – then it was ringing and she realised he had slapped her, hard.

"Do it, we had much worse in the camps, why shouldn't you have a bit of what I had while you was back home fucking niggers." He stood with his right fist clenched.

She considered fighting but he was much stronger in his wiry way and there were the boys to consider. What if he hurt them instead of her? At least they were in bed, oblivious and she desperately didn't want them to wake and witness this.

He had his prick out now and grabbed her hair forcing her head forward. She blanked her mind out and took him into her mouth almost gagging at the acrid taste. He forced her head backwards and forwards and she was almost choking and then she felt the hot spurt as he came.

He twisted her hair and held her, still with him in her mouth, "Now swallow it you whore."

As he pulled out of her he threw her down on the floor, "Now get me a proper tea."

That was the first time that the connection of violence with sex became the norm. It soon became a regular occurrence whenever he had one of his moods combined with drink. He took delight in finding a fault, was creative in doing so, and then the 'punishment' would begin. Whilst it was sexual, whilst it was retribution for her sins in his eyes, she knew that it's source lay in a prison camp somewhere in The East, a re-enactment of experience involving his Japanese captors, a reaction against the world for its cruelty and injustice. She was in her self-made prison, he was the guard, and hers sons were hostages.

She lived on her nerves, dreading the bad days, alert to the warning signs, trying to make things perfect and above all screening the boys from it. She hid the bruises, explained them away as her clumsiness. She lost weight and finally began to seek solace in drink herself, secreting it away for those moments in the darkness when she was alone with her life and needed to numb the pain, both physical and mental. She became skilled at making do on less than he gave her, spending the rest at the 'offie'. He probably knew, but he didn't care so long as she remained submissive to his will.

What made her existence worse was the fact that on the 'good' days, and they still outnumbered the bad, she could see how it could have been between them but for the war, Japs, GIs and her one mistake. On those days Richard went to work, came home sober, ate his tea and engaged with her and the boys – although she didn't delude herself that there was depth to the relationship. That was what broke her, she could see that deep within him, behind the scarred and tortured face, lay the vein of decency, fairness, and humour that she had once loved.

1947 wore on. Football had returned after the war and he started going to see Birmingham City at St Andrews. He always went drinking after the match and she became a supporter of sorts as her life on match day evenings was much better if the 'Blues' had won.

Life was hard, rationing was still in place, and it looked as if it might get worse. The weather deteriorated and bitter cold set in as 1948 dawned. The world was grey and white, people shuffling hunched through an arctic landscape.

Then she missed her period and by March she was sure. Her mind rotated the endless permutations of how a baby of Richard's would affect the complex relationships and structures within the family, especially his attitude towards the twins.

She didn't tell him at first, didn't know how to broach the subject. She could not begin to predict how he would react. Finally her body could hide its secret no longer and she resolved to tell him at the most propitious moment.

The next evening he arrived home in a good mood and had not been drinking. She had made a special effort with the meal and decided to strike when he settled into his favourite chair, seemingly content. There didn't seem much point in prevarication.

"Richard, I've got summat to tell you. I'm pregnant. I've waited till I'm sure but its certain now." She waited for a response.

For what seemed to be an eternity he stared at her.

"That's good. You can be a proper wife now," he finally responded before he picked up his newspaper and carried on reading. She had an internal debate and decided not to push the topic.

The next evening he chose to return to it. She was at the sink when she heard him open the front door, then he was standing behind her and she could smell the booze. He turned her round and with one hand grabbed her face. He pushed her against the wall. The scar was livid red as it always was when his temper rose.

"Now I've been thinking at work today and I've got a question I need answering. You'd better tell me the truth cause if I find out later that you're lying, and I will, I'll do for you and put those bastards of yours in a home. Is this babby mine or have you been whoring round again? You've got one chance to tell me and if it ain't mine I'll just kick your arse out. If you lie and I end up supporting another cuckoo in the nest I swear I'll swing for you." Richard waited.

The injustice of the accusation struck deep, "I'll swear on anything you want, I've not even looked at another man since you came home, it's yours. You won't find out anything different, that's the truth."

She could not stop herself shaking; she knew that this was a moment when her life could end and that he was completely capable of carrying out his threat.

His face inches from her; he stared into her eyes, as if he was trying to see into her soul. Then he relaxed his grip, "Okay, but don't get thinking this changes anything between us, it don't. Remember the deal, I'll provide, you play the loyal wife, you have no say in this house."

***

The baby came in September. He called her Maureen after his

grandmother. Mary had no say, and her opinion was not sought. Once more a midwife attended, but this time there were no shocks. Maureen was a perfect brown-eyed beauty, although a little underweight, her tiny beauty transgressing the cruelty of her creation, and of course Mary loved her from the moment she was laid on her breast.

Richard wasn't at the birth. He was celebrating with his mates. Rita from next door had agreed to look after the twins, despite, Mary suspected, some debate prior to the offer.

Her 'lord and master' was drunk when he first saw Maureen and his comment raised echoes of trepidation for her sons in Mary's head.

"Lovely, not a touch of the tar brush there is there? Our proper kid."

They kept Maureen in a crib at night in their room, so that Mary could breast- feed her, and although Richard complained constantly about having his sleep disturbed a routine was established.

Fourteen days later the child slept through the night and an exhausted Mary slept through as well. At 6am she finally woke and immediately checked on her.

Mary screamed at the top of her voice and tore at the blankets in the crib to clutch the child to her – Maureen was ice-cold and dead.

Richard woke in a haze – useless and unable to function in

Mary's moment of need.

Cot-death was not common and the sudden-death of the infant in its sleep, where no cause or reason could be found, left too many questions unanswered. It must have been Mary's fault – some act of neglect or attention to detail on her part. The unspoken words from friends, and even family, left Mary carrying the burden of guilt and Richard despised her all the more. She knew he hated her now.

Chapter Five: 'I Love You So Much It Hurts'

(Jimmy Wakely)

1948

The bond between the twins grew even stronger when they first began to mix with the outside world. Mary was pleased that they were so close - a unified front, although sometimes she observed that it seemed to be a relationship where Joe gave and Rob took.

When they were babies she had worried about how Joe would cope. She knew that children could be capable of monumental cruelty towards those who were different, but they had to learn to stand on their own two feet. She could not be there for them all of the time

Joe was always big for his age and could handle himself. She observed evidence of fights when he appeared with scrapes and grazes. She noted however, that he was treated with caution by his peers and surmised correctly that he had triumphed in those encounters. He seemed to shrug it all off.

No, it was Rob who seemed to suffer more because of his black brother. He was often the target for jibes and attention from the classroom and street bullies and seemed more affected by them. He was much smaller and thoughtful which encouraged the taunts. That was where Joe always stepped in on his twin's behalf.

Rob soon learnt that he had a devastating weapon to hand

and how to manipulate Joe's devotion. It almost seemed as if Joe was seeking forgiveness for being the source of his brother's shame by subjugating himself.

***

The railings around the schoolyard were designed to provide protection to the children from traffic on the adjacent roadway. To Joe they were more like the perimeter fence of a prison. Even at his tender age he needed to feel free and resented being there from day one.

Mary had insisted that Joe behave himself and that he look after his brother - at the risk of getting a sharp smack around the ear for non-compliance. Whilst Mary was not shy in inflicting corporal punishment when necessary she loved them both deeply and every Saturday night when they both sat facing each other in the tin bath in the kitchen, with liberal amounts of water being poured over their heads from a jug, she marveled at the miracle that God had given her. No 'cat-licks' for them, they had a proper wash and plenty of soap behind the ears.

It was Christmas 1948 and Joe and Rob had completed just three months at the primary school. Being a C of E church school they put great store in religion and making sure that the most was made of the festivities.

The parts had been allocated for the school nativity play and Mary turned up to show her support. She rarely went anywhere with Richard if she could avoid it and besides he despised the boys and everything that they stood for.

All of the parents sat in rows in the school hall on little wooden chairs normally occupied by the children, all of them anxious to get a good view of the makeshift stage. Unfortunately for Mary immediately in front of her was a large sweaty individual who occupied the best part of two chairs whilst his diminutive wife occupied what was left.

Mary did her best with a sideways view and fumed silently.

As the play started Mary beamed with pride as Rob made his grand entrance as 'Joseph', *'Centre-stage, that's my boy'* she thought.

The play progressed and Joe made his appearance as a slave-boy carrying boxes for the 'Three Wise Men'.

The fat man sat in front of her laughed loudly at Joe trying desperately to hang on to the T-towel wrapped around his head. The man nudged his wife, "Look at the little Pickaninny. They picked the right part for the little nigger."

Mary was not familiar with the more affectionate Portuguese derivative 'pequenino,' but knew that this man was being far from polite. Not being one to waste words Mary struck him a heavy blow across the back of the head before kicking the chair so hard that it collapsed and the fat man with it.

"That's me son," said Mary slightly more loudly than she would have wished as fifty pairs of eyes turned round to see what the commotion was.

At this moment Joe chose to throw one of the boxes at one of the 'Wise Men' for trying to trip up Rob as he made his grand entrance. At the same moment Rob decided to tip the crib over, leaving 'Baby Jesus' in a heap on the floor. The other 'Mary' on stage burst into tears and started shouting for her mother.

As pandemonium broke out Mary struck the fat man flailing amongst the chairs once more across the head with her handbag as he tried vainly to get to his feet.

Joe and Rob walked home from school with Mary.

Joe was feeling rather pleased with himself - 'Perhaps school wasn't so bad after all' he reflected as Rob pondered his lost moment of fame. For Mary's part she doubted that she would be auditioning either of them for the part of Oliver Twist, or that anyone from that audience would be making comments about Joe within her earshot again.

Mary looked at them straggling behind her and said, "Come on you two. We ain't got time to dawdle."

Joe beamed and said to Rob, "Watch out Rob. Ma might slap us round the kisser as well!"

Mary barely managed to conceal a smile.

In that instant she was happy but each step closer to home stripped that feeling away from her.

***

No school, or street scrap, no bullies, no name-calling could compete with the twin's home life as they grew. Mary was out on a rare shopping trip into town. She had a number of errands to run, and bills to pay, and Richard had agreed to watch the kids whilst he listened to the racing on the radio. It was a Saturday afternoon and he was sober. She decided that it might be good if they had time together. It would save lots of time and trouble if they weren't with her pestering for sweets and asking a thousand questions whilst everyone gazed at her and Joe.

Rob and Joe stood facing their stepfather in the empty upstairs room of their house. Two pairs of well-worn boxing gloves lay on the floor in front of them.

Richard was an archetypal bully who expressed his uncontrolled inner-anger through the amount of 'black-eyes' that their mother sported, generally on a Sunday morning after his late night antics in one of the local pubs. The twins had by now connected their mother's bruises to their stepfather's drinking bouts. Twice, Joe had tried to intervene despite Mary's protestations and had felt the belt for his pains.

Hatred of the man boiled within him but he just wasn't big enough and his mom would not permit him to get involved. Neither twin knew why, but the adult world of relationships was a mystery to their young minds, perhaps it was okay then?

They dealt with the situation quite differently. Rob shrugged his shoulders, if his mom said it was okay then he wasn't going to get involved, and get a thrashing for his troubles. He thought Joe was brave but stupid for trying.

The situation gnawed away at Joe though. Something inside

him told him it wasn't right and that his mom was hurting inside and out. He promised himself, '*One day, I'll make you pay for everything.*' Little did Joe know that the price was about to rise. Mary could not divert her husband's attention from her children any longer. Richard had decided that they were old enough to learn some lessons about life and he was looking forward to taking the opportunity of her absence to start teaching them. He also had some plans in relation to darker urges.

"You two are like a couple of girls-blouses. It's time to wise up and grow some balls, put the gloves on and take your shirts off. I'll teach you what it's like to be a man," he ordered.

They knew better than to argue, stripped off, and stood there with their arms extended to the sides, bare chests heaving slightly with a sense of fear at the unknown.

"The rules are simple. You get one punch each. Whoever stays down gets me belt. Now do it, starting with you darkie."

Joe Docker was the stronger of the two but had spent his short life protecting Rob so hurting his brother was like hurting himself. He hesitated long enough for his stepfather to slap him across his left ear as he shouted, "Do it. Unless you want me to tan your black arse."

For what seemed an age both boys rained single blows on each other, neither wanting to inflict a killer blow and both praying for the experience to finish.

At one point Rob faltered and nearly fell to the floor – his strength was failing as he regained his balance. Joe had been holding back but he was much stronger and the uneven struggle was taking its toll on Rob.

Joe made his mind up. He had to protect Rob. When the next blow landed he went down and stayed down.

"Get out you little cunt," Richard barked at Rob as he bundled him out of the room and threw his shirt after him. Rob ran and hid under the bed, glad to escape the terrible room.

Richard gripped Joe by the scruff of the neck, pulled him to his feet, and barked, "Drop your trousers you little black bastard."

From the other side of the door Rob heard the swish of the leather belt and the sharp cry of his brother as their so-called guardian satisfied one of his primeval needs. From that moment life for Joe would never be the same again.

When she returned Mary instantly knew she had made a mistake. Richard said that they had been fighting – Joe's fault for which he had been disciplined, that was all. Both boys told the same tale but in her heart she knew it wasn't true. When she pressed the point with Richard his face set into the mask that she knew boded ill for her later. She vowed that she wouldn't leave them again.

That night in bed, as Rob slept, Joe wept tears. They streamed down his face uncontrollably but they were not tears of sadness – they were of absolute fury and frustration that he was too small to take his tormentor on. He swore to himself that his day would come as he shifted uncomfortably in the bed.

***

A few months later Mary was surprised but gratified when Richard suggested that the boys have separate rooms now they were growing. *'Perhaps he's finally getting attached to them,'* she thought to herself as she agreed readily. They had a spare room - more of a box-room really, which was allocated to Joe, and Richard even found some half-decent second-hand furniture for it from a mate at work.

Joe wasn't that keen on the idea. He didn't trust his stepfather, with good reason, and the sudden transformation to benevolence raised his suspicions. He discussed the matter with Rob. He knew that if they both approached their mother and asked to stay together their wish would be granted, but Rob wanted his own room. It made him feel important and he was beginning to conceive a wish to distance himself from his protector-in-chief who drew unwanted bullying and hurtful remarks upon them both like a magnet. It was the first time that Joe had asked Rob for something and he was taken aback at the refusal.

Richard paid Joe a visit about two weeks after he had moved into his new room. Joe woke suddenly to find a hand clamped across his face. The room reeked of beer fumes. Mary was sound asleep after her usual evening 'tipple'. She had long since stopped waiting up for her husband to return from drinking, to engage in a ritual beating, and Richard had not seemed to be bothered.

Joe was alone in a living nightmare – the routine was always the same – short bursts of violent activity following which he was left soiled and covered in the sweat of a stinking version of humanity who had taken on monster proportions.

He said nothing about the abuse during the years that followed. Richard had told him that he would kill Mary if he said anything, and Joe had seen enough to believe him. Joe was used to taking punishment on behalf of others and he coped by filing the visitations in a closed room in a dark area of his mind. He was too young to understand the mental damage being done to him, damage that would return to haunt him through all his years to come.

Joe didn't broach the subject with his twin either. He was beginning to realize that their infant bond was becoming strained and he held Rob partly responsible for what had happened. It was occurring to Joe that Rob always put Rob first.

***

In September 1954 at the age of eleven years Rob and Joe started a new school. In a year that decreed that twenty-per-cent of the houses in Birmingham were unfit for human habitation Mary worked hard to make sure that they were clean and well presented. Her children were as good as anyone else's and she wanted them to make the best of their education.

As the teacher started the morning roll call the usual murmurs started with the anticipation of a new days sport. It was a ritual, the cycle of which could not be broken, and Mrs. Mills had already given up. Rob and Joe sat alongside each other in the class waiting for the crescendo to build. "Rob Docker," the teacher bellowed, "Yes Mrs. Mills," came the reply. The calling of, "Joe Docker," was always accompanied by a rise in the 'titters' of children who were unable to comprehend how one of the brothers could be white, and the other black. "Yes Mrs. Mills," barked Joe who refused to be cowed by the chatter around him. After less than two months he hated this place and the people in it.

The weaker children in the class thanked their lucky stars for the situation as it meant that for the most part they escaped the relentless bullying that took place. For Joe and Rob though there was to be no respite.

A small group of four 'hard cases' made it their mission in life to pick on the twins and being the stronger of the two, and the wrong colour, Joe generally bore the brunt. Their ringleader, a lad called Frank, had far more muscle than brain and with his entourage around him ruled the roost.

Frequently pupils would return to the class from breaks to find the words 'Nigger' and 'White Nigger Boy' chalked on the blackboard. Mrs. Mills didn't like blacks and did little to still the waters. Privately she thought Mrs. Docker to be something of a loose woman and allowed the abuse to continue. The boys were the product of their mother's loose morality and someone should pay.

Matters came to a head when Joe was absent from school for a couple of days due to yet another over-zealous beating from his stepfather and Frank decided to act. During the school dinner-break Frank, and his three cronies, cornered Rob in the boy's toilets and punched and kicked him mercilessly for what seemed like an age. No stranger to violence, Rob rolled with the punches and did his best to protect his face.

Back in the classroom Mrs. Mills enquired with a degree of casualness as to why Rob was covered in the contents of the toilet floor, and was sporting a black eye. "I fell over, Mrs. Mills," came the response.

Joe was incensed when he saw the state of his brother that evening and together they determined to exact revenge as soon as their injuries had healed. Rob was also especially keen that potential tormentors in the new school understood Joe's 'guardian angel' role.

Between them they looked like they had done ten rounds with a heavyweight boxer and at one point when they stared at each other they burst out laughing at the comparison.

Joe laughed at Rob, "You've got a face like a smacked-arse."

"Shut your face tit-head" Rob responded and for that moment they were brothers-at-arms again as they started wrestling with each other.

The following week Joe and Rob made their way to the rear of Frank's home and with a slingshot expertly smashed some of the upper-bedroom windows.

Next morning they sat in the classroom smiling quietly as Frank opened the lid of his desk. It had not been easy balancing on the chair to defecate inside it but Joe had rather enjoyed the experience.

At lunchtime, with tension building, Rob deliberately goaded three of his tormentors into a fight outside in full view of the playground supervisor, leaving Frank and Joe as observers. With all four marched off to see the Headmaster the stage was set for the remaining two to settle the score.

"Come on Frank, let's sort this out then. Just you and me," said Joe as he motioned towards the toilets.

Inside, the two squared-up to each other. Frank was slightly the larger of the two and fancied his chances. However he made the mistake of thinking that he was going to engage in a fair fight with a normal boy.

As Frank advanced Joe deftly slid the length of hard wood secreted in his cardigan sleeve into his hand and hit Frank hard in the face causing his nose to explode.

With blood pouring everywhere Joe grabbed Frank by the scruff of the neck and forced him into a cubicle, "You need to wash that blood off, Frank." Joe said quietly into his ear as he forced his tormentor to his knees, pushed his head down the toilet, and pulled the chain.

"Touch me or me brother again and I'll cut your dick off and leave it in an envelope on Mrs. Mill's desk," Joe asserted as he flushed the chain again for good measure, watching the water cascade over Frank's mop of hair.

Mrs. Mills was at something of a loss to sort out Frank's broken nose and with open mutiny breaking out in the classroom she retreated to the Headmasters office to plead for the Dockers to be excluded from school.

Later that afternoon a further confrontation took place at the school gates but this time it was between Frank's mother and Mary Docker, immediately after both mothers had been called in to discuss their offspring's behaviour.

Having spent the day supervising the repairs to the upstairs windows Frank's mother now needed to get her son medical treatment and was none too happy.

Like her son she was a large woman, with a large mouth, and was supremely confident that she could deal with Mary.

Niceties lasted seconds and Mary lost her cool one moment after being called, "Nigger Lover," at which point she landed a good punch to the woman's jaw before grabbing her hair and pinning her down to the ground, "If you like your fizzog stay away from me family." Mary screamed.

Joe and Rob looked on with pride as she slapped the woman hard twice across the face before calmly getting to her feet, straightening her dress, and walking off.

The boys followed dutifully as Joe commented, "Fucking hell mum that was great."

Mary stopped in her tracks and promptly smacked both of them loudly across their ears, "You pair need to fucking behave yourselves, and stop fucking swearing." she said and once again found herself smiling to herself at what God had given her.

Mary was no longer the slim petite woman that had turned eyes, and the stresses of living with a madman, and trying to bring up two very active kids had taken its toll. Her waist had expanded at a pace with the volume of cheap alcohol she consumed, and as her breasts headed south she lost the will to bother with make-up – if it helped to keep Richard's clawing hands off her, then all the better.

She turned and walked home with them in their usual position trailing behind her – none of that mattered to her. Mary Docker still had her boys and she loved them deeply. She could forgive them anything but was blind to the pain that one of them suffered in silence.

Chapter Six: 'Blowing Wild'

(Frankie Laine)

1953

Patrick Quinn had been a bastard for as long as he could remember, which was funny, as he wasn't one. His ma used it in combination with the Irish variation of 'feckin' on the many occasions he enraged her. His victims at school called him it under their breath, avoiding him as much as possible. His 'da' called him worse but the gist was the same - he was a nightmare.

It wasn't because he was exceptionally large. A lean and angular frame with wide shoulders promised a framework for an athletic body to come. Surmounting this was a face full of flat panes, a boxer's jaw and a mop of sandy hair that accepted no control. The eyes contributed to the uneasiness of others, they were chips of blue ice conveying a stare that never broke first.

No, everyone agreed that the problem was that the boy was 'proper yampy'. Not in an endearing, amusing manner, but in a way that made people of all ages stop and look twice when they had cause to notice him. He radiated an animal wildness that knew no bounds. Adults shook their heads, predicting a bad end, but his peers knew, as kids do, that Quinn was capable of anything.

He was a wild child, destroying such toys as he had, running amok around the streets, fighting, stealing, and poking his nose wherever it wasn't wanted. He saw every barrier as a personal affront, every other child as an opportunity for gain, challenge, or as a resource for his own use.

Unusually for an Irish family, he had only one sibling, his sister Kate, older, quieter, brighter academically, the apple of her father's eye and a comparator that he could never match up to. He hated her. The only good that came of her existence was that once his parents had decided that he was a lost cause they let him run free. They and his teachers completely missed the fact that he was in fact as bright as his sister, perhaps brighter. He just wasn't interested in schooling.

He was beaten plenty with the old leather belt his father wore, but all that did was strengthen his will, his anger, and his mastery of pain as he determined not to cry, apologise, or show any remorse. He would retreat within himself and disassociate himself from the pain, taking it into himself and storing it up, a reservoir of hate to be tapped, and dealt out to whichever unfortunate crossed his path next.

This was what marked him out. His peers were uneasy around him. They could sense something within him, a rage that burnt undiminished, that knew no boundaries, and it scared them. He was no normal school bully. Yes he intimidated, ruled the roost in his age group, and attracted followers, but he had a savagery that could not be contained.

Aged eight, little Colin Briggs had decided to stand up to him, refusing to give him his penny sweet. Quinn had waited for him after school in an alleyway with two of his cronies. When Colin adopted a heroic stance Quinn had scythed Briggs' legs from under him, and then bent his arm until he screamed with the pain and fainted. Even then, Quinn's companions had to pull him off after they realised he was going to snap Briggs' arm like a stick, and balked at being associated with that act.

Aged nine, an older boy who fancied himself as the school tough picked a fight one evening on the old bombsite that the kids used as a playground and meeting place. Everyone knew he was going to do it and lots turned up to see Quinn get his comeuppance at last. The other boy was three years older and a lot bigger. He put

Quinn down three times in the first couple of minutes but he got back up every time and the pain seemed to unleash a flood of rage.

Quinn had gone berserk, attacking the other kid with punches, kicks, and then inflicting the coup-de-grace with a half-brick to the head. Once more he was pulled off a beaten opponent when the onlookers realised that he would not stop otherwise. The boy had been hospitalised, the injuries explained as an accident on the dangerous wasteland. After that no-one tried to teach Quinn any lessons. They began to call him 'Mad Dog' Quinn, at first secretly, but then openly as word got round that he approved of the epithet.

Quinn may not have been as academically orientated as his 'sainted' sister but he was clever in a different way; an animal cunning combined a fierce survival instinct and an infallible ability to pinpoint weakness and vulnerability in others. By the age of fourteen he was out of school and beyond any civilising influence other than his father's brutal attempts at discipline and his mother's prayers, neither of which were effective.

He was in and out of Borstal, unrepentant and unreformed, annealed by the experience. Just another challenge, another, bigger and nastier pool to swim in, another chance to vent his rage at life. Borstal fanned his hatred of uniforms and authority as his constant rebellion against the rules led to some summary justice from the guards and lengthy spells alone in solitary, or what passed for it in that institution. In truth this was the only time that he felt fear as the effects of claustrophobia in confined spaces gripped him – this was Quinn's secret.

One of his father's favourite punishments had been to lock his son in their small coal cellar in the darkness for hours on end, *'so he could reflect on his sins and we can have some bloody peace,'* he often quoted. The child had sat in pitch- blackness alone with his thoughts of giant rats and spiders and being buried alive - an image that returned to haunt his dreams in later life. The regular incarcerations only added to the lava that burnt within him and he finally smashed the door open with his fists, punching the panels out and emerging with tattered knuckles and eyes that promised death. That had been the last time, but the fear remained.

Aged sixteen, and home from his last incarceration for a street robbery, his parents decided to return to Derry in the hope that a new start could be found.

***

On the 31 January 1953, they boarded the Princess Victoria ferry, bound for Larne.

Quinn was sullen and unwilling but had been persuaded to

give it a try. He had actually intended to run away for good, but a free trip to a new place was worth a try. He had a notion that it might be useful in the future if he knew some people in the North and had somewhere to escape to when he next found trouble - with access to Eire should he need it.

He was also becoming conscious of his Catholic heritage, not that the religion held any allure for him. His family was steeped in 'The Struggle'. He suspected his father had been more involved than he let on, and Quinn was both fascinated and attracted by the hardmen, the weapons, and the glory of the violence. If you fought for 'The Cause' you were a hero, lauded and lionised in comparison to the way he had been persecuted and punished.

The weather had been atrocious from the moment they boarded and Quinn soon discovered that he would never make a sailor. He made repeated trips to the outside deck despite the driving rain and eventually stayed there, leaving his family below. As the ship left the relative shelter of Loch Ryan it was apparent even to Quinn that this was no ordinary storm.

From his vantage point he could feel the violence of the wind and see the ship bucking in the mountainous seas. Occasionally he caught a glimpse of a crewmember and could see the concern on their faces. From the way the gale circled around him as he stood it seemed to him that at some point the captain had tried to get back into the Loch but had been prevented by the winds, and sea, and had decided to brave the crossing towards the shelter of the Northern Ireland coast.

He faced into the storm challenging it to sweep him away if it could. This primeval power was something he understood, it felt as if the world itself were beating him and he accepted it, reveling in the violence it awoke within him.

Suddenly the deck tilted. He waited for it to right itself but it obstinately remained at an angle. He clutched the rail. His feral instincts kicked in. He was a survivor. He weighed the options. In all likelihood the ship would be okay and he wasn't about to go jumping into that sea unless he had to. He briefly considered going below but his concern for his own skin vastly outweighed any feelings he had for his family; if they were stupid enough to sit doing nothing, so what?

He scanned his surroundings. There was a lifeboat along the deck and he pulled himself along the rail to look at it. He examined the ropes and winch mechanism and quickly worked out how to operate it. There was a tarp that he partially unclipped. A sailor, a grey-haired man in his fifties, approached him shouting above the howling winds,

"Here, you ain't supposed to be messing with that, crew members only, you should get below."

Quinn looked at the man, "If I was you I'd be fucking off out of my sight or you could find yourself taking a swim."

The man considered for a moment, "I've got better things to do than argue with the likes of you, it's your funeral if you go over the rail, just leave the boat alone." He made his way to the hatch, weaving across the rolling deck, and disappeared below.

Suddenly Quinn heard the scream of tortured metal and the

boat shuddered. The deck tilted to an even crazier angle, nearly pitching him into the maelstrom below. Salt spray and rain lashed his face. Luckily the boat was tilting his way and the lifeboat swung out over the water now only about ten feet below, some bigger waves crashing onto the deck.

He realised that something fundamental had occurred in the load area and his animal instincts rang internal alarms, fuelling adrenalin and anger. He was Patrick Quinn and he wasn't going to die here. He looked at the hatch, expecting to see others emerging, then realised that the tilt of the deck was holding the heavy door shut and that it would be almost impossible for anyone inside to lift it open. They would naturally try to get out of the hatches the other side, away from the water, with gravity on their side.

He was alone on his section of deck. He realised that the tilt was getting worse. The water was closer. He made a decision, pulled himself into the lifeboat, and began working on the pulley as the craft swung like a fairground ride.

Abruptly the ropes loosened and the winch span, dropping him into the swirling waters. He realised that the ropes still tethered the lifeboat to the ferry that now loomed over him. He always carried a blade down his boot and he began hacking at the rope until it snapped at a moment of tautness due to a large swell.

The sea caught the little boat and pulled it away from the ferry like a bobbing cork. Quinn could see the doomed ship, the decks nearly vertical now, and then it faded from view behind the squalls. He got under the tarpaulin pulling it as far over the deck as he could to prevent the boat filling with water, the will to live far greater as once again he battled with his fear of being in a confined space.

The storm abated about five hours later as a watery sun rose. The raging sea died down and Quinn emerged to view his surroundings. He was alone, no wreckage, no survivors, and no bodies in sight. Truly alone this time, no need to run away after all.

***

The subsequent enquiry found that the vehicle doors had been left open rendering the ferry vulnerable to the storm. Ships responding to the distress signals could not locate the stricken vessel until too late. One hundred and twenty eight souls including his family perished.

Quinn survived, his 'brighter' sister did not.

Chapter Seven: 'Crazy Man Crazy'

(Bill Haley And His Comets)

1953

He went back to Derry after all. The shipping company had discussed with the remnants of his extended family where they should send him after his rescue. In truth his reputation within family circles had gone before him, and no-one was that keen on taking him in, but finally a decision was reached – blood was thicker than water. Quinn's gut instinct was that Londonderry would be good for him. He had kin there at least and he would be able to milk his status as orphaned survivor.

A new world lay before him devoid of constraints now that his parents with their antipathetic mixture of Catholic morality and leather belt discipline were gone. Clever Kate was gone too; her academic brilliance had proved to be no match for his primeval survival instincts. He didn't miss any of them.

In fact they had done him a big favour by dying. He had stayed for some months with Auntie Philomena who seemed to be of the opinion that rescuing him from the sea, and the devil, would book her place in heaven. She was slightly deranged, living in a complex whirl of religion and hatred for the 'Protties'. Her husband was dead from a beating by the Orangemen and her house contained three sons, a lodger who he suspected shared her bed as well as her hatred, and several cats.

The three boys were younger than him, but one was bigger and fancied himself. That lasted three days until he found Quinn sat on his chest one night, a kitchen knife just nicking his neck, after which he rapidly converted to showing the new arrival how it was in Ireland.

How was it? It was just perfect. Everyone seemed to be as crazy as he was. Violence lay barely beneath the surface, old hatred could erupt at any time, and the law of the jungle held sway. He was particularly fascinated by the cold ruthlessness of the lodger, Thomas.

The shipping company did him a second favour. He was compensated for the loss of his little-lamented family with a tidy sum which was placed in an account that he could access himself when he turned eighteen. Before then he needed his Aunt's agreement but he was content to let it rest there for a while and had no doubt that he could persuade Philomena when the right time arrived.

It was not a fortune, but enough for a life of sorts for a while, a nest-egg for the future. It was the best thing his parents had ever done for him and he thanked them for being so obliging.

It was a mark of his intelligence that people had missed, that he put the money out of his mind until he could make proper use for it. Quinn had never smoked and avoided alcohol after two incidents where it had released the fire within, and he had realised that a life behind bars beckoned if he continued. Quinn had no intention of being incarcerated again. He knew that he would not survive a long stretch with mind intact due to his claustrophobia. Girls didn't feature either. Plenty were attracted, drawn to the flame. He had dabbled of course, but the force of nature that he was had no time for deep relationships with other human beings. He was searching for something he couldn't describe, a way to use his anti-social talents to blaze a successful path through life. The money would be there when he found his way. It stayed unspent in the Irish Bank, and he made sure that his new family knew to keep their sticky fingers off it.

Thomas the lodger ignored him at first, but after he was told about Quinn breaking a skull or two on the street he seemed to re-assess his new household companion.

Quinn found that Thomas was often there, asking about his background and his view of the world. The old bastard was clearly a bit closer to the Republican cause than he liked to appear and Quinn eagerly fed on his bigotry, encouraging his tales of youthful 'derring do'.

Eventually Thomas began taking Quinn on the odd outing and to meet some of his 'friends'. He moved packages, ran errands and messages, kept watch, fought often. One day after Quinn turned seventeen Thomas approached him in the backyard and cast a baited hook.

"I want you to come and meet an important friend of mine, could provide some ideas for your future." he floated.

"Not bothered if I do, who is he?" Quinn enquired casually, having spotted the hook but taking it anyway.

"You're a good Catholic aren't you lad, you want to help in the struggle, perhaps learn a few things?" Thomas began to reel him in.

"If it's how to crack heads I can do that already just fine," Quinn played dim.

Thomas persisted "It's a bit more than that, I think you have a talent Patrick, a talent that people look for over here and will help you to get better at. Could help you a bit and in return you help us. I like you lad, you remind me of meself when I was younger and handier. You can handle yourself and you enjoy it too, I've seen that glint in your eye."

Quinn felt the moment, savoured it. He knew exactly what 'Uncle Thomas' was involved in and it resonated with the devil inside. He was about to cross a line from youthful street tough to something bigger, and darker, and he wanted that. The proposal also potentially offered the protection from the law, coupled with the sanction for violence, and some reward that he desired. Above all else he was curious.

"Let's get on with it then," Quinn affirmed.

***

He said his name was Jimmy and he only had one eye. He sat in the gloom of a poky bar. Hard men were on the door and they nodded at Thomas then gave Quinn a long appraising look before standing aside.

"This your new friend Tommy boy? He's a scrawny little cunt isn't he? Thought you rated him, looks like he couldn't beat my Bridie in a fight," one of the men goaded.

"Your Bridie's a feckin tough little bitch and there's plenty of the lads wouldn't take her on, but I think you'll be surprised at our Pat here." Thomas countered.

The man who had spoken leant towards Quinn and stared at him eye to eye from a distance of six inches. Quinn stared back and considered poking his eyes out. The man drew back.

"Maybe, we'll see won't we?" the man attempted to recover the situation. They crossed the empty bar to the lone figure. Quinn recognised a kindred spirit instantly. He had heard that 'kiddie-fiddlers' could spot a vulnerable child across a room somehow and it was the same, he could sense a fellow man of violence.

Jimmy had a face composed of scars with a white glass eye as the focal point. He had a thin mouth, more of a slash that mirrored the one across his eye socket. He spoke very quietly and that was what impressed Quinn. It was the measured voice of a man in control of his emotions, but sub-currents conveyed menace and a deep rage that Quinn recognised.

"So, young Pat is it? Well, well. Now Thomas here has talked to me about you. Shame about your ma and da, and now you're alone. It seems you're a nasty little bastard, but you might be a good Papist despite being raised in that heathen land."

"Two out of three, I don't give a fuck about religion," Quinn replied cockily.

"But you like to give out a bit of pain here and there don't you; Tommy here thinks you get off on it. If I think I can trust you I could do you a bit of good, invest in your future, teach you some skills that you can't learn on any apprenticeship. Are you interested?"

Quinn nodded, "Maybe, but what's in it for me?'

Jimmy was reticent, "I'll be telling you that once I'm certain of you boy. I want you to do a little job for me first."

It was an innocuous nod in a dark pub that changed his life forever.

***

"That's the place." Matty pointed.Quinn and Matty, the guy from the pub door, were stood in the Irish drizzle opposite a row of mean-looking terraced houses.Matty went on, "He lives alone so there shouldn't be any problems. He needs a bit of a lesson, he hasn't been paying his dues to the church fund and he's been bragging about it, which we can't allow to go unpunished. The cunt thinks he's hard enough to go against us."

Quinn just shrugged, "How do we get in?"

Matty was enjoying himself, "There's an alleyway to the back. I'll jemmy the door, but you go in first, Jimmy's orders."

They crept through the side-entry, stopping for a moment in the shadows to pull on balaclavas and climbed the low backyard fence. Matty had the rear door open in seconds, "My little talent, amongst others. In you go son, Jimmy 'One-Eye' says it's your show."

Quinn peered around the door. It was pitch black in the

kitchen but he had brought a torch. He led the way into the hallway and stopped to listen. The downstairs was in darkness and silent but he could hear something from upstairs. He crept along the hallway, briefly checking the other downstairs room as he passed – it was empty.

At the foot of the stairs he stopped and listened again. He smiled. He recognised those sounds, the reluctant payer was not alone after all.

They crept up the stairs, Quinn leading, and made a quick check of the other bedroom – empty. Male grunting, and female cries, leaked from the half-open door to the other room. *'I doubt he would have heard us if we'd talked all the way up with that racket going on – he's got a screamer there,'* thought Quinn.

Matty was grinning like a Cheshire cat and made a mock bow, waving Quinn forward. Quinn nodded to Matty then burst through the door to be greeted by the sight of a spotty arse pumping away between white legs.

Quinn delivered a two-handed rabbit punch to the man's neck and then knelt heavily on his back pushing the air out of both bodies below him. The woman had begun a different type of scream but it was cut off as a whoosh of air was forced from her.

Quinn reached between the man's legs and took hold of his balls squeezing them - provoking a groan of pain from the half-stunned man.

"Come on out of there you dirty bastard, and keep quiet or you'll never fuck a tart again." Quinn ordered.

He pulled the man backwards until his face was between the woman's legs. "If you want I'll get him to lick you out on the way darling," Quinn laughed. The woman was wide-eyed, petrified and she shook her head. She was no oil painting, just some slag earning a coin.Matty barked at her, "You get yourself dressed now and fuck off outta here.

We know you now so one word and we'll find you and make you uglier, if that's possible - understand?"

The look of sheer terror on her face, coupled with the trickle of urine down her legs, was enough to indicate that compliance would be forthcoming.

She scrambled off the bed, nodding vigorously, and ran out of the bedroom clutching her clothes to her chest. They heard the door slam moments later.

Quinn gave the man the benefit of a good squeeze to the balls, then another full-force double punch to the kidneys, and threw him onto the floor then kicked him hard in the stomach. The man curled into a ball to protect his genitals from further damage.

Quinn produced a blade he had acquired on one of his trips around the city with his cousins.

"I think I might just take me a memento of the visit, which would you like it to be, cock or balls?" Quinn enquired casually.

The man looked up wide-eyed shaking his head vigorously.

Quinn was in his element now and this pathetic specimen in

front of him wasn't giving him the satisfaction his endless rage required, "I hear you're a bit of a hard man, above paying your way. You don't look so fierce to me, but you might say it wasn't fair, two against one, caught by surprise. Might laugh it off to your mates. Word might get round that this lesson taught you nothing. So I'll make it even. My friend here will just watch while we go at it man to man, fists only, give you a chance."

The man was recovering now. He was in his mid-twenties, and stocky. He looked at the teenager stood over him, "I'll kick your feckin head in."

He rolled away from Quinn and scrambled to his feet, then launched himself at his tormentor, arms flailing.

Quinn was caught by a good punch and felt his nose give way, but the pain just fed his anger. His innate savagery erupted and he battered the man with a hail of punches and kicks until he went down again. Quinn dropped onto the man's chest and felt ribs crack. He punched the man senseless and kept going until Matty pulled him off, "Jesus Christ, enough, we weren't told to off him."

Quinn snotted blood onto the prone figure, "I was just getting into my rhythm as well. Do we need to do anything else?"

Matty guided him to the door, "I think he got the message son."

The next day Thomas handed him a wad of cash, "Nice one, here's a little thank you from 'The Cause'."

***

Over the next few weeks Quinn was tasked repeatedly. The jobs didn't always involve violence, although violence was always in the background, he was also back to watching, passing messages, delivery runs, with Matty as his constant companion. The final job before he saw Jimmy again was a run to the border to pick up a package.

Quinn knew that this meant he had passed Jimmy's tests. It was obvious that the package was guns, he wouldn't have been allowed at such a delivery if he hadn't earned some trust.

He had been in Derry for about six months when he saw Jimmy for the second time. Same pub, but as he entered Matty greeted him by name. Jimmy once more sat in the half-light and looked at Quinn appraisingly, "Seems like Tommy was right. He was always a fine judge of character – well to be honest, bad character. You might be worth some investment. The question is whether you want to go further?"

Quinn had no doubt what he wanted. These people fascinated him. He was never going to really share their nationalist fervour, their type of hypocritical religious devotion, but they were the only people offering the apprenticeship he desired.

"We both know that I'm good at this Jimmy. I need to learn more so I can be really good at it, and I think you can help me do that. But I want more than being a hired-heavy over here. So what's your plan, what's this investment? You've used that word twice now?"

Jimmy leaned forward into Pat's face for effect. It had none.

'Something about this kid I'm not sure about, he's just too fearless,' he thought, and then continued out loud. "Well Pat my boy, let's see what you are to us. First, a history lesson. Although you don't know it, you come from a good family, very devoted to 'The Cause', your mam's brother Danny, God rest his soul, was very close to us.

You've heard your aunt speak, she is bitter because he was killed by the Protties. Your dad wasn't quite as keen, couldn't wait to follow his shovel to England. He took your mam away from here before you were born, but she was a true daughter of the Church and kept in touch always. It's in your blood boy, and that's important to us."

Quinn was surprised to discover this unknown facet of his background, especially in relation to his ma, but having now experienced the strange mix of Catholic fervour and violent criminality that these people utilised he could reconcile the apparent anomaly.

Jimmy continued, "Secondly, you were raised over the water. You know them, you're part of them, and you're English by birth. That could be very useful to us, which you'll be pleased to know means we wouldn't want you to stay over here for ever."

Jimmy went on, "Finally, you're a ruthless, violent little shit who gets off on pain. Yes I've got a few of those around me, but you have the potential to be in a different league. Matty has watched you operate and I have learnt to trust his opinion. He says you need to channel it, control it. We can develop that, turn you into a thinking man and a violent one, and that's rare and dangerous. Of course you've also passed a few little trials along the way."

Quinn nodded and there was nothing really to say as Jimmy concluded, "Before we sign up to this arrangement though, you need to believe that if you cross us we'll kill you without a second thought, and our arm is long. Dead men tell no tales and all that. You sign up to us in blood, and blood is the price you pay for any breach of contract. In return we'll teach you things you can't get anywhere else, we'll put you in touch with people, fund you, set you up, and help you. Are you up for it?"

A handshake sealed a deal that would resonate down the years to come.

Chapter Eight: 'Shake A Hand'

(Faye Adams)

1953

At Holyhead, he walked off the ferry, the family he had embarked with a year earlier a rapidly fading memory. He had cash in his pocket, money in a savings account that had been transferred over from the Trust, and a new band of brothers over the water.

Thomas had given him a ferry ticket, a train ticket, and told him to, 'get his arse to Worcester,' where he would be met.

He was in another dimension of bad to the violent and rebellious youth who had scrambled into the lifeboat. Survival had proved that his innate instincts were a lot more useful than the civilised niceties espoused by his late family. His 'employment' in Derry had demonstrated that the base animal reactions he excelled in were not only in demand, but could be improved upon. The last six months in Eire had honed him into something lethal.

At seventeen he was already in a different league to other delinquent teenagers. He was still no giant at just over six feet tall, but he was already laying muscle onto his wiry frame; he was fast, very fast, and his pain threshold had never been reached. He had been taught how to use weapons, how to fight dirty. Most of all he now began to see how the mind and body could be harnessed together so that the fury that burned so close to the surface could be channeled by thought and intent into something more precise, a stiletto.

Perfection was yet to come, but he had started on a dark road. England, in the form of a lone British Transport Commission Police officer, paid no attention to him as he walked out of the ferry terminal, but England should have. Quinn was a very dangerous young man.

Several hours later he walked out of Worcester railway station into Foregate Street and looked around him. The street scene seemed softer to his perceptions than the tensions and brutality of Northern Ireland. The people were sheep and he was a wolf but they didn't see that, just another kid shooting the breeze under the railway bridge.

A couple of teddy-boy types looked him over but they both broke stares with him first and looked away, then moved off. They could sense something and preferred easier meat.

Quinn waited where he had been told and scrutinized the face of every man who approached him, but they all just walked past. He was so preoccupied with them that he didn't notice the woman until she spoke, "You Quinn?"

He surveyed her. Late thirties, a bit plump but not bad looking, classic white skin and auburn hair courtesy of an Irish bloodline.

"Yes, Pat Quinn," he replied."Got any proof of that?" she asked in a confident manner.Quinn was irritated, "Yeah but you ain't seeing fuck all until I know who you are."The woman gave a thin-lipped smile, "Good. You have some sense. I'm your Auntie Marie.

Your Uncle Michael sent me to get you. Mike is your mother's youngest brother. If I tell you that Thomas told us to expect you would that help?"

Quinn knew his mom was from a big family and he had never shown any interest in it, so it was no surprise to him that he had an aunt and uncle in Worcester, so close to his old Birmingham home that now belonged to another world.

"I've got my passport here," he proffered it to the woman who gave it more than a cursory glance.

"Can't be too careful can we, I see you've been taught a bit over there about caution. That's good as your job now is to be a thoroughly English tearaway, and not to draw any official interest to your time abroad. Come on." She turned and walked off with Quinn following on behind.

They walked round to a cleared area that had once held buildings, probably destroyed in the war, now used as an ad-hoc parking area.

"That's ours," She proudly indicated a slightly battered Land Rover that had clearly seen a muddy field in its recent history.

"No-one told me where I was going, just to get to the station," Quinn ventured.

Marie put him in the picture, "You're going to be a farmer Pat, so get used to the idea. We're right out in the back-of-beyond. Nice and quiet, and no nosy neighbours prying into our business. That's the way they like it to be back home, and that's why they help us with a bit of money now and then so that we can afford a fine vehicle like this one." She smiled at her own joke.

Quinn could barely hear her over the rattles and wind noise so he had to shout, "How long to get there?'

Marie didn't seem in the mood for further conversation, "About twenty minutes, so settle down, look at the countryside, and shut your cake-hole for a bit." Quinn settled into the seat. They were soon out of town and he watched the countryside rolling by. Houses became thinly scattered, replaced by fields, and the roads deteriorated until the Land Rover was bouncing and vibrating.

"What's that line of hills?' Quinn indicated a grey mass on the near horizon.

"Malvern Hills, God have you never been here with your mam?" she teased him.

"I'd never been outside Brum until I got on that ferry. I'm a city boy me – streets, cuts, and gulleys."

Marie responded, "Well you're gonna find it a bit different out here. It's all farming and you'll be expected to pitch in and earn your keep."

Quinn smiled to himself. He was no farmhand, and had other plans - but he would roll with this until it suited him to do otherwise. He had all of his life before him, money of his own, a deadly organisation behind him, and no fear.

That was a much better hand than he had expected fate to

deal him. Eighteen months ago he had been staring at life in and out of prison and he knew that his fear of confinement, his hatred of the 'screws' and his temper meant that once in as an adult he might never have emerged.

Marie negotiated a tight turn into a muddy lane. Quinn caught sight of fencing and low buildings through the trees then it was lost from view.

"What's over there?" Quinn enquired. "It's an airfield, very hush-hush. They did secret research there in the war although there aren't many planes going in and out these days. Your uncle's land runs alongside the fence."

They pulled up outside a squat, solid farmhouse. To the right was a yard full of chickens surrounded by barns. A mean-looking German Shepherd on a chain stood up and barked until it saw Marie alight from the car, "Sheba, quiet! Don't mind him Pat, once he gets to know you it will be fine but he's a bastard with strangers and that's the way we like it."

Quinn followed her inside.

Marie showed him around. There was a large kitchen with a family-sized table and a wood-fed stove at the end of the entrance hall. Two large downstairs rooms, one obviously reserved for best, the other much used with mismatched but comfortable looking furniture and an open fireplace.

Marie indicated another, smaller room, and Quinn glimpsed piles of papers strewn around in a haphazard fashion.

"That's Michael's office although he's not much of a book-keeper. Come on I'll show you your room, you're lucky, got one of your own." Marie ushered Quinn up the stairs, across a square landing, and into a small room containing a single-bed, an old wardrobe and what looked like a home-made shelving unit.

Tour over, she concluded, "You can do what you want with it, use your own money. It'll do you fine. Now let's go and find Mike and Seamus, I think they are out looking for early lambing."

"Seamus?"

"Our fine and strapping son. Don't mind him if he doesn't seem friendly, it's his way with strangers and he's not in love with our friends and backers over the water."

In the porch Marie indicated a motley line up of wellington boots "You can buy your own but for now see if any of those fit."

They tramped out through the quagmire in the yard as Sheba eyed Quinn suspiciously. He liked the look of that dog and resolved to get to know it better.

"How big is the farm?" Quinn asked.

Marie was chatty now, "A good size, land was cheap after the war and Mike – or should I say our friends overseas, are still buying it when it comes up."

"So you don't own it yourselves?" Quinn enquired.

Marie's voice dropped as if she were ashamed, "No, we farm it, run it, provide a safe-house and help when there's need, and we pay no rent and get a wage. Why do you think they sent you here."

Quinn looked puzzled, "I thought it was because Michael is my uncle?"

Marie shook her head, "Well there is that, although he and your mam were never close once she married your dad. He thought we were trouble and was never keen on visiting. He wasn't too pleased when he found out we were just down the road from him in Birmingham. No, you're here for their future purposes and you'd better not forget that son. We do as we are told; you wouldn't want to cross them."

They entered a field where two figures were tending to a fence in the distance. A well-used tractor and trailer full of posts and wire sat comfortably in furrows of recent ploughing.

The two men stopped work and watched them approach. They were both stocky but the younger one was an imposing figure. He was in his early-twenties by the look of it, well over six-feet-tall, with broad shoulders and a barrel chest. He had been whacking the fence posts in with a sledge hammer that he hefted from hand to hand as he eyed Quinn speculatively without any trace of a friendly greeting.

Marie spoke to the older man, who was short and squat, and bore a face akin to a potato with a couple of day's stubble, "Michael, this here is Pat."

Quinn's uncle had an Irish lilt heavily infected with a Worcestershire burr and a hint of Birmingham whine.

He extended his hand, "Good day to you Pat. You're welcome here. Hope you like physical work – that's the way you pay your rent."

Quinn felt a firm grip, "Marie has already told me. I've never farmed but I'm not afraid of work."

Michael pointed to Seamus with his thumb, "This is me son, Seamus - Seamus say hello."

No hand was proffered as Seamus grunted an acknowledgement but made no attempt to engage further.

Sensing the tension Michael continued, "Now then Seamus, Pat here is a guest sent from over the water so you should make him welcome."

Seamus looked Quinn in the eyes, "Those cunts can fuck off and so can he, I'm sick of you bowing and scraping to them. I'll be in the barn sorting the pigs when you want me." He marched off across the field still throwing the sledgehammer from hand to hand.

Michael watched him go; Quinn could see a mixture of emotions playing across his face - amusement, anger, and fear. There was some pride when he spoke though, "Seamus doesn't like outsiders, and as he was born here his connections to our mutual friends aren't as strong as they should be. He says what he thinks but he's a good boy, works hard, and I've got no complaints about him. He's our only child and I expect he's got used to being the only cock in the roost. You and he will have to sort things out but I expect it'll be fine once you get to know each other."

Quinn shrugged; this sort of reaction was nothing new to him. It would be resolved one way or another.

Michael continued to talk about the farm, the sorts of jobs he would be expected to help with, and a bit about the area. When he finished Marie escorted Quinn back to the house and let him unpack.

Over the next few days Quinn orientated himself with his uncle's blessing, walking the farm, and the immediate locality. One side of the farm was bounded by the chain link and barbed wire of the old airfield. Within the fence Quinn could see crossed runways, surrounded by fields and woods, hangers and some nondescript buildings. A large sign on the fence promised dire punishments for trespassers. Quinn moved on, this wasn't the time to be stopped by the military and checked, neither he nor his backers wanted anyone enquiring into him too closely.

So far, his cousin had managed to avoid him other than maintaining a stony silence at the evening meal when they were obliged to eat together. He was out before Quinn got up and always seemed to be in a different part of the farm, often working with the regular labourer, Steve Richardson. They clearly had a close bond although Richardson was much older, mid-thirties.

Richardson lived on the farm, in one of the outbuildings that had been converted into rudimentary living-quarters comprising a room with a bed, old chairs and a sink. It abutted the barn where the labourer seemed to spend most of his spare time messing about with an old motorbike. Marie had called it 'Steve's garage' on their initial tour and Quinn had caught sight of tools, oil, petrol cans, and various spares parts lying around. He had already got used to the 'thump

thump' of the bike's four-stroke engine as Richardson went out or tinkered with the machine.

If Quinn tried to approach Richardson, or his cousin, and engage them in conversation they either left, or turned their back on him, and ignored him. Quinn was rapidly becoming pissed off with this situation and his anger had been on a slow burn that he was struggling to keep the lid on.

Late in the afternoon on his fourth day at the farm he spied Seamus enter the old hay-barn that was set some distance from the main yard. Seamus was alone, as his uncle had gone to fetch some supplies from Worcester. Marie was cooking in the farmhouse kitchen. He could see Richardson on the tractor in a distant field.

Quinn kept out of the sight line of the barn as he approached and quietly opened the door. He didn't know what he was about to do but he knew that Seamus wasn't going to ignore him after today, one way or another.

He could hear sounds coming from the other side of the hay bales. Seamus was hefting heavy bales around as if they weighed nothing.

Quinn moved into view and Seamus caught sight of him as he turned, "What do you want?'

"To talk." Quinn responded. Seamus barked back, "Well I don't want to fucking talk to you so fuck off." Quinn bit down on an immediate rush of anger. He was only too aware that

Seamus could do a lot of damage, not only physically, but to his plans if he played this wrong.

Quinn spoke quietly, "I want to know why you're so fucking rude and angry when we've never met before. What have I done to you?"

Seamus considered for a moment. He seemed to be in no hurry to answer. He walked up close until Quinn could feel and smell his breath. Quinn stood his ground - not the time to back off, and anyway retreat didn't figure highly in his methods.

Seamus nailed his colours to the mast "It's what you stand for more than you, although I can't see what they see in a strip-of-piss like you either. Those bastards over there think they own us, treat my parents like shit. They get ordered around, can never own this place, no matter how hard they work, and they might as well be in prison because they can never walk away. Well they don't own me, and you coming here and being forced into our house rubs salt in the wound."

Quinn never took his eyes off Seamus; he was waiting for the flicker in those green eyes that would presage an attack.

Quinn hit back, "You've decided all about me then, without even speaking."

Seamus spat the words out, "Don't need to talk - you came from them. Mind you, I was expecting something a bit more impressive, can't see why they'd spend time and money on a spastic like you. I heard you fancy yourself a bit but you look like you couldn't punch a your way out of a paper bag."

There was an inevitability about where this was going that Quinn had recognised some seconds before but as he prepared to act his arms were suddenly pinioned behind his back.

"Hello there little man, upsetting my friend Seamus?" Steve Richardson must have seen him approach the barn and followed. Seamus instantly unleashed a pile- driving punch into Quinn's stomach that drove the wind out in an audible whoosh and doubled him up. He grabbed Quinn by his chin, forcing his head up.

Seamus shouted, "Time for a little lesson, and then you can fuck off somewhere else and tell them you don't like it here." He slapped Pat open-handed.

They were both overconfident though, and had no idea of what they were dealing with. The slap wasn't hard enough to do anything other than rile Quinn, and the few seconds it, and the talk had taken, had allowed him to recover some of his breath. Quinn let the rage rise.

He whacked his head backwards, and then drove it forwards, jabbed both elbows backwards and was free of Richardson and past Seamus before they could react. He picked up a baling fork and swung the wooden handle against Seamus' skull, propelling him forward and on top of the already staggered Richardson. They both fell heavily. Instantly Quinn reversed the fork and held one tine to his cousin's neck. Seamus froze, with Richardson still beneath him.

Quinn spoke calmly, "Two onto one, that ain't very fair, and you a lot bigger than me, and him a lot older." Seamus made as if to move and Quinn dug the tine in until it made a visible dent in his skin.

He continued, "Don't fucking even think of it, I'll spit you like a fat pig. You could gamble that I ain't got the bottle but do you really think the boys over the water didn't test that? Got us a problem here haven't we? I need to stay, I've got plans, but fighting each other ain't part of them. There's a fucking world out there for the taking and we're rolling round in the fucking hay."

Quinn paused for effect whilst maintaining his hold, "Seamus, I do get it. Never had much time for parents, but I can see how it would grate, being owned by them bastards."

He stepped backwards still holding the fork pointed at the entanglement of limbs on the floor. Seamus rolled off Richardson and rose clumsily to his feet, looking at Quinn, weighing up his next move. Richardson let out a long, audible breath then followed the big man. They approached Quinn who held out the pitchfork towards them.

Quinn deliberately lightened the moment and nodded towards Richardson, "I bet you thank fuck for him rolling off you", he turned to Seamus, "I pity any woman you fuck you big bastard."

Richardson threw his head back and laughed aloud, "Pretty good move, I think its earned you a minute's talking. What do you say Seamus?"

The tension in the barn ebbed with Richardson's laugh and even Seamus half- smiled as he rubbed the back of his head, "Okay carry on."

Quinn lowered the pitchfork slightly and leant back against an upright, "I've got an understanding with our Republican friends but they don't know what I really think. I have my own ideas in here." Quinn tapped his head.

"That's a deadly game to play," observed Seamus.

Quinn was taking a calculated risk, "I passed their tests. My family background is trusted. They see an opportunity to use me because I'm English and I can live with that for now. What have they got to lose?"

Seamus snorted, "Nothing like as much as you do if you fucking cross them."

Quinn continued quietly but in earnest, "True, but it suits me too for the moment. They paid me. They want me. It makes sense to go along with it. What else can I expect from life? I hated school, I'm alone and no-one is really bothered if I live or die and all I'm good at is fighting. They're the only people who've shown any interest. The only people – including my own parents, who've said I'm worth something. So I did what they wanted, but kept my eyes open, watched, listened and learnt, much more than I ever did at school."

Seamus' voice remained scornful, "And how would that stop us giving you a beating and kicking you out of here on your arse right now?"

Quinn spoke confidently, "Well, I'm the one holding the pitchfork. I've seen how they operate. They've got fingers in every pie; people shit themselves if they think they've crossed them.

They're the ones running things and they might be doing it for God or politics but they're making a heap of money at the same time. I want a bit of that for me."

Quinn could see that both of his listeners were interested, as they hadn't bothered to stand. He went on, "I've had plenty of time to think. They're happy to set me up here. At some point they'll want things done and I can make money out of that when the time comes, but for now I'm free to do pretty much what I want, so long as I don't rat on them, or do something stupid. I've got money of my own from the shipping line. It's blood money to help me overcome the oh-so-sad loss of my family. I want to do something with it other than piss it up a wall. I haven't a clue what as yet. One thing I do know is that at seventeen no-one will take me seriously - which is where you two bastards come in."

The two men began brushing themselves off cautiously, no longer a threat. They were listening intently now.

Quinn went on, "We can be like them, but over here. I can't do it on my own though. I can handle myself but I can't take on the world alone. To do what they do you need people who ain't scared to break the law and inflict a bit of pain, people tougher than the rest. You hard enough for that?

Richardson laughed again, "Why would I though. I'm a lot older, been in the army, seen and done stuff, you're just a kid."

Quinn felt he was winning the argument, "I'm not asking you to follow me or do what I say. We'll be equal. I've got ideas, connections, and some money. There's fucking cash to be made –

enough for us all. What else are you going to do? What are you, thirty? Put your life on the line to fight for your country and what thanks did you get? You're fucking about in the mud and cold, labouring, and it looks like you ain't planning to do much else. I reckon you're owed, so take what's yours."

Richardson nodded, looking thoughtful, "Why me and Seamus though?

Quinn replied, "Because we're here, now. I was going to have a bit of a look for a while, see what the lay of the land was, but here we are, and I don't think we can leave this barn without sorting it out one way or another. I can't stay here and work on anything I'm aiming for unless Seamus is with me, and it seems you two come together. Look at us; apart we are doing nothing, but together who fucking knows? What have you got to lose?"

Seamus brushed some more of the straw off, "Nice words but how does that help me, and mine? Your 'sponsors' just about own my parents, and because of that me too."

Quinn chose his words carefully, sensing that an important moment in his life had arrived, "We'll have to be careful. They'll need to believe we're working for them, and we will, but we'll do our own stuff too. If we play this right, and remember we have time on our side, we can be so useful to them that they need us, but any side- lines mean we can stand on our own two feet. Up to you how you use any money we make. If you want, you can do it to help your parents out, save up for a farm for them if it bothers you?"

Seamus snorted again, "Sounds like a fucking dream to me –

come on Steve, I think I still want to stick that fucking pitchfork up his arse."

Richardson pondered, he had a wiser head, "Maybe, maybe not. Let's have a think about this. You don't want him here but if he doesn't stay at least for a while questions will be asked and that could cause Mike and Marie some difficulties. I know you wouldn't want that, and neither would I. They looked after me when I was at a pretty low-ebb, gave me a place to stay, and help when I was lost. I might not be here now if it wasn't for them."

Richardson paused while Seamus cogitated. Quinn could almost see the thoughts being processed. His cousin might be a giant in bulk but it clearly didn't extend to his intellect. The farmhand continued, "Secondly, we've got nothing to lose. He sticks around - we see what happens. If it looks okay that's fine, if not, then I've got a deal for him."

He moved his attention from Seamus to Quinn, "What do you say to this? We give you; say six months to see how things go. If it's okay, if we get on, if we can see some potential, then you stay, as you say equal partners. If it doesn't work then you agree to leave and spin some bullshit to cover all our backs. You can tell the Irish boys whatever you like but you go and leave us alone. Be warned if you think you can double-cross us in some way we'll find a way of making you vanish and you won't see it coming."

He looked back at Seamus, A long few seconds elapsed then the big man gave one very deliberate nod.

In fact this was a better offer than Quinn had expected, he

had been ready to fight. Six months was a long time and he just felt somehow that fate had created this meeting, in this place, with these two men, for a reason. He had always leant on his feelings and inside he was feeling a sense of fit with these two and this place.

Finally he announced, "Agreed, I'll walk if it doesn't work out. I've got a good feeling about this."

He stuck the pitchfork in the ground. Richardson stretched out his hand. Still cautious, Quinn reached forward and shook it.

"Welcome to country life city-boy," Richardson laughed.

Quinn turned to Seamus. His cousin didn't offer a hand. He shifted forward to look Quinn in the eyes, still searching for something. His voice was not friendly, "Just don't start thinking we're friends. You're on trial, so don't forget it.

Chapter Nine: 'Wild Horses'

(Perry Como)

1953

The arrangement seemed to work. Marie and Mike sensed that something had happened, but Seamus' admittedly taciturn acceptance of Quinn relieved them of a worry.

That first week, after the deal had been cut in the barn, Steve Richardson had clearly decided to take Quinn at face value. He made it his mission to show him the farm and the surrounding area. He patiently explained how to perform some of the tasks and announced his intention to teach Quinn to drive.

"You won't do nothing unless you can get about and you need to be able to work that tractor too," he said.

They started with the old Massey Ferguson and Quinn discovered to his delight that he picked up the basics quickly and within a few days had progressed sufficiently to earn Steve's praise. They then moved onto the Land Rover.

He had some trouble with the clunky gears and Steve taught him to double - declutch to get round that. The steering was imprecise and the suspension rock hard but within a couple of days Quinn had got the hang of it whilst bouncing around the farm tracks. He loved it. It was the first time he had been in control of such power and it seemed to connect straight into whatever passed for his soul.

Uncle Michael approved, "That's a useful skill you'll be needing and no mistake. You've picked it up really quickly, we'll have to see about getting you a test in a couple of months."

"As soon as you like, how do I do that?" Quinn enquired.

Michael replied, "Leave it with me; I'll go into the Test Centre next time I'm in Worcester."

Satisfied with the answer Quinn continued his tuition whenever he could, in between helping out around the farm. Another couple of days and the initial thrill of the Land Rover began to wear off - it seemed slower and more lumbering every time he drove it. He wanted to go faster, drive harder; the burning rage that lived within him sought an outlet in speed.

One afternoon, about a week after Quinn had begun driving the Land Rover, Steve came over to where he was pounding in yet another fence post with a sledgehammer whilst Seamus crouched, supporting it.

"Go on give it some hommer Pat", Steve teased him, and then turning to Seamus announced, "I've got it in the barn."

Seamus stood up, clearly excited, "I'll be over when the boy has finished knocking this in - if he ever does, get a fucking move on, I've got better things to do today."

Quinn gave the post another couple of lusty blows, "What could be better than this?"

Steve replied, "I've got Seamus' new transport, but he's got to learn to ride it." Quinn finished whacking in the post, "Can I come and see it too?"Seamus looked at Steve for guidance. The older man considered, "Don't see any reason not to. Perhaps we can see how you do on two wheels."Seamus interjected, "Not on my two wheels."Richardson was already used to keeping the peace between them, "That's okay he can use mine. He can clean it afterwards to pay for the use."

They walked across to Steve's part of the old barn and into the ad-hoc workshop. Steve waved towards a motorbike leaning crazily on its side stand,

"There you go mate. I had to get you something bigger than a Bantam or you'd have looked bloody stupid. Good bike this, Triumph Speed Twin. 500cc. Needs a bit of work but I can do that, there are plenty of bits for them about. I know where there's another one that I'm hopefully going to get for myself."

Seamus walked across to the bike and ran a hand along the tank, then lifted it upright and swung his leg across the saddle. He still dwarfed the bike.

"Can you ride?" asked Quinn.

Steve replied, "I taught him on mine, he's passed his test on it as well so he's ready to go. Fire her up and have a go Seamus, its got petrol in it and I rode it here without a problem." Richardson enjoyed the moment of being centre of both men's attention.

Seamus jumped up into the air and crashed down onto the kick-start a couple of times and the barn was suddenly filled with the pop, pop of the four-stroke engine and the acrid smell of exhaust fumes. He gunned the throttle, engaged gear, and guided the bike through the barn doors. He twisted the rubber throttle control and sped off down the entrance track to the farm.

Quinn was immediately captivated - the sound, the look, the speed, "You said you could teach me too?"

Richardson was more relaxed with Quinn now, "You ready to get on an iron horse? Sure. Let's start now. We'll know straight away if it's for you or not."

They watched Seamus for a while, cavorting backwards and forwards along the track, getting the feel of his new machine, and then Steve indicated they should go back inside.

"This one's a bit more of a knacker, but it'll do to try." he nodded towards the other bike, a battered looking item that was clearly ex-Army and still khaki green. He pushed the bike off its stand and wheeled it outside and pointed it towards the muddy track that led to the fields, "Pride of the infantry, I introduce my BSA M21 single pot. 600cc. Bit big and heavy for you to learn on – it was okay for that big fucker but you'll have to make do as it's all we've got. It needs a rebuild and I should have my new bike soon so it doesn't really matter if you drop it in the mud. You can see me right later for any damage."

He held the bike whilst Quinn got astride it. It felt right when he took hold of the handlebars and felt the weight as Steve released it. Steve explained the controls and then showed him how to tickle the carb and start it with a couple of fierce kicks. Quinn felt a thrill as the engine roared into life then settled into distinct single detonations sending vibrations through his frame.

"Can you ride a bicycle?" Steve shouted over the noise. Quinn laughed, "Yes used to all the time, and stole a few too!" Steve went on, "Right, we'll start with balancing first and then steering, forget gears. Pull the clutch lever in and then give it some revs and gently let out the clutch like I showed you in the Landy. Ride up the track a bit then pull the clutch in and brake using the foot and handlebar levers together. If you don't, on that mud you'll either lock the back wheel or go over the bars."

It took twenty minutes and he fell off three times before he mastered the basics but he was soon pulling off, braking, and then turning the bike around.

Richardson slapped Quinn on the back, "Good, welcome to the world of being covered in mud and shit, goes with the territory. Now we can move onto gears and get a bit of speed up. Just remember it will hurt if you fall off this time so don't."

Seamus had returned by now and sat astride his new steed watching.

Richardson continued with his lesson, "The main track now then, up and down like Seamus did until you can go through all the gears, turn and stop.

Quinn set off. A few times he crunched the gears, wobbled, or let the clutch out too sharply but after twenty minutes or so he could go from one end of the track to the other, turn at either end and get up to top gear and back down again. Not very fast he supposed, but the experience was a revelation.

He loved every second of this. Steve was right; it was a horse - a wild iron one! He drank in the feeling of limitless power at his disposal and the visceral connection with the machine, feeling its life vibrate through his body - and the speed! The exhilaration of acceleration, the rush of the wind as his face buffeted through it. Here was naked sensation to sate the heat that raged within him.

Richardson signalled to him and reluctantly Quinn brought the old BSA back and hit the kill button, turning it once more into lifeless metal. Quinn noticed that Seamus looked unhappy and realised that he might have pissed on his cousin's big moment. He mentally shrugged, that would resolve itself one way or another.

"That wasn't bad, you picked it up quickly. We can carry on another day. You can have another go in the Landy too," Richardson concluded.

"You can keep it, I want one of these," Quinn asserted.

Richardson brought him back to earth, "Whoa, steady on, you need to be able to use both. Can't carry much on a bike - it's not discrete, everyone sees them and remembers. You need to drive cars and trucks to be of any use round here. So far that's all you've got to offer, so think on."

Quinn was happy to allow the admonishment, "Okay, but that's the first time I've ever felt like that and I'm not letting it go."

Steve laughed, "That's fine, let's see what we can do."

The days passed quickly, with Quinn gradually learning to be of use whilst practising his driving and riding at every opportunity. He was frustrated that he had to wait on the availability of Steve's bike, but he was growing to like the older man and appreciated both the chance Steve had given him, and the introduction to the wonder of riding.

It was clear that there would be no similar offer from Seamus; in fact the relationship had worsened since that day when Quinn had first got on the bike. Something was festering with his cousin.

At first Quinn tried his hardest to ignore it, but his innate combative nature was hard to suppress and he instinctively recognised that this needed resolving one way or another, and soon.

The opportunity came when Marie and Mike went to Worcester market, which they did regularly, to sell whatever was in season. Steve had taken the opportunity to have a day off to visit his parents in Coventry and had roared off on the BSA early in the morning.

The cousins had worked in a significant silence punctuated by the odd curt command from Seamus until Quinn could take no more. He addressed the unforgiving back that he had been looking at most of the morning, "Right, that's it. I've had enough of looking at your arse, turn round you ignorant fucking lump."

Seamus swung round, his face suddenly flushed. "Who the fuck do you think you are? You come into my home and family with your big ideas, backed up by those friends of yours, who are no fucking friends of mine. You walk about as if you own the place, but you're nothing, just some shitty kid from the arse-end of Birmingham. You might have sweet-talked my parents, might have convinced Steve, but I still think you're a piece of shit with no hope who is going to be nothing but trouble for us. Steve gave you six months and I only agreed because of him, but you've done nothing yet to prove yourself and I think your time is up – now."

He lashed out with his huge fist knocking Quinn flat on his backside, head ringing.

This was the language that Quinn understood. He shook his head to clear it, could feel blood dripping down from his nose. The magma of his pent-up rage erupted. He leapt to his feet and drove forward head-butting Seamus in the stomach, knocking him down in turn. Quinn launched himself into a flurry of punches to Seamus' face and body.

But Seamus was strong, threw Quinn from him, and regained his feet, panting, and his eyes mad. He too had been blooded now. He charged Quinn who sidestepped like a matador and rabbit-punched as the larger man lurched past him. Trouble was, a punch that would have felled others just made Seamus angrier.

Seamus kept trying to get a grip on Quinn so that he could crush him but he was too quick, landing punches and kicks although he took some sledgehammer blows too, which rocked him, but he had long ago mastered fighting and pain.

It soon became clear that Seamus would never catch Quinn but for his part Quinn couldn't put him down. It was stalemate and they faced each other, bloodied and gasping. There was suddenly a change in the atmosphere, a mutual respect born of conflict.

Quinn gasped between breaths, "Big man, you take some punishment, this could go on for a long time – tell me - what's the point?"

Seamus was blowing like a racehorse, "Stop running away you little fucker."

Quinn wiped the blood from his face, "You fight your way - this is mine. I'm telling you, if you do get hold of me, if you beat me bloody, you'll have to kill me to stop me getting back up. I've never lost a fight and I'm not starting here."

Seamus spat the words "I might just like putting you out of your misery, the well would take your shitty body no problem." He paused again for breath, "You're a tough little bastard though, and quick, I'll give you that."

Quinn tried bridge-building yet again "We'd be unbeatable together wouldn't we? Think on that."

Quinn stopped himself smiling as he watched the effort of Seamus trying to think his way through the options, and saw the moment he failed in his face, "You might be useful at that. But its still six months and out unless I'm happy."

Quinn said, "Agreed. I knew it wouldn't be sorted though until we had had this out."

Quinn extended a hand, warily. He kept eye contact as

Seamus shook it, just in case, but had begun to work his cousin out now and had a feeling that the events of the past few minutes presaged a change in their relationship. This was the language that his cousin understood and trusted, man-to-man, trading blows.

Seamus took a step back "Let's get cleaned up before they get back - tonight we go drinking."

Chapter Ten: 'Money Honey'

(The Drifters)

1953

It was clear that Steve had been told what had happened and was pleased that a truce of sorts was finally in place.

Quinn rode pillion behind him down to Pershore and the pub. Pat Quinn relished the open road. Not as much fun as being in control of a bike himself but once he had learnt how to lean in concert with Steve he felt comfortable on the back.

The Star Inn on the High Street was an elderly but imposing building fronting the main road that had clearly once been a coaching inn. Two strings of fading Union Jacks fluttered sadly across the eaves, a leftover from the Coronation party two months earlier.

Seamus rode alongside on the Triumph and they roared to a stop outside the Inn. A burst of raucous laughter erupted from inside and the hubbub of many voices trying to be heard. There was evidently a crowd inside.

"This is our local," said Seamus, "It can be a bit rough and ready but most in here are alright. You won't have any trouble getting served while you're with us, anyway you look old enough, especially with those bruises." Seamus clearly found humour and some satisfaction in the damage he had inflicted earlier.

They pushed their way through the smoky air with Steve and Seamus greeting a number of acquaintances en-route to the bar. Steve acquired four pints in dimpled mugs from a barman he clearly knew well. They found a seat in a corner. Quinn was about to ask who the fourth pint was for when they were joined by a compact man who nodded a greeting to Steve.

Steve introduced them, "Frank this is Pat, Seamus' cousin. He's come over to live at the farm for a while so you'll probably see him out with us. Pat, this is Frank, he was in the Army too, although a different mob."

Quinn shook hands and noted that although Frank was about six inches shorter, he was possessed of a fearsome grip and a fearless stare. Steve continued, "Frankie here has a room over at the church, helps out with the maintenance and does the grave-digging too."

"Religious?" asked Quinn – it was not meant to be a serious comment.

Frank laughed at the thought, "No way. It's a long story but basically I was a bit lost after the war and had seen and done some things that made it difficult to come back to ordinary life. I felt like I'd been used, then spat out without so much as a thank you. I moved around for a few years doing bits and pieces then ended up here. The vicar found me sleeping in a doorway, offered me some charity that I refused so I ended up doing some work for him. He decided I needed saving, in more ways than one, and I'm pretty handy for fixing stuff. I needed somewhere to stay and put down some roots. The rest, as they say, is history, and I'm still here. Met Steve here a couple of years ago, recognised an ex-squaddie and we agree on a lot of things.

We hit it off and have stuck together ever since."

Quinn's curiosity was aroused, "So what did you do in the war?"

Frank looked at Steve who adopted a reassuring tone, "It's okay Frank, he wouldn't be here if we didn't think we could speak openly."

Frank launched into a low monologue imbued with anger, "Ended up doing some sneaky stuff. I'd done climbing when I was younger which they found useful. Also, I was a country lad and did a bit of poaching – a lot actually. I knew how to track, move silently, was used to being out in the dark and how to kill things. They liked all of those things. Unfortunately for me, they might have been valued when there were Germans to kill, and a war to be won, but they are of no use in polite society and I feel like I've been tossed on the scrapheap.

I've no time for whatever you call the people in charge of things. They use ordinary people, get rich off us, and have a nice life, thank you. I'm left digging graves, pity I never get to bury any of them bastards. No, it's always the ordinary poor people. Sorry son, but that's how I feel." His attempt at making something of a political speech at an end he uplifted his glass, slammed it on the table, and concluded, "Who's buying the next one?"

Quinn told his story, with a few appropriate omissions, and it seemed to satisfy Frank although Quinn caught him looking quizzically a few times during the evening – he had clearly spotted the gaps. They were soon deep in conversation as to the rights and wrongs of life, with regular interjections in the same vein from Seamus and Steve.

It didn't take long for Quinn to slot Frank into his plans - if they ever came off. He was ideal. Against, and outside normal society, with an axe to grind, and more than a hint of some useful skills. Quinn suspected that he had done a bit more than climb and track things and by the look of him there was muscle in that short frame.

As they were talking, Quinn's eye was caught by a well-dressed fat man in his fifties, entering the pub with two younger men. Quinn was struck by the way the man conducted himself and interacted with the regulars. There was a lot of noisy greeting and backslapping but it seemed shallow and Quinn noticed that people drew away from the man after the initial pleasantries had been passed.

The man crossed to a table in the opposite corner, with one of his companions, whilst the other fetched drinks. The table was occupied but the two lads sat there drank up and left as the fat man approached. Once he had settled his bulk into a seat, and the third man had joined with drinks, Quinn watched as a steady stream of locals approached the table, spent barely a couple of minutes in conversation, then returned to their drinking positions some distance away.

After an hour a couple of thickset, rugged-looking men wearing donkey jackets entered the pub. After looking around the room they sat at the table and were soon engrossed in conversation with the fat man. Quinn knew a dodgy meet when he saw one; he'd been in plenty in Ireland.

Quinn turned back to his drinking partners, "Who's the fat fucker on the table opposite?"

Steve glanced across without making it obvious, "Brian fucking Collins. Bent businessman, and all-round piece of shit."

Quinn ventured further, "So what's his business and why is everyone keeping clear of him as much as they can?"

Steve resisted the temptation to spit "Bit of everything really, buying and selling you know the sort of thing. He got started in the war. Got out of serving, not sure how, probably bribed someone, that's his usual trick. Stayed here and got into the Black-Market. Made lots of connections, not only round here, but in Brum too. Lately he's been lending money out and I hear some late payers have had a thumping. He's getting a bit of a reputation. Employs those two heavies, supposedly knows some tasty people but that might be bullshit, this is the back of nowhere after all."

Quinn was getting interested, "And our donkey jacketed friends he's with?" Steve continued, "I'm not sure."Frank interjected, "I know. There's lots of Paddy's about – no disrespect Seamus. Brum is packed with them, but they seem to be round here too lately. The building-sites are full of them. Last year or so they've started putting down lots of new roads, and its all Irishmen doing it. Supposed to be a big un coming down here in the next few years. Those two are with the Irish boys on the roads."

Quinn was silent for a while as the others continued in conversation. He was following events on the table opposite. It was clearly some sort of business deal and he was sure that money changed hands in Brian Collin's favour. The meeting then broke up with handshakes and the donkey jackets left.

"Now what would he be selling to Irish navvies?" Quinn mused aloud.

Frank pitched in again, "That's no secret. He's flogging them two booze and fags in bulk. Been going on for about six months. I think those two take the stuff back to Brum and sell it to their Irish mates at a profit."

"Where does he get his supplies from?" Quinn was definitely interested now.

Frank shrugged, "Don't know - keeps his cards close to his chest that one. One of the reasons people steer clear is that he's very sensitive to prying eyes and there's been trouble in the past, that and the debt collecting. Decent people don't want to get involved and the ones that owe money try to avoid him."

But I'm not decent people', thought Quinn, "Where does he keep his stuff?"

Frank eyed Quinn again and then looked across at Steve looking for a sign to guide his answer. Finding none he replied, "Got a lot of questions haven't you? If I was you I'd find something else to be curious about."

Quinn was not about to give up, "Is it just the two minders?"

Steve took up the response, "Yes, that's all he's ever needed.

No real challenge out here in the sticks. One's his brother-in-law Geoff Burton, the other's a local hard-knock called Billy Gurney - born and bred here, always been trouble. The three of them have been thick as thieves for years."

"Are they as tough as they like to make out?" Quinn had made his mind up.

Frank sneered, "They are big and can fight but that's about it. As Steve said they've never had any challenge. The local farmers, farmhands, shopkeepers, and their kids don't pose any problem, and as I said he knows people in Birmingham so seems to be left alone, probably pays something to keep them sweet. Geoff's getting a bit old for it actually, got a wife and kids, and a regular job but I guess it's a good earner on the side and it's been easy so he just carries on. Billy is just trouble, not much brain but a good soldier for Collins. He does his dirty-work and no awkward questions."

A couple of days later, Quinn approached Steve and Seamus at the farm, "I need to talk, been thinking." The three settled down on hay bales in the barn, "Here's the thing, our fat friend Brian Collins and his business is there for the taking. We should be the ones selling to the Micks and I bet I can get the necessary supplies from over the water. Collins is so fucking sure of himself he wont know what's hit him."

There was a silence that Steve broke, "How would we do it? Three on three and we don't know anything about his operation."

Quinn outlined the plan that had been forming in his mind since the night in the pub. The others listened, and questioned, but both then finally agreed. Quinn spoke again, "Tell me about Frank. What more do you know about him?"

Steve replied, "I guess I know him best. He turned up about five years ago; I told you about that and what he does. I got chatting to him in the pub one night and we realised we had a lot in common and we got on so we've been friends ever since."

"Do you trust him?" Pat probed.

Steve thought for a moment, "I think so. He seems pretty straight, hates the establishment and toffs. I think there's some war-damage in there somewhere but he keeps it hidden most of the time. Yes I'd trust him."

Seamus cut in, "I would too, he's okay in my book." Quinn said, "Has he ever told you what he did in the war?" Seamus shook his head, "Only hints but I think he was in some sort of Commando outfit. He doesn't look much but I tell you he's strong, and he can really handle himself. Doesn't flaunt it but I saw two blokes have a go at him one night a few months after he arrived and he put them both down in seconds. Word must have gone round because no-one has messed with him since. I've been out at night with him too for rabbits and stuff and I can tell you he is so fucking quiet it's unbelievable."

Quinn smiled, "Sounds like someone we should have with us. Also gives us a numbers advantage over Collins. What do you both think? Would you be willing to sound him out?"

The others both agreed that Frank Fulford should be given the opportunity to join their fledgling enterprise.

Chapter Eleven: 'Rags To Riches'

(Tony Bennett)

1953

Quinn, Seamus, and Steve entered the back-street pub and chose a table where their backs were against the wall with the whole of the saloon bar in view. They were in alien territory and taking no risks. The meet had been arranged by others and was outside their control.

The bar was half-empty but the drinkers present were definitely Irish from their appearance, chosen drink of Guinness and unmistakable lilt, which carried around the room as they laughed and joked. Seamus had taken the lead at the bar as he could put on the Gaelic persona flawlessly when he chose. Steve had been uncomfortable and kept quiet. Quinn was confident that the word from his friends overseas would ensure their safety.

After about twenty minutes a group of four men entered and stood at the bar surveying the room. They nodded and two of the men crossed to the table. The leader seemed to be a little runty man with bright eyes and a face like a ferret. Quinn knew that appearances and size meant nothing in these circles so was not surprised that the runt did the talking, "Hello lads, welcome to Digbeth, home from home to the Irish abroad. Which one of you is Patrick?"

Quinn nodded - a hand was extended and shaken. The runt said confidently, "I'm Connor. I believe we have mutual friends."

"That's right. I have a proposition they think would be of mutual benefit to everyone concerned." said Quinn. Connor held up a hand to stop Quinn speaking and looked at Seamus and Steve questioningly.

"My cousin Seamus, and a friend Steve, both totally trustworthy." Quinn reassured the stranger.

Connor nodded, "Trust is earned, but you seem to be in credit so I'll take your word for it. If it proves otherwise it's your head on the block."

Quinn stood his ground, "I understand the situation, and I always have."

Connor seemed satisfied, "Okay, let's get to the point. I'm told that you want to go into business supplying essentials to our boys?"

Quinn nodded, "It seems that two lads from around here are buying from an Englishman called Brian Collins then selling at a profit in Brum. Do you know about that?"

Connor assented, "Yes, they aren't on the payroll but they haven't caused us any trouble. They are good lads performing a service and there hasn't been any need for us to get involved up to now."

Quinn continued, "There's a need now. The problem is that the profit is going into the Englishman's pocket and further on, his suppliers. We should be getting it - and our friends over the water. That profit could be used for 'The Cause' and to help us get set up a bit better over here. The reason they sent me back was so I could build something for the future on the mainland."

Connor nodded "I understand son. Its just you're so young, but it seems they like you so that's okay with me."

Quinn shrugged. "I can't do anything about my age but I've proved myself so far and they want this done."

Quinn could sense the interest of his companions quicken. This was the first confirmation of Quinn's credibility that they had experienced.

Connor wanted to move the conversation on, "I believe so. What are you proposing then?"

As they drew closer into a huddle Quinn said, "The supply route will move across there. They get the profit and can undercut anything the Englishman can do. We will sort out Collins and take over his operation. You get the buyers to co-operate and handle the distribution. From what I hear there are lots of customers, and lots more coming, so there should be plenty for everybody and the buyers will be happy getting cheap booze and fags. Everyone wins, bar the Englishman and his suppliers."

Connor tapped a finger on the table, "What about those suppliers, know anything about them?"

"Not yet," Quinn admitted, "But we can sort that out when we deal with Collins. All I know is that he has some links back to Birmingham, so it might lead back here."

Connor stroked his chin, "I don't like unknowns and loose ends but we've a strong presence here if needs be. Okay let's put some meat on the bones."

***

Quinn, Seamus, and Steve continued to visit Collins' haunt, The Star Inn, at least once a week. Frank was now a fixed attachment to the original trio. He hadn't needed much persuading, in fact had been keen.

Quinn was riding his own bike now, only a BSA Bantam D1, 125cc, obtained and renovated by Steve. It was small but it would do while he learnt. He had a test arranged in the Land Rover that would cover bikes as well. Steve was not only teaching him to ride, but also how to maintain and fix the little bike. Driving the Land Rover was a necessary evil to Quinn, he only wanted to ride bikes and he wanted something bigger already. It was the most alive he had ever felt, and riding struck directly into his animal instincts, aggression and fearlessness.

It also marked him out as different. When he was riding with the others he felt outside routine, free as the wind. He liked the way most people noticed them, but were also hesitant to approach, there seemed to be a fear reaction. That reaction didn't apply to plenty of girls who seemed attracted to the bikes, and their riders, all of whom had acquired old RAF black leather flying-jackets that looked imposing.

The four of them had become a regular sight around Defford, and Pershore, with the occasional foray into Worcester. Frank

Fulford was the proud owner of Steve's old BSA, and Steve had finally got his own Triumph Speed Twin to match the one Seamus rode.

Together they made their usual noisy, head-turning arrival outside The Star. It was late, and as anticipated, Collins and his two cronies were at their usual table. Quinn knew that Collins had been taking note of them and in turn had made no secret of the fact that he was watching the fat man. Several weeks had passed since the meeting with Connor and arrangements were now in place.

They stayed put until closing time but didn't drink much, in contrast to Collin's group who seemed to have money to spend and sank several pints each.

Quinn and the others had invested time quietly researching their targets, pooling their knowledge and on occasion following the trio.

Collins lived alone in a well-kept cottage a couple of miles out of town. They had not been able to locate any other premises - a problem as the cottage didn't look big enough to store large quantities of illicit goods. The love of his life seemed to be a Jaguar XK140 fixed-head coupe in which he cruised around the area. He also had a van parked outside the cottage.

Burton lived in town with his family, as Frank had said. He walked home from The Star but often could be seen driving an old van around town.

Gurney walked or cycled. Either he couldn't drive or wasn't trusted to do so. He still lived with his parents in a mean little terrace of worker's cottages on the outskirts.

Last orders were called. Everyone left the pub and there was the usual milling around outside as people bade each other goodnight. Collins made a point of ostentatiously leaving in his Jaguar and Burton made off on foot. The drinking crowd dwindled. Quinn watched Gurney set off and followed at a discreet distance. The others stayed by the bikes.

Quinn had insisted that he take this part of the plan himself. He was still on trial. He waited until they had reached a deserted section of town then sped up. Billy heard the footsteps, turned and walked back until they were face-to-face, "Fucking hell, if it isn't the nosey kid. Paying too much attention to other people's business. I've been meaning to put you right about that but you never seem to be without your mates looking after you. Mr. Collins don't like you nosing in his business so you better take some advice from...."

Before Billy had finished Quinn delivered a crashing head-butt that broke Billy's nose. He grabbed an arm and swung the man around and propelled him face first into the brick side of a building. Within seconds Billy found himself face down with Quinn's knees, and full weight crushing him to the ground. He turned his head in preparation to fight back and found himself looking into the point of a blade about three inches from his eyeball.

Beyond the blade Quinn's face came into view, "You're right Billy. Time for some advice, but it's going to be mine to you. Tonight there's going to be a change of boss and you've got a decision to make. Collins is going out of business and we're taking over. We've got the muscle and the backing from some serious people. Are you listening?"

Quinn banged Billy's head into the ground one more time and continued as Billy nodded furiously, "There'll be work to be done and you are top of my list to do it. You'll get paid well, you'll be doing pretty much the same sort of thing and you'll be looked after. The alternative is not really worth thinking about, but it involves pain and unemployment. I don't have you down as a man of loyalty and honour though. Has what I've said sunk into that thick head?"

Billy nodded again. He was beaten, limp and unresisting. Quinn shifted position but kept the knife close to the eye. He pulled Billy's arms behind his back and bound them tight, "I'm going to get you up now and we're going for a walk into the park. You can sit there and think things over. I'll be back later for you to give me your decision, but I think I know what it will be. You're a survivor Billy boy, like me."

Billy was soon secured, hidden from view in bushes, ankles bound and a gag in place.

Quinn said over his shoulder as he departed, "Don't try escaping. I'll track you down and it'll still be the same decision but with a lot more pain involved.

Ten minutes later Quinn joined the others in a lane a few hundred yards from Collins' cottage.

"Sorted?" asked Seamus.

Quinn nodded, "He won't be troubling us while we do this. I

haven't hurt him too bad, just enough to get through to that thick head."

"Is he worth bothering with?" asked Frank.

Quinn insisted, "We're going to need more muscle, people to carry, fetch and deliver stuff. He fits the bill and knows the business. He'll come over. He's in it for cash and to play the hard man."

Conversation ceased as they crept quietly up the unlit lane. The half-moon just afforded sufficient illumination, limning the verges and hedges in faint silver.

At the cottage, Frank headed off towards the rear whilst the others waited out of sight. He returned after a few minutes and whispered, "Okay all lights are off. I can get to the back easily enough, there's no fence, just backs onto fields."

"Okay we wait fifteen minutes to make sure he's in bed. You sure you can do this?" asked Quinn.

Frank sounded offended, "Piece of cake. I've got what you might call a bit of 'previous' at this game."

They waited in silence with their thoughts. Quinn in particular knew the price of failure. If his plan went wrong he would be blamed and evicted from the area so that the others could carry on as before. He had put himself on the line tonight. This was the point of no return.

The minutes passed. Quinn nodded and Frank crept away again. The tension was palpable as they waited for lights to go on, and cries of alarm, but the house remained shrouded in silence. After some minutes the front door opened and a hand could be see beckoning them forward.

Frank ushered them inside and indicated the stairs. He gestured for them to wait and set off carefully, testing each tread gingerly as he went. Quinn marveled at his ability to move silently. They waited until the quiet was shattered by muffled cries and then followed the sounds of struggle into the front bedroom.

Frank was already in control. Collins' large bulk was face down on the bed, arms pinioned, and a gag in place. The compact ex-army man was proving to be very handy indeed.

They quickly bound Collins' arms and levered him upright. His eyes were bulging in either fear, or anger, or both, and he was searching for air, nostrils flaring. Quinn punched him in the stomach once, his fist sinking into the rolls of fat. Collins doubled over.

Quinn and Frank walked their prisoner downstairs to the kitchen. Seamus and Steve had made preparations. A kitchen chair sat on a large tarpaulin they had brought along for the purpose. Collins shook his head when he caught sight of it and tried to push away, but another stomach punch ended the resistance and he was bound to the chair.

Quinn leant forward, inches from the florid, round face and wobbling jowls. He produced his blade and held it within view, "Hello Brian. I'm going to remove the gag in a minute. Understand. If you shout you'll lose an eye and the gag will go back on. We'll repeat the process until you stay quiet. I don't fucking care if you live or die tonight, but I'd rather not dig a big hole to put your fat arse in. Are you going to be quiet?"

Collins nodded vigorously. Quinn removed the gag and waited. There was silence broken only by gasping as Collins caught up on lost breath. Quinn continued, "Brian. Tomorrow is going to be either the first day of a new life for you, or tonight is going to be your last. There are no other choices. I represent some people who want your business. These are people that don't take no for an answer and have sent me to do whatever it takes to persuade you. Understand?"

Collin's ruddy complexion was turning a sickly, pasty pallor and Quinn noticed some beads of sweat breaking out. The man nodded again.

Quinn went on, "Just so you know, there'll be no help coming. I've taken care of Billy and I don't think Geoff will want to play this game, he's a family man and the stakes are too high - a conversation I'll be having with him in the morning when he arrives at work. So you're alone. You've had a good run, made some money, but as a big fish in a little pool. Got away with it for years, but trading with the Paddy's has got you noticed. You've over-reached yourself."

"I was just trying to make a living," whined Collins in a tinny, quavering voice.

Quinn was soothing, "We know, that's understandable, and it's why you're going to walk away from this with some money, and all your body-parts attached - if you do what we say."

A hint of colour returned to Collins' face and calculation to his eyes. Quinn picked up the change and suddenly slapped the fat jowls hard. Collins started shaking uncontrollably, reminding Quinn of a jelly on a plate.

Quinn raised the level of his voice, "Don't go getting the wrong idea. I might change my mind. My bosses don't care what I do with you. Now pin back those piggy ears."

Quinn spoke in a flat emotionless voice, emphasizing points by prodding Collins' forehead, causing it to bounce back and forth each time, "First, you are going to take us to where you keep your stock. We are going to take it off your hands for cash."

Quinn looked around, "This place - is it rented?" Collins nodded.

Quinn smiled thinly, "Good. You've got seven days to settle up and go. I don't care where so long as I never see or hear from you again. Understand?"

Another prod produced an affirmative nod.

Quinn was relentless, "You'll tell everyone you've decided to retire. I don't want to hear anything to suggest you've either gone to the 'Boys in Blue' or tried to get friends to fight your corner. Either way you'll lose. My backers are capable of some very ugly persuasion. You know who they are when I mention the Irish don't you?"

Collins knew alright, "Bombing bastards yes, you don't live round here for as long, as I have, without knowing what they are about. Been at it in Birmingham for as long as I can remember."

Quinn needed more, "That's right, and I promise you that if you don't play ball I'll personally ensure you get it in the most painful way I can dream up. Next question, where do you get your supplies from?"

Quinn used the point of the blade to encourage an answer by drawing a pearl of blood below an eye while holding Collins head firm against the chair back.

Collins screamed "For fucks sake, it comes from Birmingham - a bloke I've known for years, from the war times, he was just a kid then, we worked the black market together."

Quinn wasted no words, "Name and where we find him?"

All resistance had fled, "Charlie, Charlie Docker. He's got a lock-up in Digbeth."

"How do you contact him?" Quinn barked.

Collins was beginning to babble now, "We have a regular meet, once a fortnight at the dog track in Hall Green, York Road, been going for years. He runs a book there, can't miss him, he stands at the front of the main stand with a sign with his name on."

"When's the next meet?" Quinn demanded. "Wednesday." bleated Collins. "Don't go, we'll be there instead." Quinn instructed. Collins sought some redemption for himself, "Don't hurt him, he's a good guy, and don't tell him I ratted him out." All resistance had drained from Collins when the blood had welled from the nick under his eye. A coward, he had found a way to stay at home in the war and he wasn't about to die in Pershore instead. Besides he rationalized, maybe it was time to retire and have a change of scenery. It had been easy up to now, but he had always known this moment would come. He wasn't a hard man and this young boy, hardly yet a man, with his icy eyes, terrified him.

Quinn extracted some more promises of compliance and administered a few more cuffs for good measure before they freed him and left.

Collins' cottage was empty within days and neither he nor the Jaguar was seen again. Before he left he had taken Steve and Frank to an abandoned air-raid shelter hidden in scrub and tree growth. He was allowed to load his van with anything other than the alcohol and cigarettes for which he was paid an admittedly cheap price in cash. Then they let him go after expropriating the padlock and keys from his possession.

Geoff Burton had experienced no difficulty in renouncing his sideline once Quinn had pointed out the lay of the land. Quinn had sensed relief and suspected that Burton had been trying to find a way out, probably due to pressure from his wife who was known to view her brother's activities with stern disapproval.

They had retrieved Billy from the bushes, cold and miserable. He was now ostensibly employed as a labourer at the farm and seemed to be making the best of the situation. In fact he seemed quite happy. He was a simple thug who liked being in the strongest gang. Quinn and Seamus were of his generation and they quickly discovered that he too desired a motorcycle. The carrot and stick sufficed for Billy and, having been bested by Quinn he showed no inclination to repeat the experience. He enthusiastically embraced an offer from Steve to teach him to ride and find him his own wheels that he could pay for from his wages.

Quinn used some of his savings cash from the insurance payout to buy Collins' stock and Billy's loyalty. Aunt Philomena was only too happy to agree when told it was for 'The Cause'. It was not only a sound investment but underlined his position as the driving force of the enterprise.

Charlie Docker, the Birmingham contact and supplier of booze, had presented more of a challenge. Quinn was no fool. He knew he had no profile in the big city, in fact he would be completely out of his depth and unlikely to intimidate Docker on his home ground.

He had pondered the problem for a couple of days after Collins left. He doubted that Docker would ever know what had happened, his buyer had just vanished and there were many possible reasons for that, including problems with the law.

The fat-man had been the go-between with the Irish and had told Quinn that Docker had never met them, in fact wanted nothing to do with that side of the business. He was happy to let his rural partner take the risks whilst he remained in the background, pocketing his cut.

Quinn's usual method was to intimidate and fight but the lessons of Ireland had not been lost on him, and he had come to realize that cunning, trickery, and exploiting other's weaknesses, greed and beliefs could work equally well.

He had contacted Connor first. That had resulted in a couple of Irish lads having a quiet chat with Docker at the next greyhound meet. For a couple of weeks it seemed to have worked but one evening a stranger had appeared in The Star asking questions. Quinn hadn't been in the pub that night but Frank was and with some discreet questioning of locals had ascertained that questions had been asked about Collins' disappearance. The interrogator had sported a deep Birmingham accent.

Quinn paid another visit to Connor's local and discussed the situation. It was clear that Connor had been instructed to let Quinn sort it out, orders from across the water, another test. Connor did however provide information about Docker.

Apparently he was another black-market trader from the war - clearly where he had first forged links with Collins. He had history of trying to be big-time, but hadn't attracted backing and was not seen as having the necessary temperament to succeed. He was a low-key dealer and small-time crook. He also had a wife to whom he was apparently devoted and was therefore doubly vulnerable.

There had been a discussion in the barn as to how to resolve the problem. Steve had come up with the idea.

Firstly Connor arranged for a note to be delivered to Docker's house. It was a threat and it pointed clearly towards the Irish. Charlie Docker had until the next greyhound meet, three days hence, to stop digging, and accept his Irish trade was over. Quinn hadn't thought it would work and he was proved correct when

Docker gave the same two Irishmen short shrift at the track.

Frank's skills were employed next. Some components arrived at the farm with a travelling Irish road worker. Frank fashioned a credible dummy device. It was viable but not wired up. It bore all the hallmarks of the IRA. Frank attached it to Docker's van and left a note under a wiper.

'Next time it will be working.'

Quinn hadn't felt that was enough. Vivian Docker bumped into a heavily disguised Seamus whilst she was out shopping. The ensuing chat made it clear that consequences would follow if her husband did not comply. Vivian was given a bullet with the name 'Charlie' carved on the casing – a traditional Birmingham warning, as a memento of the meeting.

The next time the two Irishmen spoke with Docker he was more amenable and the matter was settled. He was out of his depth and had no way of challenging what he perceived to be the IRA taking over what was after all their own market.

The business settled down into a regular pattern after that. Official palms were suitably greased. Times were still hard, as Britain recovered slowly from war, and cash spoke. Supplies would arrive at the farm by various routes and means, and were moved to the old air-raid shelter. Billy Gurney got plenty of work, lifting and driving, and Connor handled the Birmingham end of the supply chain.

Profit flowed - it was a good start. Quinn, the young orphan, had taken his first steps towards his destiny, a destiny in which the name Docker was to surface again.

Chapter Twelve: 'Shake, Rattle & Roll'

(Big Joe Turner)

1954

They all owned bikes now, even Billy Gurney. Quinn had passed his test in the Land Rover, and rode a Triumph Thunderbird 650 that he had bought for cash at a very reasonable price. He had given the Bantam to Billy as a down-payment for future wages.

Billy's twin skills of thuggery and labouring had made a seamless transition to his new employers. In fact it was clear to all that he much preferred his new biking friends to being ordered around by the much older Collins. The lure of the bikes provided heady excitement and his new friends were more his age and outlook, especially Quinn.

Considering that Quinn had only a few months ago given him a beating, Billy displayed a dog-like devotion. He had met someone who was more violent and ruthless and that sparked something within Billy that resembled respect. He had been broken to heel but didn't even realize it. Quinn kept his amusement at the fact to himself; he appreciated the unswerving loyalty and knew that Billy would prove a useful addition to both the group and himself – another brick in the foundation he was building.

The market for cheap liquor, and cigarettes, was booming as more Irishmen crossed the water to assist in the post-war regeneration of England. Some brought families over and settled.

Many operated as jobbing itinerant gangs and lived in rooms together, a particularly fertile environment for Quinn's trade. Building-sites and new road projects provided a steady stream of jobs and cash, a nice percentage of which flowed into the waiting hands of Connor, Quinn and their backers in Eire. Everyone was happy.

It was late summer, 1954, just before the first Austin Cambridge motor-car was about to be unveiled. The process of moving, storing, and selling the shipments had settled down into a routine. Quinn and his group stayed very low-key. They had decided early on to minimize their profiles for a while and so, apart from some cash for bikes, clothes, and going out, most of the cash was stashed away at the farm.

Quinn was well into his eighteenth year but could easily pass for twenty. The lean frame had filled out courtesy of laboring and fighting. He was still as quick, hit harder, and maturity seemed to have merely fuelled the fires within. It was his face and eyes though that marked him out from his peers. He had already seen and done things that were etched there, things that many men never see and do.

Mike and Marie were supportive of the new situation, especially as their masters were involved and had given their approval. The couple benefited from extra income and both the furnishings in the farmhouse and the quality of life improved. Mike was saving for a newer tractor.

The outside world knew and cared little of mundane lives being pursued in rural Worcestershire and locally Mike and Marie were popular so no-one begrudged the fact that the farm seemed to be on the up. Motorbike gangs were an unknown concept, so Quinn and the others were viewed as a group of work friends who happened to ride bikes, a very common mode of transport when few could afford cars. Quinn and his new friends viewed themselves in this way too.

Quinn's six months trial had expired sometime in July without mention. He was accepted. He had proved himself. There was a growing bond forged in criminality and adversity. No-one discussed leadership, there was no need, but it was apparent that Quinn was firmly in control of the direction they were taking and, despite his youth, was a man with ideas, a lethal support network, and a level of ruthlessness and focus rarely encountered in one so young.

In fact he was already looking for further opportunities to make money. Now that Billy and Frank were on board Steve had some help and time on his hands. He was proving to be a very good mechanic, having been Army trained, and seemed to find it easy keeping all their bikes on the road, tuned and serviced. He clearly enjoyed the work and was spending much more time on that than on the farm.

Quinn had noticed that one of the outbuildings near to the lane was something of a dumping ground for odds and ends - wood, fencing wire and the like. One evening as they ate he broached the subject after Steve left the table, "How many mechanics are there round here?"

Mike stopped eating, a fork full halfway to his mouth,

"Nearest garages are Pershore or Worcester."

"Do you know how busy they are?" Quinn ventured.

"Very, it's a pain in the arse trying to get anything fixed quickly," Mike replied, mouth full.

Quinn said, "Why don't you use Steve? He seems to know what he's doing."

Mike scooped another fork full into his mouth whilst he considered the proposition "Don't know really. He was always needed round the farm and he hasn't got the equipment either. He's a good man with motors though; he could get a job doing it easy."

Seamus had stopped eating. He recognized the sign of another idea brewing as Quinn continued, "So why don't we set him up. We've got spare cash from the booze runs lying around doing nothing, that needs investing. If necessary I've still got most of my insurance payout, although I don't think we would need it and I may have another use for that.

I've been looking at that building by the road. It looks okay and it's in the right location for access. We could clear it out, dig an inspection pit, make a fenced yard and buy some tools and equipment."

Mike demurred, "It's an idea but how do we know he would get the trade."

Seamus interjected, "If I know Pat there's more to this than a bit of car and bike servicing."

Quinn nodded, "I think we need to have proper businesses, all legal and above board, that we can use to front some other stuff. You know that our friends want us to keep below the radar and this is the way. For instance, we might be in the business of acquiring some bikes and cars and moving them on – I saw quite a bit of that in Ireland and there might be some trade from over there. We can sell cars and bikes, and maybe parts from them. Everyone uses second-hand bits for repairs so there must be money in it, especially if those bits don't cost much to start with.

I think that Steve can make money legally as well, as there are plenty of cars, tractors and bikes round here to be serviced and repaired. The building and land are there, Billy and Frank can help more round here to free Steve up and between us, and the booze cash, we can set it up."

Marie spoke from the sink, hands deep in suds, "I like the idea Michael, Steve is wasted knocking fence posts in and that building is doing nothing."

Quinn responded to the support, "The other thing is we set it up as a joint business, including Steve. So that's you two, Seamus, Steve and me. I'm not having those fuckers over there owning me any more than is necessary and I think it's a way out of their control for you two." Quinn indicated Mike and Marie.

Seamus jumped in, "Anything that can get us out is worth a go, I think we should try it, what have we got to lose? We can't keep stuffing cash under mattresses."

Mike nodded thoughtfully, "Okay I've listened. So long as

there's no risk from the bosses."

Quinn spoke reassuringly "I'll speak to them. In fact I think I'll go over, it's about time they saw my face again. They're happy with me so far and I'll sell it as another trade route. They'll see more money and jump in. I'll share the profits with them but we retain ownership of the business. They own the farm so we must give them something. Let's see what sort of a deal I can do. If we tell them about it there shouldn't be any risk."

They all indicated agreement. Within days Quinn had travelled across to Derry and once more visited Jimmy 'One-Eye', in his pub alcove. The conversation had been amiable. Jimmy conveyed the fact that his bosses were pleased with the liquor and cigarettes trade and that Quinn had won some more credibility and trust. Quinn outlined his plan and stayed with Aunt Philomena whilst it was considered. He drank with his cousins, Thomas, and Mattie, and renewed some other acquaintances. There was no requirement for blood to be spilt this time.

Two days later Jimmy told him that the business was approved. The Irish would take twenty five percent of profits as rent for the buildings. Accurate records of the true business were to be kept in addition to the false but 'legal' accounts. They would send someone over every year to 'do a bit of an audit'. Jimmy thought that there was indeed be some useful trade to be done. There were handshakes and a confirmatory drink. As Quinn stood to leave Jimmy hugged him and whispered, "It's all good my boy, but ye make sure that we get everything we're owed."

Quinn could agree with that sentiment but for different

reasons - he was now in the car trade.

His timing could not have been better. With the advent of the new Road Traffic Bill in December, and a requirement for vehicles to have MOT certificates, Steve would be kept even busier getting them up to scratch.

The weeks rolled by, became months. The building was cleared, and a fenced compound created. The front was opened up and large double doors installed. The tractor made short work of digging a pit that was then lined with concrete. An entrance from the road led to a parking area. A large quantity of second-hand and stolen tools and equipment, a bespoke motorcycle ramp, and an engine hoist complemented the new set up.

Back in Ireland the name Quinn had come to the attention of someone more senior to Jimmy.

Chapter Thirteen: 'Tutti Frutti'

(Little Richard)

1955

As 1954 faded into a bitterly cold New Year, the group became a common sight locally and had begun to visit the relatively 'brighter lights' of Worcester regularly. There was a real buzz in the air, and the first West Indian immigrants began arriving in London, attracted to the promise of jobs and a bright new future. Wartime austerity was fading; suddenly there was cash around, and something to spend it on. The largesse began to filter down to the younger generations who found their own ways to burn money.

There were however still constant reminders of the frailty of life, as seventeen people lost their lives, and forty-three were injured, when a train derailed in Sutton Coldfield at the end of January. Such things reminded them that even astride their motorcycles they were not immortal. Quinn reflected that the sea was not the only thing that took people before their time.

Quinn, Seamus, and Billy were young and stuffed with cash so they found the pull of the city irresistible. Steve and Frank went along for the ride. The fresh post- war world that had suddenly discovered young consumers beckoned. In Worcester, teenagers had started to hang around at the new cafes that had sprung up and these inevitably drew the bikers too.

They were the cocks of the roost and were gratified to

discover that the combination of money, motorbikes, and a roguish reputation acted like lights to moths for the young ladies of the Faithful City. The cafes were better than pubs for meeting girls as they were in vogue and the clientele of smoky pub bars and lounges tended to be older and male.

Quinn may have already amassed experiences that few other nineteen-year- olds had benefited from, but he was subject to the same urges.

One spring day, Steve mentioned something new that he had read about in the Worcester News, "Look at this, a café with genuine Italian Ice-Cream and coffee, plus it's got a Yank Juke-Box with all the latest stuff – or so they promise. We should take a look." Having been introduced to the UK just weeks before Juke-Boxes acted as a magnet to the younger generation, seeking the thrill of new music, in a social setting.

It was called Lombardi's. It had been a dress shop on Foregate Street, just past the railway bridge, but had been converted into a stylish café. They had ridden past on many occasions without realizing that behind the whitewashed windows a transformation had taken place.

There was chrome everywhere. There were red leather seats, and a real Italian coffee machine, sputtering and hissing behind the counter - lovingly tended by Mrs. Lombardi. Presiding imperiously over the whole scene squatted a 1952 Seeburg M100C Juke-Box that took fifty 45rpm records giving a hundred plays.

It was a visitor from another world, one of glitz, glamour,

and American excess. Its benevolent ambiance shone across Lombardi's and sent out a siren call to the young of Worcester. Mr. Lombardi spooned out large helpings of Gelato to add to the heady mix of music, coffee smells, and the fever of both sexes as they met and romanced.

There was parking on the street outside and this provided the perfect stage for Quinn and his companions to roar up on their bikes a few days after the grand opening. They nonchalantly flicked down their bike side stands in view of a small group of smokers on the pavement, fully aware that those inside were also taking notice through the large, steamy windows.

They weren't the only bikers in town it seemed. A Manx Norton with gleaming chrome tank hung at an angle on its stand directly outside the door. The group stood and admired it for a while then entered the café.

It was a bedlam - music, shouting and laughter. In one corner an impromptu dance had sprung up. Quinn surveyed the interior and led the way to a corner table. The two young occupants decided to make a move as he approached. Quinn chose the optimum seat, back to the wall with a view of everyone in the room – a habit he had picked up in Northern Ireland and never lost.

Billy and Frank set off to the serving area, with orders for coffee and ice cream, whilst Quinn surveyed the room and soaked up the vibrant atmosphere. His gaze ran speculatively over a few girls, he noted the males that could prove a threat, especially a large Teddy-Boy with a spot-ravaged face holding court in the opposite corner. Quinn had seen this character around the town before but their paths had never crossed. The Teddy-Boy culture was still going strong and their propensity to get involved in social disorder had even garnered a mention from the Home Secretary in the previous year.

His gaze was suddenly drawn to a lad about his own age who emerged from the back of the café and set off for the door with a battered toolbox in hand. The man behind the counter – Mr. Lombardi he assumed, called out,

"Son smettere di fare scherzi con quella moto c fare un po 'di lavoro nel caffe."

The youth laughed and waved a hand in acknowledgement but continued towards the door. His raven black hair and chiseled face drew admiring glances from a number of the girls as he passed through the crowd. He nodded and chatted briefly to a few of the customers, flashing a ready smile, and then exited the café as the older man's voice rang out cheerily,"Tu sei qui per lavorare, no solo per guandare le belle ragazze." Quinn knew instantly that the youth owned the Norton parked outside; a belief quickly verified as he peered through the dripping condensation on the window and could make out the youth squatting at the side of the bike tinkering.

The others returned with coffees and ice creams of a standard that Quinn had never tasted before. After finishing Quinn announced that he was going outside for a smoke – there was a prominent sign banning smoking inside. Steve joined him.

They watched the handsome youth, and the Norton for a while, and then Quinn walked over and offered a cigarette, "Nice bike - smoke?"

The offer was accepted, "Thanks, a real fag, I usually do roll-ups with not much tobacco in them – spend all I have on the bike."

Quinn detected a foreign accent, "You work here?"

The youth nodded his head, "Yes, I help out, but I also live here, up there." He indicated windows above the café, "Mom and dad own the place. It's a gamble for them but dad is pretty good at judging what's going on and I think it'll work. There's a market for good Italian coffee and gelato. We used to live in London when we first came over from Italy, rented a place, but dad always wanted his own so here we are."

"Was that your dad shouting in Italian as you came out?"

The youth laughed again, "Yes he told me to get some work done and stop messing with the bike and the girls – no chance!"

"When did you come to England?" Quinn asked.

"A few years after the war. Dad says it was chaos in Europe, everyone on the move, and he had a brother living in London who helped him to escape here."

"You've still got a bit of an accent though. Bet that gets the women interested," Quinn joked.

The winning smile flashed across the youth's face again. He asked Quinn's name and shook his hand, and was introduced to Steve who had sauntered across during the conversation "I'm Joey, Joey Lombardi."

"When did you get the Norton?" asked Steve.

Joey responded, "About six months ago, before we left London. I'd saved a bit of money – had a job at Billingsgate that paid good money. Trouble is I've got nothing here so far and I'm running out of cash to keep it running right. I'm trying to sort it myself but I'm no mechanic."

Quinn beamed "It's your lucky day. We've got a garage and we like doing bikes more than cars. What's wrong with it?"

Joey ears pricked up, "Timings out or something like that - got a misfire."

Steve commandeered the toolkit and started messing with the bike. Quinn continued to chat and decided he liked Joey. There was something about him, a charisma, probably stemming from his Italian origin. He was easy to get on with and was a fellow biker too.

The Norton sprang to life and Steve revved it several times, turning heads. He killed the engine and turned to Joey, "I don't think there's much wrong. I've got it running a little smoother but it needs the carb cleaning and the timing setting properly."

Quinn immediately offered the services of the garage but Joey pulled a face, "I can't afford a proper mechanic, I told you, I'm broke at the moment."

Quinn reassured him, "That's not a problem. Bring it along tomorrow - consider it a favour to a fellow biker. I'm sure we'll sort something out. We can have a chat when you come."

Joey hesitated for a split second then shrugged, "That's great thanks. Perhaps some payment in kind can be arranged?" as he indicated the café.

"Yeah that's a good idea," said Quinn. We like your dad's place and think we'll be here a lot from now on. It looks like it's the place to be anyway."

Steve looked quizzically from behind Joey then shrugged his shoulders and followed them back into the café where Joey joined them at the corner table. He provided a free round of coffees, provoking more good-natured Italian banter, and proved to be good company. Quinn resumed his observations of the room and his attention returned to the pockmarked Teddy-Boy who was definitely the focus of attention for a number of the denizens of Lombardi's.

Twenty minutes later Quinn had worked out what the attraction was. He filed the information away.

Before they left, Joey was given directions as to where to find them. Quinn even allowed himself to give Joey a friendly slap on the back as he took the first steps towards cementing the relationship.

It was early afternoon when Joey arrived at the Pit Stop Garage – the name had been Steve's idea. Across the fields Quinn heard the distinctive sound of an approaching bike with an engine note slightly off-key. He had discussed Joey with the others overnight so was not surprised to find the Norton already up on the bike stand, with the petrol tank removed, when he arrived outside the big wooden double doors.

157

While Steve worked on the bike Quinn motioned for Joey to join him and they walked across to the fence by the lane. The weather had finally relented and it was a fine March day with a watery sun hinting at the warmth of summer to come. They leant against the fence and this time Joey proffered a roll-up that Quinn accepted.

They talked about nothing in particular for a while, then Quinn found himself asking about Italy and Joey's life there. Quinn's existence to date, and propensity for violence, had left little space for friendship but he found himself warming to Joey once again. He had won Seamus over but his cousin wasn't the most interesting companion and both Steve and Frank were great, but of an older generation. Billy was a loyal lapdog but there was no empathy there.

Joey was interesting, and funny, and elements of his story mirrored Quinn's, although he differed in being close to his parents, *'probably an Italian thing,'* Quinn thought. The aftermath of the war sounded bad in Italy with privation, occupation - and revenge being taken on those who had supported the Fascists. It seemed that the Lombardi family had lived hand-to-mouth for a while and it had left a scar on the young Joey that manifested itself in a determination to live for the moment.

Joey explained how the Lombardi's had finally carved out a rudimentary living with a café in Milan using skills learnt before the war. There wasn't much money about and Lombardi senior's brother had extolled the virtues of life in England and had finally prevailed, helping to pave the way for a move in 1951. Joey had been ripped out of his home culture, and away from his friends, and deposited in a capital city that still remembered the scars of the Blitz and the fact that Italians had been the enemy.

The older generations in England, and Italy, were able to rationalize the past and wanted to draw a line so it wasn't too bad for his parents but it was not like that for the fourteen-year-old with the poor English and good looks. He had to fight his way through those first years and it seemed had made no friends in London.

"So here I am, starting again, no job or money, and a bike I can't afford to run – although I can speak the language now," he concluded with a smile.

"You've also got parents running a place that every kid in Worcester wants to be seen in, a bike that others would die for, and I've seen the way the girls look at you. I don't think life will be too bad." Quinn teased him

Joey stubbed out his roll-up, "Maybe. What about you Pat, and the others, what's your story?"

Quinn began a potted history of his own journey. He omitted some parts but made sure he hinted at some of the less savoury aspects. He began to test Joey's attitude towards those activities falling the wrong side of the law.

After a while Quinn ventured further, "We've got a bit of a business together, me and the others, I think you'd fit in. It would give you money, friends, and fun but there is a side to it that might present some risks from the law. It would mean that you joined us, stuck with us no matter what, and were happy to break the rules. There's no halfway house with this, you're either in or out and I can't tell you much unless you're in. Your parents can't know, and I can tell you're close to them so you'd have to be willing to hide stuff from them. We can give you a cover-story but if it all goes wrong we won't be able to hide what you've been up to from them."

Joey paused in thought for a few moments then shrugged, "I've got to make a life for myself here. Sure I love my family but I know dad had to do some things to survive out in Italy that he would rather forget. He knows it's been tough for me - that I've had to fight to survive, and I think he would be glad to see me as part of a group that can look after each other. He won't ask questions and he'll keep momma off the scent. To be honest she's got pretty good at looking the other way too. When the stakes are family survival you'd be surprised at what an Italian mother will put up with. I'm in."

Quinn concluded, "I've discussed it with the others but they'll want to talk it through with you. Can you come back here this evening?"

Joey smiled, "Got nothing better to do."

Quinn moved the conversation back to safe topics. They talked for a while longer until they heard the Norton fire up and rev sweetly. They returned to Steve. He was wiping oil from his hands and indicated the bike ticking over on its stand, "All done, sounds good, you should feel a difference. Muck in a carb jet flushed out, a new spark plug fitted and the timing set."

Joey said warmly, "Thanks Steve, How much do I owe you?"

Quinn interjected, "We can discuss that this evening." He turned to Steve, "Joey here is coming tonight to talk through joining our little business. I think he'll do well."

Steve nodded. They shook hands and Joey leapt astride the Norton and roared off.

That evening the garage provided the venue for Joey's induction interview. He was questioned at length, and in detail, by Steve and Frank, who probed his background and character skillfully. The others deferred to their experience and judgment although Quinn had already made up his mind. He trusted his gut feelings and they told him that the Italian boy was going to be okay.

Seamus probed Joey's willingness to fight and seemed only partly satisfied, "Sounds like you can handle yourself but I'll wait and see."

Billy was present but nothing was expected from him and he didn't disappoint, perching mute on the bike ramp. He was there because he was part of the group now, but he would never be a guiding mind.

Joey was asked to wait outside but it only took five minutes before he was called back in and informed that he was in, but on trial.

Quinn then addressed the group, "Okay now that's sorted let's talk business. I had a good think in Joey's café. We're doing fine with the booze to the Irish but we only get a share of the profits. When I was sat there last night what could I see?"

"Fanny?" hazarded Frank.

Quinn laughed loudly, "Yea, there was plenty of that. What I saw was kids out having a good time with money to spend. They were enjoying the coffee, ice-cream and Juke-Box - and fair play that's Joey's parent's cut, but I think they wanted more than the café was selling."

"Like what?" Asked Seamus.

Quinn turned to Joey without replying, "Who is the big pimply fucker in the Teddy-Boy gear?"

Joey knew straight away where Quinn was going, "Sid - Sid Dawson, everyone knows Sid, he's very popular."

Quinn knew the answer already, "And why is that Joey?"

Joey realized that it was just a game for the others, "Easy, he supplies the kids with fags and booze. He does it in small amounts, for instance five fags, or a small bottle of scotch. Even carries a hip flask and charges for a swig. Pays for his fancy clothes I think."

Quinn turned to the others, "What I saw was a new set of buyers. Take a good look around, there's money about, kids are setting off in their own direction, and that's a direction with money in it for us. How well do you know this Sid, Joey?"

Joey paused, "He's okay actually, despite his looks. Treats the kids fair and doesn't cause any trouble. He gives me some bits and pieces as a 'thank you' for not rocking his boat in the café. My dad knows of course, as I said he's not too particular about the law. He knows it helps bring the customers in and Sid keeps it low key."

Quinn again addressed the group, "We've got a choice here. We could just take over or we could do a bit of business with Sidney – sound him out at least. I vote we try that, as he might be useful. I'm not saying we take him in, just keep it business, after all he's a fucking Ted not a biker. It's up to you lot though?"

Sid was approached by Joey two nights later and met Quinn outside the café. Sid proved to be astute. He knew that he couldn't compete physically but he had contacts, goodwill, and a burgeoning market – assets he was willing to barter. He saw the opportunity to move up from small-time with a supply of products at an advantageous mark-up. A deal was swiftly arrived at.

Quinn upped the order from the suppliers over the water, maintaining their cut and approval. It wasn't the time to piss off the IRA, but this time Connor wasn't required so his cut was retained, doubling Quinn's profits. It was a small sideline, but added to the main booze business and the garage trade the money was beginning to flow.

So far it had been fairly smooth sailing and whenever he spotted an excerpt of Hughie Greens, 'Double Your Money' programme on ITV he was reminded of his newfound success. It was a nice feeling.

Chapter Fourteen: 'Mack The Knife'

(Louis Armstrong)

1956

During the boy's early teenage years two totally unconnected incidents occurred that were to play a crucial role in shaping the personalities of Robert and Joseph Docker. Both incidents involved violence – with one incident reinforcing the bond between mother and son, and the second demonstrating the increasing pressure on the relationship between the twins.

***

Mary Docker stood at the kitchen sink – her stress levels sky-high, as she scraped away at the potatoes. She spent half of her life staring into this fucking sink, chained to it, and chained to a man she hated and despised with every ounce of strength she had left in her body.

Mary was running late trying to do everything for the kids, keep the house straight, and acting as a slave for Mr. Richard Burns, *'Fucking twisted bastard,'* she mused. She knew that there would be consequences.

The front door opened and she froze for a second before redoubling her efforts. She remained focused as the footsteps approached.

The kitchen door swung open and bounced off the wall.

Richard Burns stood in the frame of the doorway and stared at her, '*He's pissed again,*' she thought, and turned towards him, "Won't be long for tea." Mary made what she knew would be a futile attempt to placate him.

Burns retorted, "You fucking idle bitch. I want me food and I want it now." He advanced on her and held her neck from behind in a vice-like grip with his left hand, "You do fuck-all, except feed them two little bastards, and you dare to keep me waiting," he screamed into her ear.

Her hands remained in the bowl, full of water and potatoes. In her left hand her grip tightened on the knife she had been using. She remained silent.

He took her right wrist with his free hand and spun her round towards him, "You fucking whore," he screamed, his face blood red and fit to explode. He slapped her hard across the face – his stinking breath, and spit from his mouth, invading her nostrils.

On hearing the noise Joe silently entered the kitchen and hurled himself at Burns in an attempt to protect the thing that he loved most. He clung onto his stepfather's back and tried to wrestle his arms away from his mother. Burns shook him off and he landed in a heap on the floor.

"Leave me ma alone. Leave her alone!" Joe screamed, as he jumped up and threw himself at Burns again, young fists flailing.

Mary Docker snapped – she would not knowingly allow Burns to lay a hand on her sons.

Instinctively she swung her left hand forward and with one short jab she stabbed him in the stomach - just once – no accident – one controlled strike.

Burns let out a scream and slid to the floor clutching his stomach, "You fucking stabbed me. I'm fucking bleeding."

Joe moved to stand next to his mother fists raised. There was to be no retreat this time, and no quarter given.

Mary stared down at Burns with utter contempt. It was a superficial wound and he would live, "You're not gonna to die this time you piece of shit, but if you ever lay another hand on me, or me kids ever again, I promise you, I'll stick you with this knife. I'll finish what that Jap should've done. I'll kill you and I'll be happy for the first time in bleeding years."

Burns pleaded with Mary, "You fucking yampy bitch."

Blood oozed through his clothing and fingers as he looked up at the woman who now towered over him, and seemed to have grown considerably. He flashed a look of pure hatred across at Joe who stood waiting for a blow to land, as they always did.

This time however Joe met his gaze – suddenly he saw the man for what he was and was no longer afraid – this monster would not come in the dark again.

Mary bent down and gripped him by the front of his shirt collar, "Just once more and I'll finish you, I don't care what happens to me, I've got nothing other than me kids and I promise I'll swing for you if you lay a hand on us again," she screamed, as she threw a towel at him to stem the flow.

She turned her back on him slowly, and deliberately, and went back to the sink. She rinsed the blood from the knife and dried it clean. She got the sharpening steel out of the drawer and put a razor edge on it for Burn's benefit. This was the knife that would now stay close to her. "I'll phone the doc and tell him how you fell on summat sharp. You wouldn't want people to know that a war-hero had been stabbed by a woman would you?"

Burns was slowly going into shock but even in his drunken state he knew that things had changed.

Mary Docker was done – for the time being, and Joe felt part of the winning team for the first time.

The bond between Joe and his mother grew ever closer from that moment. They had faced a common enemy and won. They had stared the devil in the face and their combined strength had defeated him. Joe had tasted revenge and liked the feeling, and if blood had to be spilt, so be it?

***

The next few months proved to be calm and quiet in the Docker household. Richard spent more time in the pub than he did at home which suited everyone. The night-time visits to Joe also stopped. It seemed that he believed his wife, for now at least.

At thirteen, and on the proviso that they looked after each other, Mary began to allow the twins to go out on their own at the weekends. She reasoned that they were better off away from

Richard's malign influence, and they both had to learn to cope with the world, Joe especially.

Saturdays therefore became red-letter days. In the mornings they caught the bus to the Kingsway cinema in Kings Heath for the morning picture show, followed by chips. If the Blues were at home they were on the bus again to St Andrews.

It was when returning from one such match that the world crashed into their relationship once more.

Returning from the game, Joe and Rob had rashly decided to sit at the front of the top deck, as the view out of the large windows was always better. Besides, downstairs was for the younger kids. They were both pretty street-wise but a bit more wisdom would have confirmed that the bottom deck would have been far safer.

They were engrossed in reviewing the day's events and failed to notice a group of six white youths in their late teens and regaled in Teddy-Boy gear, bound up the stairs and sit immediately behind them, and between the front seats and the bus stairs.

Joe and Robb were effectively boxed-in. They only noticed when the monkey noises started.

Race had always been an issue in The States and was once again reaching a flashpoint over the Rosa Park incident. In the UK, resentment against the recent influx of blacks was starting to ferment as immigrants took jobs in the public sector and railwaymen protested at an influx of black drivers. The race card provided a ready- made issue for those bent on violence.

"What you doing with that Wog?" one of them leant forward and asked Rob as the others looked on.

"He's me brother," Rob asserted, immediately regretting the reply, knowing what was coming next.

The group burst out laughing and the self-proclaimed leader continued, "That's a fucking joke. He ain't no brother of yours, you fucking liar, do you think we're fucking thick."

He stared at Joe menacingly, and with a few years on the younger boys, and backed up by his cronies, he thought he had the measure of him.

"I don't like coons," he proclaimed, "Look at him he looks like a monkey." He beamed as further laughter broke out, "If I rub his skin do you think some of that brown'll rub off." He was in his stride now playing to the audience.

Joe and Rob, now equally alert, worked out their options and Joe made the first move, "This is our stop Rob." Joe stood up.

His tormentor put his palms up to Joe's chest and pushed him backwards, "No, I think you meant the next stop darkie," as the group stood to block them.

"Before you go I think I'll have that watch you've got on." the leader said, as he drew a knife from his inside coat pocket, "Give it to me or I'll knife you."

Rob moved towards his brother but the group closed around him, "You're one of us, stay out of it or you'll get a good lamping too."

Rob knew that Joe wouldn't give up his watch without a fight as he saw Joe square up to the loudmouth.

"Who do you think you are, Rocky fucking Marciano!" the Teddy-Boy laughed.

Rob felt the blood drain from his face. For a few seconds he froze, and then acted. The sight of the knife scared him shitless.

"Leave it Joe," Rob wrenched the wristwatch from his brothers hand, a valued Christmas present from his mother, and threw it at the main protagonist who smiled and said to the others, "That's better – see the white kid's got brains, not like him just out the jungle." He again imitated a monkey, and pocketed the watch.

Joe exploded and struck him a hard punch in the eye. Joe had already seen blood, and experienced far worse pain than he was about to endure, as they closed in around him. He was purely focused on making sure that he left his mark on this bastard, who now had one of his prized possessions.

The remainder of the group launched themselves at Joe, punching and kicking him as he struggled to get through. Rob went into panic mode as one of the group held him back, making no effort to get into the fray.

As they wrestled Joe to the floor in the narrow aisle the ringleader, now sporting the makings of a good black eye, shouted "Hold him down!"

Through the melee of peoples legs Joe could see Rob standing motionless at the back of the scrum. *'Why doesn't he help, all the times I've stood up for him,"* he thought, but uttered no words - no plea for help. He had taken it for granted that Rob would be there for him and was more hurt by the betrayal than what was about to happen. He would not beg – not even to his brother.

Still struggling but pinned down, and hopelessly outnumbered, Joe was subjected to the ultimate humiliation as the ringleader undid the fly of his trousers and urinated over him, "See, it doesn't come off. He's still got a chocolate face." The youth then stabbed him in the hand, "This is for my eye, you little bastard."

One of the group shouted, "Get his todger out. Let's see if that's brown as well." Joe bucked and thrashed violently trying to avoid the clawing hands at the belt of his trousers.

The elderly white bus-conductor had clearly been aware of the commotion for some time but wasn't going to rush to get involved in a fight with a bunch of kids, especially one that was coloured, but as he heard someone shout "Stab the fucker again!" he spurred himself into action of sorts.

As they reached a bus stop he shouted upstairs, "Come on you lot. I want you off the bus."

The youths stopped momentarily and Rob ran for the stairs. Joe saw his brother's back disappearing down the stairwell and that enraged him further. He used all of his remaining strength to break free and landed another blow indiscriminately before leaping down the stairs two at a time, his injured hand dripping with blood.

As Rob and Joe got off the bus, fighting for breath, they looked up and saw a line of six white faces sneering down at them. One of them waved his watch and made a cutting motion across his throat, whilst the others broke into a loud rendition of 'Rock around the Clock' as the bus remained stationary. The conductor leant out of the back, "Bugger off the both of you." He indicated Joe, "I don't want his kind causing trouble on me bus."

Joe was still raging, "Bastards – come down if you want some more!" he screamed. The smell of urine clung to his face and T-Shirt.

Rob didn't want another round with the Teddy-Boys though. He tugged at his brother and pleaded, "Come on. Let's leg it!"

Joe allowed himself to be pulled away down a gully opposite. They walked home in awkward silence. The young Joseph Docker got home and locked himself in the toilet. He used a cracked mirror to explore his facial bruises. *'Yes there's no doubt about it,'* he mused, *'I'm brown and it'll never wash off.'*

He felt extreme hatred for the youths on the bus and cried silently, *'Bastards.'* He saw their faces laughing at him, and felt soiled.

That said, they were strangers who meant nothing to him. The bigger hurt came from the behavior of Rob who had let him down badly. Joe had not asked, nor did he expect, an apology. For Rob's part none was offered.

By the time he left the toilet he was no longer a young boy.

He told his mother that he had fallen on a piece of broken glass – Mary of course knew better, but felt powerless at times to protect him from a world where injustice and racial hatred were just normality. He just had to learn how to survive. *'Still,'* she consoled herself, *'he's always got Rob.'*

Joe sat down to eat with his white brother. More than the tea was strained.

The times were changing and relationships were changing. From that day Joe started carrying a knife of his own. He would not be caught the same way again.

After the incident on the bus Joe decided that it was time to hone his physical skills and joined the local boxing club. The place was no great shakes but there was a makeshift ring, in addition to the punch-bags, and the trainer immediately saw potential in him and showed some interest. He had never had a black boxer to train, but knew how good the American ones were.

Joe's technique was simple – as he punched the bags he saw the face of Richard Burns. As he sparred in the ring he saw the face of the Teddy-Boy who had pissed all over him.

Both techniques worked and Joe became a feared opponent.

For his part Rob decided to join the local Army Cadet Force detachment. It didn't last long but it wetted his appetite for uniforms.

Chapter Fifteen: 'Love Is A Many Splendoured Thing'

(Four Aces)

1955

The film Blackboard Jungle had crashed into the UK teenage world in November 1955, with its 'satanic' rock and roll anthem 'Rock Around The Clock'. The 'Teddy- Boy problem' continued to puzzle older heads who had never seen a teenage cult before. Further afield a 'state of emergency' was declared in Cyprus as the EOKA guerilla campaign began, and more British troops were sent to keep the peace in a part of the Empire that was more than three and a half thousand miles away.

**

Lombardi's was thriving, and with it the gang's new sideline.

Sid had proved a real asset. He was good at selling and had an instinctive grasp of how to maximize the market without drawing unwelcome attention from the adult world.

Despite that, he could never be a full part of the group. He had no interest in bikes and was drawn to other tribes. Despite his size and looks, Quinn quickly realized that the crater-faced youth lacked the internal fire and aggression that drove the likes of him, and in fact had no interest in, or propensity for, violence.

He also had a dangerous secret, one that Joey had confided to

Quinn early on in the business arrangement. Sid clearly preferred boys and was struggling with the internal agonies of accepting this revelation in a world where acting upon his desires, even in private, was vilified and still an offence in the eyes of the law.

Quinn hadn't been bothered and hadn't told the others. It was a weakness but one that he could exploit if necessary. In the meantime he was content to file the knowledge away and keep a benevolent eye on his new business partner.

Joey on the other hand, was a perfect fit. He had proved himself with his fists on a couple of occasions when other groups had tried to challenge the bikers. He loved the thrill of riding together and the new friendships he had forged. Mr. Lombardi clearly approved and a symbiotic arrangement had emerged. The café benefited from the extra custom and the bike boys keeping order, Joey had a job and friends, and the gang had a base, a market for goods - and free coffee.

It was Christmas Eve 1955, and the café was packed, windows steaming and streaming, the Seeborg blasting out 'Rock Around The Clock' repeatedly, interspersed with relics of a dying musical era such as Slim Whitman's 'Rose Marie', 'Unchained Melody' from Jimmy Young, and Dickie Valentine's 'Christmas Alphabet'. Quinn and Joey were sat in the usual corner seat viewing the mayhem.

She came in with a squat, burly male. They were arguing. Quinn couldn't hear them but his instinct for trouble had instantly zeroed his attention onto the couple. She was taller, but he looked older, in his early twenties, against her late teens. She wasn't a classic reed-like beauty, more of an Amazonian build, but she had an intelligent, interesting face crowned with russet hair cut in a boyish Audrey Hepburn style.

She was shaking her head, and he liked the way she stood up to the man, facing him down, and clearly contributing in full to the argument. Some of the other customers were beginning to take notice, and Quinn caught the eye of Mr. Lombardi, who indicated the couple in the doorway with a nod, the usual sign he wanted something done.

Quinn stood up and motioned Joey to stay where he was, "I'll sort this."

As he approached he saw the man take hold of the girl's arm tightly, clearly causing discomfort as she tried to break free. He could hear them now.

"Fucking slut, I've told you before to keep your eyes to yourself."

She slapped his face with her free hand as Quinn reached them. As the man pulled his arm back for a punch Quinn caught hold of it and straight-armed the man up onto his toes. He twisted the hand inwards evoking a gasp of pain and a profanity.

"Fucking big man you are, fighting a woman. Let her go or I'll snap your wrist."

He gave the arm another twist for emphasis. The man did let go but only so that he could try and twist around and free himself. He was strong and Quinn struggled to hold him. They danced a few steps then Joey was there, holding the door open at the behest of his father who had one eye on the damage potential. Quinn propelled the man out onto the street and hurled him away into the road.

The man stumbled a few steps then turned, snorting out breaths.

"I'll fucking kill you," he snarled, then charged head down, a tactic suited to his squat build that would probably have worked with any normal opponent found on the Worcester streets.

Quinn watched his approach then performed his trademark sidestep and delivered a crushing blow to the kidneys, and then a push that assisted the charging man into the door stanchion which shook with the impact. As the man rebounded Quinn crashed a foot down behind one knee forcing the man to his knees and delivered a double-handed blow to the back of the neck. It was over in seconds and Quinn was kneeling on the man's back.

Quinn whispered into a visible ear.

"I promise that if you don't fuck-off when I let you go I'll do you a serious injury or worse. I've done it before and to harder men than you. I think you and the girl are finished too – Oh and by the way you're barred from this café."

Quinn stood up, and backed away several steps. It took a minute or two before the man recovered enough to stand, wobbling and with blood streaming from a nasty cut on his forehead courtesy of the door pillar. Quinn could see him assessing the percentages and the risk of further public humiliation. Seconds passed then Quinn knew it was over – for tonight at least. The man shot him a look of hatred as he backed away, "This isn't over you dirty bastard!" then limped off into the evening.

Quinn returned to the café. The girl was still stood inside the door, rubbing her arm. He could see livid finger marks that must have hurt. He was impressed – not a tear in sight. She had guts.

"Come and have a coffee with Joey and me, it's on the house, Joey here is related," he said.

Joey smiled in encouragement and led the way to the corner seat. Quinn was surprised to hear a smattering of applause as he walked through the crowd. The moment passed and it was back to normal but Quinn knew that he had made a mark tonight. Word would get round.

The girl sat and smoothed her clothes. She spoke with a soft Worcestershire burr that he immediately liked. "Thanks, I can usually handle him but he was a bit pissed. I think our time together had come to an end anyway. It's 'Take Your Pick' time and as Michael Miles says on the telly, I think I'll say No!" They all burst out laughing at her quick wit, "I couldn't stand his insane jealousy any longer. You need to watch him though, he can be nasty and he'll never forgive you for showing him up in public."

Quinn shrugged, "What's his name in case I have to teach the lesson again?" "Johnny Gray. He lives in the Arboretum," she responded, slowly relaxing. "More importantly, what's your name I'm Pat, Pat Quinn?"

She smiled warmly, "Jennifer – Jenny Baker. I mean it about Johnny, he won't forget what you did, and he'll think you did it to pick me up, which will make it worse."

Quinn raised an eyebrow, "What makes you think I didn't?" She laughed and turned on a coquettish expression. "What would a nice-dressed girl like me see in a rough biker?" she teased. "Ever been on a bike?" Quinn ventured. "No, not exactly dressed for it am I?" She indicated the dress, cardigan, smart coat and heels. "It's the best thrill you could ever imagine; you should give it a go and see.

Get some better clothes on and I'll take you out." Quinn ventured further. Jenny was in no rush to jump out of the frying pan into the fire, "In this weather - no thanks. Perhaps when it's warmer. By the way I can imagine quite a few thrills - and motorbikes have never featured."

It was Quinn's turn to tease, "Okay. I'll take that as a promise – the bike not the thrills, or do I mean the thrills?"

She laughed and he liked the sound.

Another round of coffees arrived and Joey discreetly absented himself from the table and joined Sid.

An hour flew by whilst they chatted. Quinn hadn't had much time for women in his life apart from a couple of short-lived and shallow relationships. Jenny was different. The conversation flowed and they discovered a shared sense of humour. He could detect a streak of stubbornness and fire in her that had flashed across her face during her argument with Gray and it drew him somehow. Like to like perhaps.

She was a local, living on the outskirts of Worcester. Her parents both worked at the pottery company, Royal Worcester. She had a job at Kay's Mail Order as a clerk, at their offices in The Tything. On the face of it she was just like any other girl that frequented the cafe - but there was something about her that struck a chord within Quinn. Thinking about it later he decided that perhaps he had sensed a buried wildness, a kindred flame and a yearning to move outside the bounds.

He knew within half an hour that he wanted to see her again. She could not escape family duties for Christmas but they arranged to meet again in a few days. The relationship prospered and it soon became clear that this was more than a fling.

They had an obvious effect upon each other, for better and worse as the ancient vow says. Quinn seemed less insular and brooding and his popularity increased as people found him more approachable. He was different when she was around, although the effect of his growing friendship with Joey had also wrought a change that people underestimated. Almost by accident Quinn had found both a male and female soul mate in Worcester and the human relationship laid a more civilised veneer over his wild and violent core.

Dependent upon the point of view, the effect on Jenny was also marked. She had taken the promised ride on the pillion of the Thunderbird and had been instantly seduced. Gone were the pretty frocks, replaced by practical biking wear. Her hair was longer, and often held back in a pony-tail, but could also be seen streaming out in the wind as the bike roared up The Tything to the café, Quinn at the controls and Jenny now consummate as a pillion passenger, holding one-handed the grab rail that Steve had fitted to the Thunderbird.

That wild streak that Quinn had divined at their first encounter had blossomed under his tutelage and neither her parents, nor her friends, approved of the change. In fact, by April she was spending most of her time with Quinn and the bikers and was becoming steeped in their culture as it evolved.

Jenny loved Quinn and his friends, the visceral thrill of being on a bike, the feeling of belonging to something - and the sense that they were all pushing boundaries at a time when all of her post-war generation was beginning to question and probe their parent's norms and values.

Quinn had kept some aspects of the business from her to begin with, but had quickly realized that he had found a companion he could trust, and with whom he could share his thoughts and problems for the first time in his short and violent life. He had discussed it with Joey and his friend clearly approved of Jenny and suggested they take it to the others who in turn sanctioned her being brought into the operation. Quinn was grateful and realized that the decision showed a faith in his unspoken leadership.

Admittedly, he minimized the Irish connection to a business one via family contacts – there was no need to mention the Republican Army, but he gradually introduced her to the money making 'enterprises' and discovered that she had a head for figures, and paperwork, that proved her skills were wasted in the Kay's Catalogue office.

The relationship drove a terminal wedge between Jenny and her parents. Their disapproval of Quinn turned to manifest dislike, as they were powerless to stem the changes in their daughter – changes for the worse in their eyes. They tried to end the relationship, banning him from their house, and Jenny from seeing him. The house ban remained in place but they could not prevent her from going out and seeing him and her resentment of them grew, fuelled by her nature.

There were blazing rows, even an attempt to lock her in her room, but the final straw was a May morning when Jenny's mother realized with a sinking heart that the heaving sounds from the bathroom meant that one of her worst fears was manifest.

Ronnie Hilton's newly released 'No other love' played on the radio in the background like an ironic theme tune.

In the uproar that followed an abortion was suggested, and refused, and Jenny left the family home one night boiling with rage and tears after a particularly forthright argument with her father. Throughout the tribulations of those few weeks she had pleaded with Quinn to keep his distance but on that last evening he had found her distraught at their usual meeting point at the end of her road and had decided enough was enough.

They rode to the farmhouse first. They had already planned for this eventuality. Marie in particular had quickly formed a close maternal-like relationship with Jenny and, good Catholic that she was, absolutely refused to countenance any talk of abortion, counseling upon the niceties of termination and illegitimacy and persuading Jenny to decide in favour of the latter. Quinn also suspected that Marie would welcome more female company in the hitherto male dominated environment of the farm.

It was decided. Jenny would come to live at the farm and keep the records that the burgeoning businesses required. She had already shown that she was the most able of the group in this respect and they all knew that records needed urgently creating, and the growing piles of documents ordered and maintained.

Jenny, headstrong, emotional, fired up by conflict and her union with Quinn, her body a swirl of hormones, was enthusiastic. She knew that Quinn and his life was anathema to the staid normality of her parent's world and there could be no co- existence. She had to choose, and like thousands of her peers she chose the future and also like girls before her, the boy beat the disapproval of the parents.

Quinn fetched the van and they drove into a confrontation resulting in Jenny's father trying to throw Quinn out of the house, but being felled by two punches. They had thrown her things into the van while curtains twitched and neighbours stood on their doorsteps, goggling.

The public nature of the departure, with Jenny's mother hanging onto her arm, until pulled away by her bloodied father, added further to the humiliation of the encounter. Jenny stood at the van door and watched as her father dragged her mother inside slamming the door with a finality that promised no reprieve.

Her son was born on 21 November 1956. They called him Sean for no particular reason other than that they both liked the name, and Marie had a favourite uncle called that. Quinn was surprised to find that he loved his little man - much to the amusement of his friends.

Chapter Sixteen: 'All Shook Up'

(Elvis Presley)

1957

As 1957 wound onwards towards summer, and skiffle bands were at their height in Birmingham, a kind of domestic stability set in, with Marie enthusiastically volunteering to mind Sean whilst Jenny set about the books. She had a basic grounding in record keeping and had done some accounts work for three months at Kays but soon realized that her knowledge wasn't sufficient. As a result she was funded for a book-keeping course under the auspices of The Pit Stop Garage and proved competent at the work.

She was no accountant though, and her little knowledge quickly brought a realization that a professional input was required. No ordinary accountant would do for these books though, and Quinn did not want an Irish-connected nomination looking after his concerns for obvious reasons.

Frank found the answer quite by accident. By this time the garage was not only fixing cars and bikes, and building a good reputation at the hands of Steve's spanners, but had started selling them from the compound next to the lane. Part of this enterprise was legitimate and the bikers were beginning to become known in the trade due to their presence at auctions, and other forums, where vehicles changed hands.

The flip-side of the coin was a growing and lucrative trade in what was known as 'bent motors'. Some were stolen and the identities changed, 'ringing'. Others had been acquired by threats and intimidation in Eire, imported and re-registered. A third source of income was the stripping of stolen vehicles, and moving the parts on via the trade. Finally the bikers specialized in 'raids' across the country, stealing bikes, swopping their parts around and removing engine and chassis numbers then stamping new ones. Frank put his wartime skills to particularly good use in this endeavor, and a national bus strike, and dock strike, was keeping the police busy with picket-line violence.

It had not taken long for Quinn and friends to ease their way into the network of criminals engaged in vehicle theft and fraud, especially as their tight group had the facility of the garage and a growing transport infrastructure stemming from the liquor and cigarettes operations. This was easily adapted to moving other goods illicitly. In short, they were in demand.

Frank had made a good contact in Bristol - a very useful city, having a booming seaport and links to the smuggling operations of the South West. One day he had mentioned the headache of paperwork and accounts at a pick-up in Clevedon by the pier. It had been fresh in his mind due to the group spending two hours the previous evening trying to find a solution to concerns raised by Jenny about the imminent paperwork meltdown.

"I know just the man to help with that," said the contact, "Tell him I sent you and I'll get a few quid. He's a proper accountant but he comes from a dodgy family who paid his way for their own purposes when he was a youngster. He's independent now – got his own firm and a very *special* clientele if you know what I mean. He'll charge you a bit more, but he's discreet, trustworthy, and good at hiding stuff you don't want the taxman or anybody else to know about. Even better in your case, he's in Gloucester so near enough for you."

Frank reported back and accompanied Quinn and Jenny to a 'scoping meeting' resulting in Edward 'Eddie' Brough becoming retained as accountant for The Pit Stop Garage and, on a more confidential basis, the rest of the group's concerns. Quinn had satisfied himself that Brough had no links to Ireland and a highly effective and totally corrupt arrangement was initiated.

Brough might be trustworthy in criminal terms but Quinn was more confident that the fact that they could ruin each other with their knowledge meant that silence and discretion was assured, an agreement firmly cemented by plenty of cash. As a bonus, and in his own self-interest, Eddie was also happy to train Jenny up to do the basic bookwork and record keeping to his specification.

By autumn Jenny was confident in her new role and situation. Her old life seemed so far away. In less than a year she had discarded her childhood, parents, home and job. Life had cemented her into the group and her school friends were also left behind, with her boring past a fading memory.

There had been one loose end from her past. As predicted, Johnny Gray had been unable to live with his humiliation. He had turned up at Jenny's house a couple of weeks after the café incident demanding to see her. When she told him to get lost and slammed the door in his face she had been perturbed to spot him watching the house a few days later.

Quinn was quiet when told, so quiet that Jenny had made him promise not to do anything more than warn Gray off. Besotted with Jenny, and not wanting to damage their relationship, Quinn had contented himself with knifing the tyres on Gray's car late one night and leaving the message 'stay away' scratched on the bonnet.

Later that week, Quinn had been changing the oil on the Thunderbird at the garage. He liked to do stuff on the bike himself and had got tuition from Steve to the point where he now sometimes lent a hand at The Pit Stop.

Steve had gone into town to get parts, so Quinn had agreed to mind the shop whilst he took the opportunity to work on his bike. Quinn was kneeling, back to the big double door when he heard it open. As he turned he was kicked hard in the face and sprawled backwards, head ringing. It was Gray and two cronies who stood back, clearly thinking job done, as Gray ran forward and kicked Quinn in the stomach, doubling him up.

Something made Gray turn his ire onto the bike and another kick sent the Thunderbird crashing off its stand. The two onlookers applauded and guffawed but the few seconds it took allowed Quinn to roll away and clear his head. He knew another kick was coming but the furnace of anger within him was lit and the adrenalin suffused his body, dulling the pain.

He had his back to Gray now and took the next kick between his shoulder blades, using the energy to give himself the momentum to roll away again. The animalistic survival instinct had kicked in and Quinn had seen the handle of a lump hammer protruding from behind an oil drum.

The roll enabled him to grab the hammer, and as Gray rushed in for the kill Quinn delivered a crushing blow to the shin of the standing leg, whilst accepting another kick that caught his shoulder.

Gray went down like a felled tree, clutching his leg. Quinn was up and smashed the hammer down on the other leg, catching the meaty thigh, then vaulted Gray and delivered another hammer blow to the groin of the nearest man who collapsed.

These weren't street fighters like him, just a couple of local thugs and they had never met a savage like Quinn before. They had been expecting an easy victory and some bullying fun, but as they looked into Quinn's eyes they realized that their opponent was quite capable of killing them.

The second man backed away holding up his hands, but Quinn was not to be placated and launched into a ferocious attack holding the hammerhead in his right fist to give weight to his punches.

The garage door opened again and Steve was presented with the sight of Quinn, lump-hammer in hand, standing between three prostrate men, clutching legs, groin and head respectively. He shook his head in wonder,

"Fucking hell, who do you think you are, fucking Thor?" Steve enquired somewhat star-struck.

Quinn walked over to Gray and put his foot on his neck, "I told you didn't I?" His voice was full of menace.

He smashed the hammer down once again, on the lower leg,

and the crack of bone sounded like a rifle shot in the enclosed space as Gray howled in agony.

One of the men started to get up but Steve pushed him back down with a foot and insisted firmly, "You just stay there a minute."

Suddenly there was a strange silence, punctuated only by gasps of pain from Gray as he nursed his broken leg. All eyes were on Quinn because they could sense quite clearly that he had murder on his mind and was capable of carrying it out.

Steve intervened, recognizing that his friend stood at the edge of an abyss and said soothingly, "That's enough Pat, think about it - they aren't worth going down for and I don't think they are going to give us any more trouble."

Steve had unwittingly made a telling comment. The prospect of a cell and Quinn's secret claustrophobia were probably all that saved Gray's life that day. Quinn took hold of the cowering man's jaw with one hand and held the hammer poised, three sets of fearful eyes fixed on the makeshift weapon. Steve was not fearful, just hoping that Quinn wouldn't go and ruin it all when it was so good, and just for a girl.

"Look at me you piece of shit." Gray's eyes looked into Quinn's and saw the possibility of death, "I would dearly love to cave your head in right now but I'm not going to prison for you, got bigger and better things to do. This is your last chance. If I ever see you around me - my friends, or Jenny again I'll kill you, at a time and place of my choosing. You can either fuck off from here today and get on with life or spend the rest of it watching your back. If you go to the cops, my friends here will make you pay if I go down. That goes for you two as well. You came here, three on one, how would that look in court anyway?"

The two men were nodding in fervent agreement. Gray eventually nodded and Quinn stepped away, "Get him out of my sight before I change my mind."

The two men helped Gray up whilst Steve opened the big door and the trio hobbled out.

Quinn and Steve both knew that if Steve hadn't returned at that moment there would have been at least one dead body. For Quinn it was recognition that he needed his friends, for Steve a realization that Quinn was capable of anything and was indisputably the leader of the group.

Quinn also earned his nickname that day when Steve reported back to the others that Quinn, *'had looked like Thor about to call down the lightning.'* Quinn liked the name and henceforth carried the hammer secreted beneath the saddle of his bike. No police came and Gray had long vanished from Worcester by the time Sean was born.

Chapter Seventeen: 'Remember You're Mine'

(Pat Boone)

1957

As the days of 1957 shortened, life at the farm seemed almost routine. The various businesses ticked along and profits continued to accrue. They seemed to have escaped unwelcome interest from officialdom, and the law, and presented an overtly plausible veneer of working farm and garage, run by a group of friends who happened to like motorcycles.

There were occasional run-ins with other parties but there was no-one to really challenge them, and in fact they began to find 'hangers-on' appearing, particularly at Lombardi's, which was always packed. Teenage music was evolving and the Jukebox was now booming out Lonnie Donnegan's home-grown skiffle rhythms, together with Marty Wilde and Tommy Steele hits, interspersed with renditions from their American inspiration.

For the first time in his life Quinn had some roots and relationships that mattered to him. Jenny and Sean, his friends – Joey in particular, Mike and Marie, and the farm, garage and cafe. The Irish seemed happy with the arrangements although Quinn was under no illusion that their sponsorship was in any way benevolent. In fact there was resentment festering inside, a feeling of being owned and shackled, that he didn't like one bit.

He was always searching for ways to lay down some

foundations independent of Eire, and hidden from them, and his resolve to do so was hardened by a tragedy in early February of the following year that ended the period of calm.

Michael wasn't the fittest man any more, in his fifties, and both a smoker and drinker, weathered and weakened from years of working outside in all seasons. The Asian flu epidemic that started in September the previous year, and went on to kill sixteen thousand in Britain over the next two years, found him and turned into pneumonia, killing him three weeks into the New Year.

Marie and Seamus were distraught, and Quinn was sorry that Mike's genial presence no longer suffused the farm, but the death sparked other concerns in his mind. What would be the view of the future from the Emerald Isle? Would someone else be brought in to run the farm and what would that mean for The Pit Stop, Quinn, his young family and friends?

He brooded for days on the shaky nature of the main foundation of their current life and decided that Mike's funeral in Belfast would provide an opportunity. Contact was duly made with Jimmy One-Eye and word came back that Quinn should go to Dublin and not Derry after the funeral.

Quinn didn't know what to make of this and took counsel from the others, including Marie who was the repository of knowledge, contacts, and a vested interest in the result of the side-trip.

It was obvious he had to go where they asked him, untenable to refuse, but the change of usual venue made Quinn uncomfortable.

Marie felt it was a good sign - everything had gone well so far, and all dues were paid up to date. In the end she was the main instigator of the decision that Seamus should accompany Quinn to make his own claim to continue in his father's place. It was a risk, and Seamus would have to swallow and hide his true feelings, but Marie knew that there was no other way. They would want to meet Seamus face-to-face, weigh and measure him, before deciding. Marie made the contact on her son's behalf and permission was granted.

She gave Seamus a crash course in Irish Republicanism and also included Quinn in the lesson. They rehearsed scenarios and tested Seamus at length until they were satisfied. They had a plan of engagement.

The funeral was well attended and Quinn noted that Jimmy was there, no doubt to represent Michael's 'employers'. They passed a nodded greeting but Jimmy did not stay for the wake and just muttered "tomorrow" when passing Quinn on his way out of the churchyard. Quinn remained uneasy.

The next morning Quinn and Seamus set out in a borrowed car. They had debated carrying weapons but decided against in case of search. This was a moment to grit teeth and front whatever was coming.

They were met at the border by two hard-faced men and followed them not to a pub as Quinn had expected, but out into the country. Quinn was wary and the men said very little by way of welcome. They turned up a remote track and drew up outside a whitewashed stone cottage.

Quinn's senses were screaming and he was holding back the urge to take some action, when the cottage door opened and out stepped Jimmy, bearing a broad smile. Like all of Jimmy's smiles it didn't reach his eyes.

Quinn suppressed his inner unease, alighted and shook Jimmy's hand, introducing Seamus. Jimmy eyed the big man looming over him, "If you're anything like your ma and da you will be a good lad I expect."

Seamus shrugged his shoulders, " I guess you'll make your mind up on that one today," he said.

Jimmy said flatly, "For sure. Anyway, Pat, you're to meet a couple of friends of mine, you won't be told their names. These are important people and they have asked to see you."

He turned to Seamus "They also have the decision to make about you so expect some questions."

Quinn relaxed an iota. He breathed an internal sigh of relief that they hadn't come tooled up as they were both subjected to a comprehensive search by the two men who had met them at the border.

Jimmy led the way inside and they followed him into a rear kitchen. Two men sat at a rough oak table, two others stood in corners. Quinn had no doubt the standing men were carrying.

Both seated men were a lot younger than he had expected, probably late- thirties, early-forties; one was bald, one silver-haired. The bald one had a round face, bull neck, ruddy complexion and a splendid beer gut. He remained seated and studied them impassively. Quinn had met neither of them during his previous sojourn in Eire which had been much further to the south.

The silver-haired man hailed from the other end of the physical spectrum, being tall and thin, his face dominated by defined cheekbones surmounted by distinctive green eyes. He stood up as they entered and offered a hand. His voice was soft with a pronounced accent.

"Welcome. Welcome both, sit you down." He indicated two chairs that Pat noted were positioned so that their backs would be towards the men stood in the corners.

It was too late to escape; they had to ride the situation now, for good or ill. The man sat back down as they did, and Jimmy joined him at the table, introducing Quinn and Seamus as he did so.

Seamus and Quinn faced the three men across the table. The silver-haired man began, "Thank you for coming to see us. My men call me 'The General', so that is enough of a name for today's purpose." He paused for effect,

"My cousin and I are glad of the chance to meet you Pat, we've heard a lot about you and the things you've been getting up to since you left us. We would like you to talk us through it all but first Seamus - we want to know if we can trust you, and that means you go off with Jimmy here for a while so we can talk to Pat alone."

Seamus shrugged again and indicated agreement. Quinn was thankful for the preparation they had put in, and his opinion of Marie rose even higher as her judgement that they would be split up was proved correct. She had been dealing with these people all her life and knew how they operated. They all knew that Seamus wasn't the brightest tool in the box and had decided to exploit that as a tactic, selling him as part of a package with Quinn as the bow on the box. Seamus hadn't liked it but he knew his limits and so had signed up to the strategy.

Quinn was left alone with the two men and their guards. Jimmy and the two that had met them at the border went elsewhere in the cottage with Seamus. 'The General' spoke again, "Now then Pat, you just tell us all about business in England and your plans for the future. We might ask a few questions as we go."

An hour later Quinn stopped speaking and leant back in the chair, drained. It had been an interrogation without violence although they all knew that violence lurked just below the surface, waiting for a slip. He had kept to the plan and it all rested on Marie's assessment. She had persuaded him to tell most of the truth, to adopt a stance of seeking advice and approval. They had constructed a business proposition that stressed the advantages of building an enterprise that looked independent of the Irish but would offer them many advantages because of that. It was a dangerous game that required the precise negotiation of a line that presented the most to the sponsors but allowed things to go on that were not all under their control.

They also hoped that Quinn's relative youth would assist in convincing that there was no guile in his words.

The two men stood and left him with the guards. Minutes passed and Quinn knew that yet another watershed moment had been reached. They were comparing notes with Jimmy. He just hoped that Seamus had played his part.

The door opened and the two men returned. There was no sign of Seamus. 'The General' spoke again, "Okay. One thing's for sure, your friend is as thick as pig- shit but that's not a problem so long as he has you to think for him. In fact, we don't think he's got the brain cells to cross us and he looks useful in a fight too. He comes from a loyal family and blood is important so we are willing to give him a chance. The question is Pat, what about you?"

The green eyes bored into Quinn's, and they were cold. Quinn met them, this was something he was used to, facing people down and he already knew they were ninety-percent home and hosed.

"What about me?" he asked, being careful to show due deference in tone.

'The General' maintained the stare, "You're a clever lad, but are you too clever for your own good? You've done very well so far, almost too well for such a young man, but we wouldn't want your youthful impetuosity to lead you astray. We have decided that we would like you to do us a little service, just by way of a thank you for our support."

'Here we go again, another test, another chain on me,' thought Quinn as his mind raced, "What sort of service?"

The cousin spoke this time. He was curt; his voice suiting his brutish looks "The line of work you were in over here for a while. We need a message sending out, and we need you to do it, but in this case we've gone past final warning, you get the drift?"

Quinn knew exactly what he meant, and the implications. It was the final line he had to cross to prove himself, kill for them, and he had expected it sooner. If he did this deed, not only would he satisfy their expectations but also they would have a card to play if he transgressed in the future. They underestimated Quinn even now though - he had always been capable of murder so this was just one more necessity to survive.

Quinn leant back in the chair, "I can do it, but why me?"

"It's overseas and we need a clean skin, an unknown, an Englishman, not a Mick," said Baldy. "As it happens, it can also help you with a little problem you've got coming down the line."

"How's that?" asked Quinn? He was puzzled, he usually covered all the angles and he did not like the feeling that he had missed something.

'The General' took up the thread, "Part of your worth to us is the fact that you are English born and bred, it deflects attention away from us. Obviously the fact that you are a nasty, violent, criminal young bastard appeals to us too." The eyes were twinkling again, he clearly found himself amusing. "You aren't the first son of Albion we have recruited so we have come across the problem before. Ever heard of National Service?"

Quinn responded, "Of course, but being out of the country last year meant that I missed the call-up. I haven't really thought about it since as I heard nothing and figured that they'd lost me in the system."

'The General' smiled thinly "It's been a fucking shambles that's for sure, but the bastards have got their act together now. You're going to have a problem if they catch up with you. You wouldn't have noticed, but they have been debating what to do and our sources have told us that there is a new Act coming in this April that means you'll get called up if you were born before the war started, and you were – right?"

Quinn pondered, "Yes - well before."

'The General' nodded, "Thought so, you'll be getting a letter from Her fucking Majesty sometime soon. I imagine your plans don't include a couple of years in some shithole army base or fighting darkies somewhere?"

Quinn was taken aback. This could ruin everything and he was kicking himself for letting it get past his notice. He could also place a bet on how that letter would find him as it put him firmly in the grip of these cold men.

Quinn played his part in the game, "No way, and I bet you don't want me in the British Army either?"

'The General' smiled, "Of course not, and we don't want to lose you in your prime when you are showing such promise. Just to prove it's true here's a clipping from the paper."

Quinn read quickly – it seemed true. The Government were aiming to run National Service down by 1960, but had decided to call up anyone born before 30th September 1939. If these Irish bastards had a way out he had to take it but he knew there would be a price to pay.

"So how do you get me out of it?" he asked, hating every moment of being a supplicant.

'The General' had his full attention and knew it, "You stay over here for a spot more training - and then you go and do the job I mentioned before. There will be some other stuff you can represent our interests in over there, so you will be busy for a while. When you come back here there will be a nice set of documents with a new name showing that you are an Irish citizen and exempt from call-up. Who knows, you might be lucky, they might not track you down, but I wouldn't gamble on that if I were you."

Quinn knew it was a gamble he was bound to lose. All he could do now was maximise the poor hand he had. "Before I say yes, what about Seamus and the farm? I would need him and it carrying on while I'm away. I wouldn't like someone new coming in."

"That's why it's a win – win." Said 'The General', smiling genially, "We will be seen to do right by Marie and Michael - God bless his soul. Our interests continue, you do us a favour or two and when you get back you carry on with your plans with our blessing. Luckily for you, Seamus was born here – he is an Irish citizen so won't get caught up in National Service."

'Neither would Joey – he's Italian. The others are too old bar Gurney but he is expendable for a couple of years and it might make him more useful anyway,' thought Quinn. He knew he was trussed and tied but it was better than a bullet in the head. Privately he was

already thinking that he might have lost in this encounter but he would be getting training, making contacts, travelling, and finding out more of the way the Irish operations ran, which could be very useful in the future. The big bonus was that Seamus, Marie, and the others would be able to carry on as usual. He brightened, "I think that's a deal then." He shook the proffered hands. The tension in the room eased and out of the corner of one eye he saw one of the standing men take a hand out of a pocket.

Jimmy entered the room and Quinn followed him out. They met Seamus in the hallway by the front door. They were ushered out to their car. Before they left, Jimmy told Quinn to go home and say his farewells and to return to him in Derry in April.

'The General' left him with a thought, "Bit of a gift from us– time with your kid. We are family men ourselves you know."

'You aren't bothered about wrecking other families though – fucking hypocrite', thought Quinn, but he was grateful for the time, he could do a lot in the few weeks he had, and he'd spotted something before he left that he desperately wanted to sort out before the opportunity went.

Seamus and Quinn compared notes as they followed their escort to the border. It seemed that the plan that they had rehearsed had worked for Seamus and he had been able to carry off the part of a 'none- too-bright' Republican sympathiser. The fact that he was in reality dim, helped, and was the foundation of the plan that Marie and Quinn had constructed. The Irish would not see Seamus as a threat and would take him on as part of the Pat Quinn package.

They had foreseen that this meant pressure would be focused on Quinn, but not the direction it had taken. Seamus became increasingly angry as Quinn recounted his interview and the deal he had come too, "I hate those bastards – and I hate them having a hold on me."

"And me," said Quinn, "But you've got to bury that anger. We are alive, they are backing us, and you're on their team now. You and the others can carry on building while I'm away. I've had an idea that might give us some independence if it comes off, and I'm planning to build us another power base as we go on, without them realising till it's too late to stop us."

"But look what you've had to agree too, leave your kid and Jenny, go away for months, or longer, and put yourself in their power by doing their dirty work for them." Seamus protested.

"It's nothing I can't handle, but there was no way out." Quinn explained the National Service problem and showed Seamus the press clipping.

Within a couple of hours they were back in Belfast appraising a relieved Marie – skirting around some facets of Quinn's forthcoming trip. When they returned to the farm Jenny was less relieved at the prospect of Quinn being away for potentially months and they had their first real clash.

It was the first time that Quinn's 'work' had come between them and he was in no mood for compromise. He was implacable that he had to sometimes do things to survive and that was how it was going to be. Jenny had to accept that her influence and say in such matters was nil. She didn't like it but in her current position there was little alternative and anyway, she was already being forged into a prototype biker's woman.

The real wrench for Quinn was missing crucial months of his son's development. His son had breached the hard shell of Quinn, the man of violence, and stolen his heart. It gnawed at Quinn that he had no free will in the matter, but he could think of no way out of the commitment he had given. He resolved to make the most of the time he had been given and the family settled back into calm.

Seamus took over the farm tenancy as planned, and life carried on - although it soon became plain they needed a new farmhand to replace Michael. They discussed the matter and decided that it was an opportunity to grow the group and set about locating a suitable candidate.

It was Steve who found Paul Fielding. Steve had been collecting some bike parts and got chatting at the shop counter to a lanky man in his early twenties who seemed to have bathed in grease. It pervaded every visible pore and was ingrained on fingers and nails. His hair was full of it too, helping set the mop into a Teddy-Boy 'ducktail.'

Steve had gone on his bike and had parked alongside a BSA A10 - similar to that Seamus rode. Steve's expert eye had noted with approval that the bike was immaculate and well maintained. Fielding had admitted ownership and Steve had complimented him on the bike. They had started chatting as Fielding went back and forth locating parts in the labyrinth of shelves and containers behind the counter.

Steve had quickly discovered that Fielding lived in Evesham and was a mechanic at a garage in Gloucester, which was quite a trek. He was a good mechanic and unhappy at being asked to cut corners to maximise profits. It was clear he didn't like the garage owner either.

They had hit it off and arranged to meet that evening. It hadn't taken long before Fielding proffered the information that he felt trapped and underpaid in the job because he had a criminal record for assault, and no-one else would give him a chance. That sounded like an ideal qualification to Steve.

Within a week Fielding had met Quinn, Seamus and Frank. Some background enquiries had confirmed that he was viewed by the locals as a good mechanic - and a bad person, just what they were looking for. He was working at the farm a week after that, on trial of course, and seemingly joined to Steve by an invisible umbilical cord. They were inseparable, working together on the farm, or in the garage.

Quinn was content to let the others judge when, and whether, Fielding was going to be absorbed into the activities of the group, but by the time he was due to depart to Ireland he had little doubt that they would have a new, and fully involved, member when he returned.

Before he left there was that other matter to consider. Over the past years he had often gazed through that chain link fence onto the airfield that bordered the farm and the aircraft taking off, and landing, were a constant reminder of its presence.

Towards the second half of last year though, it had become noticeable that the frequency of aircraft activity was decreasing and Quinn had recently seen a small article in a local newspaper lying on a table in the pub, to the effect that the RAF were leaving Defford and it was to be sold off in parcels of land.

The scientific research side of the wartime radar development at the airfield had morphed into a private concern after the war and it was rumoured they were likely to buy the main part of the airfield. This left the rest of the base, much of which had been gradually abandoned in the post war years, as surplus to requirements. In places vegetation was already beginning to encroach and some buildings had been decommissioned.

Quinn had asked Joey to do some research in Worcester. It had revealed that the sale was to take place soon and that the unwanted parts of the base would be either returned to the Croome Estate, which had originally owned them, or sold off to locals for farming or similar.

Quinn had one of his gut feelings when he read the original article. He knew that the only way they were going to get any independence from the Irish was to have their own premises somewhere. Indeed, he had been honest in his interview with the two men in the farmhouse that he planned to do just this.

He had sold it to them on the basis that diversifying the capacity and power of his group away from links to Eire would serve both parties well. This had been the focus of the main questions at the farmhouse. They had eventually agreed, but Quinn knew that he was treading dangerous ground, and in hindsight realised that the streak of independence he had revealed was the main reason he now had to prove himself again.

Quinn now had a dilemma. He had done all of his scouting around the edges of the airbase and had identified one cluster of buildings in particular, near the entrance. Now he would be away when the opportunity arose to buy them. For the first time in his life Quinn was going to have to let someone else take the lead.

He called a meeting and explained his thoughts to Seamus, Steve, Joey and Frank. He was honest about his wish to build something outside Irish control and the attendant risks of doing so. To a man they approved, they knew the potential for danger but all of them wanted some way of minimising their entanglement with the IRA.

Quinn offered up his insurance money to fund any purchase, to which could be added the unspent earnings from their now lucrative sidelines so that this new direction would not use any Irish money. He kept an amount back to purchase his next bike. He had no qualms about using his money in this way, it was useless sat doing nothing, this way his control of, and importance to the group was cemented further and he got the major share of an asset.

Joey and Jenny were appointed to lead. Quinn trusted them most of all, and together they had all the skills required. A bank account was opened in joint names with Quinn's money, plus other earnings, so that they could access funds in his absence.

Quinn directed, "I want you to try and keep me informed, but if you can't get in touch I trust you to do the deal rather than miss it."

They spent another hour deciding how to handle ownership. They decided to set up another company with shares divided proportionately to the investment – leaving Quinn as the major shareholder and the other four as shareholders. They were the heart of the group, there was no question of Billy Gurney, or Paul Fielding, getting a part, and the women were not even considered.

Men ran things and they made the decisions. There were plenty of females hanging around by now and of course Jenny was important to Quinn, but this was business, and in 1958 business involved men - and these were not the type of men whose heads would entertain the slightest notion of women having a say.

Thus it was that Quinn handed over just about everything he had to his best friend, and the mother of his son, and then left them so that he could satisfy the Irish. They all knew the sacrifice he was making and the trust he was showing them, and this further enhanced his hold on them. Quinn never forgave the silver-haired man but also worried about him. He recognised that he had met a match for the first time in his life. He needed to be very careful with that one.

Quinn, in turn, was confident that his trust would be vindicated. He knew these people better than he had his own kin. They had been through many challenges together and were bound in blood and crime. They were his new family and he liked them a whole lot better than his old one.

So it was that in April 1958, as it was announced that National Service would end in 1960, Quinn had to leave England to escape it.

Chapter Eighteen: 'He's Got The Whole World In His Hands'

(Laurie London)

1958

Quinn found himself celebrating the first month of his 21st year in the back of beyond. He hadn't a clue where he was; all he knew was that it was green and wet everywhere he looked. He was met by a taciturn man at the ferry terminal and quickly ushered into a battered farm truck. They had crossed the border and driven for hours in darkness as rain spattered the windscreen.

Eventually the sound of the wiper-motor and the rain lulled him to sleep. He awoke to the crunch of gravel as the truck pulled up. There was no light other than that leaking from the windows of a large house. He had an impression of the shapes of other buildings and heard wind in treetops as he was led inside. He checked his watch and was surprised to find it was ten in the evening.

A stern-faced woman, who said nothing, met him and showed him a bedroom, then beckoned him into a kitchen where some sort of stew was placed in front of him. The man who had driven the truck sat opposite, and noisily consumed his helping before belching and leaning back in his chair.

He went to a cupboard and produced a bottle of Irish Whisky and half-filled two glasses. He pushed one across the table, "Here you are mate, help you to sleep."

Quinn said, "Thanks, where are we?"

His driver responded, "As to that, well you don't really need to know, and its better you don't then no-one can make you talk. Let's just say this is a very special type of school."

Quinn took a gulp and savoured the liquid fire coursing down his throat, "So what do I do now?

The man responded dryly, "Have a drink with me then get your head down. You start in the morning. You're the only one here, you're getting extra special attention, bit of a crash-course. Breakfast in here then work. You'll find some clothes for tomorrow in the room, put them on."

They passed an hour and made a big impression on the bottle. The man was good company without giving anything away, even a name. Quinn quite liked him, respecting the professionalism, even when in drink, and tucking another lesson away for future use.

The taciturn woman knocked his door early and called, "Breakfast fifteen minutes, be late and it's gone."

Quinn found clothing of a type he had seen athletes wearing in a drawer.

A kitchen chair hosted a new face. The driver was nowhere to be seen. This man looked wiry and fit, late-forties with a military haircut. He stood and extended a hand as Quinn entered, "Welcome Pat, my name's Hugh, at least as far as you're concerned. I'm going to teach you about weapons and fighting. You think you know about fighting don't you, done a bit, but we'll see. Later, after I'm done with you, there'll be some stuff on how to make big bangs but that's someone else's area, not mine."

After breakfast he followed Hugh outside and into a courtyard surrounded by long, low buildings. Hugh led the way into the first building and Quinn was surprised to enter a large, purpose built, gymnasium with a padded floor at one end, weights equipment at the other.

Hugh said, "Get used to this place; you'll be spending a lot of time in here."

Quinn had never seen a proper gym before and he listened carefully as Hugh explained how to use the weights, "I'll work through some routines with you until you know what you're doing. You need to be stronger and fitter before I'll say you are ready. It's going to be hard work but you'll hopefully find it worthwhile. You're expected to work at it every day until I'm happy."

He indicated the matted end of the gym and Quinn followed and they both removed their tracksuit tops. Quinn noted that Hugh's compact size belied the defined muscles and veins in his arms and shoulders, "Okay Pat, I've heard a bit about your time in Derry and in England, so I know you can handle yourself. If you are going to want to learn from me you need to know I can teach you something. I want you to try and hurt me.

Quinn shrugged. He had never lost a fight but he had an idea that this was about to change. He suddenly launched an attack and within seconds found himself on his back looking up at Hugh.

This went on for about ten minutes although it seemed longer to Quinn. He did manage to land a couple of blows, especially after he learnt to be more cagey in going forward and when he did so Hugh nodded in approval. He spent longer on his back though and could feel bruises forming where he had been struck. Eventually his assailant signalled a halt, "Actually Pat you've got potential, you're fast and your balance is good. I can work with that. The day you put me on my back is the day you're ready. One thing you are going to have to learn is to channel and control that temper, I could read every move in your eyes and you were rash at times."

Quinn smiled, "No-one has ever done that to me, never mind several times, what is that shit you use?"

Hugh responded, "It was my reward for being the hardest bastard the movement has. Sent me to Japan to learn about combat so I could teach others. You wouldn't believe what some of those little yellow fuckers can do and it's all balance, timing and channeling power to a focal point."

Quinn nodded, "I want some of that."

After a couple of weeks of training and fighting Hugh changed direction as they entered the courtyard one day and they entered the long building on the other side. Again Quinn was taken aback at what confronted him and his respect for how dangerous these people were increased.

Hugh surveyed the room, "Welcome to our little range and the world of guns Pat."

The weeks rolled by. Quinn grew leaner and muscled. He was a keen pupil and avid to practice. This was an unexpected bonus from his farmhouse deal with 'The General' and he knew how useful these months would be for his future.

He learnt how to shoot, gaining credible accuracy. He worked with a range of guns, shotguns, rifles and semi-automatics, learning how to dissemble, clean and re- assemble them at speed, including in the dark, how to clear jams, and to use silencers and sights.

The unarmed combat progressed to using knives and improvising weapons. By the time the long days of June arrived Quinn was in awe of his mentor. The training moved outside and Quinn learnt how to move silently, conceal himself, and observe unseen. Then it was how to get past locks, all of which made Quinn think of Frank Fulford. He wondered just where Hugh had learnt all of this, clearly military somewhere, but he resigned himself to never knowing. Fortunately for Quinn there was to be no working in confined spaces and his one secret fear remained safe.

He began to realize that the level of effort being expended upon him meant that the job he was to do was not some two-bit enforcement and that there would be no tolerance of failure. The investment in him was growing and there would be recompense in full demanded over the coming years, not just on one job.

Still, he was the perfect canvas upon which to paint the skills of dealing pain and death. He had the base material, always had, it just needed honing.

He also wondered why he remained alone with his teacher but reasoned that as the driver had said, the less he knew the lower the risk, which meant that as far as he could see, they still didn't trust him fully.

It was July before he managed to break Hugh's nose and another week before he finally got the man off his feet. Hugh got back up and extended a hand.

"That's it Pat, my work is done, you're one of the best I've ever taught and you are one dangerous bastard now. I pity any normal bloke who tries to sort you out. Just remember two things, keep that temper under control and if you kill some nobody the rope will hang you, tough or not. It's not often I come across someone who enjoys it like you do, but that can take you into a bad place, so watch it."

The next morning Hugh was gone and Quinn was confronted with his antithesis, a rotund, balding man with glasses, and halitosis, who wheezed his way around the kitchen.

Once again Quinn was led to a different part of the facility, a single building isolated across a field. Upon entering Quinn's first thought was that he had entered a mad professor's laboratory. It was strewn with what at first glance seemed like junk, but resolved itself into an eclectic collection of components, electrical and mechanical.

The little man addressed Quinn, "They want you to know a bit about making bombs. I don't know why, so don't ask me, you'll probably never have to use it. He gestured at the clutter in the room, "We'll start with timers and detonators. We don't keep explosives here but I'll talk you through them."

Quinn couldn't see why he needed to know about this stuff;

surely they weren't planning on him planting bombs? It was just another part of the deal so he listened dutifully for the next two weeks, bored stiff.

By August the little man disappeared and Quinn knew the time had come to leave. Four months of his life - and Sean's life, had passed but Quinn did not feel it had been wasted. His basic talent for violence had been crafted into something more lethal and he had played the game in the indoctrination sessions but retained his basic distrust of the Republicans. They had created a weapon that they thought was theirs, but it had a mind of its own. He knew though, that his forthcoming journey was partly about strengthening their grip on him.

His whisky-drinking friend reappeared and once more he found himself rattling along in the old truck. The man was more talkative this time - which Quinn took as a good sign. If he had just undergone a test, it seemed that he had passed.

He didn't bother to ask where he was going, as he knew no information would be forthcoming. He was not surprised when they turned up a lane and parked outside yet another remote cottage. Once again 'The General' awaited him although there was no sign of his bald cousin. Quinn noted that there was still one other man in the room at all times though.

'The General' gestured to a seat, "Hello again Pat. We've been getting good reports so we have, seems that our assessment of your potential is not misplaced. Now onto our next bit of business."

He produced a sheaf of papers, "We have interests all over

the place Pat, built up over decades, and there are loyal supporters all over the world. But our most important friends are in the New World. They retain their links to the old country and help us in all sorts of ways. Of course it's a bloody melting pot over there and sometimes we come into competition with others. We can usually talk them through and come to an agreement, but we've struck a problem recently on the East Coast."

He removed a photograph from the file and pushed it across the table, "Meet Anthony, 'Tony' Romano."

The photo was slightly blurred, clearly taken with a long lens, but was good enough to show a long-faced man with a scar on his left cheek. Quinn judged him to be young - late twenties. 'The General' continued, "We usually get on fine with our Italian friends, find accommodations to suit, but young Tony here has been making waves. He's not like the older generation. He's ambitious and seems to have decided that he can move in on our cut of the cake. He's assembled a bunch of like-minds and has become a thorn in our side. We've tried to get him brought back into line but we think our old contacts are using him to play a double game, testing our strength and resolve. Our belief is that if he is dealt with, they will disown him, but if he succeeds in taking our business they will back him. This is a significant problem for us. That's where you come in."

Quinn pushed the photo back, "Okay I know what he looks like, but I'm not just going to be able to drop into another territory and take out a big player on my own."

'The General' waved expansively, "Sure, sure, we know that and that's why we've sat on our hands till now. We've done our background work as you can see." He nodded towards the file; "Our problem is that everyone does the research so we all know each other's people. We are sure Romano will be expecting something and will be trying to get all the information he can on our operatives. That's where you come in, Mister Clean Skin."

He continued, "You will leave your Patrick Quinn name and papers with me and we will supply you with another identity. When you arrive you will check into this hotel." He pushed a slip of paper across to Quinn, "Enjoy yourself for a few days, see the sights, take in a show or the cinema. You will be contacted and given the details you need, then it's up to you, that's why we've put all this effort into training you."

Quinn frowned, "But they'll know it's you behind it won't they?"

'The General' responded, "They might suspect, but they won't be certain. You will be an English tourist who is in the wrong place at the wrong time. As long as you get away from where it happens you will disappear. Another person will leave from the West Coast and that will be your name for a while until the threat of conscription back home is gone."

'*Win – win for you though, if I don't get out alive you just deny all knowledge. If I succeed you've got a hold over me,*' thought Quinn.

He didn't like leaving his real name behind with his documents but had little choice. He was assured he could be himself again once the final draft of National Service recruits was done, which according to the news would be at the start of 1960. Until then, as far as anyone in authority in England knew, Patrick Quinn had left for Ireland in April 1958 and stayed there. Of course, given the organisational shambles surrounding call-up it was unlikely anyone would be looking for him unless someone reminded them, and the man sat opposite him held that card.

He resigned himself to make the best of the situation, as he had with the training. After all, who wouldn't want to see the States? A New World was about to open up to him in more ways than one.

Chapter Nineteen: 'Who's Sorry Now?'

(Connie Francis)

1958

A week later, equipped with fresh clothes, a wad of cash, and travel documents naming him as Oliver Kenwright from Manchester, Quinn walked off the plane at Idlewild and entered the Big Apple.

He caught a yellow taxi to the hotel - comfortable compared to English offerings. The next few days' were spent orientating himself in the big city, and learning about American culture. He walked a lot, stood atop the Empire State Building, and rode the ferry past the Statue of Liberty. He took in a show, ambled around Central Park in the sun, and soaked up the bustle of Times Square, gazing up at the man-made canyons of skyscrapers. He also did a little shopping, equipping himself with a knife - just in case.

By the end of the fourth day he had seen all he wanted. The hot weather had momentarily broken and on the spur of the moment he decided to escape the rain by taking in a movie. There was one in particular that had caught his interest for two reasons. Firstly its subject was motorbikes and violence, and secondly even he had heard of the scandal it had caused.

He had wanted to see it, but it had been banned in Britain and Ireland since it's release some years earlier. He had noticed the film was being shown at one of the less salubrious cinemas the previous day and had filed the information away. Little did he realise the impact it was to have on the future of his group back home.

He was almost alone in the cinema, but he wouldn't have noticed as he became totally submerged in a story that both mirrored and transcended his own.

It was about The Black Rebels, a gang who rode motorbikes. Their leader was a charismatic Marlon Brando as Johnny Strabler - who actually rode the same bike as Quinn, a Triumph Thunderbird. They were a family of sorts, perhaps more of a tribe, looking after each other. Quinn hung on every moment as the gang descended on a quiet American town, Wrightsville, with only one ageing lawman, Harry Bleeker.

Quinn nodded to himself as he watched the lawman have to conciliate due to the gang's strength in numbers, unity, borderline morals, and propensity for violence.

There were clashes with locals, and a rival gang, but Quinn also was reminded of home when the gang was hosted by the owner of a local bar - only too happy to take their custom and money.

It was a revelation. His life suddenly made sense; he saw now that fate had led him to Defford, motorcycles and friends. Quinn though, with his unique experiences and character, knew that he could take this idea further and stayed in his seat for a second viewing.

Afterwards he sat in a nearby café and reflected. The film was basically dramatized male high-jinks but he understood the subtler implications. The strength in unity of the group, the fear of the locals, that allowed the bikers to break the law and crash through moral barriers. It was just another type of criminal organisation, like the IRA, or the Mafia, but with the cachet of motorcycles overlaid. It was a new and exciting idea and he had seen it before anyone else who rode a bike in England.

He walked back towards his hotel with plans buzzing in his head then saw a library and diverted on an impulse. He approached the desk where a bespectacled woman with a permanent frown looked down her nose at him, "Yes young man?"

Quinn practiced being polite, "Hello, I'm a visitor from England," he put on his most charming smile and noticed a slight thaw in the frostiness.

The frown lifted, "What an interesting accent, my brother-in-law married an English girl after the war. Welcome to New York, how can I help you?"

Quinn smiled, "Well I've just seen a film I liked and at the end I noticed it was based on a true story, I wondered if you had it?"

"We can certainly have a look, what was it called?" She turned to a card index, poised.

Quinn continued, "The film was called The Wild Ones, with Marlon Brando, but the credit said it was based on a story by a Frank Rooney. It's about a group of motorcyclists."

The lady turned slightly from the cards, "I know of it of course, can't say I approve of your viewing choice but let's see – I didn't know it was based on anything more than a wild imagination."

She began leafing through the cards before giving a small cry of triumph, "This must be it, 'The Cyclist's Raid' by Frank Rooney – a short story, and we seem to have it referenced in an anthology."

She set off in a determined fashion down the corridors of books and returned holding a volume aloft, "Here we are, 'Best American Short Stories 1952'. You can sit here and read it if you like." She indicated tables and seats nearby.

The story was well written. Quinn once again drank in the details. Motorcyclists, a lot of them, in uniform garb, all wearing goggles, invade and smash up a small town, racing bikes, fighting, drinking and vomiting - finally killing a girl in a rash bike escapade.

The lone lawman is powerless and the perpetrators of the death escape any punishment because they are indistinguishable as a group and they make off into the night. The only one who breaks ranks, a young innocent unlike the rest, returns to the town to apologise and is beaten nearly to death for his trouble.

They were known as a motorcycle 'troop' – 'The Angelinos', from Los Angeles. They acted with military precision and hierarchy with a clear leader, yet ran amok like victorious troops unleashed upon the vanquished. One of the townsfolk described them as a 'private army'.

Other 'troops' were mentioned, all hailing from the West Coast. Quinn sensed there was a grain of truth behind the fiction, a new phenomenon - and vowed to investigate further once his work was done in New York and he escaped westwards.

He returned the book, thanking the librarian, and trudged

thoughtfully to his room. There was a note under the door.

It was the address of a restaurant, Italian by the sound of it, and a time when a table was reserved, 7pm. Further instructions to go to a new hotel afterwards and wait. He was to leave his current room wearing the smart suit he had been given and destroy the note.

He complied but kept the knife he had bought, just in case. He also carried the bogus identification of Oliver Kenwright. If he failed then that was his part of the deal, he was just an unlucky tourist.

The restaurant, Bernini's, was a twenty-minute walk and Quinn had to force himself to concentrate on the job at hand rather than his exciting afternoon revelations. It was clearly an upper-class establishment judging by the well-dressed couples alighting from taxis and limousines at the kerb.

He gave his name and was shown to a table for two near the window, the waiter assuring him that it was one of the best they had. The best was clearly the table in the window. It was reserved.

He decided that he might as well eat, and ordered. He obtained a beer that he left untouched, but in a prominent position. He looked around, most tables were occupied, but there was no sign of Romano. The table next to him remained empty.

He had just finished his starter when his eye was caught by a large black Cadillac pulling up outside. The head-waiter was immediately outside fawning over the group that alighted - four men and two women.

Quinn assessed them from his vantage point. He recognised Romano from the scar and noted how he possessively assisted one chattering female from the car. A second man, younger by a few years or so, mid-twenties, escorted the other woman.

The other two men were of a different mould, Quinn smiled inwardly, *'bodyguards look the same whether in Ireland or here,'* he thought. This being America he was anticipating that they would be armed.

Romano was flanked by the minders as he entered and Quinn noted how they all checked the room before Romano was shown to the table next to him by the obsequious head-waiter. Romano played to the crowd. This was clearly a regular occurrence and many of the diners were anxious to greet him.

The gangster sat with his back to the alcove wall, with a view of the room and window, his escort next to him. The heavies split up, one facing the street, the other the room. The other couple had their backs to Quinn which meant he was looking straight at Romano. He admired the planning that had resulted in his positioning and once again reminded himself what a dangerous game he played with his sponsors.

His main course arrived, and he toyed with his food whilst trying to come up with a way to provoke a confrontation that would look natural, and wouldn't involve the two bodyguards before he got involved face to face with Romano.

Hugh had taught him several ways to kill but it couldn't look like a professional hit, there had to be enough doubt to enable the

IRA, and the Dons, to move on whilst preserving reputation.

Romano solved the problem for him. The guy was clearly in love with himself and wanted to flaunt his burgeoning power and reputation. He was also a bully and a loudmouth, and it seemed used the restaurant as a stage for his performances.

Within minutes of sitting down Romano was making the waiter's life a misery and then he caught sight of a young couple at another table. The girl was very pretty and it seemed they were not part of the regular crowd of flatterers, and followers, surrounding Romano and occupying many of the other tables. They were doing their best to ignore the loud bravado and bullying from the table in the alcove whilst whispering together.

Romano caught sight of them, heads close together. They were wrapped up in each other, meaning that he wasn't in his accustomed place at the centre of everyone's attention. It seemed he also liked the look of girl as he pushed his way abruptly past his own companion and set off in the young couple's direction.

All eyes were on him now and the rattle of cutlery and conversation quietened. Quinn could sense that this behaviour was not an unusual occurrence. He could taste the rise in tension in the air.

"Hey gorgeous, what's so interesting about him?" Romano pronounced in a heavy drawl.

The couple made a bad decision; they tried to ignore him, slightly turning away. Quinn could see colour drain from the young man's face.

Romano reached the table and loomed over them. He leant forward, invading the space between them, "I'm talking to you, don't disrespect me in front of all my friends."

The man visibly swallowed and raised his hands, "Sorry, didn't hear you."

Romano, being a bully, smelt easy meat. He leant across and slapped the man hard, the crack ringing out across the now silent room. Quinn noticed some diners look away. He also noticed that the two henchmen had not moved. It seemed they played no part in Romano's sport, preferring to stay alert for greater threats.

Romano turned to the girl, "Hey sweetheart, you shouldn't be with a jerk like this, you need a real man, come and join me and I'll buy you a drink and whatever food you want."

The girl was brave or foolhardy, Quinn couldn't decide which, but he admired her backbone. She wrinkled her nose as if she smelt something rotten, "I can think and decide for myself, and if I couldn't, I wouldn't be using your brain as a back-up. Go back to your lady friend and leave me alone."

The riposte drew a small ripple of nervous laughter from one table. Romano flashed a murderous glance in that direction then grabbed the girl's wrist, dragging her to her feet. She gave a small gasp of pain.

"I wasn't asking permission, you come and sit with me." He began to drag the protesting girl away from the table. Out of the corner of an eye Quinn noticed that the men on Romano's table were highly amused but the two women were looking down at the table.

The young man stood up and protested, taking hold of Romano's arm and trying to free his grip. Meat and drink to the gangster who felled the kid with a right hook, sending him backwards across a table, plates and glasses shattering and falling. The man went down and stayed down.

Romano was now approaching his own table, struggling girl in tow. Quinn watched every step, staring intently at Romano who was flushed and excited by his endeavours.

Quinn stood up and moved around his table, putting Romano and the girl between himself and the men at the table in the window, "I don't think the lady wants to drink with you." he said in a quiet, flat voice.

Romano stopped and goggled, not quite believing his ears. He saw a slim looking man in a suit and quickly assessed the odds and came down heavily on the side of more sport to be had. He pushed the girl violently towards one of his companions, "Here - hold her for me, this won't take a minute."

He moved towards Quinn, "Who the fuck are you, get out or I'll kick your butt out."

Quinn raised his hands, palm outwards as if in fear and spoke loudly now in what he hoped was a more cultured accent, "Just a visitor from England, you are acting despicably, is this American manners? It's not too late to stop this, pay for their meal, you can clearly afford it."

Romano sensed another easy win, another addition to his reputation, "This is my neighbourhood, and I do what I want. I don't need some Brit lecturing me, time for you to leave with my boot up your ass."

Quinn read the moment of attack in the dark eyes and mentally thanked Hugh. As Romano launched himself forward, Quinn used a move he had been taught. Romano found himself being propelled face downwards towards Quinn's table.

Quinn judged the angles expertly, ensuring that Romano's windpipe impacted on the sharp table edge. He applied a little extra energy and heard the crack as the neck snapped. He knew that either impact should be fatal - both made it certain. Romano bounced back off the table and Quinn took the dead weight with him towards the door and out onto the sidewalk before anyone else reacted.

He dropped the body and had enough time to check that the bully was indeed dead before he heard the window table erupt in screams and saw movement. By the time the first bodyguard had reached his dead boss Quinn was out of sight around a corner.

Within several minutes he had covered a mile and satisfied himself that there were no pursuers. He stopped jogging and dodged into the subway. He had memorised the route that afternoon and three stops later he emerged near to his new hotel.

As he approached the desk he had a momentary thought that this was where he would get betrayed, double-crossed, but when he gave the name from the note he was rewarded with a room key. The desk clerk welcomed him, "That's all fine sir, your room has been paid for in advance and your case has already been taken up."

He couldn't stop himself checking left and right as he exited from the elevator. He approached the room door cautiously and stood to one side as he pushed it open. It was empty apart from a suitcase on the bed.

The case contained clothes in his size, toiletries, and two packages. He examined these but his recent induction into bomb making reassured him that they were safe. One contained a thick sheaf of dollar bills of various denominations - it looked a sizeable sum. The other yielded another new identity in the form of a British passport and driving licence. *'Hello Jonathan Stephens'* he thought. As he opened the passport, tickets for the Greyhound to Washington in an hour, and a flight from there to Los Angeles the next afternoon, fluttered onto the bed.

He quickly changed and bundled the suit into the case. When he reached the hotel lobby he waited until the desk was deserted before leaving by a side door unseen. He made for the bus station on foot and was lucky enough to spot some street dwellers gathered around a lit brazier in an alleyway. He proffered a dollar bill to share the fire for five minutes. The two down-and-outs looked at him and he could see the thought of jumping him flash across their minds but one look at his eyes and they took the money.

Oliver Kenwright disappeared into the brazier flames, page by page, and Quinn waited until he was sure the tramps couldn't recover anything. On the spur of the moment he donated the suit to them and left them arguing over who got the jacket or trousers.

Within twenty-four hours he was in the air. Behind him, the Dons shrugged their shoulders. They couldn't bring back the dead and Tony had been a problem. They weren't sure if it was bad luck that had got him killed but they lost no face over it.

Questions were quietly asked but when no leads were forthcoming they went back to their businesses, letting it be rumoured that they had taken out the arrogant youngster, a small but delicious bonus for their reputation.

No cop tears were shed for Romano, they too made some desultory enquiries and added the death to the gangland tally, *'who cared if some schmuck got lucky and took out that son of a bitch anyway?'* Oliver Kenwright had vanished into thin air, or the harbour more likely, with a concrete block for good measure - file closed.

Back in Eire, 'The General' sat at a table with the other ruling minds, phone to his ear. He placed it back on the receiver and smiled.

He loved a win-win.

Chapter Twenty: 'You Are My Destiny'

(Paul Anka)

1958

Quinn put on his new sunglasses as he walked down the steps from the aircraft and across the tarmac. He drank in the balmy Californian air and felt the heat beating upon his back.

He felt a small amount of trepidation as he approached the bored-looking man in the booth and proffered his new passport. The man compared the photo to Quinn, "Purpose of visit?" he drawled.

Quinn replied courteously, "Just a couple of week's downtime after business on the East Coast."

The man was clearly not done yet, "Well you've come to the right place for that. Never been East myself, what was Miami like?"

Quinn was nearly caught out until he remembered that his new passport bore a stamp for Miami Immigration two weeks earlier, "You know, big city, beach, palm trees, didn't have time to see much of it."

The man offered what Quinn supposed was an attempt at a smile, "Broads any good?"

Quinn recognized the international male code and winked, "Yes but I hope to be able to further explore that sort of business while I'm out here."

"You won't have a problem with that here, just tell them you're a Brit film producer and they'll be lining up with their legs open." He laconically stamped the passport and handed it back, "Welcome to California Mister Stephens."

Quinn collected his new luggage and traversed customs without event. The terminal was bustling and noisy but his inbuilt radar for trouble soon alerted him to a figure holding up a card bearing his latest name.

He approached a sleazy looking individual with a sallow complexion, oiled hair, and pencil moustache, a caricature spiv, dressed in his attempt at the latest fashion which he somehow managed to imbue with an air of falsehood. He may as well have had, *'don't trust me, I'm a crook'*, in lights above his head.

Quinn ventured, "I'm Stephens."

The man gave him a cursory inspection then opened his mouth in an insincere smile that revealed a very bad set of teeth, "Younger than I expected." He extended a hand and Quinn recoiled slightly at the weak, clammy grip, "Just call me Ed. My job is to settle you in and make sure you have everything you need. You sure must have done something good, I'm the best fixer in town."

Quinn decided to make the most of the conversation, "Pleased to meet you Ed. As it happens there are a couple of things I want to ask you about."

Ed raised both hands, "Nothing too much trouble for Mister Stephens today. We can talk while we drive, got you a good place to stay, right by the ocean."

He led the way to a large convertible in postbox-red with whitewall tyres. Ed launched sunglasses onto his beak of a nose and set off weaving through the traffic. Soon they reached the highway and settled into a steady cruise.

Quinn had to shout above the wind noise but he was exhilarated, California, he was really here! "So what's the plan?"

Ed replied, "Get you into your hotel, give you some funds, the lowdown on LA, and anything else you need, then you're on your own. You're booked on a flight back home in two weeks."

Ed had an unnerving habit of looking at his passenger whilst he talked, instead of the road, so Quinn resolved to keep the chat to a minimum and enjoy the ride.

Thirty minutes later they drew up outside a hotel and left the convertible to be parked.

"Another fucking film star in the making," observed Ed as the concierge drove the car off. Quinn had taken an instant dislike to Ed and regretted the fact that he wouldn't get the chance to knock out a few of those rotten teeth.

Upon entering the lobby Ed motioned to the cocktail bar, secured an alcove, a waitress, and drinks, "Okay When I leave, you check in, room is all arranged - you'll like it. Here's some dough." He proffered an envelope which Quinn took without opening, an act that clearly impressed Ed.

Ed slurped his drink and handed a slip of paper over, "If you need me call this number. It's a bar but they'll know how to find me, you are safe leaving a message. Okay so far?"

Quinn nodded, "You said you could get me anything I wanted?"Ed beamed, "Sure, especially women, what's your type?"Quinn had other things on his mind, "Maybe another time for that. Do you know any bikers, in clubs down here?"Ed was momentarily surprised then his natural confidence reasserted itself,

"Sure, I know everyone, I told you didn't I? There are a couple of groups locally, I do a bit of business with them you know, act as go-between, and a couple of them know me from way back so they trust me." He re-appraised Quinn, taking in his new clothes, and the smart businessman look that still lingered, "They aren't very nice people you know, not your type at all, if you're after some sort of tourist kick I could recommend plenty of better options, especially if it involves women - doing anything that does it for you – know what I mean?"

He gave a lascivious wink and Quinn now recognized the pimp in him. The urge to break one of his limbs re-surfaced but he suppressed the feelings. He spoke slowly and icily, "Watch my lips Ed. No girls, I can handle that side of things myself and I don't pay either. I want to meet the bikers, the worst ones you know. All you need to do is give me an introduction, vouch that I'm not a cop, that sort of thing.

One more thing, I want a bike to ride while I'm here, always wanted to try an Indian or a Harley, whatever you can find. Once you've done those two things you can get on with your life and need never see me again, so easy pay packet for you I guess. I'll even put in a good word for you, how's that?"

Ed did yet another assessment of the Englishman. He was used to dealing with all sorts of characters, low-life to high-rollers and he knew a hard man when he saw one, and this one seemed as crazy as a coot, a bad combination. He quickly decided to play along; after all it wasn't his business if the Brit got himself stomped or worse.

"Okay, okay, I get it, but I'll be feeding back up the chain that you asked for it so there's no blowback on me.

Quinn picked up a napkin and produced a pen, "Here - I'll give you it in writing if you helps." Ed thought it would help. He asked for twenty-four hours to make arrangements and set a time to meet the following evening.

At 5pm the following day Ed entered the hotel bar once more and scanned the booths. He half hoped that Mister Stephens would have changed his mad plan. He had to do a double-take before he was sure that it was his guest sat in a corner.

Quinn was wearing a T-shirt, leather flying jacket, denims, and large boots. He was unshaven. Ed shook his head; this guy was really blowing his mind. He walked over, "Hi, been shopping I see."

Quinn wasn't in a mood to waste time, "The real me, what have you got for me?"

Ed wasn't in a mood to linger either, he wanted tonight done with and this suicidal Brit out of his life as quickly as possible, "Got you a bike sorted, a Harley, belongs to a friend of mine but he's got a few so was happy to hire one out. Its old but it's in good order. It'll be outside in the morning, key at reception waiting for you. I'll put the cost on my expenses. As for the bikers, they are more difficult, but I know where they are tonight. It could be lively; they are partying, celebrating a prison release or something. Still sure you want to do this?"

Quinn nodded and followed Ed outside to the convertible.

After a ten minute journey they parked outside a bar facing the sea. It was clearly the right place, a row of bikes outside and the sounds of raucous laughter and loud music shattering the peaceful beach sounds. Quinn noticed shadowy figures further along the beach. Ed saw him looking, "Party starts here, finishes out there sometime in the morning, always the same routine."

They walked up the steps and were confronted by two large men sat on wicker chairs either side of the door. They both wore similar clothing to Quinn's and he remembered the story he had read in New York that had stressed the biker uniform worn by the outlaw bike troop. One man stood up and barred the way, "Private party - get lost."

Ed adopted his most ingratiating personae, irritating Quinn once more. He could almost smell Ed's fear, "You know me boys, its Ed, and we do some business together. Is Bobby here? He can vouch for me."

The man scrutinized Ed, deliberately ignoring Quinn. As he turned Quinn noticed the insignia sewn on the rear of his flying jacket. A curved white band bore the name 'Madmen'. Below it was a skull adorned with two wings. A further curved banner below the skull proclaimed 'Venice'. The man got tired of making Ed shake just by looking at him, grunted and disappeared inside the bar.

The man who remained seated said nothing. He took a couple of large slugs of beer from a bottle and just stared. The silence was clearly uncomfortable for Ed but Quinn did some reverse psychology, just turned his back on the man and looked at the ocean. This was going to be all about 'face' and Ed was doing nothing to help.

The sound of the door banging open spun him around. As he did so he noted the seated man reach for a pocket then relax. A new figure stood in the doorway, drunk as a skunk and swaying on his oily denim clad legs. Quinn could smell his body odour.

The drunk wasn't as big as the other two but he wore the same outfit and looked plain mean. He peered at Ed then clapped an arm around the cringing fixer "Ed my old buddy, come to party or sell us some whores?"

Ed emitted a nervous squeak of a laugh, "Bobby, good to see you. Got a dude here from England who wants to meet some bikers, heard you were drinking here tonight so here we are. This is John."

Bobby took a few unsteady steps towards Quinn, breathing an unsavoury mix of beer and unwashed teeth into his face. Quinn held his ground. This was a test.

"Why?" uttered Bobby.

There was no reason to hide the truth, "Me and some friends in England have got together in a bike group. I was over on business, seen the film and read the story about Hollister and wanted to meet some real bikers, learn some stuff to take back home, maybe create some links."

"Hollister, Hollister, I'm sick of hearing about fucking Hollister, that was nothing special, all blown up by the papers. Don't give a fuck about that, or you," the man bellowed.

Ed tittered like a girl, "Bobby, Bobby, just a favour for me please, you owe me a couple, let us in, just for a one drink, I'll let you have a free-one next time you want a girl, how bout that?"

Bobby swayed and thought, looked Quinn up and down, then shrugged and threw the door open, "It's your funeral, some of the boys are pretty lively tonight. Ed you can be sure you owe me one for this."

The noise hit them like a wave. The bar was an L-shape with a pool table in the wing of the L. The game seemed to have been interrupted by three bikers banging a woman on the table whilst others cheered them on. There was a pungent smell in the room that Quinn didn't recognize.

The bar ran across the top end of the room and it looked like the bikers were doing the serving and the drinking. A pale man was slumped against the wall at one end of the bar watching with an air of resignation as two tattooed individuals dispensed bottles, helping themselves as they did so. No money seemed to be changing hands.

Bobby noticed the direction of Quinn's gaze and shouted above the din, "Old Pete don't like watching us strip his bar but he knows there'll be a wad of dollars for him at the end and we look after him. He decided a long time ago we were better as friends than enemies and in this town he would have to pay someone for security, and we are the meanest sons of bitches around, so now this is our party place."

He led the way to the bar by forcing a way through the crowd. Quinn noticed that some far bigger men made way for him, "Is Bobby important somehow?" he asked Ed quietly.

An anxious Ed responded, "He's sort of a leader on account of he has brains when he's sober but also the meanest temper you've ever seen. Put together, that means the thick ones are in awe of him and the clever ones are scared, so they tend to do what he says. I've heard some bad stories bout Bobby and I believe every one of them. They call him Vice President, it's a club after all, and they have officers in different roles. Some of them, the older ones, are ex-military and I guess some discipline and organization has leaked into the set up."

Bobby reappeared bearing bottles of beer and indicated a table occupied by a biker with a beer-belly and a scar running down one cheek, and two females who looked like hookers. One was sat on beer-belly's lap while he lazily fondled her breast. Bobby waved at the man, "That's Crusty, so called on account of the state of his underwear. He's the cause of this little celebration – just got out after two years, put someone in hospital for expressing their displeasure at his smell."

They followed Bobby to the table, Ed reluctant, Quinn fascinated. Here was exactly what he had seen and read about. These people clearly did what they wanted on the basis that they were a cohesive group of nastiness that frightened the life out of everyone who might object. He was determined to know more but was beginning to wonder if he had bitten off more than he could chew as he scanned the room.

The party had already got wilder and Quinn was realizing that his chances of emerging unscathed were narrowing with each minute that passed. He was an interloper and he could feel eyes upon him, only Bobby's presence was keeping the wolves away, and he had a feeling that Bobby had some fun in mind.

Bobby physically booted the seated girl off her perch, "Scram," he said. He sat, leaving Ed and Quinn standing as if they were supplicants, "Crusty, here's Ed and a little English friend who wanted to come to your party, what do you say?"

Crusty looked through bloodshot piggy eyes and then spat, the phlegm landing on Quinn's boot, "Thanks Bobby, new meat to fuck, I'm already missing it. Never fucked a Brit boy." He ran his hand up the skirt of the girl on his lap "Him first then you later gorgeous."

Bobby raised his hands in an apologetic manner, "Sorry, but what can I do? It's Crusty's party, the man's gotta have whatever he wants, - I kind of thought he might like a pretty-boy like you."

As Bobby stood up, Quinn felt an absence by his side and caught a glimpse of his erstwhile friend and fixer going through the bar door at pace. He was on his own.

Crusty pushed the girl on his lap to the floor and also stood. Quinn could see other bikers closing, waiting for the show. He struck first, planting his boot between Crusty's legs then driving an elbow into the ex con's face. Crusty went down and Quinn thought that he wouldn't be fucking anyone tonight.

Quinn knew that he had one chance to get out of this before every biker in the bar came at him. He turned to Bobby who had been momentarily taken aback by the speed with which his friend had been dispatched, "You got the guts to go one-on-one Bobby, or do you have to hide behind your gang?"

Bobby laughed and Quinn realized that the man was not nearly as drunk as he had made out, "Nice move, didn't expect that, but you don't fool me Johnnie, you're thinking one-on-one you might stand a chance, but take us all on and you're a gonner.

Well that's as may be, and the usual rule is you beat on one of us you gotta do us all, that's why people won't take us on. But I don't need them to take you down."

Quinn had to admire Bobby's show at the door. Firstly he wasn't drunk and Ed now owed him a favour, Quinn would provide some entertainment and due to his unexpected victory over Crusty, Bobby could reaffirm his status as top-dog by beating, or even killing him. There was no way out now though, except through the Vice President of the Madmen.

He noted that Bobby had stopped swaying and was perfectly balanced on the balls of his feet. Quinn looked Bobby in the eye and smiled. He saw the attack presaged in those eyes just as Hugh had taught him to. Bobby found his killer chop blocked by an arm and his kick struck a blocking thigh.

Bobby danced back and began to circle looking for an

opening. A circle had formed, it was like a school playground only much more deadly. They were evenly matched in size and Bobby was as fast as Quinn too.

They exchanged a flurry of blows and kicks. Quinn's nose was broken and he could feel blood dripping. He shook his head to clear it, the man sure hit hard! The bikers cheered at the sight of blood. Bobby though had an ugly bruise forming around his eye where Quinn had caught him.

Bobby grabbed a beer bottle, smashed it on the table and lunged towards Quinn's face. He saw it coming, swayed to one side letting the bottle pass his right cheek. He grabbed the arm, reversed it into a straight-lever, forced Bobby forward and smashed his head into a pillar.

The biker went with the rebound and head-butted Quinn in the face. They separated a few paces and stood blowing like prizefighters after ten rounds. They were both hurt and stunned.

Quinn had a problem. He was sure he could win this but if he hurt Bobby too badly, or dishonored him in front of the gang, he knew he would never get out alive. He began to speak, "That's about even I reckon." he decided a spot of flattery wouldn't be wasted "I've never lost and you're the best I've fought, what say we call it a draw and have that beer."

As he spoke he monitored his opponent's eyes. He remembered Ed's words about Bobby's temper and could see the rage take hold. Quinn knew what that feeling was like. Hugh had taught him that it was both a strength, and a weakness. He could see that words would not suffice, Bobby clearly wanted blood and Quinn spat some onto the floor. He changed tack. He needed to finish this cleanly, "Looks like I'm going have to put you down in front of all your friends then, perhaps you're stupider than I thought."

Bobby charged, brandishing the bottle. He was like a rabid dog and that made him careless. This time Quinn ducked the bottle, caught the arm with one hand, and grabbed Bobby's balls with the other and squeezed. He felt the bikers legs sag as he cried out in pain. Within seconds Quinn had him on the floor, face down, and was holding the bottle to Bobby's neck. He looked up into a sea of legs and boots, "Get back or I'll take him out for good."

He looked up and saw hesitancy; some of these men were so drunk that they might think it worth Bobby's life to take him out. The moment teetered then two of the men were roughly shoved aside and a new voice spoke, "That's enough. Leave him to me. Got us a party to have and I want Bobby alive to enjoy it."

Quinn looked up. The man was older, in his thirties. Well over six feet tall with a mop of blond hair and, for his colouring, unusually dark, nearly black, eyes. No beer-belly, Quinn noted. The muscular arms revealed by the T-shirt were covered in tattoos, a mixture of military emblems, bikes and women. *'Force's man'*, Quinn thought.

Quinn decided that the initiative still lay with him and looked up, "So how do we get out of this stand off with Bobby and me still alive?"

The black eyes stared back, "Easy. You take Bobby outside,

and then we talk, one-on-one. Means you can go if it doesn't work out. Bobby, you hear that? Don't you go trying to pull any stunts now."

Bobby grunted in assent, his face still ground into the floor.

Quinn nodded towards the other bikers, many of whom had drifted away and resumed their drinking and fornicating, "What about them?"

The man hinted at his status, "They do what I say. I call what happens from now on."

It was the best offer Quinn was going to get. He dragged Bobby to his feet, careful to keep the broken bottle touching skin above the jugular vein. He backed carefully out of the doors, which were held open by the guardians of the door, who now showed a modicum of respect. Another note to himself, Quinn thought, there is discipline here, under the wildness. They hadn't left their posts during the ruckus, ensuring no outsider would witness events inside.

The tattooed man nodded to the two bikers and they resumed their seats. He spoke again, "Lets go over to the beach, give you some distance from my boys."

Quinn took in his surroundings, at a diagonal across the road, and away from the bar, the party-site on the beach that he had seen earlier. They reached a play-area and the blonde man sat on a swing, rocking gently. Quinn could see a tower for lifeguards in the distance, silhouetted against a rising moon. It was a gentle night with the sea lapping gently on the shore. With no wind he heard the fire further down the beach begin to crackle as it was lit and the tang of wood smoke reached his nostrils.

From his perch on the swing the man indicated, "Here will do. Lets talk. Smells like the beach-party will be starting soon."

Quinn decided to take a risk. This was all about 'front' and he really didn't want to walk away from this opportunity. He released Bobby and pushed him towards the swinging man, "Token of good faith."

Bobby turned, wiping blood from his face, "Goddamn it, where d' you learn to fight like that boy?"

Quinn smiled, "I had a very special teacher, if I said in Ireland would that mean anything to you?"

Bobby looked blank but the other man nodded slowly, "I think I'm getting the picture, 'John', and I bet that isn't your real name. That was some sort of Japanese fighting shit you pulled in there and I reckon our little Bobby here never stood a chance. I was watching you though, and you've done plenty of fighting, never got fazed, just calculated those odds didn't you," - it was not a question.

Quinn shrugged, "I wanted to meet you, knew it might be tough and that I might get hurt, but hopefully it'll be worth it."

The man looked Quinn in the eyes with curiosity for a while then stepped forward and offered a hand, "I'm Angelo Agnelli, first in the alphabet and President of the Madmen. I'm proud to lead this bunch of heathens. You've already made the acquaintance of Bobby King who is my right-hand man and Vice President. Tell me your proper name."

This was no time for messing about, "Pat, Patrick Quinn."

Angelo perched himself back on the swing and Bobby joined him, "Now that we ain't going to beat each others brains out for a while let's get back to thinking about what we do with you. A young Brit appears here with Ed the fixer, who despite being a repellant human being doesn't come cheap, so someone thought you important enough to look after. You're travelling under a false name, you fight like a demon, you were trained in Ireland and I just bet you've been over East, a little job maybe?"

Quinn smiled at the astute guesses, "I wish I could tell you but it wouldn't be a good idea, could get us both killed."

The President responded, "It don't matter, but it tells me you're maybe worth giving a chance. What I don't get is why you wanted to meet us so badly, so convince me."

Quinn spent the next thirty minutes explaining about his own group, and sketched out some of their interests, but most of all he talked about his love for bikes and the feeling of power that derived from being in a close group.

He spoke of the idea that the Wild Ones film and Hollister story had given him. That there could be a melding of a love of bikes, a strength in unity, and a trusted bond between like minds that could be used as a vehicle for criminality and the having of good times without interference or opposition.

Quinn concluded, "I wanted to check out the reality and the chance presented itself – may never get another one. I knew California was where it's happening; so far I'm not disappointed. So what I want is to hang around with you for the next two weeks and soak up your world, perhaps find some mutual business interests, and maybe forge some trust for the future. I've got a Harley arriving tomorrow, courtesy of Ed, so I've got transport."

Angelo rubbed his chin and looked at Bobby for a sign.

Quinn saw a small shake of the head from his recent opponent. His heart sank, all that effort was going to go to waste.

The President spoke again, "That's a whole lot of trusting in two weeks and us only just met, although you and Bobby have shared blood. We don't know you, you don't belong here, and unknowns make me nervous. I'm going to walk a few paces off and have a private discussion with Bobby - you wait here."

They walked off down the beach. Quinn could make out an animated conversation as they were silhouetted against the light from the flames that had taken hold in the pile of driftwood further along the strand.

Minutes passed, and then they turned and walked back towards Quinn. Their unified body language and determined gait indicated an agreement. Quinn braced himself for fight or flight.

The President announced, "Okay me and Bobby got a compromise. You ain't earned any trust yet but Bobby here likes the way you handle yourself. Me, I'm interested in what you have to say. Never met a biker from overseas either. So, you let us know where you're staying and Bobby here will make sure you get invites to some things. While you hang with us you keep Bobby close - for two reasons, he'll watch you, and he'll keep the others on a leash when things get wild. You have no conversations with the others without Bobby there and you keep those conversations strictly non-business, no questions. When I'm ready I'll decide if we speak further, and it will be me you speak to about those things, and I'll decide the territory we cover. If I get a hint of anything untoward you'll get a stomping you will never forget to go home with. That's the deal, take it or leave it."

Quinn's gamble had paid off, "I'll take it."

The President brought matters to a conclusion, "Okay tonight we party and you start to get to know the Madmen."

They shook hands and returned to the bar. Inside, Angelo mounted the pool table and shouted down the hubbub. He explained the deal - Quinn was in.

Chapter Twenty One: 'Rumble'

(Link Wray)

1958

That first evening went well. The group left the bar carrying armfuls of Old Pete's stock down to the fire on the beach. There was food cooked by the women, plenty of drinking that led inevitably to drunken scuffles, and as the night wore on couples began to pair off. Some of them didn't go far into the shadows and he could hear the sounds of sex. Bobby stuck with him like glue and explained some of what he saw. "Seems some women are attracted to us, not sure if it's the bikes or us. Anyhow, they have to earn trust same as everyone else if they want to get inside the club. They can't be members, that's just for men, but they contribute in all sorts of ways."

Quinn told him about Jenny and the role she played in the business back home. Bobby nodded, "Yea, that's the sort of thing, but especially the fucking. Jenny would be your 'Ole Lady', that's what we call a woman who is shacked up with one man. She's his property and everyone knows not to hassle her, that's a no-no and would be punished."

Quinn looked forward to enlightening Jenny as to her position in the hierarchy. Bobby continued, "There are others that just turn up for a good time - we have a bit of a reputation for providing good times you know. They are fair game for anyone, or more than one anyone some nights, although sloppy seconds ain't my thing. Lots are hookers of course and they get their pay in cash, food, drink, sometimes protection - seems to work for them anyway."

He paused to drain another bottle and threw the empty into the fire, "Then there are those who are after staying with us, becoming 'Ole Ladies' themselves. They are still fair game for anyone and they hang around all the time till we know and trust them. Some find a man, some don't but seem happy enough being with us." He indicated a dark haired girl watching them from the sand, "That's Sharon; she's been with us a long time, good girl. She's been asking about you. Feel free to partake, she's no-one's 'Ole Lady'. That's one way to get away from me for a few minutes anyway." He cackled, and walked off.

***

Quinn woke with a headache to a balmy Californian morning. He lay on his back in the sand and watched seagulls wheeling in the clear blue vault of the sky. Sharon was nestled against his back, her head on a rolled-up jacket. She had made it quite clear that she had never had an Englishman before, and that problem had now been resolved to both of their satisfactions. There was still heat from the nearby fire - now just a heap of embers and detritus, such as bottles, from the night before.

He looked around him and there was Bobby sat on a log, watching. The biker gave him a wave, and a smile, and Quinn joined him, "Come on, you can stand me breakfast after busting my nose, then I'll take you back to your hotel."

Quinn followed Bobby back to the bar where the bikes were parked. Quinn's eyes avidly devoured the machine that Bobby wheeled out of the line; it was huge compared with his own bike, low and mean-looking, with acres of chrome. The engine was a massive lump that evoked power; it was love at first sight.

"What's that?" Quinn demanded to know excitedly.

Bobby beamed back, "This, my English friend, is a Harley-Davidson Hydra Glide. Twelve Hundred cc's of American dream."

The bike didn't look passenger-friendly, having a single sprung seat hovering above a rigid rear-end. Quinn looked at it dubiously. Bobby kicked the bike into life and for the first time in his life Quinn heard the music of a big V-twin-engine reverberating along the street. He could feel the thump of the pistons in his stomach and remembered that he had one of these arriving later courtesy of Ed.

Bobby hitched forward on the saddle and indicated for Quinn to join him. There followed a joyously precarious ride to a local diner with Quinn hanging onto Bobby while his feet flailed in the air, devoid of foot pegs. They breakfasted in American style, at Quinn's expense, and then another slalom through the streets to his hotel where they found Ed parked up in his convertible across the street, asleep.

Bobby drew up alongside and gunned the throttle. Ed woke with a start and was clearly amazed to see a living and breathing Englishman.

"Get the man his bike sorted Ed, he's got some riding to do," shouted Bobby over the thump of the big pistons, before depositing Quinn at his accommodation.

Quinn was woken that afternoon by Ed knocking on his door. He dressed and followed the fixer to the service area of the hotel. His 'steed' awaited him. It was a Harley, same model as Bobby's, but the comparison ended there. It looked like it had been shut in a shed and forgotten for five years. It was painted in a matt green and totally devoid of chrome. It hung on its side stand, squat, sulky, and brooding. It had character though, Quinn had to admit.

"What's it like mechanically,'" asked Quinn.

"It won't let you down. Don't look much, but the owner knows his stuff engine-wise," Ed said reassuringly.

Quinn swung his leg over the low saddle and got used to the weight which must have been twice that of his Thunderbird. He stood on the pegs and kicked the engine over until he felt a piston hit top dead-centre, then jumped up and kicked down on the pedal. The big twin roared into life beneath him, sending thumping vibrations through his body and an electric thrill up his spine. He rode it around the parking area until he was confident of the handling then returned to Ed.

"That's fine, your part is done. I'll see you on my last day and hand it back." Quinn was eager to leave his company.

Ed shook his head, "You're a man of surprises Mister Stephens, and I didn't think I'd see you again. That's why I lit out soon as I saw the trouble start. Those bikers are mean as hell."

Quinn smiled flatly, "It turned out alright in the end. I guess I had to pass a test, which I did."

They shook hands and parted. Quinn changed into gear suited for riding and spent the next few hours getting used to the Harley.

Bobby was as good as his word and Quinn spent plenty of time with the Madmen as his days in California ticked away. He stuck to Angelo's rules and Bobby stuck to Quinn like glue, although that wasn't a problem as the erstwhile opponents got on famously.

Quinn waited patiently for Angelo to speak to him without avail. He kept his eyes and ears open though. Beneath the veneer of mayhem he saw organization and discipline. There was a distinct hierarchy, and Angelo's decisions were final, but he discovered that there was a ruling council of veterans and tested members, who had chosen Angelo as President, and who held various offices in the club.

Riding with the group in the sun, on the straight, endless highways of California and Arizona, was the highlight of this time. He felt invincible, unbeatable; he could see the fear on the faces of bystanders as they pulled into a town or diner. He understood the Hollister tale now, this was a new and real phenomenon, birthed in California, and he had fought his way into a privileged insight given to no other Englishman.

And the Harley! It had endless power and matchless presence. Within days he knew this was the bike for him and he also knew that everyone back home who saw it would want one.

Four days remaining and nothing from Angelo, Time was

getting tight, but at least he hadn't incurred a beating, he guessed the jury was still out. This was an extremely tight and closed group, with its own culture, and no-one got inside easily.

It was a hot Sunday and Bobby had invited him to ride out for 'something special'. It turned out to be motorbike racing at the new track at Laguna, Monterey. The Madmen had decided to make a day, and night of it, and travelled in force, the men on their Harleys and Indians led, and the women followed in several vans and pick-ups containing the essential barbeques, made out of half oil-drums, food and beer.

The track was set in a sunbaked dry lake bed. They settled on a raised hillock with a good view of the track, ousting a large group of what Bobby described as 'normals' who were not amused but thought better of taking on the intimidating bikers.

Quinn had a great day marveling at the skill of the racers and the speeds achieved. Sharon had latched onto him that first night by the fire and was good company. Bobby had a deal of knowledge about the racers, and their bikes, and kept him enthralled with tales of crashes and daring wins.

As evening fell and the crowds began to thin, the Madmen set off again to a nearby spot in the desert that they regularly used for camping. They arrived to find the same group from the hillock, its numbers doubled, in residence. This time there was no question of moving them without trouble and the bikers were in the mood for a party, not fighting, so they moved off and set up camp half a mile away.

Fires were built, barbeques loaded, and beer caps flipped. Later two of the women produced guitars and sang along. The men embarked on their usual sport of getting as intoxicated as possible courtesy of beer, and spirits - and smoking the aromatic marihuana that Quinn had first smelt in the bar in Venice Beach. This inevitably led to noise, wrestling, the riding and falling off of bikes, public sex, and a general ballyhoo that drew a deputation from the other side of the site.

The half-a-dozen men that appeared spent fruitless minutes attempting to reason with some particularly inebriated Madmen to the accompaniment of raucous cries, and cackling from the women regarding the size of their manhood's and sexual proclivity. There was only one way it could end and the emissaries from civilization were run off after some minor skirmishing.

The moon rose and the fires began to burn low. Quinn had tried some of the hash to experience its effect and understood its possibilities. As a non-smoker he found the unfiltered mix of tobacco and leaves too caustic and he was unlikely to ever pursue a narcotic that made him happy and loving. He would not be indulging again, but selling it was a different proposition. There was definitely money to be made. The overload of meat from the barbeque was making itself known so he loped off into the shadows seeking some privacy, realizing as he crossed the biker's enclave that most of his companions were in various stages of coma.

The nearest cover was halfway towards the vehicles and trailers of the others, in an outcrop of rocks. After achieving his objective he decided to use the peace and distance to review the last two turbulent weeks and to decide whether to contact Ed and get an earlier flight if Angelo didn't come across soon. California was great in its way but he was missing home and had plans in mind that needed his presence there. He sat himself on top of a rock and sucked in the quiet but alien ambience of the desert night.

His contemplation was interrupted by human noises. He could make out figures in the other camp. Quinn was a survivor and had learnt to trust his instincts. He was curious as to why there was so much movement at this time of night. He set off on a circuitous route that brought him within fifty yards of the camp, but sheltered by a stand of cactus.

There was little sleeping going on. He could make out a large group of men in a rough semi-circle being addressed by someone. Voices were raised and the topic was the Madmen. Clearly retribution was at hand for earlier slights. He stayed long enough to see tyre-levers and baseball bats being handed around. It took him ten minutes to get back to the bikers and he knew the raiding party would be hot on his heels. Most of his companions were stoned, and drunk, and would be easy meat.

The group of men crept towards the sleeping Madmen, emboldened by each other's presence and the sight of bodies sprawled around, just waiting to be punished. A number were thinking that perhaps the biker sluts would find out the answers to their earlier insults afterwards.

Some of the group was hanging back slightly, letting the ringleaders take the initiative. Quinn ran out of the shadows behind them. He had smashed two of them to the ground with blows from a chain belt, liberated from a sleeping biker, before they even registered his presence. A further two went down as he scythed through the group with the chain, whipping it in one hand, and a large Bowie knife in the other.

These were not combat-trained soldiers and the shock of his attack left them stunned for the moments he required to reach the leader, a large crew-cut, 'All- American' boy brandishing a heavy spanner. Quinn struck him in the face using the chain wrapped around his fist. As he fell backwards Quinn caught the hand holding the weapon and stuck his knife through it. The spanner fell. He was behind the leader, knife at his throat, backing away with him into the firelight, "Don't any of you move one step nearer or this is one dead boy."

Quinn cut just a little to draw a trickle of blood. He was watching the faces of the lead men. They just might take the gamble, thinking he was bluffing. Quinn had no compunction about killing again but didn't need the complications and indebtedness to 'The General' it would require to escape America and get yet another new identity.

He looked around quickly; some of the bikers were rousing but were clearly groggy and worse for wear. That evened up the odds if battle were to be joined. The moment of stalemate hung, finely balanced. Then a shot rang out, kicking up dust a yard in front of the lead man.

"I think it's time for y'all to go back to bed while you're still breathing don't you?" Angelo emerged from the shadows, stone-cold sober and holding a pistol in an unwavering hand, "Got five bullets left. That should even things up. Decision time boys, live and let live time?"

Quinn relaxed, it was over. Some of the attackers were already sloping away. The element of surprise was lost and Angelo looked as capable of carrying out his threat as Quinn.

The assailants melted away and Quinn pushed the leader after them, adding a hefty boot up the backside that sent him sprawling into the dirt. The man started to rise, fueled by anger, "Yep one-on-one, that's fair, but I promise you that I'll break your arms and legs before we finish." Quinn threw the chain and knife to the floor behind him, "And I don't need those to do it."

The man looked at Quinn and saw something in his eyes that stopped him cold. The anger drained away and he turned and ran off into the night.

Angelo slow hand-clapped Quinn several times, "A touch of class my English friend. I think you saved us some pain tonight."

Angelo was not stupid enough to hang around. There were always guns to hand in America and some hot-head might decide to make a name for himself and plug a biker - besides the law would inevitably get involved. The Madmen broke camp at speed and set off into the night whooping and hollering in various stages of inebriation.

They arrived back in Los Angeles with minimal casualties considering the state of most of the riders. Only two fell off and both managed to remount and complete the journey under their own steam.

Once they reached the city they split like a starburst and Quinn found himself back at his hotel, the events of the previous twenty-four hours a dream-like memory. Angelo had told him to meet them back at the bar later.

His reception that evening was very different. He was guided to a table filled with Angelo and beers. At last they talked. Any remaining suspicions in the mind of the President seemed to have been allayed by Quinn's heroics at Laguna.

Angelo quizzed him about life back in England, the gang, and their businesses. They shared their love of bikes and compared the relative merits of Triumph, BSA, Norton, and Harley Davidson. Quinn declared his liking for the Hydra Glide and his wish to bring it to England. He obtained a promise that Angelo would explore the possibilities. It was noticeable that Angelo skirted around the Irish. Either he knew enough to understand, or knew enough not to ask. Quinn didn't care much either way- silence was the best option.

He finally got his chance to ask about the Madmen. Angelo described how servicemen had returned from the thrills and horrors of the European and Pacific Wars and found civilian life lacking. Many of them found that once the ticker-tape parades and hero's welcomes had faded, many of them ended up in mundane jobs or without work at all. They grew resentful, and bored. They got together, at first to revisit old camaraderie, but that soon became channelled into the seeking of thrills, often fuelled by copious amounts of drink.

No-one walked in America and the cheapest and most available form of transport were the many ex-army motorbikes -

Harley Davidsons, and Indians, in the main, that were now surplus to requirements. It was a fateful and natural melding of the wild and rebellious veterans, the pursuit of action to lighten the mundanity, and the freedom and power of riding one of the great iron beasts, its V-Twin shattering the sounds of normal life.

The groups became tight-knit, calling themselves troops, and as they did so they travelled further from convention, finding strength in the anonymity of their motorcycle gear, their resolute rejection of the norms of society, and their brotherly bonds.

Eventually they began to organise, falling into a quasi-military structure with roles such as President, Vice-President, Sergeant at Arms, and a ruling council. They began to adopt badges to denote ranks, roles and affiliations, again stemming from the military. As the fifties wore on, new generations of the unruly, unwanted and disaffected were drawn like moths to a flame, adopting and building upon these foundations.

It was a California phenomenon, perhaps fuelled by the sunshine, and a lingering frontier spirit, and by the time Quinn visited there were a number of groups, loosely and unofficially confederated by their shared interests.

No-one knew for sure where the patches or 'colours' had originated, although the San Francisco Angels claimed the honour of inventing, or adopting from World War Two plane adornments, the winged skull that now adorned the backs of all the outlaw bikers.

They called themselves the 'one percenters' because they prided themselves on being in the one percent of bikers that the

American Motorcycle Association considered outside the law. They wore that badge with pride. Convention amongst them now dictated that a fully-fledged 'outlaw' member wore patches on their backs, a curved 'top rocker' bearing the troop's name, and a similar 'bottom rocker' with its home town or city. Alongside the death's head a small patch bore the letters 'MC', for Motorcycle Club.

Rituals had evolved, in order to test prospective members, or 'Prospects'. These were aimed at weeding out cops, those without the proclivity for violence and debauchery, those too closely tied into civilised society and, rumour had it, those unwilling to kill, or be killed for the troop.

In the initial stages, those wishing to join were called 'hangers on', wore no patches, and could expect to be ordered to perform just about any task imaginable. Once they were voted in as 'Prospects' they were allowed to wear the 'bottom rocker' only. Finally, after a unanimous vote of the council they became full members and were awarded the coveted 'top rocker.' The whole process could take years and once in, there was no return to that other world of morals, rules and law.

To outsiders, this was a man's world. Women could not be members, had no say, or vote, and divided into their own categories of whore's, hangers on, prospective 'Ole ladies' and those who were the property of a full member. Beneath the bravado though, the women provided an essential set of functions and services, and many exerted a subtle influence upon their male companions.

Of course, dollars were still required, and being outside of society did little to assist the outlaws in finding well- paid work.

Many drifted from menial job to job, and in and out of employment. Ultimately, they concluded that The Club had to look after its own, accompanied by a dawning realisation that their self-imposed exile from society brought its own riches that could be used for profit.

They were well organised, flexible, could travel far, and fast. They provoked a visceral fear amongst outsiders, and the upholders of law were reluctant to confront them so long as the issue was not forced. Coupled with a bond of silence and self- protection matching that of the East Coast Mafia, and a willingness to resort to extreme violence if required, they possessed all the requirements of success as a criminal organisation before they really knew it.

Angelo sketched out their many interests. They were further along the criminal evolutionary path than Quinn's group and he listened, rapt, his head full of possibilities, as the surprisingly erudite bike leader talked of the addition of marijuana to liquor and cigarettes smuggling, extortion, the use of and movement of weapons and ammunition, and the control of prostitutes.

Then it was Quinn's turn to talk through the ideas for co-operation brimming in his head for weeks. Angelo stopped him and summoned Bobby to the table. They both listened, interjecting every so often with perceptive questions about the progress of the Defford outfit, and the differences between England and California.

"Okay Pat, that's enough for now. I can see some real possibilities but I think you've got some work to do back home before we can move forward. I would need some assurances and the full support of the members before going any further." Angelo concluded the meeting.

Quinn was satisfied. He had achieved his objective, not only piquing the interest of the Madmen, but also extracting golden nuggets of learning from their experiences.

The next day he received a message to meet at an intersection out of town. He headed out East on the Harley, the sun sinking onto the Pacific behind him. Bobby was waiting on the shoulder astride his machine.

"You're honoured Pat, gonna show you something no outsider has seen. Follow me," he smirked.

They thundered out into the desert-scrub finally turning off at a nondescript track. The Harleys left a plume of dust behind them as they sped into the burgeoning darkness. About a mile from the turn-off they entered a walled compound and pulled up outside a squat building that had an air of fortification. Light streamed from the double doors and as Quinn trailed Bobby towards them he noticed that they were made of steel not wood.

"What the hell is this place?" Quinn could not resist the question. Bobby said, "Wait. You'll see." Angelo met them at the door, "Welcome to our humble home. We let everyone think the bar is our base, but since we acquired this place last year we've been fixing it up just for us. You get a grand tour as a thank-you and you keep your mouth shut afterwards. We'll have some drinks and say goodbye tonight."

As they walked around Angelo explained that they had bought the compound as a wrecked shell from the Army, via a friendly lawyer, at a knock down price. It was of no use to anyone, miles from anywhere and set in scrub that would not support any type of farming.

They had turned it into a purpose-built home for the Madmen. The compound had been made secure, as had the outer shell, hence the steel doors. There were rooms for Council members and others for those who needed to stay a night or two, or just avail themselves of a bed for other reasons. It boasted a well-equipped workshop, kitchen, eating areas, games room and the Council meeting room. It was adorned with totems and regalia of the Madmen and an array of decorations springing from the tastes and imaginations of the male members.

Quinn noticed that there were some specific areas that he was ushered past. He was still on probation himself clearly, but he nevertheless felt privileged at this glimpse into a unique, and secret culture that had sprung from the California towns and cities. He was also rejoicing inside because his modest plan for Defford Airfield had just been turned on its head.

Angelo ushered him into a final room and Quinn was confronted with a fully equipped bar with a number of the females he recognised acting as barmaids. Music boomed from a Jukebox. The room was packed and Quinn was greeted with some cheers.

Angelo gave Quinn a friendly slap on the back, "A little party in honour of you. If you were staying they think you've done enough to be voted as Prospect already, but we don't hurry and it takes months. Let's say you've made a good impression and we look forward to seeing you again."

Hours of revelling followed and Quinn allowed himself to loosen-up and indulge. He stayed in one of the rooms and was able to say goodbye to Sharon at some length.

He woke at mid-morning. The women had already tidied up after the night's carnage. Sharon provided food and a lingering goodbye, and then Angelo appeared and walked him to his bike. The President shook his hand.

"You take care, I won't forget our talk, but you've got plenty of stuff to do back home first. When you are ready contact me via Ed, I've arranged for him to see you before you go, and let you know how. Then you come back and we talk, maybe I'll come to England and see what you've got. Oh - and I won't forget my promise to look at the Hydra Glide, that's a separate matter."

Quinn felt a genuine sense of warmth, and a deal of respect towards the man, "Thanks, there's one thing I'll ask of you," he said, "Anything we do together is just us; we keep it close and no Irish of any kind. I want to have another string to my bow. Is that okay and is Ed a problem in that respect?"

Angelo laughed, "That suits me just fine. The Irish and the Italians have the East, we do our own thing out here, different business partners, and we don't want those complications. As for Ed, he gets jobs from all sorts due to his reputation, but he knows what's best where his health is involved and he's more scared of us than anyone. I'll get Bobby to have a little word in his ear."

On the night flight home, Quinn reflected upon his five months away. He had taken a life, but to a man like him that was a necessity in order to survive, and he felt no remorse. He had missed his son more than he thought he would, and Jenny too of course, but it had been worth it. He had kept the IRA on board and knew that the threat of National Service was minimal. Seamus would keep the farm. Quinn was a different and more dangerous man now, a trained-killer with a head crammed full of a unique knowledge of, and bond with, the West Coast bikers. He was a man with big plans. He allowed himself to sleep, untroubled.

Chapter Twenty Two: 'Broken Hearted Melody'

(Sarah Vaughan)

1959

Rob felt it the instant he laid eyes on Sandra. It was hardly the most romantic of meetings as they literally bumped into each other in the doorway of the pub. At sixteen Rob was still under-age for drinking alcohol and normally hung around on pub car parks with mates from school, asking older kids and blokes to buy for them, especially if the pub had an 'offie' attached, as many did. Joe had his own interests and the thought of 'dossing around' on a pub car park was not one of them.

The music scene in Birmingham was huge with loads of kids around his age forming bands and playing at numerous pubs clubs, cinemas and theatres. At these events Rob was able to get inside by mixing with the young crowds of followers of various bands. Tonight was a big event and a band he actually wanted to see rather than use as an excuse to get into the venue and drink. It was the 'Rockin Berries' at The George in Northfield.

Rob and his friends kept to the crowds who packed the lounge area. The mix of people milling around at the bar, coupled with swirling smoke from numerous cigarettes dangling from lips, or held more daintily in female hands, made it easier to blend in.

That first night their eyes met and they both stopped for half a step, then smiled as they skirted round each other. Emboldened by drink Rob had shouted at her receding back, "Oi, you here next week? I'll buy you a drink." To his surprise she had stopped, half-turned and replied, "I reckon you're kaylied, but I'll let you stand me a half next week if you've sobered up. Ta ra a bit." Then she was gone.

The following week Rob waited and hoped, without much confidence that she would show up again. When she did he went straight in for the kill, "I'm Rob – can I get that half for you?"

Sandra was two years older than Rob and slightly taller which, combined with the height of her heels did not make for a parallel universe. She wasn't particularly slim but her figure had already blossomed and her somewhat voluptuous frame screamed pure beauty at Rob. She had her long blond hair tied up in a ponytail and her red lipstick accentuated the lips that Rob felt were drawing him to them like a magnet. He was in love, or was it lust?

It was less crowded than the previous occasion and she now had the measure of him immediately and said teasingly, "I'm Sandra. Judging by your looks I think I'll have to buy you one so long as I don't get accused of cradle-snatching." Rob did not react – he was not about to spoil his chances by pulling a face.

There was a side-room, away from the noise of the band, and they sat chatting at one of the small round wooden tables, an ash-tray full of stained nub-ends taking pride of place in the centre. The conversation flowed easily. She had been with a two girlfriends who looked in on them every so often and tittered when she caught their eyes.

Sandra found Rob engaging and was comfortable. He was polite and dressed tidily. He carried himself with a presence that she was not used to from the other 'nob-heads' who frequented the place.

As the evening came to a close Rob said quietly to Sandra, "Fancy a dance?" and waited for rejection, "Daft hapath, I thought you was never going to ask!" she replied and as they merged into the middle of the shuffling couples on the lounge floor, sticky from the spilt beer of countless glasses, she pulled him gently closer towards her, and rested her head against his. Rob went to heaven.

They parted in the car park as her friends re-joined her. Rob had deliberately held back. He was not yet experienced in the ways of females but sensed that any attempt at a 'fumble in the jungle' would be met with opposition. Sandra was calling the shots and he was happy to follow. He would make do with a peck on the cheek for now.

They met regularly in the following weeks and saw a lot of bands but couldn't have named a song they played. She bought the kind of happiness to Rob that he had not known before, and a sense of individual identity that twins rarely find. This was something that he had made happen without Joe sitting on his shoulder for support. He felt loved and wanted.

After a couple of weeks she took him back to her house, a fifteen-minute walk to a place where they could hold hands and feel close.

Her parents were there and showed complete disinterest as

she made him a cup of tea in the kitchen before signalling that it was time for him to leave. On the back-step, as they stood in the shadows, she kissed him warmly and gently slipped his hand to a place that he had not previously visited. Rob went home in a daze.

The following week whilst Sandra's parents were out at the Bingo for the evening they became lovers. It was all over before it started really but Sandra was reassuring, "The first time's always a bit rushed Rob. Don't worry we'll make it last more than two minutes next time!" She laughed and pulled him close to her.

Sandra was perfect for Rob and he was devoted to her. When she was next to him he was oblivious to everything else around him. She had everything that he wanted.

In due course Rob took Sandra home to meet Mary and Joe. He made sure that his stepfather would be out at the pub; he didn't want 'that cunt' anywhere near her.

Mary greeted her warmly, whilst Joe applied apparent indifference. What Rob had failed to spot was a fleeting glance between Joe and Sandra which if analysed would have confirmed an instant attraction.

A week later Joe waited outside Sandra's place of work, manufacturers in the Jewellery Quarter in Hockley. He was taking a chance because it was Rob who had told him where she worked, but he felt driven and the risk was worth taking.

Sandra understood instinctively when she saw him waiting outside and they walked together, an appropriate space between them, to a nearby pub. In contrast to Rob his brother was well able to pass for being older, and they stood together as equals. He insisted on buying the drinks. He could tell that the barman didn't much like seeing a white girl with a black man but he was used to it and couldn't give a fuck any more.

As they talked, Sandra was torn and was not able to resolve the situation in her mind so settled for a compromise, "I can't give Rob up just like that. You'll have to accept whatever time we can get together, while I make up me mind, or walk away. That's me best offer." Joe leant back in his chair and searched the ceiling for inspiration. Finally he squeezed Sandra's hand and said simply, "Okay. I'll take what you can give – for now at any rate."

From that moment Sandra tried to manage two boyfriends – the Docker brothers.

In the early days it was just about practicable, but as the intensity of both brother's feelings towards her developed she started to find it intolerable. She loved them both, but for different reasons, and did not want to let either of them go but she gradually felt suffocated by the situation.

With Rob pushing her constantly to spend more time together she came to a decision.

There was never going to be an easy way to do it but Sandra chose the Dockers house to bring matters to a close and had decided to confront the situation head-on.

The sound of someone at the front door knocking surprised Mary, as they were not expecting visitors, and she was in the process of feeding both boys in the kitchen.

Mary opened the door and in walked Sandra. Rob stood smiling and motioned for her to sit, "Ee-ar, park your bum, I wasn't expecting to see you this evening. Nice surprise though."

Sandra delivered her knockout blow with one sentence and no preliminaries, "I've been seeing Joe for a while now and I've decided that I want to be with him. I'm sorry Rob that's it. I didn't want to hurt you."

For a moment Rob sat stunned, and mortally wounded, as the words sank in. Then he launched himself across the table at Joe with a flurry of punches that Joe tried to parry, "You bastard - You fucking bastard. I'm gonna kill you," screamed Rob. Suddenly the room was full of smashed plates, cutlery, and an upturned table and chairs, as a mammoth struggle took place between Rob and Joe.

Mary and Sandra tried in vain to pull them apart, but they were shrugged off by the two brothers who had both found an inner-strength. Rob screamed again as he reached for a knife on the floor but Joe kicked it away and put Rob into a bear-hug.

"I'll let you go if you fucking calm down," Joe shouted as he was promptly head-butted. With blood seeping from a head wound Joe tripped his brother expertly to the floor and put him in a double arm-lock pinning him to the floor face down. The blood from Joes face dripped onto the back of Rob's neck.

Mary motioned to Sandra, who stood witnessing the scene with tears streaming down her face, "Leave Sandra. Now ain't the cowing time. I'm gonna want to speak to you about this too, you can be fucking sure of that."

As Sandra left, Joe spoke calmly to Rob, whose strength was ebbing away as he remained pinned to the floor, "I'm gonna let you go Rob, and then I'm gonna fuck off outta the house so you can fucking cool down a bit. If you try to hit me again I'll give you a fucking good bell oiling, I'm telling you."

It wasn't a request it was an order, as Joe stood abruptly, wiped blood from his forehead with the sleeve of his shirt and left to catch up with Sandra. As he marched down the street he was accompanied by a string of racist expletives from the open door that struck a cold dagger into his heart.

Rob remained rooted on the doorstep in shock. As Mary went to comfort him he pushed her away and shouted, "Fuck off and leave me alone. I'm done with that bastard. He can keep the slapper," before storming off upstairs.

Within thirty minutes he had piled some clothing into a bag and left the house without speaking to his mother. At the phone box down the road he made a phone call to his Uncle Charlie. The seemingly unbreakable bond between the twins had shattered into a thousand pieces.

In the days that followed Mary tried to find a way to put her sons back together. She met Sandra in a cafe and gave her a piece of her mind for the way she had sprung the devastating news on Rob, precipitating the rupture. Having had her say she then probed the girl's feelings and intentions and was swayed by the fact she had become very fond of Sandra, Sandra's obvious love for Joe, and the careful thought that the girl had put into her decision. Mary reflected on her own disastrous love life, *"who am I to judge?'* she concluded.

Sandra's final words before they parted repeated in her head as she made her way home. " I met a boy but fell in love with a man." In her heart Mary knew it was true.

Over the following week she spoke with both her sons. Joe wore his heart on his sleeve and it was obvious that he was also head over heels and hadn't acted out of malice. Mary accepted the situation, after all Sandra was the type of girl anyone would want for a daughter-in –law, *'I won't be around forever and he needs someone to love him for what he is,'* she concluded.

Rob was implacable. He met Mary at Charlie's and agreed to keep in regular touch with his mother but was immoveable on two counts; he wanted nothing more to do with his twin, and he had left home and wasn't coming back. When Mary broached her decision to accept Sandra she could feel the coolness emanating from him and knew that their relationship would change from that day on.

As she left, Mary fumbled with her purse and tried to give Rob some money so that he wouldn't go short. He was still one of her children and whatever happened she would always be there to help both of them. His response was unequivocal, "You can stick it up your arse ma. Give it to him - you made your bed now you lie in it."

***

Mary did her utmost to stay out of Richard's reach and for the most part she succeeded. He was still a complete bastard but in keeping with most cowards since the stabbing incident he was more cautious and there had been four years of relative peace.

She should have known better however that a 'leopard never changes its spots,' and in the winter of 1959 Richard's abuse began again. She should have spotted the telltale signs, with an increase in drunken renditions of lurid tales of violence involving the Japanese, but in the comfort zone of her kitchen, site of her victory, she had gradually lapsed into a false sense of security and did not see it coming.

Back one evening from his usual 'binge drinking' session he entered the kitchen and without warning struck her forcefully from behind on the back of the head. He had chosen his moment well as he knew that Joe was out watching the recently released 'Ben Hur' film with Sandra.

The shock of the blow disorientated Mary, who struggled to turn round, but was again struck and her head forced into the water-filled sink, "Keep still you fucking whore or I'll drown you," he slurred, and followed the order with a third blow, as he unbuckled his trousers. The alcohol had provided him with a surge of strength and he once again lost control in the heady moment of sex and violence that he had become addicted to.

It was over in less than a minute and as she lay collapsed in a bloody heap on the floor she wished nothing more than to die. Richard left her where she lay and staggered off to his bed.

By next morning Richard had lost his new-found courage and left the house early, anticipating another confrontation with Joe and Mary, "Sorry if I was a bit rough last night. It won't happen again," he mumbled on the way out as Mary forced herself to stand at the sink, still bearing the bruises and scratches from the desecration she had undergone in that spot, with whatever dignity she had left.

When Joe saw the bruises and probed the cause, Mary broke down and recounted the whole incident. It took all of Mary's powers of persuasion to prevent him from searching for Richard. She pleaded, "His time will come but I won't have me son in prison for that bastard."

Mary was mortified when she was late for her period. She was normally as regular as clockwork and asked Sandra to be with her when she did the test. She had grown close to the girl and although she hated the rift between her two sons she did not blame her for it. After all Mary loved them both too. Sandra made Joe happy and had possessed the guts to confront the situation and that was good enough for her. Besides, Mary was going to be a grandmother. Perhaps, just perhaps, something good was going to come from her wretched existence

Sandra had announced her own pregnancy just one week before and was excited about her future with Joe. She was two months gone but had wanted to make sure that everything was okay and had sworn Joe to secrecy.

Mary on the other hand, was a victim of rape whose life had been destroyed. As they waited at the doctors for the result the minutes ticked by and she felt like she was waiting for the hangman's noose. The result came – she was pregnant – two people now with something in common; one child to be born from love, and one child to be born from hate.

Mary felt lost and bewildered but Sandra moved swiftly to

support her. They were family now and she would stand next to her. Sandra moved in shortly afterwards - much to Joe's relief, although he watched his stepfather like a hawk, searching for the slightest indication that the man was intending to perpetrate another one of his atrocities – but upon Sandra this time.

The odds were no longer on Richard's side now and he became subdued, no longer the master of the house, more like the lodger. Joe was all for throwing him out but Mary knew that with Richard's name on the deeds they would face problems so resisted it.

Christmas came and went as Mary and Sandra went through pregnancy together. They both loved music and Sandra filled the house with Cliff Richard and Adam Faith whilst frequently miming the words of Emile Ford's song, 'What do you want to make those eyes at me for?' to a responsive Joe. In quieter moments they discussed how fragile life was, as the murder of Miss Sydney Stephanie Baird on the 23 December 1959, in Edgbaston, hit the headlines.

Mary was not a religious person but she could not find a way in her heart to terminate the life of an unborn child who had done nothing wrong, so she had decided to have it and love it. At the right time she would get a good solicitor and with Joe's help get Richard out. She hoped that the child would work in her favour.

***

In February 1960, Sandra took a tumble on some ice outside the house and Joe spent several nervous hours at Selly Oak hospital whilst she was checked out. He was over the moon about the baby and was scared witless at the thought of anything happening to his unborn child.

Mary sat at home waiting patiently for news whilst Richard sat opposite, staring at the TV, viewing her with his usual contempt, having downed several drinks.

"In the War the Japanese soldiers used to fuck the Chinese women they had in the whorehouses even if they was eight months pregnant," he announced. Mary looked at him and suddenly wished that she were in the kitchen near the knife drawer.

"There's nothing wrong with a good fuck when you're pregnant," he persisted.

Mary stood up wanting to put some space between them, "Nothing wrong at all," his voice trailed off as he stood to block her way.

"Joe will be back soon. That's enough," she blurted out as Richard gripped her right wrist, his thoughts totally focused on one thing, "Fuck-off and leave me alone you twisted bastard or I'll keep me promise," Mary screamed but she knew that no- one could hear her, and no-one was coming.

With her free hand she clawed at Richard's disfigured face and drew blood.

This futile effort at resisting served only to excite him further, "You bitch," Richard responded as he punched her hard in the stomach and she collapsed.

Mary remembered little else about the next eight hours. Richard called for an ambulance and played the dutiful husband telling them that she fallen down the stairs and started bleeding.

That bleeding continued at hospital and she felt her unborn child leave her as the words, "I'm sorry, it won't happen again," echoed over and again in her head.

Joe sat at her bedside and watched her sobbing silently for a while before she gathered herself and clasped his hand, "Come closer Joe and listen....."

At the end of the muffled conversation Joe simply said, "Yeah. But Sandra stays out of it. She must never know." The decision was made and four weeks later they would carry out their plan.

***

A defining moment in Mary Docker's sad existence had come. She wanted nothing from her life now other than to be left alone. Now just an empty-shell of a woman she could tolerate neither the situation, nor the man who had destroyed her life.

Mary had set her stall out carefully and Joe had agreed to help her without hesitation. She felt a huge burden asking her Joe to assist her in this act but she knew that Rob would have neither the strength, will or stomach, to help her. Besides he had not set foot in the house since the argument over Sandra and had little contact with Mary, all of it shallow. She was not sure that she had the physical strength to do it on her own whereas Joe was fearless and like a lion. He would not let her down.

This night had been chosen because Sandra had been out to a family do and stayed at her mother's house afterwards. She thought that Joe had taken the opportunity for a night out with his mates. In fact, Joe had made sure he was seen in two local pubs before slipping out of a toilet window and returning home.

For Joe it was the opportunity to rid the world of a child abuser, wife beater, and his own personal nightmare. Mary was still oblivious to the years of suffering that he had endured and so it would remain – his secret, and one that would be shared with no-one. With the anger also came shame. Joe would bear the scars of his treatment at the hands of Richard for life. Killing him held absolutely no fears for Joe – the sooner the better.

As was normal Richard Burns was out drinking with the small number of cronies who were prepared to listen to his repetitive 'war stories' every night. Their company might have had more to do with his propensity to buy drinks for them, rather than his personality, of which there was little. He was still a creature of habit and would return home at 9pm to eat.

These days he was much more subdued, and a routine of silent meals at the kitchen table, followed by a stiff whisky before bed in a separate room, was the norm. No conversation took place between him and Mary – they had plenty to say to each other but it would always remain unsaid. There was no point.

The meal prepared, Mary set the table for 8.55pm and placed a large tumbler of whisky alongside the plate, with a half-empty bottle of whisky next to it, before retiring upstairs to the bedroom.

Shortly afterwards she heard him moving around downstairs. Thirty minutes passed by and her heart raced with the realisation of what they were about to do. Joe waited silently beside her. He knew what he had to do and was ready to right years of wrong – it was called revenge.

She heard muttering and heavy steps at the bottom of the stairs. Quietly she stood at the top and peeped over the balustrade, unseen. He was there, pissed as usual and about to come up to bed. The footsteps gave way to more of a crawl as he crept ever more slowly upwards. He was oblivious of her – living in his own unseen world of jungle, heat, flies, the sound of cane sticks striking bare backs, and even darker memories.

One stair riser followed by another he mounted, crawling now on all fours, seeking the sanctuary of his bed.

She waited patiently, she had waited a lifetime for this moment, and she could wait a few more seconds.

As he finally reached the top of the steep stairs he found himself face-to-face with Mary Docker's feet, and Joe Docker hunched down and focused as if ready to play rugby in a scrum.

Richard looked up, his eyes blurred by drink, and the thought, *'What the fuck are they doing?'* penetrated the fog in his mind. It was his last thought. Cleanly, and without hesitation, Joe leant forward and gripping both of Richard's shoulders firmly pushed him backwards into space.

Mary Docker watched her tormentor arch backwards, his face frozen and mouth wide open. As if in slow motion he tumbled downwards, performing what they would have described in a Birmingham playground as a perfect backwards 'gambol'. He hit the ground and lay in a crumpled heap at the bottom.

From the angle of the body he had clearly broken a leg that protruded out at right angles. Mary was sure that she had heard something snap as his head struck the floor but she had to be sure – there would be no second chances, could be no mistakes.

Mary followed him down, three handkerchiefs in her hand, and surveyed the motionless body of Richard Burns together with Joe. She made her way into the kitchen, put some rubber gloves on, and recovered another full bottle of whisky from underneath the sink. Making her way back to body she poured as much as she could down his throat, sprinkled some over his clothing, and placed it into the palm of one of his hands, before Joe clubbed the bottle onto the floor, smashing it, by holding the arm and closing the hand around the neck.

She then placed one handkerchief into a ball and stuffed it into his mouth. There was not that much of his nose left but the other two went into each nostril.

Joe took a cushion from the living room and placed it over the broken face, applying light pressure, and waited ten minutes, before Mary checked for a pulse. For good measure he repeated the process for another ten minutes, while he counted his stepfather's many sins in his mind. Finally, Joe was satisfied. Richard Burns was gone, taking his misery with him.

Mary removed the handkerchiefs before putting her coat on

to wake the neighbours next door to inform them of her discovery, whilst Joe slipped out of the back door and ran back to the pub, climbing back through the toilet window. He had been gone for thirty minutes and no-one would have noticed. He continued the evening out, downed a few celebratory drinks and stayed out of the way at a friend's house.

Next stop for Mary was the phone box to report the untimely demise of her drunken husband to the police.

Richard Burns was now in the hell that he deserved whilst Mary Docker had her own private hell to contend with. After the undertakers had left, and she knew that she and Joe were in the clear, she toasted her only love with a bottle of sherry. As she drank herself into oblivion she thought, *'Now I'm a murderer too. Whatever happened to the carefree young girl who wanted to dare the world? One mistake, that's all it took, one bloody mistake and I've been damned forever.'*

A single tear rolled down her cheek. She brushed it away and picked up the glass again.

Chapter Twenty Three: 'Cradle Of Love'

(Johnny Preston)

1960

In 1960 Sandra gave birth. It had not been an easy pregnancy for Sandra but the moment her waters had broken in the middle of the night Joe had kept her calm and driven her straight to hospital. He spent the next few hours anxiously pacing the waiting room.

Eventually the baby came, but there were tense moments when she arrived with the cord wrapped around her neck, and nursing staff worked hard doing what they do best – saving a life. Cord cut and some oxygen, and there she lay, crying on Sandra's bloodstained stomach. Sandra started crying, and when Joe arrived he started crying too, everyone started crying.

"Joe I need a cuppa," Sandra beamed.

He made his way to the canteen and on the way found a telephone kiosk to call Mary, "It's a girl Mum," he shouted down the telephone. Mary responded, "That's bostin son. I hope she's okay. Has she got all of her fingers and toes?" Mary was showing her age.

She was also resisting asking the question she really wanted the answer to, *'What colour is she?'*

Joe knew though, after all he was half of a 'miracle' birth, "No need to hope Mum – she's a beautiful little girl, and before you try to work out a way to ask, she looks white, just with darker skin, a bit like coffee with a bit of cream."

Joe finished the call and collected the tea. He always found it mildly amusing that although she had mothered a black child she came from a generation that was inherently racist but just didn't know it.

As he wondered back down the hospital corridor he reflected 'Hope – not a bad name. Not a bad name at all.'

***

In 1961 Rob got married to Lilian, an eighteen-year-old who had attracted his attention in a local supermarket that he had never been into before, and was unlikely to do so again.

She was shorter than Rob, he wasn't likely to repeat that mistake again, and slim with unusually dark curly hair that cascaded over her shoulders. Lilian prided herself on her appearance and meticulously applied subtle make-up that heightened her cheekbones and made her stand out in a crowd. All in all a beautiful girl on the outside, who was quite pale on the inside.

He frequently cursed that supermarket for providing a venue for a disastrous union.

In hindsight he realized that he had been trying to prove that Joe's betrayal with Sandra meant nothing. In fact, the unhappy marriage made things worse, adding another layer of misery and insult onto that act. lacked confidence and in reality it was already a loveless relationship even before the rings were exchanged. By that time however she was already pregnant. On the 30 January 1961 the birth pill went on sale in the UK but it came too late for Rob and Lilian who had fumbled their way through their first sexual encounters without much thought for the possible consequences.

Lilian's parents had no doubt what that meant, and Rob had no choice but to do the right thing. The only positive from the act of union was that Rob sought his mother's advice, which predictably was to do right by the child, and a small rapprochement, that expressly did not include Joe, was achieved. He met his mother on a more regular basis after that – always away from her house, so that there was no chance of bumping into Joe or Sandra.

Nine months later Rose was born – a small ray of light in a cold and already empty marriage.

Rob had been out when Lilian started to experience severe pains. She had been at home on her own and had run to the house next door in a panic screaming for help.

The neighbours had taken her straight to hospital and after safely depositing her with some midwives returned to find her errant husband.

Their knock at the door was eventually responded to by Rob - who on returning home, and finding the house empty, had decided to have a nap on the sofa.

"Your wife's in hospital – she needs you," the female half of the neighbours said curtly. She fancied she had the measure of Rob and despised men like him.

Rob declined a half-hearted offer of a lift to the hospital. He was in no great rush to sit in a hospital room for hours. He rang Mary and made his way there.

After the birth, Rob sat alone with his thoughts, looking at Rose in a cradle at Lilian's bedside. The baby and an exhausted Lilian both slept soundly.

For a moment Rob bent down and held the hands of his daughter very gently. He could feel the perfectly formed fingers moving slightly in his hand, *'You've got little donnies ain't you?'* he thought. She was a beautiful child. He experienced a rush of emotion that he quickly suppressed. The moment passed.

When the pill became available on the National Health Service Rob insisted that Lilian go on it. He didn't want to repeat the same mistake twice and she complied without protest. Her job was to look after the child and that was enough for her. Rob had greater ambitions to follow.

***

Joe Docker, at heart a decent and noble human being, had been wrestling with his conscience about Sandra and the fall-out with Rob - and losing. There was no doubt that he loved his new family deeply, but the rift with his twin had struck deep and preyed on his mind. He also needed to find work to support Sandra and Hope. He wasn't the type of man who expected his mother to provide and he knew that Mary was sliding into alcoholism as she tried to come to terms with what she had done with her life.

One day he was walking through town and saw a poster that

seemed to offer a solution, a job, money, training and some time to think. Like thousands of other refugees from crime, debts, or broken love, he took the Queen's shilling, joined the Army and, after initial training, was posted to Cyprus.

Sandra didn't like it, but she knew that she could not expect Mary to support her forever and that Joe needed to be the provider and have time to work through his feelings. She and Hope were happy staying with Mary in the meantime. She fervently prayed that the next three years of Army service would allow her husband to reconcile his inner turmoil, and that he would find himself.

She loved Joe and realized that he was struggling, not only with the manner of his split from Rob, but also with his unique situation as he matured into a world that seemed to offer him nothing but hatred. He was a black man in a white world in appearance, but a white man from a white family inside.

***

Joe was the only black face in his platoon and the sergeant in charge made sure from day one that he didn't forget it – John Ryan didn't like black people, and now he had a target.

Like many of his kind Ryan was a natural bully. He suffered from 'short man's disease' and was forever lifting himself up off his heels, trying to find those extra inches that had eluded him since birth. A short clipped moustache and a peaked- cap - peak slashed at the front, completed the picture. Straight out of 'Bootsie and Snudge,' his bark completed the picture.

"You should be fine here with the heat Docker, but take care.

The locals don't like 'niggers' and if you so much as go near one of their women you'll get your long shiny black cock cut off and shoved in your mouth. Do you understand me?"

This was not a question, just a statement of fact, and Joe had already learnt that answering back just got you extra duties. Cleaning 'shit houses' full of flies and mosquitoes, was to be avoided at the expense of a loss of pride.

"Yes Sergeant!" came the well-rehearsed response.

Joe spent endless hours with his section sitting in a tent adjacent to the Water Tower at the top of the hill in Trachoni Village, just a couple of miles from Akrotiri. He didn't know what they were supposed to be guarding but nobody cared. Some of the locals used to pass by begging for food.

One in particular, Demitros, who worked at Ayios Mamas church, in the centre of the village, found a novel way of succeeding. He was a married man but childless, however he used to gather children at the church and march them up the hill to be introduced to the soldiers as his 'family'. Usually the youngsters would then skip back down the hill like mountain goats, carrying cheese, chocolate and any other food they could coax from the troops. The British soldiers did not notice that the 'family' members used to change from time-to-time, - *the locals all looked the same anyway'*.

On other occasions Joe would patrol around Akrotiri, and the area of Fassouri Plantation, in open-backed jeeps, rifles at the ready. They were not welcomed by many Cypriots who regarded them as an occupying force - even though most of the soldiers were just homesick young boys. On occasions rocks would come flying from the orange groves at the sides of the roads, thrown by some invisible young 'Costas' or 'Andreas' anxious to be free from the yoke of the British.

Joe would sometimes get a pass out of camp and would make his way alone into Limassol to try to find some peace away from the constant banter and childish behaviour of his fellow squaddies. Some parts of Limassol were out of bounds but Joe was not one for following the rules and took his chances.

One evening he sat alone in a small bar just off one of the narrow side streets near to the Old Port. The only other occupants were three young Cypriots, dark- skinned, with curly black hair, and huge hands from working the fields. They spoke quietly between themselves, and Joe understood nothing. If he had done so he would have left.

The words "Malakismenos – Poustomavros – Skato Egglezos" floated across the room as they occasionally smiled in his direction, and he smiled back.

One more drink and he left walking slowly on the cobbles towards the castle. He heard nothing but felt the heavy 'thwack' of a blow across the back of his neck, followed by the thud of heavy boots on his ribs as he fell to the floor, and lost consciousness.

Next morning Joe was up on a charge before his commanding officer sporting two black eyes and some very sore ribs. He was given extra 'shit house' duties from the officer and no sympathy, "You're a fucking nuisance Docker. We need to knock some sense into you," said Sergeant Ryan as he marched him away.

Joe nursed his injuries and kept his mouth shut for a few days but he was acutely aware that he was very much on his own. Ryan had made sure that 'niggers' were not to be associated with.

It was a Saturday evening, and one that Joe would add to the list of things that he would remember for the rest of his life. He had just returned from the shower block and was drying himself by his bed. Four other squaddies eyed him, with more than just idle curiosity, until Ryan entered the room of the accommodation block, "Well, well Mr. Docker what do we have here?" Joe struggled with his towel as Ryan ordered him to attention in the half-light. One soldier went to hold the door as three others closed in silently.

"You need a lesson Sambo – we don't like 'golly-wogs' in this Army and you're far too cocky for your own good. My advice is don't struggle," uttered Ryan, as Joe was filled with the dread of what was to come. It was all too familiar and he watched the specter of Richard's ghost leering down on him.

Before Joe could utter a word he was attacked and pinned face down on his bed by the other three. Struggle as he might he couldn't move and sheer panic set in. "Take this as a taster," said Ryan, "You should stick to this when you get home and leave all the white women alone. You'd make a lovely bum-bandit." Seconds passed and then the pain became unbearable as he felt Ryan's hot stinking breath on the back of his neck.

After it was over Joe lay in the darkness feeling a mixture of pain, anger and disgust. He now had three secrets in his life to take to his grave.

Joe knew that there was no point in complaining. It was the word of one black man against five white men. It wasn't the last time that they came in the night for him. If he resisted Ryan would beat him, or worse inflict torture with a broom handle, but no injuries to the face – it wouldn't do for the officers to see.

If he didn't resist they would take it in turns whilst Ryan constantly cursed his colour and the heritage of Joe's mother. On one occasion they even smeared him with white toothpaste and took it in turns to brush his skin with it. Just a little 'in-joke' to see if they could change the colour of his skin.

Joe was the closest he had ever been to being broken, three years was going to seem a very long time.

He was alone.

Chapter Twenty Four: 'Working For The Man'

(Roy Orbison)

1962

On the 22 August 1962, Rob Docker woke up to a new dawn and joined the police service as constable '117'. Given the trauma of the last few years, and the break-up of his relationship with Joe, he was glad to have a sense of purpose and somewhere to escape to.

Getting into the job had not been easy, as his working-class background and broad Birmingham accent were not to everyone's taste. The force had experienced a large influx of recruits from Scotland and Wales as deprivation drove families to look for work in the Midlands, or the richer South. These groups looked after themselves in the job and if you weren't in the Scottish 'mafia' or the Welsh 'mafia' you needed to consider aligning yourself to other elements.

Rob was bored silly by the thought of playing golf, or joining the 'Buffaloes' or 'Masons', so for now he kept his own counsel whilst he watched and learnt. He had also figured out that a lot of opportunities would arise over the next decade as those who had joined the service immediately after the war left on completion of their thirty years' service.

Fortunately for Rob his mother knew the mother of one of the recruitment officers and they made sure that Rob appeared before him for the medical and initial written examinations. Rob was not short of intelligence by any means, but a slight amendment here and there on the medical form, together with some conveniently placed answer sheets in the exam room, ensured that good luck did not need to take part in the process. After all what was the harm in helping the family of a friend, and why to mention his black heritage when he was clearly white for all to see?

Rob's initial training course had not been a happy experience as both the drill- sergeant, and class instructor, took a dislike to him from day one. He suffered the humiliation of being constantly bawled at on the parade ground by an ex-military man who clearly viewed his red sash and the slashed peak in his cap as a sign that he was superior. Most of the recruits were frightened by the physical presence of this man and showed it, but Rob was not afraid and paid the price for his lack of deference, with extra early morning parades, and the endless shining of boots.

Likewise, his class instructor, who hailed from Cardiff, and suffered from a rather large ego, which did not match his height, determined to do his best to make Rob suffer, and demeaned him in front of his peers at every opportunity, "We know how to deal with thick 'Brummies' here Docker – if you last six months I'll be amazed," was his favourite catchphrase. Rob took it in his stride and waited whilst those around him thanked God that they were not the focus of attention from a man who was inherently a bully and a coward.

Rob knew better than to confront this unwarranted hostility full-on, and studied hard as a means of distraction. He ultimately took the 'book prize' for best academic student on the course, and had great pleasure in posing with the Training Centre commandant for the customary photograph, as his prize of a splendid English Dictionary was presented. The class instructor looked on from the sidelines barely able to control his displeasure.

The end of course 'evening ball' was a sight to behold as the camp was flooded with invited guests from various nurses' homes, and officers struggled to get to grips with the complexities of dinner suits and bow-ties. Rob relished the evening, but as his colleagues sank deeper into an alcoholic haze, he drank from bottles and maintained a clear head.

Just before midnight Rob left the warmth of the main building where the event was taking place and walked unobtrusively towards the dimly lit staff car park. He had already had his fill of Cliff Richard and the Shadows, and Elvis, and listening to the newly released 'Lovesick Blues' by Frank Ifield had just about finished him off.

He had already determined what car the drill instructor drove. It was the extra- clean one with some fancy leather bench seats – his absolute pride and joy. In keeping with his character the 'drill pig' also always parked in exactly the same place and as he approached the car Rob slid the white drill gloves and a sharpened key from his pocket. It took him a matter of seconds to traverse both sides of the car with deep scratches to the bodywork. For good measure he positioned four nails under each tyre and after punching a hole with a screwdriver in the driver's door he sprang the door lock and proceeded to urinate over the front seat.

The next morning as Rob exited the main gates of the Training Centre he felt the warmth of the early morning breeze and allowed himself a brief smile. At about the same moment, a short distance away, the wife of the class instructor picked up an envelope that had been addressed to her, which lay on the floor below the letterbox of her married quarters. She wasn't that used to receiving correspondence. That sort of thing was normally dealt with by her somewhat controlling husband, who was also not shy in administering a bit of corporal punishment when he felt that she was in need of it.

She opened the envelope carefully and found a single sheet of typed paper, the contents of which described in detail her husband's infidelity with not one, but two, females from the recent recruit intake. For a woman who had suffered for years and had revenge in her heart it was a moment to savour as she folded the paper and put her coat on, before making her way to the Commandant's office.

Rob never looked back from that day, nor did he ever disclose his activities to another living soul but one thing was for sure – whoever crossed Rob Docker from now on was a marked person. Like his brother, he had found that he had no limits to his quest for revenge when someone wronged him. Rob was already a 'wrong-un'.

***

Nine months into the job Rob Docker liked being in uniform, and still took great pride in turning himself out immaculately. Working on a unit covering the outskirts of Birmingham City Centre he was all too aware that he was still one of the new boys on the block but he kept his head down and quietly went about making his mark.

There were no flash jobs for Rob – for the time being he would be walking the streets alone on foot patrol, well and truly 'on his tod'. Some of the other probationer constables stuck with a bit of traffic to ease themselves into things but Rob wanted prisoners, in fact he very much enjoyed the exercise of power over some poor 'scrote' when he banged someone up who was unfortunate enough to cross his path. Also, a summons report for traffic was one thing but a prisoner in the cell-block was where you were seen by senior officers.

Many of the officers on the unit had nicknames, which were deliberately derisory, but for some reason the other officers in his team found it difficult to put a label on him. His two sergeants were fine with him, but he had already incurred the wrath of his inspector who showed his dislike to the point of contempt. The Inspector was old school, and on night duty would always close his office door after the parade and sleep until one hour before the shift finished, when he would wake up and demand a cup of tea. Not a bad life really.

Rob had made the mistake of arresting someone wanted on warrant one evening which required the Inspector's attendance in the cell block. He was not best pleased and made his feelings known. As far as Docker was concerned the guy was a waster who was holding down an inspector's job that someone else could have – maybe it would be him one day.

The thing that brought the unit together was public order, better known as a good scrap on the streets, and when an officer was in trouble the unwritten rule was that you dropped everything else and made for the location. This was the 'law'.

One Saturday evening, at turning out time, Rob was on foot patrol at the back of Broad Street when a pub fight started in Summer Row. Rob Docker ran with his helmet in his hand to make it as fast as he could.

Minutes later he arrived at a scene of absolute mayhem as a crowd of fifty- plus people milled around outside the pub, cursing and up for a fight. The battle lines were drawn as the combatants weighed each other up – fifty on one side, and a dozen in blue on the other. The officers knew from experience however that a dozen determined officers were enough. Like in the film 'Lawrence of Arabia', which was to win seven Oscar awards, a small band of determined, and organized men, often prevailed against many and won. It was one of Rob's favourite films of the time.

The crowd bayed for blood, and as was often the case the shortest and smallest officer on the unit suddenly darted into the crowd and dragged a man out backwards by his collar. The officer punched him hard in the stomach for good measure and he went down 'like a sack of spuds'. Bundled unceremoniously into the back of a van the score line started at 0-1 to the police.

Unbeknown to the officers this was to become a bit of a family affair as other brothers, sisters, and even their drunken mother emerged onto the front line to demand his release.

Rob quickly identified his own target, another brother, and as the man stepped forward to protest he grabbed him from the rear and pinned both arms behind his back. No time for handcuffs, he steered the prisoner towards the nearest police vehicle, as the driver came round to assist him. Try as they might they couldn't get him inside as his body went rigid. The older officer shouted, "Just give him a pisser son. Lamp him one before he puts one on you." Rob obliged with a less than subtle blow to the lower abdomen, and the prisoner collapsed inside.

Seven members of the same family were arrested and duly deposited in the cells, screaming and banging on the metal doors until the effects of alcohol and the heat of the confined space forced uneasy sleep.

During a delayed meal break Alan, one of the longer serving PCs said to Docker, "You did ok tonight. These silly fuckers think that they're going to get done for being drunk and disorderly but we're gonna charge them with affray." Docker knew what was coming, "Leave the evidence with me Rob. I'll do me pocketbook up and you can sign it later. We just need to make sure that all the evidential points are covered. Done up like a kipper. Do you get my drift?" Docker nodded.

"You'll do fine Mr. Docker just fine." the words rang in his ears and resonated.

During the course of the fight another probationer was spotted in the darkness of a nearby doorway. For whatever reason he didn't make it to the fight and unfortunately for him he was now a marked man.

One of the old-sweats summed up the situation, "As useless as a 'fart in a colander. The fucking titty babby's in the wrong job."

'How easy it was to be in or out,' Docker reflected.

At 6.30am the unit gathered in the yard at the back of the station – all bar one of the team who left quietly, cutting a lonely and isolated figure.

Docker had signed the pocket book – there was no going back now and he had tasted his first experience of 'noble cause corruption'. It didn't taste too bad.

"Come on Rob we are off for a pint," said Alan, and by 7am Rob found himself sat in a pub just off Broad Street in a cluster of tables. The pub gaffer had pulled himself out of his pit and opened up for them. It was a weird feeling sitting in 'half-blues' sipping a pint, at that time of the morning, but it tasted good and in any event he wasn't paying for it – no-one was.

Docker had a good feeling in his stomach – he was one of them now and trusted. Now he could move forward.

***

Most officers craved the warmth of a cosy front police-office, especially when it was 'pissing down of rain' – commonly known as the 'policeman's friend'. If he had a penny for every time the weather was predicted with that phrase, 'it's a bit black over Bill's Mother's,' he would have been a rich man.

Rob however loved foot patrol. He enjoyed the solitude which gave him time to think and plan his life – nothing was left to chance.

Out one late evening, as the light was fading, he found himself in Rotten Park Road, just off the Hagley Road. As he walked past the red telephone box he noticed a young black female standing inside, in her early twenties. Nothing unusual in that except that she wasn't making a phone call.

Rob's sixth sense registered the situation immediately and the fact that she was wearing a skirt short enough to have been mistaken for a large belt compounded his theory.

Without breaking pace Rob continued onto the main road, and out of sight, before doubling back and hiding in the front garden of an adjoining house from where he could observe the scene.

Dealing with prostitutes, more commonly known as 'brasses' was not strictly within Robs remit, but he was never one to observe rules and he continued to watch as, the female left the box to stand on the curb, arms folded and looking both ways.

After a few minutes a battered green Ford Escort drove slowly up the road towards her and came to a halt. The passenger window was wound down and after a brief discussion with the driver the female got inside and they drove off.

Rob waited.

Almost exactly thirty minutes later the car re-appeared at the phone box and came to a halt briefly to allow the female to get out, before driving off. Rob had the registration number if he needed it but for now his focus was on the prostitute.

Rob waited until she had stepped back into the phone box and then made his move. Swinging the door open he announced abruptly, "Your under arrest for soliciting prostitution. I've got you bang to rights with that last punter, so don't try messing me about. Where do you live?" She nodded; she knew that she was defeated already, "In a flat just down the road."

Docker responded, "Right we'll go there first then. Unless you've given me the right address there's no bail for you and if you try legging it I'll cuff you."

Something didn't feel quite right to her even then, but he had the power of the uniform and she had nothing – not even the support of the pimp who routinely controlled her with violence.

She led Docker a hundred yards down the road and into a dingy downstairs one-bedroomed rented flat. As she switched the light on a cursory search of the room showed the electricity meter cupboard open in the corner with a broken padlock dangling from the open, and empty, cashbox.

"You've got more than one problem now luv, and you can stop looking at me with a face like fourpence. If you don't like being nicked why don't you fuck off and do your business out of sight – like it used to be, round the back of Rackhams." He paused for effect, "Any road up, abstracting electricity is an offence under the Theft Act. Stick the kettle on and we'll sort this out." Rob ordered.

She knew that to survive she had no choice. Her last client had paid £20 for a 'knee trembler' at the back of some nearby lock-up garages. Her next client demanded full sex and didn't pay a penny. Robs price for ignoring the 'abstract electricity' offence.

Prior to leaving, Rob extracted details from her of the man who had given her a recent black eye and later that week he made sure that he was given the benefit of a routine stop-check as he was about to park up outside the flat in Rotten Park Road.

Rob listened to all the bullshit and then arrested him for driving whilst disqualified, no insurance, and being wanted on a commit warrant. This man was going nowhere except straight to jail for ninety days. As he placed the man into the back of a police vehicle Rob could have sworn that the curtains twitched inside the flat.

***

On yet another occasion Rob had rather a strange experience following an encounter in the gent's toilets at Five Ways. He was bursting to have a 'piss' and whilst standing at the urinal in full uniform he suddenly felt the presence of a pair of eyes on his back and a muffled whimpering sound.

Having put himself straight, and done up the belt on his heavy raincoat, he stepped back and immediately kicked the door of the nearest cubicle open as hard as he could and came face to face with a man, trousers round his ankles, and penis erect, whose rather bloodied nose had just connected with the door. Clearly the hole in the cubicle door had provided Rob's victim with a view that he couldn't resist.

"Ay up what have we got here then - You dirty yampy bastard," Rob announced as he dragged him to his feet and punched him in the stomach. As the man bent double Rob connected his knee with the man's jaw, sending him reeling back across the toilet seat, and collapsing in a heap onto the floor, which was covered in years of slime and filth.

Rob paused to determine his course of action and then said, "Decision time me poofta friend. You need to decide whether you get done for being a fucking pervert, or for being drunk and disorderly and resisting arrest. If you take the first I'll make sure that all your friends and family know what a dirty little wanker you are."

Twenty minutes later in the custody block Docker announced to the custody sergeant "One in for D & D and resist arrest sarge. His breath smelt of alcohol and he was unsteady on feet, eyes glazed, speech slurred and swearing loudly in a public place. He was violent on arrest and had to be restrained." Another tick in the book. Rob was well chuffed.

***

On 8 August 1963 the Great Train Robbery occurred and Rob read every article about the crime that he could find in the national newspapers. These were proper criminals and he had an insatiable thirst for understanding the criminal mind that he hoped would put him one-step ahead in the future. These were real villains and tasty at that.

***

On 28 August 1963, Martin Luther King made his famous 'I have a dream' speech during a march in Washington as President Kennedy tried to push through his Civil Rights Bill and race riots erupted. As Rob reflected on events in America he felt no connection at all to the issues – the reality was that as far as he was concerned he was white and if Joe just happened to be the wrong colour that was his problem, and he deserved everything he got.

***

Rob's two year probationary period flew by, and in between putting villains away a stroke of good luck placed him nicely with the 'powers that be'. He had been working in the front office on nights about eighteen months into his probation, a task he hated, but one that he was sometimes required to perform. As he sat there bored to death he suddenly heard the sound of breaking glass followed by the smell of burning.

Dashing outside, he saw the remnants of a broken bottle as flames shot up the wall of the building and engulfed the window frame of the office directly above his head – the one where the inspector slept.

Docker ran up two flights of stairs shouting for help as he went. A fire extinguisher was wedging one of the upstairs doors open and in full-flight Docker grabbed it without breaking his stride and used it to smash at the door of the inspector's office, which to his surprise gave way with ease. The room was full of smoke from the blackened and burning window frame as pieces of hot glass spat across the room. Rob grabbed the dazed and crumpled inspector and had great pleasure in launching him unceremoniously through the door as the flames started to take hold.

With the sound of sirens in the background and other running feet Rob tackled the blaze with the extinguisher, and in so doing suffered a slight burn to one his hands which later required medical treatment. The inspector gathered himself in time for the arrival of the fire brigade and assumed his customary position of self-importance.

Expressions of thanks and appreciation were in short supply that night but the job loves heroes and after a glowing report from one of his sergeants the inspector was duly obliged to pose for a photograph for the media, with a bandaged Rob Docker, shaking hands with the man who might well have saved his life. The inspector hated this, 'jumped up little cunt,' getting all the attention, but could do nothing about it, although he had his arse in his hands for days afterwards about it.

The mystery of the petrol bomber was never solved but Rob Docker came to realize the power of the media through his 'heroic' exploits and in particular developed a close relationship with one of the newspaper reporters, Jane Smith, who gave him a nice 'front page spread' as well as spreading something else for him.

For her efforts Rob undertook to provide her with inside information and Jane provided some creature comforts that Rob was not receiving from Lilian, who was pre-occupied with bringing up a largely unwanted child. It was a mutually useful relationship that was to last for many years.

***

In 1964 Rob Docker had plenty to celebrate – the end of his probationary period as a police officer, receipt of a Chief Constable's award for bravery, becoming twenty- one-years-of-age, and managing to maintain an affair under the nose of his devoted wife who fulfilled the role of committed mother, and total doormat, that he wiped his feet on regularly.

He also had the christening of his Rose to look forward to.

To celebrate after the church service, Mary and Lilian arranged a party in one of the back-street pubs, which was meant to comprise a mixture of family, friends, and police colleagues. It was just the sort of affair that Rob hated.

In pride of place at the top table sat their three year-old daughter. Whilst Rob had certainly not bonded with the child in her early years they were gradually becoming closer and Rose stayed next to him in the room. At a respectful distance sat Jane the reporter, and part-time mistress, who immersed herself amongst police officers with Lilian oblivious to her presence. Rob got a thrill from the danger of having Jane so close to him.

Mary had an ulterior motive for wishing that the party would be a great success. She sprang her surprise on Rob as they were just about to cut a cake and deliver best wishes – Joe strode through the door.

"How you doing brother?" he announced as he cautiously extended his hand towards Rob.

Rob instinctively clasped his hand and for a few moments they both exercised their full strength in trying to squeeze the life from each other's extended fingers. There was no outright winner but they remained joined to each other, momentarily re- kindling their twin's bond. Robs colleagues looked on quizzically at the sight of a black man extending friendship and greetings towards a whiter-than-white Rob.

Tension rose palpably in the air as the gathered assembly looked on with curiosity, except of course for Lilian who wished that she were somewhere else. "What do you want Joe?" said Rob in an almost inaudible whisper as his daughter started clinging to his trousers.

"Mum asked me to come so I'm here – it might have escaped your notice but I am your brother. Mum wants an end to all this. What's your problem? Are you worried about shaking the hands of a black man in front of your 'pig' mates?"

Rob leant into the ear of Joe and said softly, "Leave Joe – this ain't your ground. It's mine. Leave now while you can still stand. One wrong word from you and me and these drunken fucking mates of mine will sort you out and throw you out. Just fuck off quietly unless you want to upset my daughter."

Joe stood in silence for a few seconds then replied in a low voice, "Now you listen before I go. You're a sad fuck Rob. I looked after you all those years but you hadn't got the guts to stand with me when I needed you. Yeah I stole Sandra, it wasn't out of spite, I loved her and she loved me, but you can't accept that can you? I realize now it's always been about you, never a thought for anyone else.

You can't even bury the hatchet when our mom, who put herself and her body on the line to protect us from that evil bastard, wants you to. I could ruin you here and now with a couple of words, but I pity you for the shame you feel, having me as a brother – so I wont say a word. Enjoy the rest of your selfish, mean life, hope you can live with yourself when the career has finished, hope it's all worth it." In just a few moments he summed up all of his anger in one short speech.

He turned abruptly on his heels and marched out through the goggling crowd. Mary Docker looked on feeling desolate – there was to be no reconciliation today. It could so easily have been one of the better moments of her life – the reunification of the family, but Rob exercised no such thoughts. Forgiveness was not in his nature. He turned to those within hearing.

"Just some Wog I locked up trying to spoil the party, I'll sort him out another day. Let's drink! Can anyone borrow me a fiver to get a round in?" he joked, whilst inwardly fuming with anger.

***

That same month Rob had his own personal tragedy to contend with – one that stayed with him until his last day on earth.

Rob was at home on a rest-day and was up and about early. He always felt claustrophobic on his days off and had been out in the garden, trying to keep the goldfish pond that he had created in the back garden of his police house in some semblance of order. There was something peaceful about fish and it gave Rob an excuse to get away from Lilian's idle chatter that mostly left him feeling 'brain-dead'.

As was her wont Rose was sat in the back kitchen in her pyjamas making a mess of boiled eggs and 'soldiers' whilst Lilian busied herself hoovering. Almost the perfect family scene, except that it wasn't.

"Rob – there's someone on the phone for you from work," Lilian shouted down to the end of the garden.

Rob made his way back inside, door left ajar, and as he brushed past Rose sat at the kitchen table he tickled the back of her ear, causing her to giggle uncontrollably. Without doubt his love for the child was growing by the day – she gave unconditional love and wanted nothing more than to feel close to her 'dad'.

He remained on the phone for a good ten minutes in the hallway trying to sort out what to do with a prisoner that he had circulated as being wanted on warrant and who had been arrested in Leeds. He would have preferred to have been called in to deal with it but the duty inspector declined to pay the overtime so that was it.

Rob went back to the kitchen and Rose was no longer there. The sound of hoovering continued upstairs.

"Lilian is Rose with you?" Rob shouted.

They found her face down in the pond, and despite frantic efforts by Rob to administer mouth-to-mouth, Rose was pronounced dead on her arrival at hospital. Something died inside Rob as well.

Neither Rob nor Lilian could find any comfort in each other's presence and whilst she did not have the courage to say what was in her head Rob knew exactly what Lilian was thinking, *'the bastard loves his job more than he loved his daughter'*. To escape the silence that enveloped the house Rob did the only thing that gave him any release – he reported for duty.

The funeral took place a week later and Lilian chose the

music, 'Take Good Care of My Baby' by Bobby Vee, to accompany the small coffin being carried into the chapel.

Mary had insisted that the whole family attend and would tolerate no resistance from Rob. For his part Joe kept a polite distance, with Sandra and Hope huddled against him, a perfect family picture which did not go unnoticed by Rob, even in the depths of his own personal despair.

Rob's shift was on nights that week and after one night of listening to Lilian sobbing he went back to work next day, no further thoughts of compassionate leave in his mind.

He had a job to do – the night sky closed in around him as he drove silently to work - it was looking Black over Bill's Mother's again.

The relationship between Rob and Lilian deteriorated rapidly thereafter. In his opinion she spent all her time lounging around while he had to go and earn the money to support her. It came to a head when he returned home late from duty one evening to find his tea in the bin, not for the first time. She was in bed asleep and he simmered all night before exploding the following morning.

"What's the matter with you then. Why have you got your arse in your hands?" Lilian snapped back, "I'm sick of cooking meals for you and then throwing them away. I can't be bothered anymore."

Rob looked at her with contempt and suddenly snapped, slapping her sharply across the side of the face, "I'll fucking tell you when to stop cooking. I go to work every day to provide for us whilst you sit on your fat arse all day doing fuck all, so don't push me." Lilian burst into tears, "And you can stop that blarting. I'm going to work." Rob had crossed another boundary.

Chapter Twenty Five: 'Leader Of The Pack'

(The Shangri-La's)

1964

Quinn surveyed his domain. The compound, the parked bikes, the workshop doors and further afield, the disused Defford Airfield runway with its new buildings. He spent some time assessing the huge white mass of the new radio telescope, wondering what the fuck it was for, but decided there was no money to be made out of it and his eyes moved on. He had missed the small article in the Malvern Gazette a couple of years previously,

'SCIENTISTS from the Royal Radar Establishment will now be able to explore the Universe more accurately than ever before. This deeper investigation has been made possible by the construction on Defford Common of a radio telescope interferometer at a cost of over £240,000. The equipment, sited on the former airfield at Defford, is built on two railway tracks to facilitate movement. Not only will it be able to improve radio and radar techniques in tracking ballistic missiles, earth satellites and 'space ships', but it will also observe radio signals originating from stars and other heavenly bodies.'

He was slouched in his chair, feet on the conference table in the meeting room of the Club, where only Council members had seats, gazing past the grilles on the only window.

It was a rare moment of reflection in what had been a

whirlwind few years since his return from that first trip to America. He was not a man of culture, but even he had heard of a ' tide in the affairs of men'. The last few years felt more like catching a wave and surfing it like they did in California.

More by luck than planning he had caught a massive breaker when he had gambled his life in the Venice Beach bar and later at Laguna Seca. Its surge was still carrying him forward even now, in 1964, as The Beatles and the Stones crashed into the consciousness of every teenager, and Mods and Rockers fought pitched battles on the beaches of England.

The first piece of good news upon his return from America in that autumn of fifty-eight had been that the old airfield had indeed been divided up into lots and sold off, together with some parts of the neighbouring Croome Estate.

Most had gone to the private company that was the anointed heir to the wartime research establishment, and it was they that had built the new buildings in the middle of the main runway. These squat blocks were a good mile from where he sat and the people who worked there maintained a studious separation from the activities of their biking neighbours. The radio telescope sat on its rails between him and the buildings.

Some of the sale lots had been designated for locals and Joey had had the sense to use Seamus' role as farm tenant as a cover for the purchase of the set of peripheral buildings that Quinn had been eyeing prior to his departure. Jenny had enlisted Eddie Brough to set up a company called 'Defford Farmers' into which Quinn's insurance money and club cash, laundered courtesy of Eddie Brough from the various businesses, had been deposited. There had been no other bidders for the low-grade buildings. The local interest had been welcomed by the vendors, who would have been surprised at what had become of the site had they retained any interest.

The plot boasted angular, featureless, flat- roofed concrete blocks that had once housed the guardhouse and the telephone exchange for the wartime base, but had not been used for years other than by the local wildlife, especially a healthy population of pigeons. The buildings sat within a compound with a good fence, courtesy of the old top-secret wartime airfield. Quinn had spotted their potential as a secure, and low-key base, away from any official interest, one that was not indebted to the IRA. Quinn had also wanted his own place for Jenny and Sean.

That final night in the Californian desert six years ago had enhanced his plans and the example set by the Madmen had been successfully transposed to Worcestershire. Firstly though, he had completed the transformation of his erstwhile friends to 'outlaw motorcyclists'.

They had not been easy to convince, having not witnessed the phenomena unfolding around Los Angeles and San Francisco, but his views had currency and weight. They had all felt the benefit of his leadership and he had earned their trust by putting his life on the line for them by going to New York.

After some debate and explanations he had prevailed, creating the first such group outside the West Coast of America. He had thought of a name in 1958 before his plane landed. It was a rare legacy from his mother who had often professed, '*You've a black soul and you'll have a bad ending Patrick Quinn'* - before she asked his father to administer punishment for his latest transgression.

The 'Black Souls' were formed from the original members, Quinn, Seamus, Steve, Frank, and Joey - the 'First Five' as they became known. Quinn had been unanimously voted in as President. Joey had no opposition as Vice-President and Frank's knowledge of weapons had won him the post of Sergeant-at-Arms. Seamus had no official post but self-appointed as group disciplinarian. The rules of normal society may not have applied to them, but they had their own Code of Conduct and it was fiercely enforced.

Together with Steve, who led on vehicles, the five formed the ruling council for the first few years. Billy Gurney had proved himself and was nodded through to full membership but he did not hold council status, he would always be a follower.

They had eventually expanded to a ruling group of seven; a deliberate odd number in an effort to ensure a decisive vote although Quinn, as President, had a casting vote if necessary. The group had no problem in attracting recruits and as Quinn sat that morning taking stock he could count on fifteen full-members, four prospects, plus some 'hangers on', a formidable force.

Two new members had been added to the Council to bring it up to strength. Tony Rogers, known as 'Egghead' was endowed with a sharp intellect, unfortunately coupled with homicidal tendencies that precluded him from any sort of career in normal society, but precisely the qualities valued by the Black Souls.

He had a rare skill with numbers, and a talent for organising chaos, and had been given the title of Treasurer with Jenny as his assistant. Jenny had to accept that a full male member with a vote on the Council was going to be the lead for such an important function in the increasingly complex business affairs of the organisation.

Graham Devlin or 'Leper', a tag earned due to an interesting collection of skin conditions, which were not assisted by a heroic and determined lack of personal hygiene since becoming a full-on outlaw biker, had arrived suddenly one morning with a shipment of goods from Eire.

He bore a note expressing a non-negotiable request that certain people would be very grateful if Quinn could take him on for the long term. Quinn was initially suspicious and spent an uneasy year ensuring that Devlin was kept well away from certain parts of the operation whilst he gradually verified the facts.

It seemed that Devlin was the son of a high-ranking officer in 'The Cause' and had been groomed to follow in his father's footsteps. However even in those circles young men rebelled against their parents, in his case a very dangerous stance to take.

He had then transgressed with an older female who, 'liked a bit of rough'. Unfortunately she happened to be married to another significant member who was not overjoyed when he found the two of them in bed.

Devlin had been permitted to live because of his father's status, but a Judgement of Solomon exercised by the ruling council had exiled him permanently to England. Quinn had discovered that his silver-haired nemesis, 'The General', had something to do with

Devlin's arrival, probably as a nil-cost future option in the schemer's plans, but the affair had alienated Devlin to such an extent that he initially refused to have anything to do with 'The Cause' until Quinn pointed out the advantages of appearing to be remorseful.

Devlin went on to prove himself a loyal and useful member. Having been steeped in the culture of the Republican Army he knew their thought processes and had been schooled in violence from an early age. Happily he took to bikes instantly and filled the seventh council post within two years of his arrival.

More importantly, Devlin had also been able to name, 'The General', as being Dermot McCann, and had confirmed that the holder of Quinn's reins was indeed high in the echelons of the IRA, controlling the movement of goods to and from the mainland. Devlin cultivated an on-going relationship with McCann at Quinn's behest – he wanted to know as much as he could about the man who was holding him to ransom.

The rest of the full members shared a passion for bikes, a distrust or rejection of normal society for a spectrum of reasons, and a propensity to use violence before compromise or negotiation. They had all found their home within the Black Souls.

They were not fully formed 'Hell's Angels' yet, that metamorphosis would not be complete for a few years, and knowledge of the existence of such beasts would not burst upon the world until Hunter Thompson's' book of the same name in two years' time. They were the base metal, waiting to be forged by the white heat of the Sixties, and that decade's rejection of the values of the past, its music, drugs, fashions, and philosophy. The bikers never would espouse the 'Summer of Love' and 'Flower Power' within their creed though.

Their numbers still included Paul Fielding, now known as 'Grease', the mechanic who assisted Steve in the garage, the nickname stemming from the ingrained dirt that provided a second skin.

'Tramp,' - George Collins, was a carrot haired individual who took filth and debauchery to new levels, including one notable occasion in a full bar when he vomited into a pint glass then drank it for a bet prompting dry retching all around.

Harry Jones with a squint was probably clinically insane and certainly only touched reality on rare occasions, rode his bike like a maniac, and would do anything for the Club, to the point where the other members had to take care not to voice any idle musings out loud just in case Jones carried them out.

'Fatty' Wilson, a huge bear of a man with a barrel chest, and gut to match, who could pick up his bike under one arm and carry it up a flight of steps into his flat.

They were colourful, unruly, unfettered from the bonds of normality, and a truly daunting prospect to behold.

The California connection had prospered. Angelo had kept his word and Quinn's Harley had arrived, together with a cache of spare parts. As predicted, everyone who saw it wanted one and they had been able to set up an import trade from California.

The machines arrived in the form of parts and Steve

assembled them, using manuals that Angelo had thoughtfully included. The Madmen were sourcing the parts by stealing complete machines from out of State, breaking them up, and shipping them via their criminal conduit. It was easy to get them freshly registered in England and there was next to no chance of a machine being traced once it had been cannibalised and the engine and chassis numbers erased and re-stamped.

Quinn had visited California on several occasions now, and Angelo and Bobby had been hosted by the Black Souls in return. Steve had spent several weeks learning about the big bikes in California until he could strip and re-build them in his sleep.

The bond between the groups had been further bolstered by a lucrative trade in Marijuana, imported amongst the Harley parts. Sid was no longer a lone-wolf at the café and had developed a tight network of sub-dealers kept in line by fear of the Black Souls. Despite not being a member or a biker he was one of the most loyal followers Quinn had, as a result of Quinn frightening off an older man who had discovered Sid's secret and tried to blackmail him. The man had decided against the plan after a meeting with 'Thor' and his hammer one night.

Sid had incorporated the dope to run alongside the booze and cigarette trade very nicely. They were also beginning to add pills into the repertoire as 'uppers' and 'downers' became fashionable. Quinn respected Sid's business acumen and thanked his foresight in keeping him on the team rather than just taking over in Lombardi's all those years ago.

Drug supplies came not only courtesy of the Madmen, but

from burglaries of chemists, forged prescriptions, and a couple of corrupt pharmacists paid in cash and girls. They had eventually moved the trade away from the café at Joey's behest and to spread the risk amongst the City's pubs, clubs, cafes and street corners.

Girls. The group attracted them. Some were hookers and the bikers quickly realised that they could provide security and management for the ladies of the night. The girls appreciated the protection and the fact that their existing, often unsavoury pimps, were efficiently excised. The bikers treated the tarts fairly, and by 1964 had set up a 'knocking shop' run by a fearsome Madame called Lulu in a large terraced house on the London Road.

Another stream of income came from what was euphemistically known as 'street banking'. They were awash with cash and plenty of people shunned by banks wanted to borrow it. Interest rates were high and defaulters dealt with harshly.

To complete the 'business' functions, they had also begun to provide security on doors and this was expanding into granting 'protection' to licensees, often sorting out problems away from the premises and encouraging troublemakers to drink elsewhere. The doors also provided a useful outlet for illicit goods.

The Black Souls were in essence a criminal organisation veneered as a bike club, although there was no doubting their love for the machines, and the hedonistic lifestyle that went with them. They were free; they had cash, women, a base, comradeship, and the knowledge that they were feared and unbeatable together.

The totems of outlaw biker culture had been imported into

England with Angelo's approval and connivance. A 'top rocker' proclaiming 'Black Souls', the bottom, 'Worcester', surrounded the winged death's head on their backs.

They had the 'One Percenter' badge and the '13' standing for the thirteenth letter of the alphabet, 'M' for Marijuana. White cloth badges with red edging bore their nicknames. Quinn had a signet ring designed, bearing the letters 'BS' entwined in gothic style produced by a local jeweller. As part of the ceremony full members were presented with one on the day of their induction. Quinn kept one back to give to Sean on his eighteenth birthday.

Over in California, the disparate biker groups had begun to coalesce and form their own structure and culture, led by the troop from San Bernadino, or 'Berdoo', the Hells Angels. They had a joint council and Angelo had gained approval from the others for the Black Souls to wear the regalia, the only group outside the USA to be accorded that privilege.

Quinn was strict in trying to keep the Black Soul's activities low-key, but it was inevitable that they would come to notice. To date it had been manageable, although they had all seen the inside of a prison cell, mainly for violent conduct. Luckily Quinn had only got a short stretch and had managed to keep the lid on his claustrophobia, although the experience had yet again caused him to vow that he would never see the inside of a cell again, no matter what it took.

It was worth the short spells of imprisonment to maintain their reputation, deliver enforcement as required, and to ensure that the group were viewed as violent nuisances rather than criminal entrepreneurs. Prison went with the territory, a badge of honour. They bore it with perverse dignity and caused no trouble for the guards, all part of staying off the radar.

In reality, no-one 'normal' was particularly bothered about the bikers and their 'businesses' so long as they kept to their own haunts, restricted their beatings to other scum, and avoided confrontation with the police.

They had also acquired a useful network of contacts via prison, their criminal dealings, and the use of liberal amounts of cash, or girls, to bribe or blackmail. There was a solicitor on a retainer, local councillors, and the beat constable whose life they made very easy. He in turn portrayed them to his colleagues as a misguided, but loveable bunch of rogues, and gladly pocketed any sweeteners offered.

Quinn rose from his seat at the head of the conference table and walked through to the main room, looking around with satisfaction. The old blocks had been transformed. The ex-military shell survived but the attentions of the bikers and their cash had added grilled windows, steel-skinned doors, and social facilities including a bar, darts, pool, an expensive record player, a kitchen and eating area, and living quarters both casual and permanent. The compound fence had been upgraded and a substantial set of gates replaced the old wooden barrier from wartime days.

It was also Quinn's home now. Together with Jenny and Sean he occupied what was basically a bed-sit within the complex but with full use of the whole area. It represented a high standard of accommodation for the time. The other permanent residents were

Joey, who understandably wanted to distance his parents from the Black Souls, and Frank who had transitioned from his church residence, or 'from heaven to hell' as he was fond of quoting. Seamus and Steve lived at the farm and Fielding occupied Steve's old quarters at The Pit Stop. The others made their own arrangements but there were rooms available at the clubhouse for crises, crashing out drunk, or one-night-stands.

Quinn doted upon his son, and his relationship with Jenny had matured and strengthened beyond the initial attraction. They had never married; the question had not arisen because she was smart enough to realise what she had linked herself to, and that the bonds involved were stronger than vows taken in church. She had sacrificed her old life and persona and could never return. There was to be no Burton and Taylor marriage for them.

Her father had died without forgiving her, and her mother blamed her for breaking his heart. She had not been invited to the funeral and had not tried to go. In response she had created a Jenny to match her new life. She was the queen of the biker women, and not just because of her link to the leader. She was smart and had cultivated a style that combined compassion for the females -many of them had significant problems, coupled with a dedication to the Black Souls that was pursued with a ruthlessness that matched Quinn's.

He was no ordinary man, and there were two strands to their relationship. She had realised that she could never control, or set bounds upon him, but that was part of the attraction. She accepted that there would be other women, but she knew that he trusted her implicitly and no other woman would replace her, and that was enough. He was devoted to one person in his life and that was not her, but it was their son, and no-one else could be the mother of the one thing that Patrick Quinn had ever loved in his life.

As Quinn emerged into the compound he spied Sean playing in a small area that had been made into a play area. Life was good, better than he could ever have expected when he jumped into that lifeboat all those lifetimes ago.

Only one thing clouded the picture for Quinn; he constantly felt the claws of the IRA, personified by the silver-haired McCann. The consignments made plenty of profit, and had been diversified recently, beginning to include drugs and pornography, but it grated continually with him that he was not free.

It would not be for some years that the ramifications of his youthful deal and it's later strengthening via the blood of a New York gangster, would begin to bite, but Quinn could already sense trouble brewing and he was rarely wrong about that. He knew he was in league with the devil but that his spoon was nowhere near long enough to sup from the shared bowl.

Chapter Twenty Six: 'From A Jack To A King'

(Ned Miller)

1963

He was a walking contradiction. A man brimming with resentment, and internal conflict, born of both nature and nurture. He was black and white, sexually ambivalent, with a nobility of spirit, if not action.

Autumn 1963. He returned to a world awakening to a new era. Even now he was brimming with contradictions, having spent the last three years regimented, he was suddenly free to make decisions - at a time when all boundaries were about to be pushed or broken as the 'Swinging Sixties' dawned.

Joe sat on a bench overlooking the building-site that was the centre of Birmingham. The planners seemed to be achieving what the Luftwaffe had failed to do. He watched the old city being swept away, recognising that he had reached a watershed of his own. Would he make a new start, or return to the past?

Mentally he counted off the issues. They came to mind easily – he had spent many nights pondering them as his discharge approached but had put off any decisions until he had escaped the confines of the Army and could set his thoughts free.

He had known for a long time that he would not stay on past his three-year stint. It had been a disaster and tested his mental strength to the very limit. He recognized now that he had needed an escape from the effect of taking a life, and the agonies of estrangement from his twin brother, but ironically had fled to another kind of prison with its own unique brand of punishment.

That first year in Cyprus had been hell. The sadistic bullying at the hands of Ryan and his cronies, suffused with racism, and homosexuality, had amplified and reinforced conditioning from his past, royally fucking his head up.

Despite his size and strength, he had meekly put up with it because it had destroyed his will to do otherwise. The fault of that lay with his stepfather and his white twin, and was etched into his soul. He had been twice betrayed.

He had been the stronger twin and had adopted the role of protector to Rob from infancy. He had adored his sibling and had learnt in childhood that he was of lesser worth, a guilty secret, the black sheep, destined to be the punch-bag of society and his stepfather. That being the case, he had resolved that a few more blows on behalf of Rob would make no difference, and had routinely put himself between Rob and punishment, whatever the form.

He got used to physical punishment. Anything inflicted by his peers was a pinprick compared to that meted out by his stepfather. The damage wasn't the bruises, but the fact that, unbeknown to his mother, the physical abuse from Richard had taken an altogether darker direction that had warped his sexuality. That was the first betrayal. Ryan had unwittingly knifed an old wound.

The second treachery had been the slow and sickening realization that his love of his twin was not reciprocated, and that Rob had coldly and clinically used him. He had begun to suspect the truth as they both matured, and it was clear by their fifteenth year that Rob was embarrassed by his black brother and had chosen to reject him in favour of his new, white friends.

That had wounded. By the time Sandra made it clear that she was interested in him, Joe had little compunction in stealing her away. He knew it had not been a righteous act, but he felt that he was owed something, so took it. Rob had revealed his true feelings in the cataclysmic argument and had left the next day to live with Uncle Charlie. Rob's last words yelled down the street as Joe marched away were seared into Joe's memory,

"You're not me brother, you fucking nigger freak. I never want to see you again, so stay away from me."

So he had run away, in a state of mental anguish and turmoil, straight into a nest of vipers. If he had paused to think, he should have realized what his reception into Her Majesty's Forces would be, but he had been desperate to escape.

Mentally weakened, he had put up with the abuse for two years until one day he snapped and put two tormenting squaddies into hospital. Ryan had moved on by then and Joe had been court-martialed and imprisoned for six months. When he emerged there were only six months to de-mob day and he had been moved back to England.

He arrived at his new unit with a reputation and had faced

down the first attempt at racism by breaking a nose and letting it be known that he was capable of worse. The man went down like a sack of spuds and stayed down.

Joe then announced to his peers in the dormitory, "Any more argy bargy and someone else will finish up with a face like a bosted arse. Any other fucker who starts getting on me wick will get the same. Now, leave the coon alone you bunch of spastics, or feel the pain."

His fellow conscripts had assessed the likely outcome of tangling with a crazy six foot six inch, fifteen stone madman and decided it wasn't worth the trouble. It was what he should have done years before, and he was left alone with his thoughts to eke out his last six months

And now it was decision time.

Firstly would he stay with Sandra and Hope? That was easy although he knew that he would lead a double-life as a result. He loved them both, and possessed a broad streak of fairness, and sense of justice, that far outweighed any vestiges of decency possessed by his police officer twin. Irony piled upon irony. The liar and cheat was a cop but no-one saw past his white skin. The protector, with at heart a noble soul, could never follow him because of the colour that damned him.

No, he would stay with Sandra and Hope, do right by them, and find a way to satisfy his other urges without hurting them. They still lived with his mother and she would need looking after, that was one debt he could repay and it was a sound base to build from.

Secondly, he had tried to be white but it was plain that he would never be accepted. Racism in every form, at every age, had taught him a hard lesson. He could not overcome his appearance and he was tired of fighting. He knew about the struggles of his black brethren elsewhere in the world and his own experience mirrored theirs, albeit in the more traditionally English format of prejudice, rejection and abuse. He felt empathy with the black struggle. It would be a waste of his life to continue trying to be a 'coconut' and fall between both stools - people could not see past the skin to what lay within. Henceforth he resolved to follow his true father.

Thirdly, what was he going to do? He had no interest in earning a pittance in a factory whilst putting up with the prejudice of both bosses and fellow workers. He was no Einstein, but even if he had possessed a mighty intellect, the colour of his skin meant there was no way of using it in a professional vocation, they were closed to his kind. He was fed up of rules and being controlled.

As he pondered, a brightly-coloured sign caught his eye.

'BE PART OF THE NEW OUTDOOR MARKET

STALLHOLDERS REQUIRED'

There was a number to call and a promise of reasonable rates. He looked down from his vantage point and now he could make out the roofs of the stalls set in an open plaza. Fate owed him a lucky spin - perhaps this was it. He could be his own boss. He wasn't afraid of hard work, could handle himself, and could probably afford the initial outlay on stock and the stall from the money he had put aside whilst serving.

His mother had provided the keep for Sandra and Hope, in return for their company and help, and he suspected, as a thank-you for his help in removing the cross she had borne for all those years, the late and unlamented Richard Burns. It had enabled him to save, with Sandra's full approval, and he had dutifully put aside most of his pay.

He had never drunk much – he didn't like the feeling of losing control, or smoked – he had tried once but hated the taste and had never tried again. The official government announcement that there was a direct link between smoking and cancer was still months away and many still enjoyed having a 'drag' at every opportunity, in fact it had been sold as having health benefits for many years.

Joe had continued the boxing he had started at school, in the Army, and neither of those vices assisted the training. There was no incentive to socialize with his tormentors, and their mute supporters in the Army, so he had very little to fritter his cash upon. After three years he had managed to accrue a tidy little sum.

His only expenditure had been a cheap guitar and Bert Weedon's book. He had spent the hours learning, and whilst he would never be a brilliant player, he found he did possess an instinct for rhythm and blues.

He stood up, took one more look at the market and resolved to catch the bus home and speak to Sandra. He sat alone on the bottom deck and realized that people were not just avoiding him because of his colour; he could sense they were frightened by his size too. Before, he would have resented it, but now he began to consider the uses to which being an intimidating outsider could be put.

He tried to stem the excitement of his market stall idea, he had been disappointed by life too many times, and then it suddenly occurred to him that he had no idea what to sell on it – fool! He cast around for inspiration and suddenly Uncle Charlie came to mind. He still carried on the trading activities originating from the wartime black market and he had always supported both twins, never differentiating between them.

Yes, he had taken Rob in when the split happened, but that hadn't lasted long and Joe had heard that there was a distance between them since Rob had turned blue. He suspected that Charlie still sailed close to the wind and wouldn't want a cop too close, blood or not. Joe had received regular letters from him whilst away and knew he would get good advice and possibly support from that source.

By the time he alighted from the bus he had also worked out that he could avoid the issue of skin colour prejudicing the renting of a stall by asking his mother to front the application. He strode up the pavement towards the terraced house in Moseley Village with a new purpose.

Six months later he was getting used to the early starts. His stall was on the end of a row nearest to the alleyway containing the toilets, next to the fruit-and-veg man. It was steady but not busy to start with, but at the end of May 1964 Prince Philip had opened the Bull Ring Shopping Centre and the crowds had followed, gawking at the shiny new modern concrete labyrinth that Birmingham had become. His timing had been right. There had been empty stalls before, as the building work had put people off, but now it was done there were plenty of buyers for his socks, hats and gloves.

Charlie had suggested it, He had a reliable source of textiles coming in from abroad – some contact who had links to the Far-East where they made stuff dirt cheap, and the Brummies' snapped them up. It was cash all the way and the bare minimum of the takings declared. Charlie had stood him some credit to start with but he had already covered that and things were looking good. He was getting on really well with Sandra, Hope was a charmer, and his mother was glad to have him around. He would recall that first year on the stall as being surrounded by a golden halo.

He was also into the lively local music scene. Birmingham had a multitude of groups and singers stretching back to rock and roll and skiffle days. Live music venues abounded, many of them in the old dancehalls and cinemas. They were all white though, playing white music, although he knew it was all based on the good old rhythm and blues appropriated from the blacks in America and sanitized for the white buyers.

He was part of a black group, still playing his r&b. There were seven of them, four playing, three crooning and they were doing okay with regular gigs around the circuit. They were something a bit different and whilst there were nights of abuse and diving out of the back door in a hurry, most times it was good, and they had started to attract a regular following, many of them 'coloured,' as the Brums termed them.

As the spring mellowed into summer even the Birmingham weather relented and his takings faded. He needed a new line. Back to Charlie, this time with a suggestion,

"Got an idea. You got any contacts in the States Charlie?" Charlie laughed, "Blimey, flying high ain't we? Importing already?"

Joe persisted, "I've spotted a market no-one is into. There's money to be made."

"And I ain't spotted it in all these years in the trade, but you do within months?" Charlie countered.

Joe nodded. "You ain't the right colour, or age, and you don't move in the circles I do."

"Hark at you! Stop going round the Wrekin and cough it up, what's the big idea?" said Charlie.

Joe's voice lifted, imbued with excitement, "Music. It's booming, records and groups. Look how much The Beatles and all the others like them are making, and I bet there's plenty in the background creaming it off."

Charlie's brow furrowed, "How does that fit with a market stall, you gonna stand on it and busk?"

Joe laughed, "Nope. Never in the reign of pigs pudding! That's the clever bit. You wouldn't know, but all these kids in groups learn everything from America - the tunes, the rhythms, the riffs and how to play. The way they do it is by getting hold of records and playing along to them. Problem is, it's all based on black music, Blues, that sort of thing, and all the good stuff comes from the Southern States. It's like rocking-horse shit to get hold of, and one record gets passed around loads of people."

"I wouldn't know where to begin." Charlie remained unconvinced.

"But I do," said Joe, "I'm in the middle of it, all me mates are black musicians. I know loads about it. I know if we can get hold of a supply of the good stuff it'll be like black gold and it'll fly off the stall."

Charlie made some enquiries and it transpired he did know someone importing from America, but comics - those Superman and Batman ones. Joe hadn't seen anyone selling those around town either so suggested giving them a try.

By August the socks, hats and gloves had been relegated to a third of the stall. They made a comeback that winter but could not compete with the imports. Joe had cornered the market and the cash flowed in. In the spring of 1965 he took over a second stall just for the records. He manned that one and employed one of his fellow musicians, Winston - who blew a mean horn, on the other one.

He had a mean look to match that deterred opportunistic shoplifters. Winston was also the right colour, a team player, laid back but totally focused – there was nothing half- soaked about our Winston.

They thrived in the shadow of the new Rotunda.

Several evenings a week they still played. He loved being up on stage but there were still regular occasions when the audience was hostile, and the management of the venue was either unwilling or unable to do anything about it. There also began to be trouble between the growing following of blacks, and racists in the majority white audiences.

Things reached a head one Friday in a pub in Hockley, a white working-class area where resentment at the influx of immigrants was tangible. Tension had been rising for months and he knew as soon as he walked on stage that trouble was brewing. Half a dozen blacks were at the front glancing uneasily at a vociferous group of drunken white youths, and men, surrounding the bar who were making comments about 'coons' and 'darkies' that carried across the general hubbub as they were intended to do.

There were boos from that direction when Joe's group appeared, and comments about 'nigger music'. While they finished setting up Joe walked to the front and spoke to one of the regular black followers that he knew.

"Listen our kid, it looks like trouble Lloyd mate, and you got no way out other than past them."

Lloyd was a sizeable individual with the beginning of what would be later described as an 'Afro' but he looked worried, "We gonna get our heads kicked in, too many of them, I told the others we shouldn't have come but it seemed like giving in."

"If it all cracks off, you and the others get on stage and head left, there's a back door, I'll nip off and make sure it's unlocked." said Joe who smiled and whispered, "By the way don't get using that shiv I know you're carrying. We don't need any attention from the pigs do we?" he winked.

Joe still routinely carried his own knife but always remembered well the old saying from a fifties criminal Billy Hill *'I was always careful to draw my knife down on the face, never across or upwards, Always down. So that if the knife slips you don't cut an artery. After all chivving is chivving, but cutting an artery is usually murder. Only mugs do murder.'*

They were halfway through the first number, a Jackie Wilson cover, when a pint dimple mug sailed through the air and smashed on the stage. Shouts of, *'Get the wogs,'* were accompanied by a charge towards the stage by about twenty-five of the noisy white gathering.

The six blacks saw them coming and leapt onto the stage, closely pursued. Joe said goodbye to his guitar and smacked a youth across the chest with it, hurling him backwards. It snapped across the neck - which he used to stab into the stomach of another, doubling him up.

The band, and their fans, retreated into the exit corridor, Joe at the rear. It was a narrow corridor and the assailants were forced into single-file. Joe was taken aback by the savagery in their faces but they had not reckoned with facing a boxer, one-on- one, and he left two more on the floor within seconds.

They backed out of the exit and slammed it shut. Luckily it opened outwards and by the time Joe backed through it the others had found some wooden batons lying in the pub yard that they used to brace the door. They all piled into the group van like a world record attempt and careered out of the yard and past the crowd that had disgorged from the pub. Joe hated running away and they had left all their instruments behind, but that could be sorted out later.

Joe, Winston, and Lloyd returned the next morning and banged on the pub door until the licensee's head appeared through an upstairs window and told them to piss-off. Joe tried negotiation but in the end had to threaten to put all the windows in before the door was opened.

Joe noted that the licensee had a face 'as long as Livery Street' as the man shouted, "You're all barred for life, fucking troublemakers. And tell all your mates, no more coloured's in here, no more jungle music."

Joe just about refrained from planting one on him, "We want our instruments. You know we done nothing, but you're just like all the rest of them, might as well have been one of them."

The licensee couldn't meet his gaze, "Just take your stuff and go."

***

Word got around and bookings dried up. The licensee had put the poison down and people were keen to believe any story painting 'coloured's' in the wrong. Everyone knew they were no good and didn't it prove their jungle drum music belonged to the devil? They couldn't have played anyway, all the instruments had been trashed including Winston's pride and joy, his French horn.

It was the injustice that really hurt. They had lost their

instruments, gigs, and the pleasure of performing, and all because of their skin colour. It became clear that the whole thing had been a set up to curb any black performers, music, or fans carving out a niche in Birmingham. It was all part of a baseless philosophy that abounded in the factories, and public houses, blaming immigrants for everything from stealing jobs to bringing in diseases. This was received wisdom and those who didn't agree kept quiet about it.

They met up regularly in the weeks that followed, in a safe pub in Handsworth, and were gratified to find that their supportive following were keen to see them perform. Word had also got around an indignant local Caribbean community who were as determined to stamp their culture upon their new home as the indigenous population were to stop them.

Their problem was that the colour white dominated the music scene and, despite some being privately appalled at what had happened, the promoters and licensees could not afford to step out of line.

The answer was so obvious that no-one had thought of it until Joe the businessman, always looking for an angle, approached it from the market perspective. Twenty odd of them were sat in the smoke-filled public bar, the sound of dominoes being smashed down on the tables with a flourish by the older black guys. Joe was in the centre of the horseshoe seat they all occupied. Voices had become raised amongst some of the more hot-headed who wanted to visit retribution on the site of the fight and its perpetrators. Joe stood up and motioned for silence, then bellowed "Quiet!"

His exploits on the night of the fight had earned him plenty of respect and the intervention worked.

"Right," he said, "If we go back there and smash the place up, break some heads, you know what happens, honky and his law will come down like a hammer on everyone, involved or not. That's what they want us to do; it's their territory, their world. No, we need to be smart about this and I've got an idea. I just need to know how much backing I'd have."

An hour later there was more shouting, but it was excitement not anger that provoked it. Joe had lit a fuse.

***

Joe stood on the opposite side of the Soho Road and wondered if he had taken one gamble too many. He had to admit it wasn't an inspiring edifice but it had been cheap. Who wanted an empty pre-war dancehall closed for ten years?

He did. It was a golden nugget covered in shit. Firstly it was slap-bang in the middle of black Birmingham, the reason why it was closed, and a bargain price. The whites had the money and none of them saw investing in Handsworth as worthwhile. Everyone knew the area was going down the pipe - full of darkies with no money. Who was going to go dancing there? - Certainly not the daughters of the good white citizens of the 'Second City'.

Secondly, behind the peeling paint, rotting windows, and shattered signage lay a sprung dance-floor with a stage that had hosted the long departed big bands powering the fox-trots and waltzes. The place had foundered in 1956, just before the rock and roll explosion that could have saved it. A Bank had ended up owning it and it had lain forgotten on their asset books ever since, apart from bills for rates and complaints from the council about its decay. Joe had offered a derisory amount of cash, expecting to negotiate but they had snapped his hand off.

He smiled to himself - just occasionally being part of a shunned minority had its advantages.

***

There wasn't much money remaining to fix it up and Joe was expecting trouble, so he left the outside alone and put boards over the windows. This had the effect of making the front a blank canvas apart from a reinforced double door.

Winston wasn't impressed, "Looks like a fucking hole in a wall."The name stuck. Joe didn't want signage that could be smashed so one of the boys who had some artistic talent painted 'The Hole In The Wall' over the door in rainbow colours. There was plenty of help to be had for free, led by Lloyd and the others he had saved from a beating in the pub. They were fuelled by injustice and determined to have a place of their own.

By December they had restored the dance floor and stage, and had a lucky find, the original chairs and tables had been stored in rooms upstairs. However, the upholstery had provided nesting material for mice and Joe hadn't the cash to replace it. The grapevine hummed and one morning an almost circular figure appeared and asked to see Joe.

Hyacinth was Jamaican, with a huge smile, and breasts the size of small zeppelins.

"Hear you got a problem with chairs boy," she smiled.

Joe showed her the moldering pile, and the fixed benches in the alcoves covered in pigeon crap, springs protruding.

Hyacinth shook her head, "What you need are some women who can sew and some fabric. I got a proposal for you."

They missed Christmas opening. It took until February before Hyacinth and her many friends finished applying the material Joe had purchased from the rag market - good old Uncle Charlie again. In return Joe agreed free use of the place in the daytime for the women to meet. It was no hardship; he wanted his place to be something for the locals to use.

While the women sewed, the men had finished the heavy work. They were ready - not before time, as Joe's coffers had run low. He was under increasing pressure financially, a fact he kept hidden. By February 1966 he estimated he had enough left to bankroll 'The Hole' until May.

The market stall was no Carnaby Street and couldn't sustain the cash required any longer, and he had already cut his family expenditure to the bone. He was supporting the fledgling dance-venue, Sandra, Hope and his mother, on socks, records and comics, not a viable business model even with the huge amount of free help his friends had provided.

The building was ready, but now the cosy Caribbean bubble surrounding it was pricked by the real world, the white world. He had expected problems and he wasn't disappointed. There had been mutterings, and a small article in the Birmingham Post, whilst objective and fair, had raised awareness that a venue run by and catering for 'West Indians' was rising from the decaying remains of the old Stardust Dance Hall on Soho Road, Handsworth.

The reaction from certain vocal quarters of the local white population was predictable, depressing, and laced with hypocrisy. Lurid predictions of 'jungle style excesses' perpetrated against the backdrop of the 'devils music'. Fears for the safety of white women, and the greatest irony, demands that 'immigrants', all of whom were non-whites, and had recently alighted from a banana boat apparently, shouldn't be allowed their own place and culture.

They should be made to conform if they wanted to live 'over here'. This conveniently overlooked the fact that dark skin colour precluded entry to many establishments and could attract a kicking on the street at the wrong time or place.

Joe had anticipated, and prepared, for trouble of this kind and the building was impregnable. The rear protected by a high wall and substantial gates, and nothing to damage on the unprepossessing frontage. He had already recruited Winston, Lloyd, and three other 'handy' and sizeable men named Everton, Gladstone, and Alvin to provide security, confident they could handle any problem at the door.

No, the problem came from another quarter - officialdom. He needed a licence to operate a dance and music venue, and he needed a liquor licence to run a bar. The revenue he needed to survive could only flow from those two pieces of paper.

The granting of these cash lodes lay in the hands of the

Birmingham Licensing Committee, a body renowned for its conservatism and 'whiteness'. Joe had first applied in the autumn of 1965 and had waited weeks for a reply, then an avalanche of requirements for the building and its operators arrived.

The last of Joe's cash, plus a small loan from Charlie, had rendered the building compliant and an inspection had been arranged. The Chairman of the deciding Panel duly arrived, an obnoxious individual who found fault with everything and spent the tour squinting down his prominent nose, his face bearing an expression of detecting an unpleasant smell he couldn't quite place. Joe knew that Alan Foster- Smythe called the shots and also that he had no chance.

A few days later he received a list of issues and conditions that the most righteous of white establishments would not have satisfied and he hadn't even started on the liquor licensing process.

He caught the bus back to Moseley, arriving with a mind to pull the plug. How could he win when prejudice imbued every edifice of society? It was a neat, self- fulfilling prophecy. Blacks were only good for manual labour, bus driving, that sort of thing. If they tried to better themselves they crashed into the bulwarks of white society and rebounded, proving the point.

Sandra eventually cajoled the truth out of him. She was an eminently practical woman who ferociously protected her family, untroubled by notions of legality, or justice. She loved Joe and this was the first time she had seen her husband defeated. She knelt on the floor in front of his slumped seated figure and shook his hands from his face – the strong woman.

"You better snap out of this Joe, or I'll give you such a slap. I won't have you moping around with a face like fourpence," she joked to break the silence.

"How can I beat the system? It's been shitting on me from the day I was born. No-one sees past the skin." Joe bemoaned his plight.

"I do, and I don't see a quitter. That's not the man I married," Sandra soothed.

"It don't matter what I do, no way is that stuck-up white prick going to give the club or me a licence, never in a month of Sundays, he'll just keep on finding faults." Joe was completely dejected.

Sandra kept his hands in hers, "You're going about this cack-handed. Find someone who would be acceptable."

"That means white and of good character, how many of those do I..." Joe stopped mid-sentence, "Charlie. He's the right age, on the surface respectable – at least he's never been caught. Best of all I'd trust him with me life. Good idea but still not enough, it's the nigger club idea that's frightening the locals."

She nodded, "Okay it's a start. So how do you get a lever on this man?" Joe shook his head, "Can't think of anything I can offer him.""Everyone's got summat to hide Joe, specially people like that who seem to have the sun shining out their arses. Find out what it is." Sandra was slowly providing him with hope of another type.

Joe reflected on the truth of that statement, but ironically it was his own dark secret that provided the key he needed.

He started asking questions about Mr. Foster-Smythe. For several weeks nothing, then one evening he succumbed to desire and went in search of male company in the bar near the Hippodrome Theatre. The place was frequented by actors, and dancers, and was a meeting place for casual hook-ups, a secret kept close by those who risked exposure and prison in pursuit of their sexual orientation. Joe was well known, popular and in demand. Everyone was an outsider and it was a rare location in the city where being black carried no stigma.

Luckily he was sat in an alcove, and the pub was packed, when he saw Foster- Smythe walk in. The licensing justice forced his way through the crowd, ordered a drink and stood at the bar. Joe ensured that he was out of sight but watched keenly. He believed in no deity but he offered up a silent prayer that Foster-Smythe was not on licensing business. He whispered to the two men sat with him.

"There's a grey-haired man in a tweed jacket stood at the right hand end of the bar, don't make it obvious, but you ever seen him in here before?" Joe enquired.

They returned a few minutes later. They both knew him.

The Hole in The Wall officially opened on Friday 27 May 1966, a Bank Holiday weekend, with a concert of local black bands - many had never played live before. Joe's old group headlined, but Winston remained on the door, and Joe had realized that being the owner precluded performing, there was too much else to do. There had been no problem finding replacements though.

Joe had been nervous throughout that make or break day, but when he finally summoned up the courage to open the double doors he found a queue of several hundred strong outside. The crowd knew they were on public trial and there was excitement with order as they all filed beneath the wooden panel bearing the legend.

'Charles Eustace Docker - licensed to serve intoxicating liquor'.

Joe felt Sandra take his hand as they proudly watched the citizens of Handsworth experiencing their own venue for the first time. He had told Sandra that he had caught Foster-Smythe being unfaithful to his wife.

It was after all true. He had just omitted the detail that the photographs had featured notorious male-prostitute 'Bobby' giving the magistrate a 'blow-job' in an alleyway.

Joe Docker now owned a club, but after watching the first episode of Alf Garnett's 'Till Death Us Do Part' on TV, less than two weeks later, he feared that it would be some time never before the average white working-class man would be gracing him with their presence.

Chapter Twenty Seven: All You Need Is Love

(The Beatles)

1967

"That's a World Cup Willie if ever I saw one!" The young man looked up. The England mascot had been aimed at children and its creator would have blanched had he seen the situation. "Don't talk with your mouth full; I'm not paying you to crack jokes." Joe took hold of the man's head as he finished thrusting. Ever the outsider, even Joe had been touched by the euphoria sweeping the country following Geoff Hurst's decisive goal, and Nobby Stiles' gap-toothed jig. He had been out drinking and as usual, that had weakened his resolve not to indulge his favourite vice.

Anyway, why shouldn't he be happy? For once he seemed to be having some luck.

The Hole in The Wall was making money, and plenty of it was in cash. He had been able to employ a couple of his 'brothers' to run the market stalls allowing him to concentrate on the club - and Winston to oversee a fledgling business in security. Demand was growing for door-staff and large, intimidating black men fitted the bill.

The demand for live black-music at the Club was insatiable. An office had been created upstairs where Joe now spent most of his time finding, and booking acts, and keeping a tight grip on the finances. He missed the market, its smells, sights, and sounds, and the ready comradeship of the other stallholders who had accepted him as one of their own, but he had moved on, had time to think, and he saw opportunities to make more money everywhere he looked.

The name of the club had proved accurate; it was a doorway, and the jungle it led had been waiting for a beast like Joe. He had plans.

***

Quinn had plans too, and 1967 was going to be a big year for the Souls. He and Joey had just returned from California with an official Charter from the Angels. Another first. It was an honour, and a status to be jealously protected. The oxygen of publicity had made the Californian bikers infamous across the world, drawing condemnation and adoration in equal parts.

They were vile, rootless, criminal, frightening – fascinating, free, envied, with a hedonistic lifestyle that many secretly coveted. Monster bikes, the open road, easy- women, booze, drugs, parties, fame, they embodied the time, with the exception of the 'love is all you need' rubbish, spawning followers, imitators and those who saw a money-making opportunity.

Ironically, their anarchic and wild origins had been subsumed by a realization that they were being exploited. The result was a set of rules enforced by harsh discipline, a need to squash opposition, guard the image, its totems and regalia. They had lawyers now to enforce copyright, negotiate deals, and to keep them out of jail. They were a corporation, albeit different to anything on the planet to date bar the Mafioso - and the Black Souls were part of the franchise.

The Souls had evolved with the times. Hair was long, beards abounded, tattoos covered arms, backs and in some cases faces. Drug use was common and growing both within the group and in teenage culture. Rules of supply and demand applied to crime too, and the provision of the exploding array of illicit substances had overtaken, and was replacing, alcohol and cigarettes. The bikers were perfect facilitators. A closed group with savage punishments for transgressors, they were feared, mobile and could outrun and outfox any police interest.

The IRA hadn't liked it at first, but had abandoned any pretense at appalled Catholic values when they assessed the profit margins. They had connections everywhere and the network was easily adapted to move drugs along with guns, alcohol and cigarettes.

Everyone was awash with cash, some of which found its way to corrupt politicians, officials, police, lawyers, smoothing out any difficulties encountered.

Quinn didn't need any chemical euphoria. He had Jenny, Sean, power, status, and money - pretty much anything he wanted. Something inside him, that old survivor's voice, told him that drugs were bad news, a point proven by the change in his best friend.

Joey was no longer the nice young Italian with the ready smile. Quinn couldn't place exactly where the decline had begun. He had been alone when they first met him that day outside the café and the Black Souls had become a surrogate family, especially after his father died of a heart attack in 1964.

His mother had run Lombardi's for a while but her heart hadn't been in it and she eventually returned to her family in Turin. The Club had bought the café, kept the name and two of the women ran it.

Joey seemed to have a gap in his life that nothing could fill. There were plenty of women but none of them lasted long. These days he seemed to prefer using prostitutes for one-night stands. He indulged every vice, every experience offered by the life he had chosen but he still sought something elusive. Quinn had tried discussing it but Joey couldn't even put it into words, there was something missing, just out of sight.

Using drugs had been inevitable, dope at first, then amphetamine, lately LSD. Quinn kept a close eye on him, friend or not, he came second to the Club, but so far Joey seemed to be handling it.

Quinn had another problem on his mind. The Club was very successful and was now behind the café, the garage, several bars, one brothel, a promising protection racket, and a breakers-yard, on top of the commodities they were transporting, importing, transmuting, and selling. They had outgrown Worcestershire. The dynamics of the business needed bigger markets and one of the biggest lay on their doorstep.

They had friends in Birmingham amongst the Irish; otherwise it was alien territory, potentially enemy territory – Quinn arranged a meeting and picked Seamus and Joey to go with him.

The Mermaid in Sparkhill was Irish through and through. A

casual visitor's welcome was likely to be gauged by the contribution he made to 'The Cause' when the collecting tin appeared. The three bikers had arranged to meet a trusted intermediary who turned out to be not Irish but Scottish, albeit a staunch Catholic, as he made plain within minutes of meeting them.

He also rode a bike, a shiny new BSA that spoke of ready-cash. Ronald Fraser was thirty but looked fifty. Thinning sandy hair, missing teeth, ferret face and nicotine stained fingers. Wafts of halitosis accompanied his pronouncements, delivered in an accent so heavy that Quinn needed every sentence repeated. He didn't inspire confidence and before they left the Mermaid, after an introductory pint, Quinn had already decided that this Celtic warrior was not about to feature after tonight. Quinn was a master at preserving himself above all, and Fraser may as well have had the words 'bad risk' floating above his head in neon lights.

Fraser had set up a meet at another pub, which he assured them was 'biker friendly'. Quinn had quizzed him about any affiliations but the man seemed to be a loner whose lifestyle had deposited him into a role of underworld facilitation and ragged diplomacy, a charmless version of 'Ed the fixer'.

The New Inns sat on a road junction in Acocks Green, a blocky building possessing no dignifying features and a customer-base of veteran drinkers, underage kids getting tanked up before breaking some shop windows on the way home, and its very own group of bikers who regarded it as 'their pub'. The licensee had relinquished control to them years before, rationalizing his abrogation of duty by the custom they brought in and the security they provided. They kept order and until the night the three Souls walked in, that arrangement had worked just fine. Life was about to change.

There was a row of bikes outside and they parked, adding to the line. The three Black Souls were not wearing any colours for this trip so Quinn didn't anticipate problems; a biker pub seemed to be a good choice, as they would go unremarked.

The large lounge was packed with Friday night drinkers and smoke hung heavy in the air. No-one thought about passive smoking in those days, and if you didn't smoke you still stank of it as it got into your hair and clothes. It was just normal. Fraser looked around then nodded towards a table in the corner.

He introduced them to a man whose dark complexion and suntan spoke of warmer climes. He had jet black hair, a Mexican moustache, ostentatious gold watch, rings and bracelets, and two gold teeth which he flashed as he stood and offered a hand to the three visitors, "Welcome, I am Ahmet, but everyone calls me The Turk. Thank you Ronnie, would you fetch some drinks for our friends and then leave us to talk."

Fraser obeyed, and whilst they waited, exchanging pleasantries, Quinn scanned his surroundings with an expert eye. He quickly tagged the three men at the nearby table, clearly minders of the man sat opposite him. Probably tooled up, but if this Ahmet was the player he was supposed to be Quinn would have been disappointed if he had not brought protection with him.

He was watching Fraser at the bar when one of the bikers appeared through the crowd from the direction of a rear alcove hidden from his view. A tall, thin figure with shoulder length hair falling in generous curls to his shoulders, sporting a goatee beard and moustache. The man was wearing a biker leather with a cut-off over the top. An array of metal badges adorned the lapels – 'biker medals'. He leant against the bar talking to Fraser, and Quinn saw him nod towards them. The man was served before Fraser. As he turned away, a dimple glass in each hand, Quinn had clear sight of the rockers on his back bearing the Legend 'PAGAN PRIESTS BIRMINGHAM'.

Fraser returned with the drinks."Who was that at the bar and what did he want?" asked Quinn."He's the leader of the local bikers; he was asking who you were," Fraser replied. Small alarm bells began to ring in Quinn's head."And what did you tell him?" Quinn retained his composure."Just that you were some friends from out-of-town doing a spot of business," Fraser responded, carefully choosing his words – or so he thought.The man was a fool.

Quinn met Joey and Seamus' eyes, there was a problem and they knew it too. Tonight's business had to be dealt with first though. Fraser was dispatched to sit with the minders and the conversation began.

Ahmet was Turkish, and Turkish drug dealers had the fortunate geographic gift that their country was at a nexus of international transit routes for opium and hashish. Heroin was still not widely used in Britain but the hippy era was doing wonders for dope sales. Ahmet had some product and a market. Quinn had another source of the product, a transport network and needed a bigger market.

They could have been rivals, it could have meant blood being spilt, but instead they came to an understanding. Drug dealing was a simple business really. You got hold of more stuff, you moved it to the sales point, you expanded your market, and your profits grew. If there were rivals you did a deal with them, or took them out and took over.

They may have been from different countries but the international language of criminal profit was better than Esperanto. Ahmet was no fool. When Quinn suggested cutting out the middleman, indicating Fraser, he agreed.

The Turk joked, "Geri zekali – he's retarded" for the benefit of Quinn's amusement.

A further meeting was arranged, and then a disagreement was staged for the benefit of Fraser and any other watchers. Ahmet stormed out with his minders shouting "Siktir git. Cehenneme git. Orospu cocugu!!"

Quinn had never been cursed in Turkish and told to fuck off. He quite liked it.

Fraser returned to the table, "No good?" He was used to being paid on results and sensed failure.

Quinn shook his head, "Nothing doing. He didn't want to let us in, said there were already too many players in Birmingham."

Fraser didn't like the sound of this, "What you going to do about it?"

Quinn placed his hand on the man's shoulder, "I don't need a bloodbath; it would affect our other businesses. It's easier to look elsewhere; there are plenty of other towns around."

The Scotsman looked relieved, "Okay, sorry it didn't work out."

Quinn reassured Fraser, keen to see the back of him, "That's not your fault. Tell the others thanks for trying and that this is one where we step back. You can go now, we'll have another drink. It's alright in here."

Fraser took the opportunity to escape gratefully and scuttled out of the door. Seamus summed up the departing man, "Wanker.""Yes Seamus, and stupid. Not someone I want around when we're about to cut the Irish out of a deal." Quinn smiled thinly."It's risky," said Joey "We're putting a lot of faith in this Turk."Quinn made it clear in which direction they were going,

"Maybe, but I doubt it. He wants to make more money. He has his own tight set-up. It's in his interest to keep it between us. As we talked I saw how it could work. He's the smokescreen. We keep this one for us. The less we are tied up with those mad bastards in Ireland the better. It suited us in the early days but we need to grow our independence. The Black Souls need to be free." Quinn emptied his glass, "We've got a more pressing problem here don't we?"

The others nodded, "We can't allow it, makes us look weak, and anyway the rules are clear," said Joey.

"Time for a stomping?" The big man sounded keen.

"Maybe. I'll get another drink and see what happens." Quinn stood and collected the three empty pint mugs. The staged argument had drawn attention and a number of eyes monitored Quinn as he walked to the bar. He was fairly certain what was about to occur. He saw the barman's eyes look past him and the pints were put down a little too fast, causing the suds to slop onto the bar.

He turned, there were three of them, goatee-beard in the lead, "That piece of shit Fraser tells me you're from out-of-town, what you doing here?"

Quinn spoke quietly giving nothing away, "That's my business I think."

His principle aggressor retorted, "You wanna watch your mouth. This is our place and we say what goes on here." he turned, displaying the patches, "Know what this means?"

Quinn smiled, "Into a bit of black magic are you – orgies and the like?"

It was not the expected response, "You heard of Hells Angels boy? You should show some respect." The man was becoming more agitated.

Quinn nodded, "I heard. You got a charter says you can wear that rocker?"

'Goatee' was momentarily taken aback, "You better believe it. Now what the fuck,"

Quinn interrupted, "Cause if you ain't got a charter any real

Angel has to take those colours right off you, part of the law."

The man stared closer into Quinn's eyes trying to see whether there was any trace of fear, and said with less confidence for the watching audience, "No Angels other than us round here."

"You're wrong there," said Quinn as he head-butted goatee and burst from between the two bikers either side of him. He was out of the door with a good head start before they recovered. Quinn had assessed that the alcove containing the rest of the group was out of direct line of sight of the bar and had gambled on the 'red mist' provoking a chase before they realized what was going on.

The two Pagan Priests burst through the double doors and the Souls were waiting. Seamus and Joey had slipped out earlier, had their three bikes running, and had pushed the whole row of Pagan bikes over like dominoes. They had their Duplex chain-belts ready.

By the time goatee appeared his companions were down and getting a chain whipping. A Duplex belt not only looked good but functioned as both a whip, and an iron bar. Quinn grabbed the still-dazed biker and threw him face-first into the pub wall then smashed his boot down onto the back of a leg, forcing him to the floor. He took hold of the flowing hair.

"Beautiful curly locks," Quinn announced, as he wound his hand into them and pulled Goatee across the car park on his back. He produced the hammer.

"I'm called Thor on account of this," He smashed the lump down on an arm, the crack echoed and Goatee screamed.

He flipped the wounded Pagan over and ripped the cut-off from his back, "We'll be in touch. We are the Black Souls and we do have a charter from California. You got some thinking to do about wearing these and how much pain you want."

All that remained when the other Pagans finally came looking were three wounded men without colours, and a haze of exhaust smoke settling gently upon the tarmac.

**

Joe was in his office contemplating his next move, facing two scared-looking young men. He was oblivious of the fact that worlds that had been parallel were now converging, his crime-twin Patrick Quinn being driven ever closer by the economics of the business.

A year since Geoff Hurst and 'they think it's all over,' he was secure in his Handsworth fortress. Sure, there were other club owners in Birmingham, but none of them had the skin colour to compete in his market, and he in turn was happy to carve out his niche. There was enough money for everyone and the main-men in town were bright enough to agree a demarcation of interests that was working well, in fact they were complementary.

Joe had decided one club was enough and had diversified, always being careful to keep to his roots, where he had support from his black brothers and sisters.

He owned several pubs, a betting shop, and a used-car dealership that had a monopoly of sales locally. He charged fair prices, looked after the customers and in turn they would only buy off 'one of their own'. Lately he had begun to explore the market for sex, both written and real.

He had realized that there were a lot of white guys who wanted to sample something different, and had opened 'Second City Escort Agency', run by Sandra and populated exclusively by stunning black women who were much in demand. Sandra had proved to be a natural 'Madame' and had suggested the massage parlour that fronted the prostitution business.

The law had come sniffing around a couple of times but he had contacts now, and the interest petered away to nothing. His mind was not on prostitutes today though.

There was change coming, and Joe knew that he had to adapt. A new confidence, a pride in being black was in the air, and he had begun to see these 'Rastafari' appear. The sixties were a time of cults and a religion that encouraged the use of dope to broaden the mind was not the strangest. It was the dope that was presenting the problem, and opportunity, and Joe was wrestling internally as to how to proceed.

At heart he was a decent man. His standards and operating rules would not have found approval in a church or court but he tried to be fair and deal as he was dealt. His people, his community, trusted him, he looked after them, and in return they were loyal. So far his businesses had not conflicted this stance and those who had challenged, or tried to rip-him off, had been punished without ruffling the veneer of Joe Docker, successful black businessman.

But the world was changing and he had to keep up. The old Caribbean immigrants were fading out of the limelight and their children, aware of their rights - steeped in fashion and notions of freedom, were taking their place. And they wanted drugs, specifically dope.

He had kept away from the trade, didn't like it, but when Winston had found two dealers operating in the club, and the door staff were being approached constantly wherever they were working, it was time to recognize that the time had come to decide.

He had interrogated the two youngsters whilst Winston glowered at them. They tried to be nonchalant to begin with, but the casual production and placing of a gun on his desk brought Joe the desired effect.

He had nipped this particular bud just in time. They were effectively freelance, buying from an uncle who brought small but regular amounts in from Jamaica and sold some to cover his own use. They told of a few others using cafes, street corners, and bars to deal, but it was clearly small-time and disorganized.

Joe thought it through whilst they sat waiting for him to pronounce judgment. He couldn't stop it - that was clear. It wasn't just a Rasta thing. The hippies wanted all the hash they could get. It fuelled their lovey-dovey flower power culture. There was a power vacuum right now, but where there was money to be made there were always sharks circling, ready to take a piece of the action. Someone would appear, and they would become a challenge to Joe's position.

Joe came to a decision, "Right you two, here's how it's gonna go down."

It didn't take long. He was the man with the power and credibility. He had the muscle, a network of contacts and venues, a mini army of doormen and a ready supply route from the West Indies. He imposed organization and discipline, and another source of profit flowed.

***

A few miles away, Quinn was engaged in a war. It was impacting upon business but that wasn't the cause of it. The Black Souls had signed up twice, once to the Irish, and once to the Angels, a coin with two-sides, and the Souls balanced trickily upon its edge. They were the foundations upon which the Souls stood, but they also demanded their dues.

Quinn's attitude towards the two 'partners' could not have been more different. He had fallen into the IRA when he had nothing else. It could not be denied that it had literally been the making of him, and it had been bearable until that first meeting with 'The General'. That day had brought the crushing realisation that he had been caught in a net from which he could find no escape. Sure, he had built an independent business via the Madmen, but the only way out from 'The Cause' was in a coffin, along with his fellow bikers.

Only the original five founders of The Souls knew the truth about the Irish. They had decided many years ago to keep that secret close – too damaging to the reputation, loyalty, and philosophy upon which the Souls were based, the charismatic alternate lifestyle that drew in recruits and enabled their profitable criminality.

Recently he had become increasingly uneasy about some of

the packages being transported by his people. He knew the situation across the water was deteriorating and couldn't shake off the feeling that the bikers were being inexorably drawn into disaster. But that was a problem for another day.

His local war stemmed from the Angels. The rules were absolutely clear on the subject and were enforceable with extreme prejudice. The Pagan Priests had committed possibly the worst transgression bar betraying another Angel. Only full Hells Angel members of a club officially chartered by the original Chapter in California were allowed to wear the insignia on their backs. The colours were to be removed from imposters and renegade groups disbanded - or subsumed if their members were up to it.

In the weeks since that first clash Quinn had done some research via Ahmet, who was already proving to be a very useful contact. It seemed that The Pagan Priests had originated from a group of biker friends who met regularly at the New Inns. The colours had suddenly appeared about twelve months before and the group had declared themselves 'Hells Angels'. Quinn surmised that the recent notoriety of the brand in the media and especially that book by Hunter Thompson had been the spark.

The Turk reported that they were about twenty-strong and involved in some low-level criminality, but were mainly disposed to lording it around the local pubs, causing trouble, and indulging a visibly hedonistic lifestyle. Without challenge they had grown in confidence and Ahmet's view was that they needed sorting out before they attracted any more recruits.

They had already started asking questions of Ahmet and he

was expecting a clash of interests in the near future. Luckily the staged fall-out with Quinn had passed muster. The Turk described himself as a 'double-agent' trusted by the Priests but actually working with the Souls. He had seen too many James Bond films in Quinn's view.

The outfit that The Turk described had no proper organisation and the pub was its home. Goatee beard, real name Charlie Miller, was self-appointed leader. He was accepted it seemed because he had originated the idea, and the name, and had a protector with the unlikely name of Archie Shaw who preferred to be known as 'The Bear'. This giant had not been present on the night Quinn beat up Miller and was itching for revenge. He was described as a man-mountain, six foot six tall and about eighteen stone with a fearsome reputation.

Ahmet was uneasy, the Priests were growing fast in numbers, reputation and influence, and the charisma of the 'Hells Angels' was bestowing its attraction upon them.

An ultimatum had been sent and rejected. There was no negotiation allowed, the Black Souls were the real Angel's only representatives in England and they were responsible for enforcing Angel law. If they couldn't do so they proved themselves unworthy of their Charter.

The move into the Birmingham market courtesy of Ahmet had proceeded well enough. He provided product, sub-dealers, premises, contacts, and market penetration. The Souls also had their own product from the US and facilitated low-risk transport, dealing, enforcement, and scouting out new markets that The Turk could not penetrate.

No-one wanted to stop them and they could outride any cop. Supervision of sub-dealers came with a healthy dose of intimidation and enforcement. They operated without wearing colours, in twos and threes, looking to remain below the radar. The unlikely co-operation between Muslim and Angel was working like a dream.

The Pagan Priests were the only cloud in the sky. They frequented many of the key premises and they were nosy as hell. Out-of-town bikers suddenly appearing pinged their radar. It took only three weeks before two Prospect Souls got a good kicking by about ten Priests outside The Greet pub in Tyseley. They carried no colours to be taken, but both were chain-whipped and their bikes trashed. No words were needed.

Quinn had led a sortie in response. Intelligence from The Turk led to a group of Priests being ambushed at a house party in Sparkhill. Three Priests were hospitalised, and a female received a fractured skull from a young Prospect after she got in the way of a blow from a tyre lever. The house was trashed and panic-stricken party goers spilled out onto the street

The Bear and Quinn had briefly faced-off in the street outside, but Miller had assessed the odds and retreated, the big man following.

Yesterday, another Black Soul, 'Tramp' had been run off the road by a van minutes after leaving the Clubhouse. He now resided in a ward in Worcester with a broken leg. Even worse he had been washed.

Quinn was sat in his usual place at the head of the Black Souls Council table. There was unanimity that this was a war that must be won, but disagreement as to the means. After everyone had a chance to speak, some with raised voice and thumping of the table, he delivered his decision – almost a speech rallying the troops for the coming battle,

"We can't afford to lose, we can't afford to carry on like this either, it's bad for business and this tit-for-tat will kill both sides, the pigs must be loving it. It brings us to their attention, gives them excuses to hassle us in all sorts of ways. They can decide if it suits them to investigate, like they did when Terry got sent down for nobbling that girl at the party, or sit it out and watch us do their job for them and beat the crap out of each other. No, there has to be a once and for all meet that decides it. Let me tell you what I've thought of." He had their attention.

Once more messages crossed. The Priests were hurting more than the Souls and a number of their 'members' and 'hangers-on' were having second and third thoughts about what they had signed up for. Unbeknown to Quinn, Charlie Miller was becoming isolated and pressured to conciliate, and his position as unelected leader was preserved only by fear of his loyal, giant friend. They accepted the offer of talks.

Stourport-On-Severn was suggested and accepted as neutral ground. The town was a regular haunt of bikers from Birmingham on runs to spend sunny days parading in the parkland by the river and drinking in the pubs. The Priests were familiar and comfortable with it.

It was late August, a muggy, hazy evening, when the Priests rolled onto the riverside car park. A three-line-whip had resulted in seventeen bikers, and a number of females, in the convoy of bikes, and one battered Transit van that still bore the dent from Tramp's bike.

The grass banks and walks were busy with couples walking, there were groups sat around enjoying picnics, and there were already a number of bikes present so the arrival of the group didn't occasion any more reaction than a subtle movement away that left an empty area near to where they milled around their metal steeds.

The Souls arrived at the appointed time. Neither gang wore colours by agreement. Why make the cop's job any easier?

Details had been agreed beforehand. Quinn and Seamus walked forward and met Miller and The Bear between the ranks. A historian would have remarked that similar scenarios had been played out before battle numerous times before.

Miller began to speak but Quinn cut him off, "You shut the fuck up. You're a piece of shit not worthy to be called President of a Chapter. I could take you apart in two minutes. No, you take a few steps back unless you want to fight me in front of everyone, and I'll make you crawl."

The Priest's President looked into Quinn's eyes and saw no quarter. Quinn knew his type, and had expected Miller's sideways look towards the hulking man beside him. The Bear was actually growling. Quinn addressed him, "Ah yes, and the power behind the throne. You want to fight me don't you, and this coward will let you, like he always does. You must be thick as pig-shit but they're all terrified of you so I reckon if I beat you in front of them that's it."

The Bear grinned and pushed Miller backwards. The Pagan's President stumbled and fell onto his backside and a ripple of laughter arose from both groups. Quinn knew that Miller was finished from that moment, whatever happened next.

The two protagonists circled each other and the watching Priests and Souls fell silent, united in fascination.

The big man suddenly charged. Quinn silently thanked Hugh for the weeks of training and The Bear found himself on the floor. Quinn delivered a kick to the head and danced away. The process repeated itself until The Bear was blowing heavily, bruised, bleeding and raging. The watching Priests couldn't help but begin to root for the smaller man. Most of them had felt the power of the Bear's fists and they were enjoying seeing him being played like a bull by a matador.

The bull blew blood down his nose, "I'll break you in two when I get hold of you, you little fuck."

Quinn continued to circle, "You haven't even got close yet, and you won't you big wanker."

Quinn watched the eyes and saw the red mist descending. The Bear charged blindly, head down. Quinn dropped the hammer from his sleeve and felled his assailant. The giant dropped like stone.

Quinn marched towards Miller, "Your turn."

Miller ran. Quinn caught him as he tried to get onto his bike, grabbing a handful of the luxuriant curls for a second time, dragging the man backwards and hurling him to the ground in front of his Chapter members.

Quinn nodded towards the watching Priests, "Right, prove you're worthy to lead them. Get up and fight."

Miller stayed down. Quinn booted him between the legs. He put his boot on the man's head and turned to the audience, none of whom had moved.

Quinn barked, "Time for you all to decide. This is how it's going to be. The Pagan Priests can continue under a new President but you become affiliated to the Black Souls. We are chartered by the California Angels so that gives you the right to wear the colours. The Soul's Council rules but your new President gets a seat on it."

A stocky man with a full-beard stepped forward, "And I suppose one of you will be The President so why the pretence at giving us a say?"

Quinn held up a hand, "Not necessarily. Let me finish." He lifted his boot. "Get up Miller, or I'll break something for good measure." The man complied.

Quinn held out a hand, "Colours – now!"They were handed over meekly, completing the public humiliation.Quinn raised his voice so all could hear, "Right, Miller, you can go. I don't care what you do so long as you don't wear patches or get in my way ever again. You might consider changing your postcode but that's up to you. As for the rest of you, decide now. Go with him and leave your patches behind, same deal. Stay and you are signing up to be Prospects for the Black Souls. If you don't want to do that, don't think you are up to it - this is your chance to leave without any problems."

The stocky man spoke again, "I'll stay but you still haven't answered the question."

Quinn gave Miller a helpful push towards his machine and walked up to the man who held his ground. He read the name badge on his cut-off, 'Filthy Phil', "at least someone else has got the balls to stand up for your Club. You might just make the draw. Watch and decide."

Quinn turned and walked back to where The Bear lay on the ground. The big man was fully conscious and had been watching the proceedings, "You cheated using that." He indicated the hammer.

Quinn smiled, "Firstly we never said anything about fighting fair; secondly I'd prefer to say I speeded up the inevitable conclusion. We could have spent another fifteen minutes buggering about till the cops arrived."

The Bear tried to recover some self-respect, "Not sure I agree, I might have caught you in the end."

"Maybe another time. What do you think of your mate now, worth fighting for?" Quinn nodded towards the departing Miller.

The Bear responded, "I wasn't fighting for him; he was President that's all."

Quinn held out Miller's cut-off with its President patch "That's why this is yours if you want it. Take it and you don't have to Prospect for us, plus you get a seat at the table. You know your people - know who might make it and who won't. The war ends, you run the Priests, we work together. There is plenty of business to go round. What do you say?"

Chapter Twenty Eight: 'The Mighty Quinn'

(Manfred Mann)

1968

It was the drugs that brought them face-to-face for the first time. Joe, the reluctant dealer, had kept to his own strict rules. He kept the trade tight, safely confined to the Afro-Caribbean world where he was respected and strong. He knew the cops couldn't get inside - there were no black faces in blue.

Joe had carefully created a secret business structure to facilitate importation and supply. He could plausibly distance himself from it, claim ignorance if the wheel came off. There were a number of individuals who were willing to take the rap for him in return for money, protection and security for their families. They all knew that they could not achieve the same rewards in any other way. In 1968 legitimate avenues of enrichment were closed to those with a black face. Their parents had been brought over to drive buses, clean, labour in factories, not compete with the white upwardly mobile.

Winston was the lynchpin of Joe's chosen few. The security business was the core of the distribution network, using door-staff at pubs and clubs in concert with street dealers. If a problem with the law arose Winston would claim that Joe knew nothing about the drugs.

***

It was in the city-centre where the problems began. Joe had cultivated good relations with those of a similar ilk in town. They respected each other's territories, agreed business demarcations and helped each other out. They knew that Joe had Handsworth and the blacks sewn up; he in turn had no aspirations amongst the white businessmen.

They had regular meetings and Joe had earned their respect through his fairness and ruthlessness. All of them agreed that profit came from stability and working together to stop the law from getting a foot in any door.

It had worked out well with the drugs too. Joe had conceded to Winston's urgings to increase market size by allowing the creation of a white sub-dealer network in city-centre venues where they had door staff placed. It was a franchising operation servicing a large and lucrative market. A percentage was paid to Joe's business colleagues in town, the owners. They turned a blind-eye and had no expenses or management problems - to them it was pure profit, no risk.

The whole franchise operation was kept entirely separate from the black dealer structure - and Joe, by the simple expedient of handsomely paying a number of white 'middle-managers'. To any observer or investigator these individuals would appear to be the main-men. Any temptation on their part to take on that role in reality had been dealt with by making examples of a couple of chancers. It was a fool who would upset both black and white concerns at once.

Organised crime had effortlessly leapt racial boundaries and all was calm. Greed outweighed philosophy or social boundaries. The norm was what they decided it would be.

On a non-descript Saturday evening in early 1968 the phone rang in the office of Second Security Services, a converted shop on Soho Road. A message was relayed to Winston. There was a problem at a pub in town and the doormen needed to know how to handle it.

Winston gave it minimal thought and, slightly puzzled that such an issue had required his attention, made the obvious decision.

As a result, two Pagan Priests found themselves ejected from the premises by four doormen. There was a brief scuffle, that ended all-square, and then the doormen returned to the doorway. The two parties eyed each other for a tense moment then the two bikers walked away. Just another minor incident in the life of a bouncer, Winston had no further calls and gave it no further thought.

Two nights later eight bikers appeared. A quiet Monday, there were only two doormen on duty. Winston didn't get a call this time. The first he heard was when the two bouncers turned up at The Hole in The Wall, beaten and ejected from the door.

He listened as they explained, and realised that he had misjudged the situation. He dismissed them, then found Joe in his usual position, on a stool at the end of the main bar, holding court.

Joe sensed trouble straight away; Winston was not the type to run to the boss with every issue. They went to Joe's office.

"We got a problem. I made a bad call Saturday night and it's come back to bite tonight. I'm not sure if it's a big problem or not, but I don't like the feel of it, could damage our - your standing if we don't sort it." Winston explained what the doormen had told him.

There was no dress code at the pub and the two bikers had got inside without a problem. The franchised dealer, a weedy kid used to getting back-up from the doormen, had been operating in his usual alcove by the toilets. He suddenly found his personal space invaded by two intimidating figures making it abundantly clear that he should vacate his seat and leave his gear behind. No hero, he bolted for the door.

The four bouncers had been confident of handling the two bikers but were aware of the reputation of bike gangs and their avowed right-wing tendencies. These two hadn't looked like the usual jumped-up kids strutting about in leathers, they were older, meaner looking, and seemed unlikely to back down in a confrontation with black men. They were also the first challenge to the neat business model Joe had set up and appeared completely confident in taking over someone else's patch.

Unfortunately the details of the message hadn't reached Winston so he had not understood the nuances of the situation.

Joe made a call, asked some questions. He didn't like the answers.

Across the city Quinn was ensconced with Ahmet, getting answers he didn't like either.

The Turk was not happy, "This isn't the backwoods of Worcestershire. These are serious people who won't frighten, or back down. I thought I'd marked out the areas to deal in - your two went off-script going into that place. Why didn't you speak before sending an army in to sort it out, you've declared war and you don't even know who you're fighting?"

Quinn shrugged. He had faced down, or overcome every challenge bar 'The General', and he would solve that particular problem one day too. He was frightened of no-one, no reputation. The Black Souls brooked no opposition and he had never lost.

Quinn tried to placate Ahmet but only up to a point, "They had some gear left and went in to the pub to suss it out. Some punk was selling so they took over. The bouncers had a go, and you know that we never let an attack on one of us go unanswered. I don't need to ask your permission."

Ahmet chose his words, "Never said you did. We're partners and business is good. Part of that success is my knowledge of this city and its dirty underside. I could have advised you, nipped this in the bud, but now we have a bad situation."

Quinn was puzzled, "What? Just because we stomped a couple of jumped-up nigger doormen?"

Ahmet winced inwardly but ignored the racist overtones. Most of the biker's Swastika wearing, and Nazi posturing, was done to upset normal citizens rather than for political reasons but it was true that there were no non-white Angels and some of them had very extreme views. He put up with it because the business needed him too, but he knew that the current situation could be much worse if it sparked a race-war.

He went on, "If you'd asked first I could have told you that those doormen work for an outfit that's got fingers in a lot of pies, and an understanding with some very influential people. Those people in turn got an understanding with my people, everything was calm and everyone was happy. You've just lobbed a brick into a nice calm pond. You stamped on their toes. You've insulted them, challenged them, and worst of all threatened their business. They won't accept that."

Quinn sneered, "I've met big men before. They lost."

Ahmet insisted, "Allah belani versin -This is their territory. We don't need this." He did not enlighten Quinn that he had just requested that God damn him. Quinn shook his head, "You can leave that Turkish shit out when you're talking to me. If we beat them we can expand into the city centre."

Ahmet made a last attempt, "Pat, Pat, just walk away from this one. I'll get a message to them, say it was a mistake."

"The Black Souls don't walk away from anything." Quinn leaned back in his chair, "You'd better tell me what you know." It wasn't a request more of an instruction but as they concluded their business and Quinn left, Ahmet could not resist muttering under his breath, 'Allah bizi senin gazabindan korusun.'

Whether God would in fact protect him from Quinn's intentions remained to be seen but the answer was not long in coming.

***

Two weeks later, and the biker President was back with Ahmet and seething. He had been outflanked and he wanted to punch someone. The bikers had found the city-centre closed to them.

The doors of the pub where the original confrontation had taken place had remained implacably closed for 'refurbishment' ever since. Quinn knew that this was bollocks but couldn't argue with a door.

Attempts to enter two other premises led to inconclusive skirmishes. Suddenly the cops began taking an interest in bikers in town. Stopping them, hassling them, and making life difficult. Someone was pulling some strings.

Quinn decided to go for the throat. It had worked before. He knew the name Joe Docker now. It sounded familiar but the memory of Charlie Docker had faded and he never made the connection. The offices of Second City Security were petrol bombed as a warning shot. It didn't work.

Two nights later the house in Sparkhill used by the Priests as a base got the same treatment. It was payback with interest though – the brothel in Worcester got the same treatment. The Clubhouse had to be put into lock-down with twenty-four-hour guards. The Black Souls were on the back foot.

For the first time since his painful lessons from 'Hugh', Quinn lost control and let the volcano of anger inside him erupt.

Saturday night. One-thirty in the morning. The Hole in The Wall was heaving. The phalanx of bikers rumbled into Handsworth wearing full colours. They drew up in a line opposite the entrance. Quinn, Joey and Seamus slowly crossed the road as Winston and a group of followers emerged from the door barring the way.

Winston barked, "You ain't welcome here boy. Take your

filthy friends and fuck off."

"I want Docker out here now." Quinn demanded. Winston laughed, "You're in no position to make demands.""Oh but I am." Quinn indicated the line of bikers opposite "We'll walk right over you. How many you got here, ten, twenty fighters? All mine fight and they fight hard. Will your punters help out? I doubt it. No - you get me Docker right now."

A voice interjected, "It's okay Winston." The line parted and Joe emerged. "I'm Joe Docker."

They stood assessing each other. Quinn saw a tall, well-built, black man, immaculately dressed in suit and tie. He noticed that the hair was unusually straight for a black man, and flecked with grey.

Joe had done his research. He knew who really backed Quinn, knew the Black Soul's track record of fear and intimidation - backed up by extreme violence. He knew that he was dealing with no ordinary greaser frontman. He knew danger, that this had to be handled just right.

Their eyes locked. Neither looked away, neither saw fear.

Joe made the first move, "What do you have to say to me that requires this ridiculous display Quinn?"

Quinn stormed, "I'm telling you to back off. You can keep this shithole part of town but we take the doors in town and the trade that goes with them."

Joe struck a thoughtful pose, "And your bargaining chip is

what? A bunch of hairballs in fancy dress? No - you listen to me. You're out your depth. You got no contacts other than the Turk and he knows what's good for him. You got no favours to call in, no basis for business. Under those leathers and pretty badges I think you're an intelligent man, a businessman like me. You can't be a fool to have come so far."

Quinn pushed forward until their faces were inches apart. He was not exercising his usual control and it showed, "I got me and I'll sort this man-to-man, here and now, if you got the balls."

Joe threw back his head and guffawed, "You see! You're talking a load of tripe. You don't understand the situation. This is my patch. You bring your disgusting racist playmates, covered in Swastikas, into our part of town and threaten me in front of all my brothers and sisters. You think they'll run away from you? Take a look around and tell me why I would wanna go rolling about on the pavement with you?"

Joe took a step back without breaking eye contact. Quinn noted the change of stance, the balance, recognised a boxer's stance. The man was ready to fight if necessary.

Quinn had been fixated on Docker, waiting and watching for an indication of an attack that hadn't come. A worm of doubt entered his mind and began to gnaw away at his confidence. His surroundings began to register and he too took a wary step backwards.

There were a lot more people on the street now, all of them black, and none looking at all cowed by the bikers. Joe and Seamus looked uneasy.

Winston was by Docker's side now, and Quinn found himself looking at the wrong end of two dark tunnels as Winston displayed pure hatred, "I'm just itching to blow your white balls back across the road you honky fuck."

"Now, now Winston, not so hasty," said Joe. "Mr. Quinn is thinking, I can see the cogs turning."

More people were spilling from the club, others appearing from side streets and a nearby pub.

Joe spoke again, gesturing to encompass the crowd and made his speech, another rallying cry – the one thing that the two men had in common, the ability to lead and for others to follow.

"These are my people. We've been through hard times together you see. No- one understands persecution and injustice like a black man in a white country. I look after them and they look after me. This is what you don't understand. You can't win against a people united. You can't come here without me knowing. You can't beat all of us. We see you white boy, we see you as soon as you come into our neighbourhood with your racist friends. There's no hiding place for you and we'll crush you. My friends in the city will help. They don't want you in their pubs and clubs, they're happy with the current arrangements. I've discussed matters with tem. The deal we offer is this...."

Quinn began to move forward again but Joey caught his arm, "Let's listen, it can't do any harm." Joey was taking a big risk, but as Quinn's closest friend he was the one most likely to be listened to.

Joe was now enjoying himself, "Thank you, wise advice. Ah yes, Vice President Lombardi, how is the café going?" Joey made no reply.

Quinn was silent but seething – but now with his opponent and his right-hand man.

Joe continued, "Where was I? The deal, yes very generous in the circumstances I think. You carry on with the Turk as before. You carry on with your Irish friends as before. You get no problems from us. The police interest disappears. Your reputation is intact. As far as everyone knows or cares we've dealt as equals.

In return you keep out of the city, out of Handsworth and out of my businesses. No more attacks from either side. We call what happened a misunderstanding and life goes on. If you say no, if we fight here and now, Winston will blow a hole in you. Your people are outnumbered and outgunned. When the police arrive I assure you that the conclusion will be that you were the aggressors, after all you've travelled here to provoke a confrontation. The police will decide to close you down. They'll make life so difficult for you, with our help of course, that your allies will find you too hot to continue trading with you. Your story will end. Your call '*Mister*' Quinn."

All around them continued the hubbub of the crowd, the traffic, and loud soul music leaking out of the double doors. Yet in their world of confrontation there was silence. All eyes were drawn to Quinn. His anger was palpable, the effort to contain it obvious, but as they waited the heat in him seemed to evaporate and the eyes became icy.

Quinn had been here before. On someone else's territory, playing by someone else's rules in a different game. His mind returned to that day so long ago sat across the table from 'The General'. He had been willing to commit murder, sign up with a real-life devil in order to achieve his ends. He had used that start to his advantage though. He could do it again.

Quinn replied flatly, "I agree."

He turned and walked across to the bikes without once turning around. Only Joey and Seamus heard him vow, "I promise I'll kill both of those bastards when the time is right."

Joe returned to his office. Winston followed once he had assured himself that the Black Souls had left and no tricks were to be played. Joe was pouring a scotch. He gave the glass to Winston and filled a second then took a large mouthful and said, "I bloody need this."

Winston was still pumped up with adrenalin. "Yeah plenty to celebrate, nice job." He raised his glass in salute.

Joe did not respond in kind, "Celebrate? No just relief. I had one chance and pulled it off. Just about convinced him to walk away but it was close. Not a man I would like to cross too often and a man with the most dangerous sponsors, especially in this city. We were so close to ruin there I could taste it. A war with the bikers and Irish would be disastrous. No, Winston, Quinn has killed and is quite capable of killing again.

There is something about a man who as taken another life, a mark upon him. He won't forgive or forget and that moment of defeat will gnaw away at him. I fear there will be blood spilt because of this."

Chapter Twenty Nine: 'With A Little Help From My Friends'

(Joe Cocker)

1968

Andreas Markou was a short stocky guy, but what he lacked in height he made up for in courage, and the ability to charm women into bed. His long-suffering wife had given up trying to change his behaviour and concentrated all of her efforts on bringing up their son and daughter. They would have the best that money could buy in terms of education, and she would stand next to her errant husband as the dutiful wife when weddings, christenings and funerals dictated it. Appearances were everything and Eleni knew that her first duty was to her family. Even the threat of routine domestic violence did not detract her from that - after all Andreas was always careful not to mark her face.

The Markou family left Cyprus in 1960 after the Island was granted independence from Great Britain. His left-wing views were not welcomed in some quarters and the day that a bomb went off underneath his beloved 1958 Morris Minor car, outside his home, signalled that it was time to leave.

He would now have to monitor the success of his beloved football club Omonia FC from a distance; their following was so large that they became known as the 'Chinese'. Most Cypriots also followed a UK team so the positive at least for Andreas was that he would be able in future to watch the progress of Manchester United more closely.

The Markou family made their home in Birmingham, taking with them nothing more than the contents of two suitcases, which included a .38 revolver and twelve rounds of ammunition that had been 'liberated' from the home of an auxiliary Turkish Cypriot police officer in Nicosia, during the EOKA campaign, and passed on to him for safekeeping.

Above all else, Andreas was a grafter, and eight years later had moved his 'Fish and Chip' business from the sleepy outer suburbs of Birmingham to the outskirts of the city-centre itself, on the main road out towards Handsworth where there was lots of passing foot-trade on the way home from the pubs and clubs. There was one thing that English people loved as much as eating fish and chaps, and that was a kebab, and the black punters were no exception.

Six days a week Andreas laboured surrounded by fat-fryers and the constant 'hub-bub' of customers, many of whom were that drunk from a good night out that they could hardly speak let alone eat. Amongst them would be his prey, young impressionable girls who fell for his 'special prices,' his broad smile, and his tactile approach. Some were regulars but most he saw only once, however he was a predator and if there was a chance to take one up to his room at the back of the shop, for a short break he took it - even better if there were two.

Sunday afternoons were a different issue. This was his day for playing cards in the back room with fellow Cypriots who, in their usual manner, would exchange loud memories of home with copious cups of 'sketos,' black coffee, ice-cold Zivania straight from the freezer box, and the skills of playing Pilotta to keep them occupied. A trick-taking thirty-two card game, normally with four players, this was not a game for the faint-hearted, and large sums of money could be won, and lost, as friends became opponents.

This was a man's world and there were no women in sight, but after a good session they often found time to visit 'Poutanes,' local prostitutes in the red-light district in Balsall Heath, before returning home to be served their evening meal by their loyal wives.

***

As Winston entered the Fish and Chip shop Andreas knew instinctively that he was facing a challenge. He was on his own at the time preparing things for the midday rush of office workers. No courtesies were extended. Winston simply announced, "I work for Joe Docker. We look after things round here and we make sure that there is no trouble for you. To do that you need to meet our expenses and we expect to receive twenty five pounds per week from you every Monday."

Andreas stared back from the opposite side of the counter, "I am Andreas Markou and I work for no-one. Tell your boss to go fuck himself. I'm not paying."

Winston reached behind his waistband and produced a short cosh that he displayed for effect, "You might wanna change your mind. It would be a shame to see such a nice place get messed up." He leant over the counter and stared into the face of the man opposite.

Without warning Andreas used all of the strength in his short, but muscle- bound arms, to pull the hot fat-fryer from its metal casing and threw the boiling contents into the face of his tormentor.

Winston Livingstone lurched backwards screaming as he clutched his already peeling face. At the same time Andreas jumped over the counter and propelled him through the front door and into the street, before locking the door and placing the closed sign on. He would not be selling fish and chips today.

Joe visited Winston in the Accident Hospital and got the gist of what had happened as he mumbled through swathes of facial bandages. He would not be winning any beauty competitions in future.

Three days later, at 3am in the morning, three figures crouched at the back door of the Fish Shop before forcing it open silently with a jemmy. Swiftly they moved from the back room to the kitchen area. The contents of a Jerry Can full of petrol was spread along the floor and a single match did the rest as they left. At the same time an envelope was pushed through the front letterbox at the home of the Markou family in Erdington.

Andreas found the letter himself after being disturbed by the phone call from the police informing him of the fire. The note inside simply read, *'Savvikis and Maria next – everyone pays one way or the other'* He folded it carefully before placing it in his pocket and looked for his phone book. He rang a number in Larnaca.

They say that 'there are no free meals in Cyprus' and Andreas had a few meals that were owed to him. Within one week a good friend had arrived. This was a man who was unfamiliar with the art of making fish and chips, but was well versed in the skill of making bombs, learnt from his days in EOKA fighting the British.

Costas had no love of the British and even less for black ones. He had been involved in the first attacks on the British establishment in Cyprus on the 1 April 1955 and still believed strongly in the concept of Enosis and unity with Greece.

Forty-eight hours later a bomb placed in the doorway of The Hole in the Wall exploded at 6am. It was deliberately designed to cause damage at a time when the club would be closed although a passing postal worker finishing a night shift had a close shave when passing, blown off his bike and across the carriageway. Luckily the road was empty.

At the same time an envelope was pushed through the home that Joe shared with Sandra and Hope. The ever-alert Joe heard the clink of the letterbox and went downstairs to investigate, gripping a baseball bat in one hand. He read the single sheet of paper the envelope contained, *'Next time it will be Hope. There will be no end until there is an end.'* A phone number completed the message.

Business had been good for Joe since the face-off with the bikers. That deal had been kept because no follower would dare cross his iron-willed leader. Joe had earned respect and further business from his partners. They liked a man who could sort out problems without unnecessary bloodshed and the unwelcome attention it drew. As he read the note Joe thought of that night outside the club and the tightrope he had successfully walked.

***

Joe met Andreas on the canal towpath in Gas Street Canal Basin.

As agreed they met alone – there was no mutual fear between them and this was after all just business.

It wasn't in either man's character to lose face but the conversation confirmed that neither of them was going to win. If Joe murdered Andreas then his family in Cyprus would feel obliged to search for, and kill his killer. Popular opinion had it that some of the people of Larnaca came from generations of gypsies, 'Gyftos', and that they would pursue a vendetta whatever the costs. Likewise if Andreas murdered Joe he would find himself permanently looking over his shoulder as the black community in Birmingham sought revenge for one of their own.

A truce was called – one single handshake and they parted with Andreas muttering, 'bastartomavro,' under his breath as he walked off to rebuild his business. 'Opios anakatonete me ta pittoura ton tron e kotes,' he reflected, – 'who is part of the wheat will get eaten by the chickens'.

Manchester United had won the European Cup so it wasn't all bad news.

Unfortunately for Winston he would not so easily be able to rebuild his face, but in the great scheme of things he was a negotiable asset, and was well rewarded for his loyalty. The scars actually added to his fearsome appearance, and street credibility, so he was eventually able to see them as a badge of honour.

Costas went home with one debt settled and with the black, 'mavro,' 'son of the bitch,' – 'gie tis poutanas,' sorted out for the time being. He still had work to do in Cyprus.

Little did he know that six years later following the invasion of northern Cyprus by the Turkish military in 1974 he too would make his home in Birmingham.

Chapter Thirty: 'Street Fighting Man'

(The Rolling Stones)

1968

Joe habitually took himself off for a walk along the canal towpaths just off Broad Street where he now had a satellite office managing the bookings for his club and other venues. It was also very convenient for Joes more nocturnal activities. The artistes and bands seemed more comfortable in the city centre than Handsworth. The time spent walking gave him the peace and solitude that he often craved.

Any outside observer would think that he had forged himself a better life since his return from the Army. He had a beautiful and loyal wife, business was good, and his daughter Hope loved him unconditionally.

Both Sandra and Joe protected her fiercely. Even whilst pregnant with Hope, Sandra had withstood the barbed comments from the more ignorant in society. It would take more than misplaced humour that she was, 'carrying a chocolate bun in the oven,' to rattle her.

Outwardly, Joe was confident and self-assured but beneath the surface he suffered in silence.

He suffered because of his relationship with his brother, the fact that he was a black man living in a white man's world, his sexuality, and the fact that by the age of twenty-five-years he had already committed murder.

Strangely he thought less about the murder, which had been committed to some extent as an act of revenge, but nevertheless he had crossed a line that few cross and he took no pleasure from it. That night outside the club, Quinn had seen it, and in turn Joe had instantly recognized that the biker President had traversed that boundary too, although Joe suspected with less trouble to his conscience.

Joe had also been permanently scarred by events in Cyprus, and the experience of being a black man, with scarcely suppressed gay tendencies, married to a white woman, did nothing to simplify his agonizing.

The thing that he thought about every day though, felt in his heart, was the loss of his brother. As a twin he had always felt the closeness that Rob apparently did not feel, and it hurt him to have no contact. He was desperate on occasions to feel normal, and to be able to share his thoughts with the one who had followed him from his mother's womb, but he felt rejected and alone. For a man who was afraid of no- one, he felt quite vulnerable.

There was a nip in the early-evening air but Joe didn't mind as he hunched up into his jacket. He had potential acts to see, bookings to make in the afternoon, but this was good thinking time and he wanted to make the most of it. As he rounded a corner his thinking time came to a halt.

Underneath one of the bridges three white men had a young

black female cornered. She clutched her handbag in front of her chest, her face frozen with fear as they jostled her, just feet away from the filthy water.

"Leave me alone you scum," she screamed as one of them tugged at the straps of the bag.

Joe had seconds to react and decided that with the odds of three to one, introductions would not be required and 'Queensbury Rules' would not be observed.

He launched himself at the back of the one closest to him, spun him round and hurled him unceremoniously into the canal.

Before his head had even disappeared beneath the surface Joe turned towards a second attacker and almost lifted him from the ground with an uppercut, followed by a jab to the face. The sound of bone crunching confirmed a successful delivery and the man was left with just a thin piece of gristle sticking out from above his lip where it had previously been connected to his nose. He screamed in agony as the blood pumped down his chin and onto his chest. For good measure Joe kneed him in the groin and he went down and stayed down.

As the first tormentor tried to drag himself towards the opposite bank of the canal, Joe confronted the third man, who by now had backed away from his victim but had decided on fight rather than flight. On his right hand he wore a brass 'knuckle-duster'. Designed to preserve a punch's force by directing it towards a harder and smaller contact area, a blow resulted in increased tissue disruption, and more likelihood of bone fracture on impact. A leftover gift from his father's service in World War II, this man felt powerful when he wore it.

"Come on you black cunt – let's be having you then," he beckoned Joe towards him.

Joe took the measure of the man. He was big, but too many pints had given him a flabby belly, and whilst his bald head made him look more like a football hooligan, Joe saw no threat.

Reaching with his right hand towards the back of his trouser waistband Joe drew a small pistol, and clasping it with both hands, pointed it square on at the man standing just ten feet away from him.

"Your move white boy," he said calmly.

"Don't. Don't," the failed-robber screamed throwing his hands up in the air and backing away.

"What's the matter you little prick – has your bottle gone? Leave that knuckle- duster on the ground and take this piece of shit with you – now!" Joe said, indicating to the man on the floor.

As his attacker bent down to pick his friend up, Joe kicked him hard up the backside and sent him sprawling, just to complete his humiliation, before kicking the knuckle-duster into the canal. He grabbed the wrist of the frightened girl and headed off briskly in the opposite direction.

After putting some distance between them Joe stopped and spoke quietly in reassuring tones before finding a taxi and paying for the girl to get home.

"Just remember bab – none of this happened and no police please," he whispered as she got inside the cab, still in shock, but happy to be safe. Joe didn't know who she was, but she in fact frequented the club, and her account of the incident swept through the 'street telegraph,' adding to Joe's legend and confirming his status within the community.

***

In 1968, the year of Enoch Powell's 'River of Blood' speech at the Midland Hotel in Birmingham, Rob Docker was appointed as a detective constable at the age of twenty- five. He was doing well for himself but the nature of the beast was that Rob was a restless spirit, and always wanted more in the way of success. He was already the archetypal 'bent copper' who got good results. He justified his own actions by virtue of the fact that in his own mind he had never fitted anyone up who hadn't deserved it.

When the phone call came in asking for him personally it was not a surprise. He was by now a commodity with some value to those that needed the sort of help that the police could provide, often unofficially. One of the club owners in the city- centre needed his help and Docker arranged to meet him later that evening at his premises – on his own.

They duly met and over a whisky the story was related. It was a simple and straightforward one but serious. One of his door staff had taken advantage of a drunken customer and in the process of trying to help her he had taken liberties. To put it in more technical legal terms he had taken her into one of the back rooms at the club and violently raped her.

She had made a complaint to the police and now the club owner wanted it to go away – it was not good for business and the doorman was a relative. His job was to protect his staff from the wild allegations of some 'young scrubber,' who was obviously asking for it. It had been just some 'slap and tickle' with a bit of skirt who had been flashing her knickers, as far as he was concerned.

Docker gave it some thought and, despite the risks, decided on a plan of action that would result in a win-win - for Rob Docker, and for Rob Docker. It would cost the club owner £1,000. There were expenses to be paid and it would take time to obtain a retraction from the complainant.

Docker made contact with the officer in the case, who was a good friend, and trusted colleague, a man on the same team - who was also on the take. They came to an 'arrangement,' and Rob Docker adopted the case on the basis that his colleague was struggling with a high workload. This gave him access to the victim whom he met on several occasions but always on his own.

She trusted him, after all he was a police officer, and she wanted to be co- operative. Living on her own, her family knew nothing about the allegations and, as Rob Docker began to groom her, he gently started to prey on this aspect of the case.

As part of the legal process, Docker explained how she would be called a liar in court, and how the doorman would undoubtedly say that she had willingly had sex, in fact perhaps even encouraged him, a slapper who just wanted a shag. Her sexual history would be questioned in open court, and of course the media would be present to report the facts in the press and on television.

As Docker carefully repeated each scenario the victim became more and more distressed and unsure, as was the intention. She reached out to Docker for a solution to her dilemma – there was no-one else to turn to.

Rob Docker had the answer and he delivered it with two simple messages "I could take a statement from you saying that you no longer wish to make a complaint and that under no circumstances will you go to court to give evidence. This'll stop the court case and your reputation will be protected. On the other hand, I have the means to protect you in the future, and to make sure that this man pays. I'm in your hands, you must do what you think is the right thing, up to you kiddo."

The next day, Rob Docker visited the victim again, but this time with a female officer, who took the retraction statement; just some split-arse from the police- women's department whose day Rob had spoilt by lumbering her with doing some work.

Docker sat quietly next to the victim reassuring her. That was the end of the court case.

***

Docker made two phone calls, one of which was to the club owner, to make some arrangements to collect his money, whilst the second took much longer.

Two days later the doorman stepped out from the club into the cold air at three in the morning, and pulled up the collar of his leather jacket. He was happy with himself. It had been a good night and, being the sexual predator that he was, he had managed to get a few more phone numbers from some of the mini-skirted girls who liked attention from a man in authority. He had also clipped the ears of some of the drunken lads who knew better than to retaliate – he had bounced a few off the walls of the club in his time. Yes, it had been a good night's work.

He made his way to waste-ground at the back of Broad Street, where his car was parked, and just prior to getting in he stopped to light a cigarette. One long inhale as he looked up to the stars and savoured life.

He heard nothing, but suddenly felt something cold in his back that he instinctively knew was the figure eight of the barrel of a sawn-off shot gun, "Don't move a muscle you cunt, and don't look around or I'll blow your spine away and then your head," the voice commanded him.

Frozen with fear, he did as ordered and then darkness surrounded him as a hood was placed over his head, and his hands were secured from the rear. A gag was placed over the hood and he was as close to suffocation as he might ever be.

The doorman was bundled into the boot of his own car, where his legs were secured, and he had time to contemplate terror during the short fifteen- minute drive, whilst a second vehicle followed.

They arrived at Hockley Port and drove into the deserted goods yard. Three men lifted the doorman from the boot and carried him a short distance to one of the railway lines whilst a fourth looked on, shotgun in hand.

His body was laid across the line, feet resting on one rail whilst his head rested on the other – it was a classic suicide position, the only difference being that he was secured to the line with strong thin rope.

Once again the voice came, "We'll be back in one hour to collect your head and feet. It won't be a pretty sight, but you'll not know anything about it my son. Keep your ears open for the next train. By the way you seem to have shit your pants."

The four men withdrew in silence only a short distance away and watched the pathetic figure writhing in desperation, with just the occasional sound of choking as he struggled for breath.

Exactly sixty minutes later they went back to him. The doorman stiffened as the hood was cut away and he found himself looking up at four men wearing 'clown' masks. He had always been afraid of clowns. In the darkness he felt his bowels move again, and a damp patch grew large in his groin as urine trickled down his ice-cold legs, as he pissed in his pants. They sat him upright.

Slowly and deliberately, one of the men removed his mask and stared intently into the face of the terrified doorman and said, "You need to remember my face and you need to understand the importance of my words. You're not wanted in Birmingham and this morning you'll leave for good. You forgot where to draw the line boy. You've upset some important people. If you fail to go I've been ordered to kill you within seven days. Do you understand?"

The doorman nodded vigorously, no semblance of any fight in him. His tormentor continued, "You need to know we are serious though my friend," and without pausing he reached behind the doorman's back and took hold of the little finger of his left hand upon which he placed a cigar-cutter. The round hole fitted neatly over the finger and as he applied pressure he sliced halfway through it as the doorman writhed in agony, blood spurting from the wound.

His attacker stopped and said, "Next time it will be your cock before I kill you my friend. It is my promise to you. We'll be leaving now and once we've left you can move in fifteen minutes. Then fuck off and don't come back. Go and find the bright lights and some other little girls to play with."

As they departed, the doorman's hands were freed and a single ticket to London Euston was thrown at his feet.

***

For Rob Docker it had been a good result all round with a few quid in his pocket, a rapist off the streets of Birmingham, and another 'port in a storm' when Lilian was giving him a hard time. After all, the rape victim was in debt to him now, and he fully intended on settling the debt as and when it suited him.

Chapter Thirty One" 'Proud Mary'

(Creedence Clearwater Revival)

1969

In early 1969, Rob achieved promotion to the rank of uniform sergeant, but a family issue involving Joe once again marred his satisfaction at his success. No-one noticed anything untoward though; Rob was not one to show his feelings.

He was in his office when the call came through. He had several prosecution files to check and some paperwork to catch up with so any interruption was an irritant.

The voice on the other end of the phone was matter of fact "She hasn't got long to go. You need to be here. She's asking for you."

Rob frowned and whispered to himself, "Fuck it," as he terminated the call without pleasantries and gathered his coat from the back of his chair. "I'll be back later," he announced to his team, "Get your arses into gear and sort some jobs out while I'm away. I want to see some bodies in the cells by the end of the week, so less gassing and more doing." Rob had made his point and walked out. Behind his back one of his more foolhardy detectives was brave enough to make some 'wanking' motions with his hand.

Joe was sat at his desk, a solitary figure in his office in Birmingham, surrounded by photographs of himself with smiling

VIPs and a mix of failing, and up and coming artists. All for effect, most of them were just passing ships in the night. He had little time for the status that the pictures represented; it was just a business necessity. He felt the loneliness of the office acutely. His receptionist startled him from his deep thoughts, "Mr. Docker, you have a phone call. It's from the hospital." Like Rob he listened to the same message, but different feelings were evoked.

He had been close to his mother and understood very clearly the implications. Calling his manager in, he gave him strict instructions to get on with things and that he should not be disturbed.

One hour later, Robert and Joseph Docker found themselves facing each other across Mary's hospital bed.

No conversation. No connection, just an uneasy silence as they waited for the inevitable. The bond between them had been sundered forever.

Rob passed the time counting the number of flowers on the wallpaper in the room, in much the same way as IRA suspects counted bricks in the RUC interrogation centres in Northern Ireland, maintaining their silence whilst being questioned. It helped count off the minutes towards the inevitable conclusion, and had the second benefit of avoiding unnecessary eye contact with his brother, who was sat gently holding his mother's right hand.

Mary Docker had been a strong woman but now she seemed to have shrunk within the bed, and her body occupied barely half of the mattress. Her daily evening trip to the 'offie' for a pint of sherry delivered in a lemonade bottle, and consumed within an hour of purchase whilst she lay in her bed, had finally taken its toll. Liver failure would be the official cause of her death – physical and mental abuse, sadness, heartbreak, and living with the guilt of being a murderer not being recognised medical conditions at the time. She was only forty-eight, and was near to completing one of the longest suicides in history.

She was peaceful as the effects of morphine dulled the pain deep inside her enlarged stomach. Her eyes half-open, she breathed gently but with a slight rasp in the throat from the effects of smoking tip-less cigarettes. One breath – one rasp – one pause – one breath – one rasp – one pause.....

The hospital staff had already briefed them that it was a matter of time – but how much time to die? Not long it would seem. The brothers were alone with each other and their thoughts. They had both discouraged family from attending the end, ironically acting in concert as twins without realizing it. Sandra and Charlie had been to say their goodbyes earlier, and had been glad to leave the brothers to their unwilling reunion over Mary's wasted body.

One breath – one rasp – one pause – and so it continued as the clock on the wall ticked incessantly.

Suddenly, Mary Docker opened her eyes fully and stared at both of them in turn, "You pair have to sort this out. There has to be an end to this." There was silence in the room as neither chose to speak first. Her voice grew louder, fuelled by a last desperate surge of inner strength, "Promise me, make your peace."

Joe squeezed his mother's hand gently and quietly said,

"Don't worry mum. We will. It'll be okay." Mary turned to Rob and looked deep into his eyes, "Of course mum - we will," he responded maintaining a steady gaze. Rob was after all a practiced liar.

Mary, satisfied, returned to semi-consciousness.One breath – one rasp – one pause – as the clock continued its slow rhythm. Each time Mary Docker drew breath the bedclothes rose slightly and then deflated. One breath – one rasp – one pause and then the next breath.Rob became mesmerised by the movement of the bedclothes.

One breath – one rasp – one pause – one breath – one rasp – one pause... Then the pause became permanent.

Rob waited. He had seen many dead bodies but this was the first death that he had actually witnessed. He waited for the cycle to begin again but nothing happened. She was gone.

For Joe this was not a new experience but before he had been in control and now he was not. Joe bent his head slowly, the tears welling up in his eyes, as he remained holding his mother's hand. Not willing to let go yet, or to leave her.

Rob stood up, "Let me know what half of the funeral costs are," he announced, and left the room.

This was one 'death bed' promise that would not be kept. There would be no reconciliation. In fact Rob's lie in response to their mother's dying wish added another slight to Joe's list.

As Rob left the room all Joe could smell was the stench of a rotten apple. He could truly swing for the bastard, such was the level of his hatred for the man at that moment.

Rob returned to his office – he had some files to deal with and some bodies to nick.

***

The funeral passed off quietly. A respectable distance was maintained between the two brothers as they sat listening to a man of the cloth saying nice words about a woman he had never met. A thirty-minute ceremony followed by a burial in the Docker family plot with her mother and father and that was it.

Just dust now, but at least no more pain, and the perpetrator Richard had been cremated and the ashes flushed down the toilet, so he wasn't there.

The lifeless body of Mary Docker may have been buried, but the enmity between the twins hadn't gone into the grave with her. There were no more bridges to cross as the warring brothers went their separate ways.

Chapter Thirty Two: 'Come Together'

(The Beatles)

1969

On the 12th August 1969, one hundred and twelve people were injured in rioting in Londonderry, and on the 10th September 1969, seven thousand troops were deployed to the Province. 'The Troubles' had begun.

Quinn had been monitoring the situation with growing unease. He knew what the extra packages arriving with the usual consignments meant. For only the third time in his life he felt powerless. It was stupid. He could beat any man in a fight, the Black Souls had been successful beyond his expectations, but he could do nothing to stop their slow slide into participation in a war – on the wrong side.

He reflected on the decisions taken long ago that had led to this moment. A cocky youth, who had eagerly signed up in a pub in Londonderry, thinking he would be in control. The building of his business, founded upon help from the IRA. The deal he had done with 'The General', to keep the farm for Seamus. The murder he had committed, another signature in blood.

There was no way out. For good, or ill, he was entwined with the Republicans and they seemed determined to unleash a hell he had no appetite for, or belief in. Not for the first time, a feeling of impending doom swept over him. He had played the game and won big-style, but there would be a price to pay.

***

By 1969 Joey Lombardi had changed but not for the good. The decline that had worried Quinn had accelerated, fuelled by Joey's heroin habit and increasingly violent sexual appetites. Neither presented a problem in an outlaw biker gang where nobody could be described as 'normal', but they made Joey an increasing risk, one that was about to blow up.

Joey played the role of Vice President to the full, enjoying being in charge and the power that the patches sewn onto the black leather jacket gave him in the presence of normal citizens. He could see the fear in their eyes and it made him feel invincible. Even the lesson he had witnessed outside The Hole in the Wall that night had failed to check his headlong race towards disaster. In fact he had by now convinced himself that his role in persuading Quinn to walk away from Docker's club door was actually a victory. He was becoming a legend in his own mind.

The Italian Stiletto knife that he routinely carried also added substance to his inflated ego. After Italy's surrender in 1943 these knives had become an instant hit with American GIs and as some returned home, via England, they began to circulate on the streets.

Originally crafted in the North-Eastern Italian town of Maniago, the spring mechanism created 'shock-and-awe' amongst those suddenly finding themselves facing a deadly blade when the trigger mechanism was pushed. Joey had practiced this move many times, and still enjoyed a thrill when he saw the effect.

It started out as just a normal day in the life of a Hell's Angel. Joey had completed a run early into Birmingham to visit some contacts that provided bike parts. He was in no rush to go anywhere and spent some time at the 'Golden Eagle' pub in Hill Street, a regular biker pub, where he enjoyed several bottles of Double Diamond Burton Pale Ale. The keg version had been launched in the 60s but Joey preferred the feel of the bottle and felt that it fitted his image better.

Several bottles became just a few more, and his thoughts turned to other things, namely his continuing interest in acting out his fantasies shagging prostitutes. He was partial to one of the black girls working at a nearby massage parlour and was looking for a 'happy ending' to the day.

Screwing a black woman was about as deviant as an Angel could get, given their tendency towards white power, and Joey was nothing if not deviant now. He could have gone down to another favourite haunt, at the bottom of Balsall Heath Road, however his motorbike was not the best transport for picking a prostitute up, and the area around Varna Road was starting to look like a building site so he opted for comfort.

Also, the girls down there were white and came from Scotland, or the North West, and whilst conversation was not exactly a priority he struggled with the accents and preferred something 'home grown' and of a darker hue.

Sandra peered through the spy-hole and spotted a familiar face. Joey was 'pissed' but she could normally handle him, and saw no reason to lose a customer and the chance that he would reveal some information about the Black Souls that Joe could use.

Sandra used a working name at the brothel so Joey was blissfully ignorant that every time he indulged his sexual fantasies he was plugging into a direct communication with Joe Docker. It was his bad luck that Joe had come to collect Sandra one evening and had seen him leaving, recognizing him from the confrontation with Quinn.

It had been a quiet day for the girls, apart from the busy lunchtime period when office workers took an alternative break. Sandra was looking forward to spending some time with Joe, who somewhat unusually had promised to pick her up and take her for a meal. Being the Madame of a massage parlour was not to everyone's taste, but for her it was strictly business, and she kept a tight rein on the girls.

Joey's usual girl was in, and he was away for thirty minutes before presenting himself back at the front entrance where Sandra was waiting.

Joey hadn't scored any 'Horse' that day and was feeling it. His mood was deteriorating as the craving for a fix rose. As he tucked his T-shirt into his jeans he snapped, "I'm not fucking paying. The slag wouldn't take it up the arse so I had to slap her a couple of times. The dirty cow wanted me to wear a fucking rubber Johnnie – the fucking cheek of it!"

At that moment the girl in question staggered into reception. It was clear that it had been more than just a couple of slaps. Joey liked violent sex and had been carried away with the moment, the screams and sobs, the fear. It really turned him on. The darkness in him had surfaced.

Sandra took one look at the girl's broken face and lost her customary cool, momentarily forgetting who she was talking to.

She shouted into his face, one finger pointed within an inch of his nose, "You don't come ere throwing your weight around, you piece of shit. You don't touch my girls, and you pay. This ain't a fucking charity for sad losers who can't get it at home. What's the matter with you - can't you get yourself a girlfriend to fuck with."

Joey swayed slightly as the words hit home. No fucking woman was going to speak to him like that and get away with it. He slapped Sandra hard across the face with the palm of his right hand – a blow which sent her reeling backwards and into the wall, which she struck with the back of her head.

The girl started screaming hysterically and ran from the reception.

Sandra went down hard and stayed down in a disheveled heap. Barely conscious she lay with her skirt pulled up revealing long legs, the sight of which were strictly reserved for someone else.

Joey's eyes lit up, "Maybe I'll have some of this instead," he slurred as he staggered forward and gripped Sandra's hair with his left hand, whilst attempting to grope her breasts with his right. She fought back and it aroused him further. He forced her down onto the floor and slapped her again, hard, "Nothing wrong with a bit of meat in the right places. Let's have a look at those tits then."

Suddenly Joey's world began to spin as he received a blow to the neck and was placed in a stranglehold – Joe had arrived.

Joe maintained his grip on Joey Lombardi, hauled him off the semi-conscious Sandra and frog-marched him to a back room. The now recovered, but permanently scarred Winston had been driving Joe's car and his face split into a wide smile when he walked through the door and saw who Joe was holding.

Joey was expertly tied to a chair by his arms and legs, and a cloth was thrust into his mouth, a technique that Joe was already familiar with.

Leaving Winston to stand guard over him, Joe tended to his wife before sending the girls home and closing the premises. Joe was furious inside and ice-cold out. He loved Sandra and the thought of someone violating her left him with a feeling of rage that he fought to control. The fact that it was a Black Soul made it ten times worse. Any thought of the truce he had so carefully negotiated evaporated, he had vowed after Cyprus never to take this sort of shit from anyone again, especially not from a white man.

He sent Sandra home with Winston and returned to the back room – this was something that he would do alone.

Joe calmly stated the facts, "No-one puts a finger on my wife and you're gonna pay. The words must have penetrated Joey's befuddled mind because his eyes widened as he realized what he had done and who was stood before him. "Now, are you man enough in your fancy black jacket to take your medicine," said the aggrieved husband. He removed the cloth and Joey spat violently into his face.

"Be it on your own head, sonny boy." Joe went to work.

Joe struck hard with one punch and the cracking sound of Joey's nose breaking confirmed that it had achieved his purpose.

With the cloth re-inserted Joe went about his business, beating Joey methodically on his legs and back with a length of rubber hose – "I'll stop when you beg for mercy and forgiveness?"

After each round of blows Joe removed the cloth and faced Joey – the same question was asked. Twice more Joey spat in his face and on the fourth he shouted for mercy as the tears rolled down his bloodied face.

"Stop, you bastard, stop. I'm sorry," he screamed.

Joe stopped and surveyed his artwork. He had burnt off some anger now and his mind was beginning to sort through the possible implications of this evening's work.

"I'm going to release you now and you're gonna fuck-off to whatever cess-pit you live in. If you ever come near here again I'll kill you. You was there that night outside the club. You know the score. If I was you I'd be keeping this to myself too, I don't think Quinn would be too happy to have to re-think his decision cause of your dick, you yampy fucker. Do you understand?" Joey nodded, his eyes fixed firmly to the floor.

Joe untied Joey and turned around before propelling him towards the door of the room – he had vented his fury and wanted this finished. He wanted to get home to Sandra.

Joey made the worst decision of his life – or rather the short life that he had left. As they moved towards the door Joe saw Joey's hand move to his jacket pocket and heard the swish of the mechanism as the blade of the knife locked in Joey's hand.

He smashed the biker's already broken nose hard into the door, and as Joey struggled to stand he received two 'rabbit' punches into the side of the ribs.

The knife fell from his hand as he lost his footing and went down. Joe kicked him twice in the head and for good measure smashed his broken skull with the upturned chair. Finally he picked up the knife intended for him, held Joey's head back and slashed him across the throat. As the knife hit the carotid artery blood shot several feet towards the ceiling. It was a bloodbath and Joey had paid the ultimate price for his ego, his addictions and his affiliations.

Joe collected himself quickly – the last blow had been deliberate so there was no question of shock setting in. Once again he had not killed in rage but because in the final analysis he had wanted to. Now he had to cover his tracks. He knew that if Quinn found out he would not stop until he had taken at least one life in revenge and all Joe's careful work would be undone.

He made a phone-call to his house and Winston returned. They worked efficiently together to wrap the body in a dustsheet Winston had bought with him, and it was taken to a wooded area in Cofton Hackett, in Joe's Ford Capri, where eventually the foxes would disturb the shallow grave and a police investigation would start.

Joe had been careful about forensics, and after two days the telltale signs at the massage parlour had been expertly removed and a fresh coat of paint applied. Sandra remained at home recovering and it remained one of Joe's many secrets. Joe told her he had administered a slapping, and that Joey would not be visiting again. He liked to tell his wife the truth, just not all of it.

For his part, Winston became the new owner of a nice ring with the words 'BS' on it, and a nice earner from selling Joey's bike to a dealer with a reputation for not asking too many questions.

Who said crime didn't pay?

***

It was 1970, and Joe sat pondering in his office as the phone rang. It was a fairly brief conversation – no point in wasting words. Joe concluded, "Thanks Malcolm – that's very helpful. I'll see you right."

Another phone call followed, "Get your best stuff off the shelves and move it next door. You're getting a visit in the morning." Joe concluded his instructions to the 'Adult Bookshop' manager close to the railway station.

Porn was a great earner and a perfect set-up for Joe who financed the operation but kept his distance and left it to his 'squeaky clean' manager to take the rap when raids took place. The man was paid well for his services and most of the time the police never got past the forfeiture stage, with rare prosecutions. The arrangement suited both of them, the manager was somewhat of a connoisseur of 'X' rated magazines and was like a bear in a honeypot and loved his 'work'.

As predicted, a team of plain-clothes officers turned up next morning as the shop opened. They were armed with a warrant issued under the Obscene Publications Act 1967 and removed stock from the shelves, content that they had a result. All they needed to do now was to spend hours cataloguing it.

In the Seventies, before the advent of the video cassette, there was a growing market in the take-home pleasure of an 'adult' magazine filled with favorite anonymous stars 'in action' with much of it purporting to originate from Sweden or Denmark, and the somewhat appropriately titled 'Climax' much in evidence. Occasionally the officers had to deal with the extremes of 'snuff' movies but such recoveries were thankfully rare.

Within an hour the stock that had been moved to the empty retail unit next door, which Joe also owned, was put back on the shelves, and a new order placed with their supplier in London.

As far as Joe was concerned, Malcolm Reid was a fat cunt that he despised, but needs must, and he would be paid in kind for his services in due course. Reid had a liking for one of the girls at the sauna so it cost Joe very little to retain his loyalty.

***

In 1970 Rob Docker took one step closer to getting back onto the CID when he was appointed to run a plain-clothes 'street crime' team. He felt like a dog with a new bone. The message from his superintendent was simple, '*Sweep the streets. Keep them clean. Get results.*' These days' skinheads were frequenting the streets and they provided Rob with a steady stream of prisoners.

***

The doorways smelt of stale urine, the floors littered with chewing gum, cigarette ends, and crushed empty cans of alcohol. A strange place to hold a briefing but for the two sergeants, and six constables, gathered there it was not going to be a long affair. Rob Docker was not really up for this, he was a 'thief taker,' and nicking punters for 'importuning for immoral purposes' was not up his street. He had however promised his fellow Sergeant, Dave Jones that he would lend a hand with his team, and a promise was a promise.

"Whatever you do, for fuck's sake don't get your dick out," Dave stressed as he split the officers into pairs. "Stay together, pick your man, and wait for them to do all the talking. Stand at the bog but just make it look as if you're holding it. No wanking movements, no smiling, and no winking. Don't come out until you've got a body. Give them enough rope and they'll hang themselves." Not the most technical briefing Rob had heard but to the point.

The toilets opposite the Crown pub in Station Street, which became known as the 'Silver Slipper', were the favourite haunts of men seeking the thrill of sexual contact with another man in a public place.

The pastime of 'cottaging,' was a way for many men who led double-lives to relieve the tension of everyday life.

Rob Docker felt his heart sink as he descended the steps into the toilets, *'Fuck this for a game of soldiers,'* he thought, as he was faced with a row of filthy urinals occupied by men of all shapes and sizes.

Three cubicles to the right were clearly also occupied as muffled sounds emerged from the darkened spaces. In truth they needed no locks on the doors and there were none. These were not private places and the roughly fashioned holes between each cubicle wall ensured that for those wanting to participate there was no privacy. Big enough for an eye to look through, or a penis for the more adventurous, they took their choice.

Rob's partner was a PC who would simply follow his lead. He had worked with him for a while now and the lad knew exactly how to play it. Rob picked his target – a tall man in his late forties, clean-shaven, with short greying hair, who had an anxious, but determined look about him.

There was just one urinal between him and Rob - who could clearly see him playing as he fixed his stare on Rob's groin area. Rob stared back but kept his body close into the urinal. The game continued as others came and went. Docker likened it to a chicken farm where heads were constantly bobbing up and down and pecking away furiously at feedstuff in their trays below.

Eventually Rob's target well and truly crossed the evidential line as he turned full-on towards him with his erect manhood in full view and uttered the immortal words of Gary Glitter, "Do you wanna touch?"

Rob moved swiftly, his partner closing in behind him, "You're nicked," he exclaimed and literally dragged him back up the stairs, back into reality and the bite of a cold grey evening.

As they reached the street level, their prisoner started pleading with them to let him go. He didn't struggle, which was a shame as Docker would have liked to rough him up a bit, but he wouldn't stop asking the officers to give him a chance. The response was a curt, "Just shut the fuck up you cunt. Tell it to the beak."

On arrival at Steelhouse Lane, Rob pulled rank and left the PC to book the prisoner into custody whilst he went for a pint in the police bar in the basement of the building. He needed to take the taste of the shithouse he had just been in out of his mouth.

Ten minutes later, and after wasting £5 in the fruit machine, he was about to finish his second pint when the PC hurried in and made a beeline for him. "There's a problem. He's in the job. He's a skipper in Warwickshire. The twat had still got his warrant card on him when I emptied his pockets out. The custody sergeant wants to know what the score is from you before we go any further."

Rob stared down for a second at the dregs of his nearly empty glass and finished it off. It wouldn't be difficult to 'cuff the job' by minimizing the evidence a little bit, dusting the prisoner down, and putting it down to a 'learning experience'. He could save the man's job in a split-second, but Docker had bigger fish to fry and he couldn't think of a better way to tell the world that Rob Docker was above reproach and one hundred per cent straight.

Docker declared firmly, "Fuck him – the only way he's leaving here tonight is with a charge-sheet in his hand instead of his dick." That was the end of the conversation as he turned away from the officer to order another pint.

Two weeks later a woman was walking her dog along a well-trodden footpath near to the village of Henley in Arden. She loved the fresh air of the countryside and it was perfect for her lively cocker spaniel to expend some energy amongst the many trees, and the tangled undergrowth. Suddenly the dog veered off into a small copse and out of view. Despite appeals to return, all that the owner got in reply was the constant barking of the excited dog.

She scrambled through the bushes to reach him. "Jesus H Christ," she exclaimed as she suddenly came face-to-face with the body of a grey haired man hanging from a tree. Face contorted, red and purple, etched with the pain of the last few minutes of his life, as the body swung silently in the light breeze. Ordinarily a peaceful location, there would be no peace here again – not for this man nor his family. Neither would there be a court case for importuning, as the prosecution would formally offer no evidence when the case came up for hearing.

When Rob Docker heard the news he gave it no more than a second thought. Compassion was not his style and as far as he was concerned the man had only himself to blame. *'He would have been better off jumping in front of a train,'* he mused, *'much quicker, especially if you adopt the crucifixion position'.*

Dave Jones's prophesy during the briefing had come true.

***

Weeks later, Rob found his services were required again, "I need another favour Rob" ,said his colleague Dave Jones. "We're gonna hit a Sauna tomorrow and I'm short of staff. We'll deal with the 'bodies' but I just need a few more to make sure that we have control when we go in with the warrant."

Saunas were really a polite term for running a brothel and the one off Bristol Street had been doing well for some time. The plain-clothes team had already been in to do some 'testing' of the services available. They were supposed to get the girls to come up with the 'price list' for services rendered before making their excuses at the critical moment and leaving. It was normal for expenses to be provided – you couldn't go into a sauna without any money could you? Sometimes some of the money got spent – needs must to secure the evidence as they say.

Rob couldn't refuse his colleague, and at 1pm next day they assembled in yet another doorway around the corner from the sauna. This was a good time to hit the place as lunchtime office workers from the city would often pay a quick visit prior to going back to their loving wives at 5pm.

The object of the exercise was to catch some of the punters in the act of having sex with the girls, but to do that they had to get in through the secure door quickly. They expected to find the 'Madame' and three girls.

Minutes later one of the PCs from the Plain Clothes team, who had previously visited the premises, pressed the buzzer and waited for the door to open. Either side the officers hugged the walls of the building.

A chain rattled on the door then it was opened silently by the 'Madame'. The officers poured through the door and up the stairs, with two of them staying behind to secure the startled woman. Rob recognized Sandra straight away. He hadn't seen her for a long time, but in an instant a number of long-buried feelings poured back into him. She looked good. He hated her. He had never really closed the wound of rejection. That act had sundered the twins, changed their lives.

She recognized him too, "How you doing Rob." She proffered a weak smile hoping, without much hope, that he might rescue her from this situation.

Luckily he had been at the back as the officers bundled into the building and no-one noticed that she knew his name. He turned over the options in his mind then decided.

"Well I'll go to the foot of our fucking stairs! All right Sandra, I had you down for being a slag - nice to be proved right after all this time." Docker almost spat the words out.

She had been about to say something else, but shut her mouth as if he had slapped her, as the words hit home.

Perhaps she had been about to ask for help. That was one of the options. He had considered how he could use this unforeseen windfall, but the chance of revenge, however petty, had over-ridden any schemes he could have come up with.

He didn't want to help Sandra, or his brother, whatever he could extract in payment. No-one in the force knew about Joe – his existence was a vulnerability that Rob had buried and he had no desire to indulge in any sort of relationship. He enjoyed cuffing Sandra then walked her outside and handed her to a waiting PC,

"Stick her in the back of the car. Don't get too close, she might have the clap." He returned to the premises. The search so far was going well. Dave quickly filled him in.

Bedroom One – one punter – one girl – both naked – good start. Bedroom Two – one punter – one girl astride him having sex – result. Bedroom Three - One girl found on her own, smoking quietly in the corner.

Short skirt, legs crossed and a resigned look. No evidence, so she had been told to stay put whilst the search continued.

Rob remained in the outer corridor with a PC whilst the other officers secured their prisoners. It was their job so he fully intended on doing the minimum. His attention was drawn to a fourth bedroom at the end of the corridor. The door was ajar and he could see a young Chinese girl sitting on the bed looking scared. He decided to have a closer look and entered the room. "Please don't take me. I'm illegal. They'll send me back," she pleaded.

Rob motioned to the PC in the corridor, "Stay here and gimme ten minutes – I'll sort this out." He closed the door and inserted the bolt on the inside. Docker did not speak Chinese but he didn't need to, "Chop, chop – move your backside over a bit." He sat down on the bed.

When he was done, Docker left the room and joined the team who were in the process of gathering the prisoners downstairs to be transported. Shortly afterwards Sandra and two of the girls were taken to the nick. The other girls were left behind, no evidence, not worth the bother. He had made sure that the Chinese girl was not taken.

Rob Docker reflected, *'Interesting work with benefits,'* as he headed for a quiet drink to finish the day off, and waited for the call that he was looking forward to. It came the next morning.

Rob was enjoying himself, "Swear to God I didn't know that it was your place, wasn't my job, I was just helping out."

Joe stormed down the phone, this time it was his turn to lose control, "You've never been honest about anything, and I don't believe a fucking word you say. You could have stopped it, tipped us off, but you had to have your little moment of payback didn't you?" Rob said nothing but part of the assertion had struck home.

Joe went in for the kill, "You're fucking pathetic. You still can't take the fact that she chose me over you, even after all this time."

"I think this conversation is over. It's not my job and I can't do anything for her before you ask. In fact let me make it clearer – I ain't gonna do anything. Cards on the table Joe, I think your precious Sandra is going to finish up with a CRO number." Rob replied coldly, after a pause during which he swallowed his emotions.

"Nothing changes does it Rob? It was always a one-way street. I'll sort myself out, like I always did." The phone went dead as Joe slammed it down at the other end.

Rob kept an eye on the case and wasn't surprised when there was insufficient evidence to convict Sandra of running a brothel. The two girls had been acting independently without her knowledge apparently.

It seemed that Joe's reach had now lengthened somewhat - Rob made a mental note for the future.

***

Rob loved the bustle of the city-centre with its transient population and resident characters. He also enjoyed being out with his team of four officers who displayed unswerving loyalty, and thought nothing of meeting force with force. One or two of them were a bit too handy with their fists but Docker set the rules and they obeyed. If someone was going to receive a bit of 'instant justice' there had to be an, 'assault police,' charge at the end of it to cover any injuries.

Saturdays presented a different type of challenge for Docker and his team as the increasing emergence of football violence was added to the mix. Birmingham City FC had a large and loyal following, including an unusually violent group who would later emerge as the feared 'Zulu Warriors'. Football hooliganism was in its infancy and organized pitched battles, and the fencing of fans, were far in the future but the fresh shoots were showing, and growing, as the decade of love marched towards its end.

Hundreds of fans would regularly make their way back into the city-centre after watching the mixed-fortunes of the team; most of them looking for a pint, or a bus or train home, whilst a sizeable minority had other things on their mind.

Rob led by example, and at 5pm on most Saturdays he and his team would loiter in plain-clothes in the vicinity of New Street Station looking for suitable targets. On this particular day Rob observed an 'up and comer', a young white lad, chest puffed out, leading his own little troupe of hooligans from the glass doors at the station, and on in the direction of Station Street.

They had just been ejected by the British Transport Police, and the plan undoubtedly would be to do a circuit of the surrounding streets before re-emerging on the station via the exits from the Birmingham Shopping Centre – but not on this occasion.

Rob hated anything connected to football and today he was in no mood to show mercy. As the group approached the steps leading down to Station Street the young leader raised his right arm to point the way forward to the group of some fifteen behind him.

That simple wave of the arm was good enough for Rob who launched himself at the individual, closely followed by two of the team. The remaining two officers put space between them and the now leaderless group.

As Rob reached the youth he grabbed him with one hand by the scruff of the neck and shouted loudly, "Police you're nicked!" In one move Rob's free hand swept into one of his prisoner's trouser pockets and he palmed the small Stanley knife in effortlessly.

Silenced by shock the youth was bundled against the parapet wall whilst his comrades in arms simply melted away. "Search him," Rob gave the familiar instruction to one of his officers whilst he applied handcuffs.

The recovery of the knife, favoured tool of hardened hooligans, who thought nothing of inflicting severe slash injuries to opponents, brought further shock-waves to the individual. All colour drained from his face as he tried to protest his innocence.

On arrival at Digbeth, the custody sergeant asked for details of the offence for which the prisoner had been arrested to which Rob calmly replied, "This tosser was seen leading a group of Birmingham City supporters from New Street Station towards Station Street. A bunch of Aston Villa fans appeared at the top of the steps and it was clear that a punch-up was about to happen. The prisoner raised his right arm and shouted, "Come on let's get the bastards" to his group at which point we put ourselves between them and I made the arrest for threatening behaviour. On being searched we recovered an offensive weapon in the form of a knife."

The prisoner remained silent. On the way to the station Rob had already whispered in his ear and told him that if he kept quiet he would arrange for him to receive a caution, whereas if he created a fuss he would make sure that he didn't get bail. 'Hobson's choice,' for the youngster, who had been well and truly stitched-up.

Rob was lying on both counts but that would only become apparent after he had made a confession of sorts and received his charge sheet.

Two days later Joe was approached at work by one of his cleaning staff who was crying, "What's the problem Sheila?" he enquired.

"My son got arrested and charged at the weekend with football violence but he's been done up like a kipper. I'm worried he'll get Borstal for it," she responded in floods of tears.

"Let me make some enquiries Sheila and see if there is

anything that can be done." Joe said trying to calm her.

Joe liked to look after his staff – they were his family and always repaid his loyalty towards them. He put a phone-call in to Malcolm and waited for a response.

The call back was not to his liking and darkened his mood considerably as he sought out Sheila.

"I'm sorry Sheila, there's nothing I can do on this occasion. Me best advice would be to tell your son to plead guilty and get it over with." He put his arm around the cleaning lady, "I'm sorry."

He had no intention of ever speaking to his twin again. Rob Docker was two up at that moment and Joe didn't like it.

Chapter Thirty Three: 'He's Gonna Step On You Again'

(John Kongas)

1971

In 1971, at the age of twenty-eight, Rob Docker got the job that he had wanted since joining the police service – that of detective sergeant in Birmingham city centre.

***

Standing in doorways was part of normal life for Rob Docker. It gave him a few moments to step out of the crowd and to gather his thoughts. It also meant being able to turn the volume on his police radio up slightly so that he could make more sense out of the constant chatter on the air. To the untrained eye, at best, they would have observed someone with their left ear slightly lower than their left shoulder, where the radio sat snuggly unseen in an upper jacket pocket. To most they were simply invisible.

As was the norm these days Rob was out with a young PC. Fit and fast, he could outrun most and stand his ground if confronted. Somewhat jaded from a heavy session on the beer the night before, Docker had already commented that the lad, 'looked as rough as a badgers arse,' but his partner took it in jest and would do the business when the time came. Rob felt safe, and confident that they could deal with most things and if the power of speech failed, brute force would normally prevail.

They were looking for some 'bodies' and the city-centre was fertile ground for teams of shoplifters, 'heavy' beggars, and drunks.

Standing at the top of the ramp leading from New Street into the Birmingham Shopping Centre they were suddenly in luck, 'Three suspects just left Rackham's – one security guard assaulted. Three white males, one blonde hair wearing a red jumper, and one carrying a rucksack, heading towards New Street' - the radio blurted out.

They waited patiently, their senses sharpened by the prospects of some activity. A quick moment of reassurance as Rob patted the handcuffs nestling in his pocket.

Minutes later two of the suspects emerged from the crowds at the bottom of the ramp heading towards them; the one wearing a red jumper, and the one with the rucksack. They were walking quickly scanning Corporation Street behind them as they hurried along, no doubt starting to feel with each step that they had made it.

Rob Docker and his partner waited patiently and as they drew parallel with the two officers they were grabbed and spun into the doorway. "Hold your horses. Police officers – you're under arrest for assault," Docker announced, and swiftly both were handcuffed with their hands behind them.

Street arrests needed to be made quickly whilst there was still that element of surprise. Once the sense of shock had worn off suspects would invariably weigh up the odds to see if it was worth trying to leg it. It wasn't going to happen on Rob Docker's watch and he had drilled it into his team, *'Strike and strike hard, there'll be plenty of time for talking later,'* was his motto.

The pair stared sullenly at the officers as they waited for transport to take them to the 'nick'. These were not first-timers, and they knew the score. Apart from an initial protest from one of them that they had done, 'fuck all,' they chose to remain silent, but the eye contact between them spoke volumes to the trained eye.

On arrival at Steelhouse Lane, they were lodged in the cells in the Central Lock-Up so that Docker and his team could sort out the facts, and to give them time to acclimatize to their surroundings. Neither of them had asked for a brief which was a good start, as the presence of a solicitor would only complicate things for Docker.

It didn't take long to work out that the suspect with the rucksack was bang to rights for the job. He had stolen goods in his bag from Rackham's, and fitted the description for the assault on a security guard who had tried to stop them leaving the store. When it came down to it there wasn't much at all on the second so the odds were that he would walk. Docker knew this but the suspect didn't, and Rob wasn't one to miss opportunities.

Docker gave instructions to his partner to deal with the 'rucksack man' but told him to make sure that he was only released on police bail, pending further enquiries for the time being, even though there was in fact already enough evidence to formally charge him.

Ten minutes later Docker sat facing the suspect in the red jumper across a barren desk in one of the interview rooms. He didn't have long as this interview was not one that was going to appear on the custody sheet record. Not one to waste words, Rob got straight down to business, "With that red jumper on you was lit up like a

Christmas tree today George," he announced, "As they say, you're well and truly fucked. Bang to rights I'd say."

George made his second mistake of the day; the first was getting caught "Me mum told me not to speak to strange men."

Rob slapped him even-handedly across his face, barely lifting himself from his chair."

George protested again, "You're barking up the wrong tree. I've done fuck all and you haven't even cautioned me yet." Rob reached casually across the table again, grabbed him by the throat, and held him there for a moment in a vice-like grip before releasing him, and gently easing himself back into his chair.

"Take it for granted that you've just been cautioned you little shit," Rob responded, as he looked into the eyes of his suspect.

Rob went straight for the kill. "I already know that you're on a bender, and with a six month suspended sentence, plus what I charge you with today, you're going to prison for twelve months, so shut your stupid fizzog and listen to me very carefully. You've two choices – play silly fuckers and I promise you'll get charges for conspiracy to steal and assault. No bail and straight to jail. Your arse will be so sore by the end of the week from being fucked by some old lag in Winson Green Prison that you won't be able to sit down, and you'll be so slack that you'll need a sanitary towel up it to stop shitting yourself. So either you get used to the idea of sucking cock or listen to option two. Are you listening to me?" George stared back – he knew what option two would be, but at this point he was scared shitless.

Docker continued, "If you play your cards right I'll bail you today pending further enquiries, and your mate will get the same treatment, so you both leave here with the same piece of paper. The difference is that the other little cunt will be back here in a couple of week's time to be charged. You'll answer your bail but you won't be charged. The price for that is that from today you sign up to work for me. I look after you, and you look after me. I want the names of every little toe-rag operating in the city-centre and you can start with a few before you leave."

Rob paused for effect, "I don't have time to waste so I'm putting you back in a cell for ten minutes and then I want an answer. Either get used to having a shit in the corner of your cell every morning, with no bog paper, or do yourself a favour and make a few quid in the process. You must have a few old scores you want to settle."

Eleven minutes later George was signed up as an informant. He needed to survive – anyway it could be worse and now he had some protection as well. He could also return a few favours to some of those who had ripped him off in the past over the proceeds of shoplifting.

***

As Rob Docker entered the yard he was eyed up with some interest by three men in blue overalls, working amongst the skips and piles of scrap metal. He did not need to introduce himself – the suit and tie gave it away. Although he could also have been from the Inland Revenue there was something about the measured pace of a police officer that the men instinctively recognised.

Detective Sergeant Rob Docker was on his own today, and for a reason. He was looking to establish a relationship with the owner of the scrap-metal yard and he didn't need any witnesses to the negotiations.

Without breaking stride he made his way to the office, knocked and entered. Behind the desk was a short balding man, overweight, with heavy gold chains adorning his right wrist and neck, a large gold signet ring with a black stone, and even a couple of gold teeth which flashed as he opened his mouth to speak. Don had been making a good living for years and wanted people to know it.

The all too familiar handshake out of the way, Docker announced, "I've come to have a butchers at the scrap-metal registers." Pleasantries over, Docker sat quietly and methodically going through the entries for scrap metal looking for the telltale signs that they were receiving stolen property. Don looked on nervously, fiddling with his gold rimmed glasses, and occasionally rotated the signet ring.

Finally Docker looked up and said, "Don, I think that you've been a bit of a naughty boy. There are too many 'John Smiths', or 'Jack Jones', with iffy car registration numbers for me liking. Don – you're not keeping a tight ship. It won't do Don."

This was not what Don wanted to hear as he shifted nervously in his seat and protested lamely, "The bloke that was here before you didn't have any problems."

Rob leant forward to give emphasis to his key statement for

the day, "Listen Don I'm here now so I don't give a fuck for what went on before, and how things used to work. I'm here to tell you how things are gonna work from now on."

Docker now had Don's full attention and went on, "Every month you're gonna give me a decent job. I don't care what other knocked-off gear you have in here but once a month I want a good result, not just some tatter who's had a bit of lead off a church roof. You'll phone me when they come in and I'll come down and give you a hard time before I nick the thieves so you're covered. I'm gonna register you as an informant so there'll be some money in it for results, but it's a partnership if you get me meaning and I'll decide what you get paid – after all said and done with all that gold you don't really need it do you?" Don nodded in response.

Rob continued, "If you fuck me about I'll put a panda car outside your front gate and put you out of business. If you try to play me off with some other twat I'll come for you and bury you. I'm not on the square and don't play golf so I don't give a shit who your friends might be." He paused, "Well Don do you think that we're gonna be friends?"

Don reached down to the drawer of his desk and pulled out a bottle of whisky. This was language he understood, "Why not?" he said.

The deal was sealed with a double and Docker signed the registers and marked them as being in order.

As he was leaving Docker concluded, "If any other coppers come in here refer them to me. This is my patch. I've also got a thirsty team so at Christmas I expect more of that. A couple of crates should do it."

Don responded and took out some crisp new banknotes from his top shirt pocket, "Here, get something for your family. I don't suppose that they see much of you." The notes hung in the air for a split second in his hand – that split second where honesty or corruption prevails. In Rob's case there was no hesitation and moments later they were in his pocket. "Cheers – have a good day, I think we're gonna get on just fine. I'll wait for the first phone call."

Don watched Docker leave the yard, "Bent bastard," he muttered, as he reached for the key to the safe where he kept his personal diary containing the important telephone numbers. He had many contacts in the Force but he sensed something in the eyes of this man that alerted his instincts to the fact that he would need to be very careful – it was time for another whisky.

Rob Docker did not linger – he had another five visits to make, and more men with gold bracelets to develop a relationship with – Rob Docker's way of course.

Not a bad business this - 'any old iron' – 'any old iron,' he practiced his best tatters shout in the car and laughed at his own childishness.

***

It was pitch-black but Rob wasn't worried. He had already had contact with George and knew what time the team was coming in, and how many there would be. Rob's biggest problem was the cold – mid December 1971 and it was bloody freezing, but the Parcels Yard at Curzon Street was crammed full with pre-Christmas deliveries and was a magnet to thieves. There were parcels everywhere, on the decks, and in the delivery vans parked within the huge shed – and all guarded by one old guy who never left the gatehouse and certainly wasn't looking for a fight.

George had confirmed that the team of four villains, plus himself, would be coming in via the elevated railway tracks overlooking the yard itself. He would be driving the van, whilst another would stay on the elevated section with a grappling hook, also acting as a lookout. The remaining three would drop down a ladder to gain entry. They were well out of sight of the gatehouse and would be able to plunder the parcels at their leisure.

Rob got on well with the local British Transport Police CID officers based at Birmingham New Street Station, and occasionally had a drink with them in the station bar, on the bridge link, or in the nearby Tavern in the Town pub. They always did him a favour, and put him in First Class if he was travelling by train with a prisoner escort, and showed willing when a job came in. His peers referred to them in a derisory fashion as 'railway coppers,' not proper ones like they were, a bit like the 'hobby bobbies', that liked to come out as Specials on a Friday or Saturday nights. Rob however saw the benefits that they could offer.

Docker calculated on two officers per prisoner, plus a BTP dog handler, and a fierce looking Alsatian who looked more like a lion than a dog. They came into their own in these environments and Rob was glad of 'Sabre's' extra pair of teeth. He wasn't one for history lessons but had once been told that they were the oldest dog section in the history of the UK police. Mind you some of the old-sweats at New Street Station looked as if they had been there since 1908.

His mixed team of BTP and local officers sat waiting patiently for the signal to go – some behind piles of parcels inside vans, and others placed at the furthest end of the yard, adjacent to the Birmingham to London Euston line, to cut off any escape.

Rob sat in the gatehouse, using the privilege of rank, and waited alongside the security man who was enjoying the excitement. Almost on cue at midnight a brief muted crackle on the radio and the words, "They're in," put everyone on their mettle. Rob had already briefed the team to give the thieves ten minutes to get well and truly hands-on – he wanted them to be caught red-handed.

"Parcels being carried back to the wall," the radio crackled once more. One of the thieves was in the process of attaching a parcel to the grappling hook, whilst the other two struggled behind with other boxes. "Go-Go," Rob shouted and all hell broke loose.

The three thieves in the yard had no chance and whilst one of them fancied himself as a runner the BTP dog handler proved that his dog was faster. All three were taken into custody whilst the one with the grappling hook ran back to the waiting van and screamed at George to get the fuck out of it.

The plan had worked perfectly – three bodies, and George's own role had been covered well enough, by allowing the fourth suspect to escape. Just to be safe, Rob left the prisoners with the BTP to be dealt with. They could have the collars and he would split the informant payment with George. There was no point in showing out unnecessarily.

It was time for a scotch – or even two when he got back to the office. His new- found friends in the metal trade meant that he always had a couple of bottles in his desk drawer.

After all, the only other thing he had waiting for him at home was Lilian – it was a no-brainer really.

Chapter Thirty Four: 'Back Stabbers'

(The O'Jays)

1972

On the 30 January 1972, thirteen people were shot and died during the course of a civil rights march in Derry, which became known as Bloody Sunday.

During the following two weeks, Quinn was kept busy by his PIRA masters, running 'materials' between the West Midlands and Hampshire. Quinn was very careful with the Black Souls to keep the level of their knowledge to an absolute minimum. One rider would simply be provided with a sealed package, and an address, and two other bikers would be nominated to provide an escort. All of the bikes were on false plates and they ran without displaying colours. They were told to stop for no - one, and certainly not the police.

As far as most of the gang was concerned they were simply ferrying drugs, or weapons, but in truth it mattered not to them and they complied without question.

On the 22 February 1972 a bomb exploded at Aldershot barracks.

During the following months Quinn organized a couple of official weekend runs to the Province, and the Black Souls stayed on campsites near to the coast in the Bangor area. Ostensibly they were having some fun and they certainly made the most of it as the locals simply steered well clear. The return trips by ferry entailed the distribution of further packages, and on one occasion two 'new' Black Souls made the trip on the back of bikes. Both were delivered to safe houses in Birmingham.

***

Police Constable James Delaney had a heavy Northern Irish accent, and came from a good Catholic family. Religion however was not uppermost in his mind as he sought the solace of a few pints in one of the Irish pubs just off Deritend.

He had been a police officer for four years, mainly working in the city-centre, and had a reputation for being tough. When 'red mist' occurred in front of James's eyes you would do well to step out of his reach, as many a drunk had found out to their cost.

Unfortunately, Delaney also had a propensity to let his headstrong habits spread to his mouth in drink and after a few pints he had an opinion on everything, which he felt compelled to share with whoever was in hearing distance.

Standing at the bar, it was not long before he was giving his views to the lone barman on everything from the troubles in Northern Ireland, to the rights and wrongs of Birmingham city-centre's thriving gay community, who were becoming increasingly visible.

Seated behind him were two men engaged in quiet conversation. Their ears pricked up when he proclaimed about how he was in the job and cleaning the place up. In another corner of the room sat Quinn. This was not his usual watering hole but he knew the licensee and had just completed some business with Connor who had already left. He fancied a Guinness and the opportunity to listen to a few Irish folk songs on the Jukebox in the corner. He knew the two 'boys' had been keeping an eye on Connor as he talked with Quinn – the usual bit of insurance, but Quinn had no intention of engaging with them. The less contact he had with bloody PIRA the better.

From his position he was able to watch the actions of the loud officer, and the reactions of the two men seated behind him. Quinn had learnt always to have a clear view in front, and the safety of a wall behind him.

It wasn't long before Delaney headed into darker waters as he began to articulate how much he despised the IRA, and all that they stood for, and that being a Catholic himself, the only thing that he despised even more was the UDA.

"Bring back the death penalty and hang all of the bastards, that's what I say. Top the lot of them," he announced, before heading off to the toilet at the rear of the pub.

As the room went quiet one of the two men spoke briefly to the barman, who went over to one of the outer doors and closed it. Quinn's attention span increased considerably as he recognized the signs of battle to come, and settled down to see whether the cop's fists matched his mouth, which he doubted.

Delaney returned to his position at the bar and ordered another pint, which was served in silence. He loved the taste of a long cold drink and as he raised it to his lips, head tilted back, he was suddenly struck on the back of the head with a glass which shattered on impact. He struggled to find his feet as blows rained down on him from two directions. Finally he fell to the floor where the thud of fists and boots continued.

Quinn sat there – an interested bystander to a ritual beating. As he had thought, the man was all mouth.

"Hold him still," one of his attackers shouted to his partner, and as he was pinned down Delaney felt the full force of a pint glass being crushed and ground into his face.

"Remember that you fucker, and don't come in here again unless you want to go home in a box. This is a gift from your Catholic brothers."

Delaney lay on the floor blinded by his own blood, and totally oblivious to the departure of the two men, followed closely by Quinn who had no intention of sticking around to be a witness. After they departed, the barman casually phoned for an ambulance. He would of course have been changing a barrel when the attack happened, which left the officer with forty stitches, and a scar for life which stretched from his right eye to his jaw.

Some would have said that Delaney had got what he asked for, but the reality was that the attackers had crossed the invisible line. Having a punch-up with the police was par for the course but a wanton attack on an off-duty officer could not be tolerated. Whilst no police officer worth his salt would have put himself in that position he was a brother-officer and such things needed to be dealt with.

When Rob Docker heard about the attack he paid a personal visit to the licensee, "Put in a fucking nutshell," he said, "You'll deliver some cunt up for this or I'll close you down. I'm not having some scumbags ruling the roost on my pitch. You've got seven days."

Later that day Connor made a call to Quinn, "I need a favour Pat. If they close the pub down it won't be good for our business. I can't put the boy's who did this up to the police, and by now they'll be back over the water – their job is done in Birmingham."

Quinn took a moment to reflect on how much he hated these people, "Leave it with me. I know someone who fits the bill. I'll sort out your sacrificial lamb."

Two days later Quinn sat in the living room of a maisonette in Northfield. There were more black bin bags in the room than there were in the rubbish bin outside. The place stank of decay. Quinn had two members of the Chapter with him to emphasize that this was a business visit and Liam, the forlorn resident, dreaded what was to come as they chose to remain standing. He had been at the wrong end of Quinn's unhappiness before, and the £5,000 drugs debt he owed the Black Souls weighed heavily on his mind.

"Liam my friend, I'm gonna do you a good turn. I'm gonna clear what you owe in return for a small favour," said Quinn, as Liam's face dropped, knowing the size of one of Quinn's 'small favours'.

Quinn commenced telling him the story of James Delaney, and his scarred face. Quinn went into the details of the incident three times before he was satisfied that Liam had digested sufficient details and the minute facts which only a person who had been at the scene of the attack could have known.

"Now then Liam, in two days' time you'll present yourself at the desk of the front-office at Digbeth Police Station. You'll tell them that you've come to give yourself up for the attack on the police officer, and that a detective called Docker is looking for you. Make sure that you emphasise that fine, 'Top of the morning,' Irish accent of yours. Do you understand?" Quinn concluded.

Liam drew in a sharp intake of breath, "Do I have a choice?" he said weakly. Quinn responded, "You will do this and your debt is cleared. You'll get eighteen months for GBH and be out in twelve months. You'll be fine, they'll feed you so full of methadone while you're in that you won't know what day of the week it is." He paused for effect and then went on, "Don't do as I say and my two friends here are going to break both of your legs now, and then piss all over you for the fun of it. After that one of them will give your arse a good rodgering. Then you'll still owe me £5,000."

Quinn and his boys left a few minutes later, their business concluded, and two hours later a man with a heavy Irish accent called 999 from a telephone box. The conversation was short as the emergency services operator responded, "Listen and write this down. I'm only going to say this once. There was a picture of a copper with his face smashed in with a glass in the papers. The person you are looking for is called Liam and comes from Northfield – that's all I know. There's a detective called Docker looking for him." The line went dead.

Two days later Liam emerged from forty-eight hours of seeing the world through a heroin induced haze and presented himself at the desk at Digbeth Police Station.

Docker had his man – job done, another tick in the box too. He was getting a reputation as a detective who could get results and nobody was going to question his methods while they worked. It was all about checks and balances and Rob knew which levers to press.

***

Rob waited patiently. He was out of his comfort zone but the robbery was planned for the outskirts of Birmingham and he couldn't pass it over to anyone. He needed to be in control of this one.

Several nondescript cars were parked up in secluded locations in the area, each carrying two men armed with .38 revolvers inside shoulder holsters under their jackets. Their ears were glued to the police radio – this was no time for idle chatter. Nearby, a street-cleaner meticulously swept the grass and paved areas next to the small sub-post office in a small run-down shopping precinct. The cleaner pushed a trolley containing rubbish bags, but one of the bags contained a heavy object that was definitely not for cleaning.

Two women sat nearby on a bench with a pram with a young baby inside. Someone with a trained eye would have noticed that it was a well-behaved baby that did not cry or even stir. One of the women pushed the pram back and forth whilst they engaged in animated conversation. Other young mothers played with their children in a small run down playground oblivious as to what was about to happen.

The raid was set for the noon arrival of the GPO delivery van that would bring a substantial cash delivery for benefits payouts. It would be enough for a nice extended holiday in Spain for a few months and sort out some other pressing problems. The robbers had already done two dry runs, and they were happy that they would be facing one security officer as he made the short walk from the vehicle to the premises.

There would be three men on the actual robbery – the driver of the stolen vehicle, and two others who would be armed with a pick-axe handle and the weapon of choice for the day's aspiring robber – a sawn-off shotgun. The gun was double - barreled and loaded with two cartridges. One would be discharged for effect into the air, and the second was for anyone who was foolish enough to get in the way.

At the briefing Rob had given very precise details of the offenders and what their plan was. To those listening intently it was obvious that this was a job where an informant was involved.

Rob was meticulous in his planning as specific officers were allocated to take out the two robbers who would confront the security guard. He would tackle the driver with some of his own team – trusted servants who had already been briefed separately.

At 11.55am a green Ford Cortina drew up in one of the parking spots. Stolen that morning from Selly Oak, it would be used for the first mile after they had left the scene, before they swapped to a second vehicle parked up in Weoley Castle – or so two of the robbers thought.

The three occupants sat inside the vehicle smoking – pumped up with adrenalin, and the effects of a 'spliff' - ready for action. They peered intently through the windscreen waiting for their target.

On cue the GPO van drew up five minutes later. The driver got out and removed a cash container from the rear for the short walk.

He paused for a few moments to adjust himself, and scratch his balls. He wasn't used to this uniform – his was normally blue. With the old nerves going, he was bosting for a slash but it would have to wait.

Two men launched themselves from the Cortina and bounded towards the security officer both weapons clearly in sight. "It's a go!!!"Rob shouted into the radio.

The team had been briefed to take them out well before they reached their intended target and that's exactly what happened.

To shouts of "Armed police, get down on the floor," the street cleaner, the two females with the pram, and the security guard produced pistols that were aimed at the two suspects. As women hurried their children away from the playground the two gave up without a fight as cars screamed in from all directions to secure the scene.

Legs spread wide, and arms in front of them, they buried their faces in the grass as reality set in. Next to them lay the loaded sawn-off shotgun that would guarantee a ten-year prison stretch –

they were, to put it mildly, well and truly fucked – tucked up like a fiddlers elbow.

Rob and two of his team ran towards the getaway car as the driver made a break for it. He was off like a rabbit heading for some alleyways that led into the council-estate; a jumble of cul-de-sacs and void premises. It didn't take long for him to increase the gap between himself and his pursuers. Just long enough for everyone to see that the police officers were a bunch of fat bastards who needed to get themselves into a gym. Then he was lost from sight.

"Hold your horses," Rob gasped at his pursuing colleagues "He'll come another day."

The two prisoners were to be dealt with by local CID; there was no sense in drawing attention to Rob's presence – one less question to be asked at their trial. After the ritual expressions of thanks to the firearms officers he left the scene - quietly satisfied – another good result under his belt. Time for a snifter in the bar at the station.

At 5pm Rob answered the phone in his office, "You done good," he announced to the voice on the other end of the line, "Just as we planned George."

Laughing, the response came back "I thought for a minute you fuckers were gonna catch up to me. I had to be on me toes real quick."

Robs planning and the informant's ingenuity at finding two impressionable young men who had let their greed, and need to pay off drugs debts, overcome common sense, had paid off.

Rob had a result and the informant would be paid out handsomely for an armed robbery. He would of course be splitting some of the payout with Rob.

The offence would never have happened but for the partnership between the police officer and the criminal, a joint enterprise pushing legality to it's limits, but who would ever know?

***

Rob Docker read out the antecedents for Liam McDonagh following his plea of guilty at Birmingham Crown Court. He stood indicted with causing grievous bodily harm to off-duty PC, James Delaney, under a statute more commonly known in legal circles as Section 18 of the Offences Against the Person Act 1861.

In sentencing him to four years in prison the Judge commented, "This was a despicable and unprovoked attack on an off-duty police officer and I must pass a sentence befitting the crime, and one will act as a deterrent to others." As the Judge ordered him to be taken down Liam collapsed in the dock.

***

Docker checked in at the gatehouse at Winson Green Prison and went through to the visitor's block. As a police officer he was able to get a separate interview room and the prison officers let him get on with it once Liam had been ushered into the room.

Liam was not well and Rob knew it. Too many dirty needles and the unprotected sex had left its mark. Liam was merely surviving day to day.

He was not best pleased to see Docker again, but any time out of his cell was welcome, as was the pack of twenty cigarettes that Docker slipped into his hands underneath the table. "If you've come to get me to clear any jobs for you, you can fuck off," Liam retorted, as he slid the packet inside the waistband of his trousers.

Rob looked at him steadily, "Liam just listen carefully. I took some of your clothing back home recently. You know, the stuff that we had as exhibits. A little bird tells me that you ain't coping very well in here, in fact you look shit. I've come to make an offer – are you listening?" Liam nodded.

Docker went on "When you come out I want you to work for me. I think you're right in the middle of what's going on, and you know the Irish stuff too, and I'm interested in that."

Liam shook his head, "No way, if them fuckers found out I was a grass I'm dead."

Rob spoke softly, "Liam, Liam, look at yourself. You've got what, another two years in here? Do you think you'll ever walk out at the rate you're going? I know the Governor, personal friend of mine. I can swing it that you get moved to the Hospital Wing, get methadone, then a cell of your own, and parole as soon as possible. Call it an investment for the future, I got a good feeling about you, I think I'll get the payback to make it worth me while."

Liam looked doubtful so Rob ploughed on. "Of course the alternative is to carry on like you are, in fact I can make it as much worse as I can make it better. You won't last and we both know it. Work for me and I'll protect you when you get out too, so long as you come up with the goods for me. There'll be some money in it for you as well."

Liam's world was full of bastards who used him and here was yet another one lining him up for the same thing, and yet he had no strength to protest.

The deal done, Docker insisted on a bit of good faith up-front from Liam. In addition to a couple of small-time dealer, the name Patrick Quinn now appeared in his notebook for the first time. He looked like an interesting prospect for the future. Certainly worth having a look in MIDCRO records to see if he had a file.

Docker stood up to leave, "Oh by the way, you can stick your write-offs up your arse. We've already got our detections for the month. I'll sort things with the Governor to show good faith and I'll be back to see you and have our next nice long chat."

***

Whilst Rob Docker was busy cementing his own reputation as a top-drawer detective sergeant, a former colleague was busy trying to climb the CID ladder himself. In reality Alan had peaked as a constable and was looking for something better than noble cause corruption to satisfy his needs.

Alan was entering a new phase of his police service, and relishing his role as a newly-appointed detective constable. He prided himself on his appearance and liked to think of himself as a bit of a ladies-man so needed to keep up with the latest fashion in kipper ties, three-piece suits and cowboy boots. Not so his wife, who had suffered from the effects of childbirth, and not quite regained the size twelve figure that was his preference. Far too much meat on the bones. Still, plenty more fish in the sea was his maxim, and he would play the detective card to the hilt to explore his options.

Some police officers were outrageous flirts and some predators – Alan was definitely the latter.

His CID attachment had gone well and he had managed a good arrest rate. Arresting people was one thing, but having enough evidence to charge was another. Alan however had no problems in this area, and was well versed in reaching the evidential thresholds which needed to be met, by fair means or foul.

Carrying all of his worldly goods in a box file, and wearing a thin fixed smile, he entered his new office and was surveyed by more than a dozen pairs of curious eyes.

He walked through into the detective inspector's office and presented himself to an aging pot-bellied man with grey hair, who was still suffering from the remnants of a good session from the night before, and was playing with a pile of papers scattered across a disorganized desk. The office smelt of stale tobacco and the overfull ashtray on the desk pointed towards a forty-a-day habit.

A number of yellow Personal Assessment Forms for officers lay festering on the table – just detail that he couldn't be bothered with, even though he held the career ambitions of decent, hardworking officers in his hands.

It was a short conversation, "That's your detective sergeant" he said, pointing his finger at a balding man with glasses sat outside, "That's your desk, keep your nose clean, and do as you are told. You need to fit in – any road up we're a team here so let's see if you're a team player."

Alan was dismissed summarily and after brief introductions to his sergeant, and those around him, he made his way somewhat dejectedly to his desk. He was the outsider and he felt it keenly.

He started to spread the contents of his box onto the desk and positioned the blotter pad square on. He liked straight lines but the liking didn't extend to his working practices. He pulled open the top left-hand drawer and placed his CID diary carefully inside. In the drawer below he placed his pocket book, and several black pens, plus the all-important red pen for payments to informants. In the top right-hand drawer went a pair of handcuffs and a torch.

Alan pulled open the bottom drawer to deposit some outstanding court case files awaiting 'Not Guilty' hearings. As it opened he saw a small brown envelope.

As curiosity got the better of him he instinctively turned his back slightly towards the other officers in the room. Shielded from view he opened the envelope with one hand still in the drawer, his left arm firmly resting on the top of the table. He saw a typed note that said simply, *'welcome,'* and behind it nestled a wad of crisp new ten pound notes.

Slowly he closed the drawer and continued making the desk his own. No pictures of the family, the wife, the children, the dog – nothing.

Alan turned and crossed the room to talk to another detective constable whilst behind him an officer casually walked into the DI's office and closed the door. Message conveyed, Alan had passed his first test – others would follow.

It was pretty straightforward really – take the money and stay. Leave the money in the drawer, and you either got transferred subtly, or life became extremely difficult – simple.

From the DI's office came a familiar shout, "Get some work done you bunch of spastics. I don't wanna hear you lot cackling all day."

His first day passed quietly and at 5pm he spent a couple of hours drinking in a local pub with his new family.

Driving home later he opened the window of the driver's door and vomited without stopping. The brown envelope sat comfortably inside his suit jacket pocket. It had not been a bad day.

It didn't take long for Alan to settle in and soon he had another good little sideline going which he wasn't about to share with anyone else.

On his area there was a debt-recovery company who specialized in getting payment from 'hard to reach' individuals. They got paid a good percentage of the going rate for recovered goods and used any means in the book to achieve their targets.

Alan's role was simple. When the company had the registration number of a creditor's vehicle they fed it back to Alan so that he could complete a Police National Computer check enabling him to provide them with address details of the keeper. At £10 per check he was providing a totally illegal service that was pure profit for himself. A few quid he could salt away for a rainy day, and besides he liked a flutter now and then in the bookies.

As far as Alan was concerned he was performing a public duty and he had no difficulties in finding spurious reasons for performing the checks. If necessary he could always fix it so that someone else's name went down for the check.

***

If it wasn't so serious Joe would have found it mildly amusing. He did not relate to being some form of Sicilian 'Godfather' figure but it appeared that others felt that he had some influence.

As the man sat before him in his office pleading his case he found himself presented with two relatively small problems.

The man wanted his son to get bail for an attempt robbery on a sub-post office in the south of the city, and he wanted a false passport so that the errant young man could do a runner and leave for Spain.

Joe listened to the tale of woe as the man described how his son had been caught bang to rights by the police, as he was about to rob a security van delivering to the sub-post office. His son had previous convictions and was looking at ten years if convicted. He had been the one holding the loaded sawn-off shotgun; the driver had legged it and got away, whilst his co-accused was a first time 'druggie,' which would leave him to face the music. His father was gutted by the prospects facing his only son.

Something about the story appealed to Joe's better nature and he made a quick decision. To get the man bail would cost the man's father £500 as someone would need to get paid. The passport he would arrange free gratis on the proviso that the man would owe him a favour in future. There were no free meals in this business and Joe would collect on his favour in due course.

After the man had left Joe made a call to his friendly magistrate and the price was agreed. It would need to look right and sureties would be expected to come forward, in the knowledge that they would lose their bail money. Bail conditions would include the surrender of the accused's passport, and a condition of living at home, and reporting at a police station.

None of these would cause any concerns, as the would-be robber would be on a pre-arranged flight to Spain before it was found that any of the conditions had been breached.

Joe made one more phone call to the man's father. He told him to sack his lawyer and provided him with the name of another to be contacted immediately and provided with details as to when to make a bail application. It was that easy.

Joe had no means of knowing it, but he had just made the score 1-2.

Chapter Thirty Five: 'I Gotcha'

(Joe Tex)

1972

It wasn't in Quinn's nature to be sentimental, but the death of Joey had struck a chord inside him - the pain of which would not leave him. He had been under no illusions that Joey's disappearance was anything other than unnatural, and the discovery of the body, three years later, in 1972, had just confirmed his worst fears, and also brought with it some unnecessary attention.

'What a way to finish up – being chewed by a fucking fox in the middle of nowhere.' Quinn reflected.

Cofton Hackett was just on the border with Birmingham City Police, and West Mercia Constabulary, and it took some time for them to decide which force would take primacy. No-one wanted an unsolved murder on their books if they could avoid it but Birmingham City had the resources, and a possible missing person report to go with the leather jacket found in the grave, so they took it on.

Quinn had got one of the women to pretend to be Joey's lover and report him missing back in 1969. There was a last-known sighting at the pub in Birmingham City Centre, but police enquiries had met with a blank, and the papers, such as they were, remained on file.

It wasn't long before Quinn and the Black Souls were receiving attention from the murder investigation team, but he knew it was coming and had put steps in place to make sure that any extraordinary business was put on hold, at the same time advising his sponsors across the water to keep a low profile for the time being.

The officers worked methodically, interviewing each member of the club as a T.I.E. – 'Trace, Interview and Eliminate,' enquiry, and got absolutely nowhere.

The bikers had been made a specific line of enquiry by the old detective chief inspector in charge, but he knew that his officers would struggle to get a foot through the door into their world and was not hopeful of a breakthrough. He wasn't too bothered either, *'one less scumbag in the world to worry about.'* In the end, all of the bikers, including Quinn, provided an alibi for their movements on the day of the murder and the enquiry team moved on.

Quinn however did not. He would move heaven and earth to get to the truth although he was not expecting much help from the former.

Someone had murdered a good friend, who had shown him loyalty and friendship. Despite what he had become, Joey was a founding member, the Vice President and a true Angel. His murder could not go unanswered. Revenge would take place in accordance with the Code. Quinn would not rest until justice was done – that was his kind of justice, and not to be confused with the law of the land.

He was confident that the way forward was to find out what

had happened to Joey's distinctive Harley Davidson. He put the feelers out amongst his contacts, assisted by some pressure, threats, and the calling in of favours owed.

Eventually this resulted in an anonymous phone call from a biker based in London. He confirmed that he had purchased the bike from a dealer in Birmingham some three years previously. Although it was on false plates he was confident that it was Joey's bike but the name of the dealer was all that he was prepared to give. He was giving the information out of loyalty to the biker fraternity and a healthy dose of fear of the Angels, but that was it, and he would not be in touch again.

Quinn prepared carefully for his visit to the bike-dealer in Small Heath and took three of the Black Souls with him. They used cars so as not to attract interest, and dressed down for the occasion in jeans and T-shirts – no identifying leather jackets.

The dealership was not a grand affair – just a dozen bikes on a small forecourt, and a small shop for motorcycle parts with a counter at the front. They found their man sat in his back office with his feet up on the table, digesting the remnants of a bacon sandwich, and studying the contents of the Sun's page three.

Whilst one biker secured the front door Quinn and the other two went to work. This was not a time for pleasantries and Quinn wanted to be in and out as quickly as possible. Whilst the other two held the struggling man firmly by the arms in the chair Quinn gripped his mouth firmly open and went to work with a pair of pliers.

He wasn't interested in asking the question first as he needed the man to know that he could, and would, inflict pain and that any threats made would be carried out.

A gag in the mouth stifled the cries of pain as blood oozed from the man's mouth.

"I'm leaving here in five minutes with the name of a person who sold a vintage Harley Hydra Glide to you three years ago," Quinn declared, as he held the bloodied tooth and the pliers in the face of the terrified man. "If you lie to me I'll take all of your teeth out one by one and then cut your cock off."

The man nodded furiously and Quinn thrust a pen and paper into his hand.

"If you speak to anyone I'll burn this place down and then burn you and your family alive. Do you understand?" Through tears of agony the man nodded twice.

Driving back, Quinn studied the piece of paper, *'Winston Livingstone, comes from Handsworth,'* – now things were starting to slot into place. So the truce had been broken. That suited just fine. It was time for a reckoning.

Fate had decreed that he now had the opportunity to not only avenge the death of Joey, but also to take revenge for his loss of face at the confrontation with Joe in Handsworth.

Winston Livingstone's days of pointing shotguns at people were numbered – Quinn was going to enjoy this.

He moved quickly and after a few phone calls arranged for Maggie and Shirley to pay a visit to the club. They scrubbed up well and the transformation from jeans, T-shirts and leather jackets, to high heels, short skirts and equally short tops, which left not very much to the imagination, surprised some of the Black Souls. Both of them done-up like dog's dinners.

They were under strict instructions that the first trip was to be just a 'recce' and the two girls spent the next few hours listening to some very unfamiliar music and fending off unwanted attention from pissed youngsters, and older men, clearly married, who were just looking for one thing. They struggled with the Reggae beat and found Soul dreary. No rock music.

Maggie and Shirley in turn were just after one thing, and when they found Winston inside, arms folded, playing the hard man as he watched over the dance-floor area, Maggie muttered 'bingo,' and hissed under her breath as she spotted the ring on his left hand. He wasn't that difficult to identify with the scars from a chip-fat fryer still etched into his face, but the ring sealed his fate.

The two girls played the innocent with him for a few minutes, asking for the toilets as they were new in the area, attending a training course, and after exchanging first names they left with big smiles on their faces. As Winston watched them walk across the dance floor he also managed a smile of appreciation. Nice bits of skirt. One of them had an arse like two peaches in a bag.

The following week the two girls went through the same routine but this time engaged Winston in more conversation and some casual flirting. Winston couldn't believe his luck – the potential for 'two for the price of one'. Before leaving, Maggie made it clear that the following week their course would be finishing and that it would be their last visit. At the same time Shirley delivered the last piece of the honey-trap as she whispered into Winston's ear, "Perhaps we could say goodbye properly next week," and patted him on the bottom as she walked off.

Quinn discussed the plan with the four Black Souls who would accompany him, plus Maggie and Shirley. Three of the bikers were those who had known and loved Joey in their own way, Seamus, Steve and Frank. They had insisted, and it somehow felt right that the original crew should avenge the murder of their fifth member. The fourth was a new Prospect called 'Sharpie' who wasn't the brightest tool in the box, but was a strong man, eager to please and had made it known that he would do anything to get his top rocker. He was also a 'clean skin' with no previous convictions, and Quinn wanted to test his mettle.

The plan was agreed and there was no question of turning back – their evening would end in murder.

***

Maggie and Shirley spent time chatting, drinking at the bar and dancing the hours away. Winston had jumped at the chance of giving both of them a lift back to their accommodation and had even arranged to leave the club at 2am instead of checking around and closing up. They made it clear that Winston was on 'a promise,' and he couldn't wait to have them all to himself. He could already smell the bacon.

At 2am the three of them left and, after collecting his car, Winston followed directions from Maggie and Shirley to the Lee Bank area. Maggie sat in the front next to Winston whilst Shirley sat giggling in the back seat, leaning forward between the front seats, exposing her breasts beneath the short top, and teasing Winston constantly. *'This was going to be truly a night to remember.'* He smiled to himself as Maggie stroked the inside of his left leg.

It was a ten-minute journey and as Maggie directed them into a dimly lit cul- de-sac to park up Winston was feeling excited. He was totally preoccupied by the attentions of the girls and failed to see a black Transit van, with no lights on, move quietly across the entrance, as he drove in, and remain stationary with the engine running. There was no way out.

Winston brought the car to a halt and switched the engine off. "Where to then girls?" he turned to Maggie with one hand on her leg.

"To hell you black fucker!" screamed Shirley from the back seat as she looped a thin cord over his head round his neck, and pulled back hard against his headrest, clinging on with all her might.

As the air choked from Winston he gripped the cord with his right hand struggling to free up his windpipe whilst Maggie clung onto his left arm.

Within seconds the driver's door was pulled open and Winston was dragged from the car into the roadway and a beating was administered.

Quinn had given strict instructions that the girls should leave immediately, and without speaking, adjusting their unfamiliar clothing as they went, they walked off into the darkness. A car had been parked up by arrangement with the ignition key left in, in a nearby road – their job was done.

Quinn stood towering above one of the two men he had sworn to kill that night outside the club. He felt no rage, just deadly cold, and Winston saw no mercy in those ice blue eyes. Joe's words came unbidden into his head,

'There is something about a man who has taken another life, a mark upon him. He won't forgive or forget and that moment of defeat will gnaw away at him. I fear there will be blood spilt because of this.' The irony was, Winston was not the one who had spilt blood first, but he was about to pay for Joe's moment of anger.

Quinn interrupted the brief reverie, "No shotgun or crowd of spook friends to protect you tonight lover-boy?"

Quinn struck Winston hard in the mouth and stuffed a rag between his bleeding lips to silence him. There was never much likelihood of Winston getting to his feet but Quinn needed this to be over quickly, and as he drew back the other three stepped in stamping and kicking Winston with their steel toe-capped boots. One direct stomp on the head broke bone.

All four of the bikers were holding lengths of bike chain that they wielded expertly to flail Winston's still body. He was already unconscious and no doubt close to death as Quinn bent down and whispered in Winston's ear, "For Joey you bastard!" He plunged a knife into the right side of his neck.

As the black van started to reverse slowly towards them, Quinn wiped the blood from the knife on Winston's shirt and pulled the 'BS' ring from his finger. The job was done and leaving the lifeless figure in the middle of the road, they climbed into the van.

In the end it proved to be a night that Winston Livingstone would not in fact remember.

Six floors up in the ugly tower block that overlooked the cul-de-sac, Elsie Grant looked out from her bedroom window doing what insomniacs of her age always do, have a good old nose. She had watched the black van for some time and could see the front-seat passengers sat smoking, and when four men eventually left the vehicle to walk into the Close her interest increased.

Elsie was no stranger to unusual activity, the area was rife with drugs-dealers, and street fights were routine, but she knew instinctively that these men were up to no good, and it mithered her whilst she made her mind up what to do.

Thus it was that Elsie was the only other person on earth granted a birds-eye view of Winston's last moments on earth. She reached for the phone to dial 999.

Chapter Thirty Six: 'The First Time Ever I Saw Your Face'

(Roberta Flack)

1972

As they drove towards Worcester, elation turned to despair as they came face-to-face with a police road-block just outside Bromsgrove town centre. With five of them in the van together, and all tooled up, it wouldn't take a brain surgeon long to make the connection with the fight in Birmingham.

The inside of the van was like an armoury, and although Quinn had just enough time to conceal the knife under the driver's seat, any thoughts of trying to fight their way out of the situation quickly diminished when a couple of dog vans turned up to support their colleagues, whose 'Christmas' had come all at once.

With the two Alsatians straining at their leashes, the five men were lined up, handcuffed, and transported individually back to Birmingham, as more police vehicles arrived.

Quinn sat in the back of the police vehicle, to the left of the driver, with an officer sat next to him. Nothing was said and he stared out of the window trying to collect his thoughts. He remained convinced that the death of Joey had needed to be avenged but he realised that he had placed everything that he had worked for, including his family, in jeopardy for the sake of it. He again felt the cold fingers of fear that stretched all the way back to a boy in a coal cellar. For a man like Quinn this was an uncomfortable feeling – his

'Achilles heel'.

Quinn spent several uncomfortable hours banged up in a cell alone with his demons before he was spoken to. On arrival he had been stripped and made to wear a white paper suit before his clothing was placed individually in large brown paper bags.

All of his belongings including his belt, his wallet, and two signet rings bearing the initials 'BS' were removed, one from his finger, and one from his pocket. His boots were left outside the cell door. Every half an hour a uniformed officer dropped the hatch on the steel door to peer at him and then slammed it shut again. They were in no rush. Quinn tried to remain outwardly calm but inside he was in turmoil – he couldn't stay in this place much longer.

Quinn sat on the wooden bench with the grey blanket wrapped over his shoulders staring at the closed grey painted door and the open toilet next to it. He wasn't in control here, even the chain for flushing the toilet was outside the cell, and he didn't like the feeling. He certainly didn't like the smell of stale piss and shit. He had asked for a 'brief' when the custody officer had informed him that he was being detained on suspicion of murder but none had been forthcoming.

In the confined space Quinn was living his worst nightmare.

In other cells nearby, but out of earshot, four other 'Black Souls' gathered their own thoughts. For 'Sharpie' in particular, this was a new experience and although he tried hard to suppress the feelings he was shit-scared.

As Quinn wrestled with his phobia he tried to remember

everything that he had been taught in Ireland about interrogation techniques. This would be a real test for the 'code of silence'.

Finally the door opened and Patrick Quinn came face to face with Detective Sergeant Robert Docker for the first time in his life.

Rob was well prepared and ready with a game plan.

"Follow me Pat," he said quietly and turned away deliberately with his back to Quinn who was obliged to follow in his footsteps. The mind games had already begun.

Docker took him to an interview room within the cell block, and beckoned him towards a chair. He closed the door and a uniformed officer stood outside.

"What's this, no good cop - bad cop – where's my brief? I asked for him hours ago." Quinn tried to wrestle some control away from the police officer.

Rob looked mildly amused but very calmly stared straight into Quinn's eyes and said, "I don't believe in them games Pat – they're strictly for the kids. There's only one cop here and it's definitely a bad cop situation - and by the way you won't be getting a brief. There's no record on the custody sheet of you asking for one and me hearing ain't what it used to be these days."

Quinn pushed the chair back angrily as he rose to his feet, squared up to Docker, and shouted, "I'm not frightened of you, you bastard I'll fucking eat you for breakfast in court, and you can expect a visit at home too."

The door opened but Docker waved the officer away.

"Sit down Pat and fucking listen, or go back to your cell. It's all the same to me – and by the way I hate me wife so you'd be doing me a favour, and me kid's dead already so you can't touch her."

Quinn was unsettled – he was used to getting a reaction and this man was having none of it. He sat down.

Rob went on, "Pat, we do things by the book here – my book that is. My bosses want a result. A man's been murdered on our patch and we simply can't have that. As it happens I know you quite well. I know that you have a family, that you exert power and influence, and you can get things sorted. I like that in a person. I also know that you've some interesting mates."

Quinn struggled to gain control, "Get to the point – I don't need a CV writing."

Rob smiled thinly, "It's dead simple Pat. You won't be leaving here without a charge sheet in your hand. That charge sheet will either have affray written on it or murder. You have a choice but if you choose the first you'll be grafting for me and I'll make sure that the Judge gets a letter from us telling him what a useful informant you've been. If you choose the second the only place that you'll be seeing your good lady and Sean in will be in the visitor's room at Winson Green Prison – that's of course if they can get a Visiting Order to see you."

"You're fucking joking," Quinn exploded, "You can't prove murder."

"No good bleating about it now Pat, the dirty deeds been done, and you are well and truly in the frame. By the way Pat I *can* prove it," Docker persisted "You made a mistake taking that ring off Winston's finger. It's got his blood on it and I've already got five witness statements to say that he owned it, and was wearing it the last time he was seen alive.

That's the straight bit of evidence, but you also need to know that when I say the word your clothes will match forensically to the dead man, and when I say the word the hair samples I'll remove from your bonce – by force if necessary, will be found on the dead man's clothing."

Quinn stared at him defiantly giving himself time to let the words sink in.

"You need time to do a bit of thinking Pat. You know how it works, you're not averse to a bit of creative thinking as I recall. Remember the copper that got done in the Irish pub Pat? Very clever – a man after me own heart," Rob paused, "There are five of you and someone is going to have to have the murder. I'll even let you decide which one if you see a little bit of sense. You know how the game works Pat, it's not personal. Just think of it as an opportunity – a way out of a mess."

"You cunt – you think I'm scared of the likes of you. I'll have your fucking guts for garters," said Quinn.

"No I don't Pat," Rob said soothingly "I don't think for one minute that you're frightened of me. Let me tell you a little story though. Some years ago I read-up on the Kray twins and some of the big villains. Fascinating stuff. Real hard villains, some killed for pure pleasure. What I learnt though is that you have to look for the weakness and we all have them you see Pat, we all have them."

Quinn glared at him but felt the sweat start to rise on his forehead.

Rob continued, "I've read everything there is to read about you Pat, simply everything, and guess what, you have a little weakness don't you? It's on one of the custody records from one of you previous little episodes, and the records of your time in Borstal, ain't it Pat? In big red letters, you're fucking claustrophobic Pat – you don't like small spaces, and I got lots of them available and waiting. Not quite the big man that they all think you are. I can make sure you spend the rest of your life in the smallest space you can imagine, and I bet you can imagine that really well."

The uniformed officer returned Quinn to his cell whilst Rob sat in his office contemplating his next move. For the purposes of the custody record Docker had merely been collecting antecedent history from the suspect.

After thirty minutes, two of Dockers detective constables took Quinn from his cell and interviewed him at length. It was all very formal and with no offers on the table. No solicitor and no let-up even though Quinn tried to maintain, 'No Comment,' responses in an effort to irritate them but they smiled confidently throughout.

Two hours later Rob arranged for Quinn to receive a visit from Jenny – just five minutes but just long enough for her to break down in front of him sobbing uncontrollably.

Rob faced Quinn again across the interview room table, "You don't look too well Pat. I guess it's a bit hot and sweaty in that cell. The offer on the table won't change and it's the best that you are gonna get. If I was you I'd bite me hand off before it's too late. Work with me and I'll look after you. Fight me and you are fucked. No bail straight to jail. I'll be sending the forensic boys in to see you soon, by which time it'll be too late. I wonder what they'll find under your fingernails Pat, or on the soles of your boots – they just love looking for blood spray patterns Pat."

Rob left the room and the same two officers returned for a further tedious round of questions. Relentless and monotone, one of them actually said, "I hope you enjoying counting bricks Pat because you're gonna have plenty of time to do that soon. And by the way I just love boring people to death so you just take as long as you like. This is the interview record for court Pat, and shaping up nicely it is too."

Quinn's mind was racing – he wanted to beat seven bells of shit out of them, beat these two twats to death, and smash Rob Dockers face into the nearest wall. He was full of hatred and ready to explode again but he was a practical man and a survivor. He was also in agony from the confined space of the cell and despite fighting and winning many challenges in his life the horror of claustrophobia gripped him to the point of despair. Quinn made a decision.

"Get me Docker – I'll only speak to Docker," he announced.

Docker sat alongside Quinn on the cell bench. He showed no fear of the man who had just killed Winston Livingstone in cold blood, and Quinn flushed visibly as defeat stared him in the face.

There was always that moment in the eyes that good interrogators could detect, before capitulation, and Rob had seen it.

"Perhaps we could sit in me office Pat – it's a bit more cosy in there," said Rob quietly, sensing success.

They spoke freely for thirty minutes after which there was clarity and a way forward. Quinn would sit down with the two 'clowns' and admit to playing a minor role in the disturbance involving the death of Livingstone. He might even throw a bit of self-defence in. "Now we're cooking with gas" said Rob.

The thorny question of who would be the focus for a murder charge was agreed upon, and Quinn would get bail with conditions once he had appeared at court. In the interim Docker would arrange for Quinn to be supervised in a detention room with the door open – all very civil.

Before that, by arrangement, Quinn was placed in the cell being occupied by 'Sharpie'.

He studied the young Prospect before him and felt more than a tinge of guilt as he persuaded him to take the rap for the murder, "You've got no previous and with a good brief and the arrangement I've negotiated it should be dropped to manslaughter. The most you'd get is seven years, and you'd be out in half of that. It's either that or we all go down together and that means the end of The Chapter, and I know you don't want that. If you do this I'll give you your top rocker the day you come out and you'll be respected as a righteous brother the rest of your days."

'Sharpie' wanted desperately to belong to something and to

be someone. The offer of a monthly allowance to be paid to his pregnant girlfriend clinched it as Quinn bear-hugged him and concluded, "You're truly one of us now and we always look after our own. You've got balls. You'll do well when you get out." Inside Quinn was gutted – this was not the way it was supposed to be.

For his part, once they had 'Sharpies' confession written down, Rob would see to it that the ring was removed from the evidential chain for the time being – they were in business. Docker might be more bent than a fish hook but now he had a specimen fish on the line.

Quinn added Rob Docker to the list of men that he hated in the world, but also started a new one for those that he feared. The man had an empty space where his soul should be.

In contrast Rob had a couple of well-deserved pints, and watched an episode of 'Van Der Valk' on TV in the station bar, before cracking on with the paperwork.

***

After the first one it had become much easier, and with the court case over he could start looking forward again. True to his word Docker had produced a letter for the Judge when Quinn's case had come to trial, and he had received a suspended sentence. The final story had been of a fight in the street that had gone too far, with unfortunate results for Winston. As far as the Police were concerned it was a neat job. A nasty piece of a black bastard was dead and a scumbag biker in jail for a few years, everyone a winner.

Quinn hated every second of dealing with a man like Rob

Docker, but he also realized that he could make use of the situation, like he had with the Irish. Sometimes you just had to roll with the punches - then hit back hard when the time was right.

There were no cosy meetings in pubs for Quinn and Docker – this was strictly one hundred per cent business, and Quinn wanted to spend the least time that he could in the company of the man he despised for what he was.

Quinn always removed any trappings of his biker existence when going to meet Docker and drove a car rather using his bike. The routine was always the same with a late evening meet on the sprawling car park at the back of the Wholesale Markets. Quinn would wait, staring from the front seat into the darkness until Rob made his appearance on foot and slipped into the front seat.

The cosh under Quinn's seat gave him a degree of comfort as he sat in the shadows waiting. He itched to use it. *'One day,"* he thought, *'One day I'll see you into your grave.'*

Initially, Quinn had given up someone that was wanted by another police force for a serious wounding. He knew where the guy was staying with friends and simply provided the address. Not so painful really, and he owed the man nothing.

After that he started taking out the opposition, indeed anyone who represented a threat to the growth of his business interests. He provided the names and sometimes, if it was a drugs dealer, he set up a buy so that Docker was guaranteed a result.

For his part Rob passed most of the jobs to the Regional Crime Squad so as to put some distance between himself, Quinn, and the information. The RCS were happy to get jobs given to them on a plate and Rob's reputation grew within senior CID circles.

Rob always made claims for payment for the activities of his informants, the difference being that in Quinn's case he received nothing for his information – just the pleasure of Rob's company. He would simply sign the paperwork for receipt of cash, none of which he ever saw.

***

After years of relative success Quinn now found himself trapped in a relationship with a corrupt police officer, and knew that this man would not think twice about exposing him should the need arise.

The splits which had emerged in the preceding months between the Provisional, and Official Irish Republic Army, had simply added to his problems but some fairly direct conversations with 'The General' had resulted in him nailing his colours firmly to the PIRA camp. They represented the future and he calculated that the old guard would not survive.

The problem with this was that PIRA were pushing all the time after internment was introduced on the 11 August 1971, for spectaculars on the mainland to make the British pay. The deaths of British soldiers, or police officers, in Northern Ireland were simply not enough and PIRA calculated that the deaths of innocent people would help to focus the minds of the politicians.

The stress of living with extreme claustrophobia, being an agent of PIRA, an informant for the British, and the President of an organised crime gang left very little room for sweet dreams, and a relaxed life. With so many backs to constantly watch Quinn rarely found himself with a clear head.

The transition from simply providing information on criminals to that of exposing terrorists had been much easier than Quinn would have imagined. He had no love for his masters, and his status as an informant gave him a degree of protection as well as the opportunity to take revenge.

Rob Docker had given clear instructions to Quinn that whilst he wanted to know about all of his PIRA activities he also needed to know who else would possess the same knowledge. Docker would determine on this basis which jobs might be allowed to run and which ones would not. His bosses got told what they wanted and needed to know.

Quinn did not need to be reminded that with one false move his number would be up and it would be the death of him – it would not be a pleasant one.

***

After Winston's murder, Joe held a meeting with trusted friends within the community. He had no desire to set Handsworth on fire in a war with the Black Souls and his sixth-sense told him not to rush headlong into battle. Besides which, he had waited to see if justice prevailed when the case came to court.

When Quinn walked free and he realized how, he decided to take time to think things through carefully. His twin was everywhere, the spider at the centre of a web of corruption and murder, and Joe knew better than anyone how ruthless, cunning and dangerous Rob Docker could be when his own arse was on the line. That made things complicated. Winston's death would not go unanswered but the response would be of his time and making.

Chapter Thirty Seven: 'For The Love Of Money'

(The O'Jays)

1974

Sandra's girls were handsomely rewarded for their efforts and by 1974 the business was doing well. Although still only thirty-two years of age herself, Sandra was regarded as the mother-figure, and she knew every detail of their personal lives. Even prostitutes have families, and many of them were in loving relationships. Experts at achieving 'happy endings', they were also experts at gathering useful information.

Sandra chose her girls carefully. As well as having good figures they also needed to have a great sense of humour, and to be able to provide for all tastes.

She had once interviewed a girl who came wearing a short fur coat. The girl had a face a bit like a smacked arse but legs that went on forever, and a beautiful trim figure with large breasts which some of her clientele would be pleased to get their hands on, "You know what they say, fur coat no knickers," she had quipped to the girl who, quick as a flash had responded, "I thought it was red shoes no knickers. Anyway do I need any for this job?" They both collapsed in fits of laughter – she got the job.

The reality was that many of the punters never got to experience full sex, and indeed one or two were actually happy with the experience of just having a good chat with a beautiful woman who would normally be beyond their reach. After the experience with Joey, Sandra tried to discourage clients with more extreme tastes, so whilst voyeurism was acceptable, sado-masochism was not.

"What sort of day have you had?" or, "Are you busy at the moment?" was usually enough to get the clients talking. The girls were good listeners, inherently sympathetic souls who empathized with the men who entered their lives for a maximum of one hour per session and then left again.

After each session Sandra debriefed the girls over a cup of tea. She kept a card on each client, and built up a steady picture of knowledge on each one. Police officers, Judges, MPs, sports personalities, they were all there, and Joe perused the cards every now and then, to identify people who could potentially be of use to him in the future.

Most of them loved someone in their lives, often their wives, who of course did not understand them, always their children, and for the slightly more complicated one or two, their mothers.

Arthur Mason was one of the more straightforward. In his late-fifties and slightly overweight, wearing spectacles, he was the epitome of 'Captain Mainwaring'. In keeping with the fictitious Home Guard captain he just loved the feeling of power. Arthur just wanted sex, with the occasional bit of spanking, and set time aside from work each week to go and visit his favourite girl at the sauna. Before long his usefulness became apparent – he was a Bank Manager.

Three months into his visits Arthur received a letter in the post, at his home address, which when opened revealed an invitation for Arthur and his wife to attend a charity boxing match at The Albany in Birmingham. A free meal for a good cause appealed to Arthur and appealed to his misplaced sense of importance.

Joe spared no expense, but deliberately kept a low profile. It was a cracking event, black-tie, good food, free drink, some quality boxing, and some very attentive hostesses for the evening – just up Arthur's street.

Arthur of course did know Joe, but disliked him personally for no other reason than the fact that he was black. He was however scrupulously careful not to display his racist attitudes overtly as they shook hands at the beginning of the evening.

Arthur played the dutiful husband and for the evening put his wife on a pedestal that she rarely occupied these days. As the daughter of a rich Birmingham businessman however, she had a nice inheritance coming, so he tried his best to keep her sweet.

The boxing finished, and as people were gathered in small groups across various parts of the club, Arthur was approached by James Hathaway together with his wife. James was on a regular retainer as Joe's solicitor and was sharper than a razor blade.

James shook Arthur's hand firmly but whilst maintaining his grip said, "Arthur, perhaps we could leave the women chatting for a few moments. I just need to speak to you on a matter of some importance." It was more of an instruction than a request as James guided Arthur gently towards one of the empty cubicles.

Arthur was not at all happy and went blood red, intoning pompously, "Mr. Hathaway I can't think what business you might want to discuss at a social event. I am not here to talk about work related issues and I object to being dragged away from my wife."

James was practiced at dealing with confrontation and soothed, "My sincere apologies. I really do understand. I have merely been asked to deliver some paperwork to you personally for you to consider at your convenience. Please do contact me if I can assist further."

Two small brown envelopes were placed into Arthur's hand as James indicated his departure, "Any road up, enjoy the rest of your evening."

The last thing Arthur Mason wanted was to be seen in a club with two brown envelopes in his hand and he fumed as he slipped them into his suit pocket.

Back home, Arthur's wife had her statutory cigarette, and one final large glass of white wine, to complement the copious amounts of gin and tonic that she had consumed, then went upstairs to bed. Within five minutes he could hear her snoring loudly from his chair in the living room where he sat dejected with a large tumbler of whisky.

Above all else Arthur was not a stupid man, and during the drive home had already worked out in his own mind what was going on. Alone with these thoughts he reached inside his pocket and took out the envelopes as his stomach churned violently. This was no wind-up and Arthur's dirty washing was about to be displayed.

He tore the first one open and was presented with seven black-and-white photographs of a smiling Arthur 'naked to the world' and in various sexual positions with his favourite girl. *'God knows where the camera was hidden in the room'*, he thought, but there was no mistaking it was Arthur and the picture of him being slapped on the bottom was particularly difficult for him to digest. Frankly he had not realized how pathetic he had looked.

The second envelope contained one hundred pounds and a typed note. *'No-one needs to get hurt Arthur, this is simply business. If you go to the police the remaining photographs will be sent to your wife and the Birmingham Evening Mail. In due course someone will be in touch with you to arrange for some deposits to be made at the bank. We look forward to working with you.'*

Arthur poured himself another whisky as the word 'shit' bounced around in his head over and over again, and he contemplated a new career in the world of money laundering.

***

It was a busy week for James Hathaway who often acted as a messenger for Joe. He didn't mind, as the risks were low. After all who was going to find anything strange in a solicitor speaking to criminals, police officers, or members of the judiciary?

James met Malcolm Reid in the pub opposite the Victoria Law Courts and stood quite openly in conversation with him in the busy bar area. It was always full of solicitors and police officers putting the world to rights after a hard day. One more or less made no difference. James detested Malcolm but tolerated him and knew the basis of his worth to Joe.

"A pint Malcolm?" James ventured. The ritual response came, "Go on then you twisted me arm." Malcolm never paid.

They talked about the validity of Red Rum winning the Grand National, John Conteh being the Light Heavyweight Champion, and whether the erotic film 'Emmanuel' would be worth seeing. At the right moment however James lowered his tone and gave Malcolm his instructions in very simple terms. How the task was delivered was up to Malcolm.

The following morning Malcolm made an early start at work and under the pretext of depositing some exhibits into the property store he carried three cardboard boxes inside and closed the door behind him. He entered details of two of the boxes into the property book and placed them neatly into one of the racks. Studying the book carefully he found what he was looking for and after pinpointing their location on the shelves he carefully removed two ledgers and placed them into the third box.

Before returning the keys he made the short trip to his car at the rear of the station and deposited the box into the boot of his car.

Scrap metal registers were key pieces of evidence to any police investigation in proving that a dealer had been behaving dishonestly, and would be one of the cornerstones of any criminal case.

This was one prosecution that would be going no further and one more favour owed to Joe by a grateful dealer who would be well-chuffed.

Chapter Thirty Eight. 'Behind Closed Doors'

Charlie Rich

1973

In 1973 the pot-bellied man with grey hair moved on and Rob Docker achieved the somewhat rare distinction of being promoted straight from detective sergeant to detective inspector to replace him. Quinn's information played no small part in his elevation.

He started as he meant to go on.

Rob surveyed the two young detectives across the desk. He hadn't invited them to take a seat so they knew that this was not a good sign.

"Well boys a good result I see from your prison visit at the 'Green'..."They relaxed – perhaps it wasn't going to be a bollocking after all."Eighty theft of, and from, motor vehicles cleared in the city-centre – yes very impressive."

Rob surveyed the paperwork in front of him – eighty crime reports neatly tied up with narrow pink ribbon used for prosecution files.

Contained within each report was a copy of a statement under caution made by a serving prisoner in Winson Green Prison. Within each copy a couple of lines were highlighted which amounted to an admission to that particular offence.

The officers were asking for these offences to be 'written off' under item 10 of the Home Office Instructions as being inexpedient to prosecute due to the fact that the person admitting responsibility was already serving a sentence. Eighty cleared crimes would make the detection figures look pretty good for the month.

"Shut the fucking door," Rob barked sharply.

As they stood facing him he turned his wrath on them, "Listen you pair of cunts. Are you trying to drop us all in the shit? I signed a prison visit request for one hour. How the fuck can anyone admit eighty offences in one hour, and then put them all down in a written statement. You got him to sign blank pages didn't you? Then he wrote the caption at the end so that you could fill the rest in later. You must think I was born yesterday." They stared at the floor.

Rob wasted no time in giving instructions - page one was to be amended and initialed to show that the statement was in fact just three pages with considerably less detections. The last page would be retained,

"Rip the rest up you twats and go back next month and do the fucking job properly.

If I so much as get a whiff of Complaints and Discipline round here I'll ship you in myself. Now fuck off and get your act together. I'm prepared to deff this one but next time you're out." They were dismissed.

***

One by one Rob reviewed his staff and explored their strengths and weaknesses. All in all they were a solid bunch of individuals who worked hard, and displayed great loyalty to the job, and in due course to him.

There were certainly some 'characters' amongst them, and more than one with a drink problem that would have raised eyebrows in a doctor's surgery, but they covered it well and were always there when the going got tough. They were all pissing in the same pot together and he was acutely aware that if one fell they all fell. He wasn't just throwing his weight around for the sake of it; he was trying to protect them – and more importantly himself.

One of his Detective Sergeants, Malcolm Reid fitted both characteristics. He was a larger-than-life character with a large girth and a 'beer-belly' to go with it. Wherever his 'belly-button' was it certainly didn't match where the belt on his trousers rested, and as a result he had a continual habit of pulling his trousers up until someone found the answer and brought him a pair of brightly coloured bracers.

With twenty-five years' service, much of it in the city-centre, Reid knew everything, and everyone that you needed to know. With just five years to go he wasn't interested in anything except being left alone to finish his time in the same place. His long-suffering wife had divorced him years before, and living on his own in a one-bedroomed flat, his work was his life, and he was never in a rush to go home.

Most importantly for Rob he made it clear from day one that whatever help he could provide Rob with he would get it. He was on-board with the new gaffer and that was one less thing to worry about.

What Rob did not know was that Malcolm Reid had already sold his soul to the devil in the guise of Joe, and was even more corrupt than his new boss. To Malcolm of course, the fact that both his 'bosses' were called Docker was just a coincidence.

**

Rob had also inherited his old colleague from his shift days as a probationer, and whilst he had quickly put Alan in his place, he sensed that he presented both a threat and a risk to him.

He sat brooding quietly in his office and surveyed the problem before him. Outside in the main office Alan was leaning back in his chair holding court, with his tie pulled down to one side, and oblivious to the attentions of his line manager. Alan now considered himself to be no longer the new boy on the block and liked to convey a sense of supreme confidence, masking a laziness and ineptitude that Rob viewed with disquiet.

He might be on the team but he was a liability, and Rob had to find a way to deal with it quickly. There were no margins for error in the way Rob played this game.

The main problem was that Alan could not keep his mouth shut when he had supped a few pints. He liked the feel of rolled-up bank notes in his pockets and he liked those around him, particularly those in short skirts, to know that he was loaded. This wouldn't do for Rob who was also attracting complaints from the scrap-metal dealers, who disliked being squeezed by a 'nobody'. It was one thing to pay – it was another thing to pay too much.

Rob shut his door and made a phone call, "Liam, I got a job for you. Meet me at 5pm in the usual place."

Rob and Liam had maintained a constructive, and rewarding, relationship since the drug addict had come out of prison. Liam had benefited from several payments for information received. Sometimes he didn't even know what the information had been about. He just got put forward as the source and was paid – less thirty per cent for Rob of course.

They met in the usual pub – Rob was not a fan of dark corners - too obviously shady. He brazened it out in lively places where it was difficult for people to overhear conversations or remember your appearance.

Liam listened to the plan intently. He wasn't that keen on getting involved in this one but he knew better than to think that he had a choice in the matter.

Rob went over it twice and then got Liam to repeat what he had to do. A couple of pints later they parted.

Two days later Rob paid a visit to the Complaints and Discipline Department by appointment. He didn't want to make it too easy for them so he focused on 'lifestyle' issues and described a man who wore good suits, drank too heavily, and liked to play the field. He threw Alan's vehicle in for good measure – which was worth well above the wages of a mere DC. He also suggested a review of PNC might be in order.

The Head of Complaints was new to the department, from a uniform background, and ambitious. He was looking for CID scalps in particular and Rob fed his appetite, "Thanks Rob I owe you one." he concluded at the end of the conversation.

Exactly one week later, a phone call went into C&D from Liam. He wanted to make a complaint about a 'bent-copper' who was trying to force him to 'fit people up' for robberies and was taking 'back-handers'. Two pieces were now in place in the jigsaw puzzle.

Piece number three came two days later when C&D investigators, the incorruptible 'Elliot Ness's' of the police world, discovered that Alan's car had been paid for in cash.

Rob had a phone call from his contact in C&D and they discussed the next move – Rob was now trusted and seen as 'squeaky clean.'

A week later, Rob arranged for a number of officers, including Alan, to go out early looking for a couple of suspects, leaving him alone in the office. Prior to confirming with C&D that the office was empty he went to Alan's desk and using a duplicate key, and wearing gloves, unlocked his desk drawers.

A brown envelope containing cash was placed in the bottom drawer. In a separate drawer, wrapped in cling film, he placed a small block of cannabis resin, and hid it underneath a 'Write-Off' file that appeared to be gathering dust. The phone call was made and he waited.

Thirty minutes later a team from C&D arrived. Rob had insisted that everyone's desk was searched to ensure that sources were protected. The chosen few had already been pre-warned, so apart from some of the other staff getting a bollocking for hiding exhibits and late paperwork in drawers, the scene was well prepared.

C&D set about their task with vigour, and when it came to Alan's desk they were all over it like a rash as the 'bagging and tagging' exercise started and the cash and drugs went into exhibits bags. Then they sat and waited.

Alan returned thirty minutes later with his team. He displayed his usual cocky attitude as he sauntered through the door, "I'm fucking knackered. I'm getting too old for smashing doors in." His smile froze and his jaunty step faltered as he saw four officers clustered around his desk.

They ushered him away quietly and Rob gathered his staff together to brief and reassure them.

Alan never came back.

He went onto 'gardening leave' after being interviewed under caution. Whilst it was always going to be doubtful that the prosecuting solicitors would run with a corruption charge, the drugs would be enough to offer him the honourable way out – resignation from the Force and another case which would not be in the public interests to prosecute.

Weeks later Rob had a phone call from the assistant chief constable overseeing the work of Complaints and Discipline, just back from his Command Course at Bramshill Police College, "Good work Rob. We need to rid the Force of the small number of corrupt officers in our midst. Stop it before it spreads like cancer. Your efforts have not gone unnoticed. We will need some extra people in

Special Branch in the near future, and I hear that your good reputation as a thief-taker has been noticed. Have a think about it."

***

Rob Docker shook the hands of Alan's replacement warmly – well he would do, it was a woman. Getting into the CID for female officers was nothing short of 'dead men's shoes', with one per CID office. They had no chance of progressing on merit alone and to survive had to learn to be as tough as the men.

Using skills that belied her name Claire Wise had survived and with a bit of support from her husband, who was a senior officer on another division, she had finally got the posting that she had cherished, and the title of detective.

Rob allocated her to Malcolm Reid's team. It was a deliberate challenge to see how she would shape up, but her distaste for the corpulent womaniser who drank too much was obvious.

At the end of her first day she was invited to buy the customary round for the team, in the police bar, and Rob attended to observe and judge the opportunities. Reid was as subtle as a brick and after a couple of pints Claire was obliged to steer his wavering hand away from her waist a couple of times. "We're going to get on just great," said the delighted fat man.

Reid made matters even worse when he told a colleague that he would, 'love to slip her a crippler, or might get her to give him a knee trembler,' not realizing that she was standing directly behind him at the time.

Claire turned on him, "You can slip one off your own wrist cause I won't be doing it for you!" She had made her first stand.

Rob spoke to her quietly at the end of a fairly light drinking session, "Just let me know if you have any problems with him Claire, he's normally harmless but I'll look after you. Tell your husband not to worry and please give him my regards." A thin, but reassuring smile crossed his face; Rob was never one to lose an opportunity to ingratiate himself with a senior officer.

***

They had a busy couple of weeks keeping observations for a team of blaggers doing post office robberies - long hours and not much to show for it. Claire got more than her fair share of the boredom being the new person, but knew that complaining would not be good form.

On the Friday at the end of the second week, an armed-robbery took place at a sub-post office just outside the city-centre. As luck would have it, the get-away car of the two robbers broke down outside a doctor's surgery, and they had to make a run for it.

They hadn't got too far when a passing traffic car literally fell over them and detained one almost immediately. The second managed to escape into a nearby tower block and went to ground still holding a sawn-off shotgun.

Rob's team arrived on the scene quickly and, as the world and his dog arrived, the tower block was cordoned off and contained.

"Come with me Malcolm," Rob ordered and they made their way to the lifts, "Press the top button. I'm not about to let the uniforms take all the glory. We start from the roof and work down."

A more foolhardy exercise one could not imagine but Malcolm blindly followed and they began the painful process. The only positive thing for Reid as he started sweating profusely was that they were going down and not up.

Six floors down they found the front door of one of the flats smashed in and Rob walked straight in to be confronted by the second robber holding the shotgun in front of him.

This was a scene that Rob had seen so many times in the movies where negotiations take place and the armed man is finally persuaded to put down the gun and go quietly.

That was in the movies though, and before the armed man could react Rob smashed him straight across his wrists with one downward strike of his trusty cosh, whilst a second upward strike hit him square on the jaw.

As he went down, for good measure Reid kicked the man between the legs and tore the weapon away from the crumpled figure that lay bleeding and moaning on the floor, "Have that for good measure cunty bollocks," he announced to the failed-robber writhing in agony.

"Fuck me it's loaded boss," Malcolm asserted as he displayed two cartridges in the barrels, and promptly kicked the unconscious prisoner again.

Both prisoners were taken into custody, one via hospital, and Rob gave instructions that Claire should become the investigating officer, which also meant completing the prosecution file. He had a method in his madness.

They had some good witnesses from the post office, outside the doctor's surgery, and the two traffic officers, and Rob gave instructions for an Identification Parade. He wanted this one watertight.

The two traffic officers arrived and Rob intercepted them as they came through the station door. He took them into a small office off the main CID crew room and placed two photographs on the table in front of them.

As he was talking them through the process Claire entered the room without knocking, a thick bunch of papers under her arm, she had been using the room to catch up on paperwork. It took her two seconds to digest the scene and it's implications, "My apologies, I was just going to get the ID paperwork sorted," she stuttered, and turned on her heels.

"No problem Claire, the officers are ready for the ID parade when you are." Rob calmly asserted.

In the meantime Malcolm had managed to have a useful chat with one of the witnesses who he had offered to collect from home. The man was a stalwart pensioner who knew right from wrong and was sick of all the parasites in society who engaged in crime. The old man knew his onions. He could be counted on.

Three witnesses positively identified the two offenders, plus a couple of possible identifications from the post-office staff. Both men were charged and kept in custody.

Later that evening Claire went to see DI Docker in his office. "Shut the door Claire. How can I help you?" He pointed towards a chair. "I'm a bit out of my depth here sir with this file and the evidence and all. I'm getting a bit stressed with what I should be doing." She chose each word carefully – this was a survival exercise rather than a bridge burning one.

"There's no need to be stressed Claire, we look after each other here. Whatever help you need I'll make sure that you get it." Rob already knew what was coming but maintained the charade of a statesman.

"I'm not sure about what I saw sir, you know the photographs and that...." she tailed off.

Rob leant forward and held his hands just inches from hers on the desk "I'm not sure what you think you saw Claire, but I can assure you I always do everything by the book. Ain't nothing to worry about at all. Now, it's been a long day and I think a drink is called for."

Taking her shoulder he ushered out of the office and into the arms of the waiting sergeant, "Malcolm – the bar if you please. Drinks are on me. Then I could murder an Indian."

Once again Rob observed Claire with interest as she suffered more attention from Malcolm whilst clearly her mind was elsewhere. Even after getting a light tap on the bottom from the fat DS, she seemed a million miles away as she fended him off, and later declined to go with them to their favourite restaurant.

He recognised the signs all too well, *'Not one of us at all, pity,'* Rob made a decision.

Two weeks later Claire Wise was transferred to the new Family Protection Unit that was badly in need of a female detective. Rob wished her well – she was too much of a risk. They would have to look for another split-arse.

***

Quinn had been busy. There had been several trips to London with 'packages,' but after a number of explosions in March 1973 he received a directive from 'The General' to stand down for a few months. Police raids in the capital had intensified and a number of arrests were made.

In July 1973, Quinn was tasked again and the 'Black Souls' were kept busy acting as couriers throughout the West Midlands.

Docker started to press Quinn for more and more information. Whilst they had disrupted some activity, and Docker had been able to engineer some low level arrests, he was still hungry for the 'big one,' a PIRA bust to add to his glowing record.

Towards the end of August, a delivery was to be made to a house in Shirley and Quinn decided to check the contents out before sending it on. This was not without risk, but the confirmation of high-explosive gave Docker something positive to go on.

Just days later, as the young terrorist delivered two carrier bags full of explosives to the doorway of a shopping centre he came face-to-face with a number of armed police officers screaming at him. No chance of escape or using the pistol secreted in his coat pocket, he was caught bang to rights – Docker had his result.

His moment of glory turned out to be brief as other PIRA operatives in the city placed explosive devices in a 'tit-for-tat' act of revenge. The air was full of madness and every newspaper headline underscored the fear that innocent people were living with.

As autumn came, another bomb exploded in a busy shopping centre and a young boy died from his injuries. Quinn had known nothing at all about the plot but it didn't stop Docker from threatening him with exposure if it ever happened again. Quinn left the meet thinking, *'I'm a dead man walking,'* as Docker insisted that he got closer to the action.

Quinn, always attuned to trouble, knew that the increase in PIRA activity presaged disaster for the Black Souls and in particular the President. The delicate balancing act he had so assiduously, and cleverly performed, was unraveling. The incompatible demands of PIRA, informing for Docker, his role as leader of a Hells Angels Charter and running the criminal organization were about to combust - and the result would be spectacular and fatal.

Quinn the survivor knew that to ask more questions would attract the attention of PIRA intelligence officers and then Dermot bloody McCann, it would be the beginning of the end.

***

A quiet Christmas and a few days peace with Sean and Jenny provided some respite, but even that was to be short-lived. On Christmas Day he took his son for a ride out to The Malverns and they spent some time alone, sat at the top of the hills surveying the patchwork of fields laid out beneath them. It looked so peaceful. His eye was drawn northwards towards Birmingham. *'I wish now that I'd kept us out of there,'* he thought. *'That's where it all went wrong, fucking Dockers.'* Not for the first time he marveled at the coincidence of the shared surname of his enemies, and once again dismissed it. How could they be related after all?

He watched his son as the lad walked around the summit, taking in the views towards the Black Hills and Wales. Sean was a good-looking teenager now, tall and clean-limbed with Jenny's dark hair, and Quinn's ice-blue eyes, a striking combination that boded well for the future attentions of women.

He had a teenager's opinion on everything, and a broad streak of rebellion inherited from his father. Quinn didn't think he would be following his path into the Angels, and he was glad. In the end there had been a lot of good times, money, girls, status, all those material things, but an older and wiser Quinn sat on top of the hill and realized that he was still empty inside. All he had was this youth, a fragile scrap of life that he was drawing into increasing peril.

Quinn loved the boy unquestionably and wanted a good future for him, but Quinn's world had a distinct lack of goodness in it, and try as he might, he couldn't think of a way out other than in a coffin.

***

Rob was twenty minutes late and Quinn idled with the car radio trying to find something to occupy his thoughts. He smiled to himself briefly as Gary Glitter's "I'm the Leader of the Gang," came on but it was not to his taste in music and he didn't get past the first chorus before he changed channels. David Bowie didn't last much longer and he switched the radio off, irritated by the delay.

The passenger door opened and Rob slid into the front seat. "How you doing Pat?" Rob enquired – no apologies for the wait forthcoming.

Pat was in no mood for pleasantries, "I'm surviving, no thanks to you, but you're well on the way to getting me killed and at the point where I've nothing to lose I'll come for you first, you bastard, so think on that."

Rob smiled, "Keep your hair on. Great minds think alike, I've been having the same thoughts and I need you to have summat to lose, plus you're fuck all use to me in the ground so I've brought you a couple of presents. I'm going to give you a break for a few weeks, let the heat die down. On the last job there were questions being asked which were a little bit too close to home. I don't want to burn you so call it a small holiday."

"That's very fucking big of you Docker," retorted Quinn, who hated the fact that Docker wasn't frightened of him. It made him feel vulnerable.

"Second present, just to show good faith, here's a little something to cement our arrangement" – Rob pressed a small brown envelope into Quinn's hand and said, "Open it. It was taking up space in the property store so I thought that you might like it back."

Quinn looked inside the envelope and saw Joey's Black Souls ring.

"I don't understand. That's your evidence. What's to stop me walking away now or even better shipping you in to the Complaints people?" Quinn enquired.

"Nothing at all Pat," Rob responded, "Give it a go if you fancy your chances and I'll make sure that everyone in your shitty little world knows that you're a 'grass'.

I suspect even a man like you would last for about a week. You see, I don't need the evidence any more, I got the power of life and death over you – and your family."

Quinn stared back sullenly, he had known the answer, just wanted it spoken.

"Same time, same place in three weeks Pat. Don't come empty-handed. We'll leave the Paddies alone for a while but I've got some Customs guys who are interested in what's being imported into Birmingham so get your ears to the ground." Rob concluded the conversation.

No pleasantries extended, or expected, Rob stepped from the car and disappeared from view as Quinn fumed, angrily throwing the envelope and ring into the glove compartment, before slamming it shut and driving off.

***

Ordinarily Quinn didn't allow Sean to touch his car. He wanted the boy to be clean when he started driving and was trying to keep him straight. That didn't however extend to driving the car around the local dirt-tracks just as Quinn had once done around the farm, and

Sean, like he had, enjoyed the power of the engine and sense of control.

On one such excursion Sean reached inside the glove compartment searching for the prospect of some abandoned cigarettes. As he rifled through the various bits of crap that filled the compartment a brown envelope drew his attention.

Sean understood the significance of the gold 'Black Souls' ring and whilst he was curious as to why it had apparently been abandoned he wasn't about to miss the opportunity of possessing such a valuable asset. He slipped it into his pocket and replaced the envelope. Quinn, mind elsewhere, never checked it was still there.

***

1974 bought with it a veritable onslaught by PIRA on the mainland, with attacks in Birmingham, Manchester, and London.

On the 4 January 1974, as midnight approached, a warning message came through to say that there were two bombs in Birmingham City Centre, including one in an empty unit in the Birmingham Shopping Centre opposite the Army and Navy Recruiting Offices.

As two British Transport Police officers approached the location they watched in 'slow motion' as the shop windows bowed visibly and an explosion wrecked the premises and corridor, showering the officers in glass and debris from the roof space and hurling them to the floor.

One of the officers was suffering from a previous injury to

his foot which had slowed them down. Had they arrived a minute earlier they would have been struck by the full force of the blast. It appeared that their angels had been watching over them that night.

Elsewhere in the city-centre, a local officer picked up a duffle-bag from outside a sweet kiosk and was in the process of opening it when he heard the combustion begin and hurled it away from him. It exploded. His quick thinking saved his life.

In February, the IRA campaign on the mainland continued at a pace with bombings on the M62 in Bradford, where eleven servicemen were killed, and explosions in Buckinghamshire.

On the 6 April 1974, bombs exploded in Birmingham City Centre, and at the Birmingham Power Box. BTP officers searching at track-level one floor below heard the sounds of windows exploding above their heads and gave thanks to the layers of concrete that had afforded them some protection. Brave men and women armed with nothing more than a wooden truncheon found themselves pitted against determined terrorists armed with weapons, and high explosives, who simply melted back into the community after each attack.

Elsewhere, a conscientious security officer, well known for wearing an over- sized hat, reported finding a duffle-bag containing wires and batteries in a doorway below the Army and Navy Recruitment offices in Navigation Street. The bag contained high explosives and he was keen to pass his find onto BTP officers who arrived to examine it. They were equally keen for him to put it down on the floor and to put some distance between themselves and the bag before calling for Bomb Disposal Officers.

***

In June 1974, Rob Docker was at last seconded to the Special Branch, as the IRA bombed Westminster Hall in London. In truth it wasn't his 'cup of tea' at all but it brought him close to senior officers and the people who could influence his future. He remained ruthlessly ambitious and was determined to go further.

It was clear that there was an active PIRA cell operating in Birmingham and whilst explosions were to take place in the South East, Manchester, and in and around London, Rob knew that on his own doorstep they were a facing a major problem.

In the middle of July 1974 bombs exploded at the Rotunda, and at Nechells Power Station, and three unexploded devices were also found.

***

Quinn knew full well that he was just one cog in the wheel of terrorism but the rise in attacks meant re-supply and he continued to play the dutiful courier and facilitator, whilst at the same time feeding Docker with information.

On one occasion he went a step further, and interfered with a package containing timers that subsequently failed to go off on three devices planted in Birmingham.

The Rotunda had by now assumed an iconic status as PIRA made a determined effort to reduce the building to rubble, but it remained defiant – a symbol of Birmingham.

Life rushed by as Quinn struggled to keep the various strands of his life and businesses together. He sometimes wished that he had stayed in America but everything that made him the person he had become was here in England. He was still searching for a way out from between the implacable rocks of PIRA and police but had made no progress, the problem seemed insurmountable other than by dying, and that would leave Sean and Jenny exposed and vulnerable.

He had too many fingers in too many pies. If it had just been himself, he may well have decided to go out in a blaze of glory, settling all the old scores in an orgy of violence, but he had others to think about now, and Sean had become the only thing in his life that he valued.

At the beginning of November 1974, Quinn took a call from 'The General', "I need you to get your hands dirty on a couple of jobs. The boys are getting too much attention and we need to provide some distraction before the big ones."

Quinn was given his instructions and duly collected two much smaller incendiary devices from a safe house in Acocks Green. It was a solo-effort and he rode silently through the night to leave one in the city centre near to Snow Hill railway station, where it went off in the early hours, after a discreet evacuation had taken place.

The second device he delivered into the hands of Rob Docker who waited covertly with some bomb disposal officers at the location of the intended target. He quite enjoyed putting a bomb in the man's hands – just a pity not to have blown the bastard up.

Docker now had a complete device and access to the identity of the Birmingham-based bomb maker. Things were looking up.

Rob had already arranged for a small 'controlled explosion' to take place at the target location, so as far as the media and PIRA were concerned it was two attacks, two explosions and Quinn was protected.

Quinn prepared himself carefully for the phone call to 'The General' but received nothing but praise from his self-appointed guide and mentor. Nothing had been clocked, "Take a break Pat. Go and find some sun, and I suggest that you stay out of Birmingham for the time being. The boys are going to be busy."

Quinn resisted the urge to ask for further detail, McCann gave nothing away and it would just raise his suspicions.

In hindsight, that would prove to be a mistake that changed Quinn's life forever.

Chapter Thirty Nine: 'This Town Ain't Big Enough For The Both Of Us'

(Sparks)

1974

Late 1974, and life was pretty good for Andreas Markou. As a successful businessman he had the respect of his countrymen who had made their home in Britain but never had, and never would, forget their roots.

Eleni continued with the facade of bringing up the perfect family, and the children were growing, and doing well at school. Just to put the icing on the cake, he had a new English girlfriend who was happy to see him twice a week as long as she got well fed and had some money in her purse for new clothes.

Status is everything for Cypriots and so when the phone call came he determined to make the most of it. An opportunity to cement a growing relationship that had begun in enmity but now found its foundation in mutual respect.

"I need a favour Andreas," said Joe, the reluctance in his voice clearly showing.

"And what might that be Joe?" he enquired.

"I need to arrange a meeting with someone who is making life difficult. It's not good for business Andreas. It needs sorting before things get totally out of hand but the meeting has to be on neutral ground. Could we use your place?"

There was no hesitation in Andreas's response, "Of course Joe. We all need to make a living. If I do this though there are some conditions which are not negotiable."

A weary Joe enquired, "And what might they be?"

"They are quite simple," Andreas went on, "Firstly if you come to my place you will be my guests and you will eat and drink at my table. Second you will both bring your families with you and I will bring mine. It will be a good way to control tempers don't you think my friend?"

Joe reluctantly agreed, something he would have cause to regret later, "What else?"

Andreas concluded, "You will arrive at the time decided – no earlier and no later. Neither you nor your 'friend' will wear jackets – I want no knifes or guns in my place unless they belong to me, so make it clear that both of you will be 'clean'. If you do this then I think that we can have a nice party and you can get your business done in private after we have eaten."

Joe confirmed, "I'll get back to you once the other party has been spoken to."

Andreas smiled to himself, "Of course Joe – and just one more thing. If I do this both you and your 'friend' will owe me one favour each. Nothing big of course, just a bit of help in the future perhaps moving a few things around."

Two days later Andreas received confirmation that the meeting was on for the following Sunday afternoon at 4pm with all of the terms agreed.

At the appointed time Joe arrived with Sandra and Hope. Whilst Sandra was used to the business, Hope had no idea, and was excited about the prospects of a Greek meal out with her parents – an afternoon of normality.

Quinn for his part arrived at the same time as instructed, with Jenny and Sean. They had travelled into the city by car and Quinn struggled with the crisp and newly ironed shirt that Jenny had purchased for him. Sean was also looking forward to the prospects of doing something normal with his parents. This was going to be good.

The fish and chip shop was closed and the blinds drawn down so that prying eyes would not be able to observe the strange gathering.

Eleni was there with Savvakis and Maria and she busied herself in the back room making last minute preparations to the meal. Cypriots built houses that would stand for centuries, and ate every meal as if it were to be their last one. Today was to be no exception.

Apart from the three families there was just one addition to the party. Marios was not in the same league as Costas, who was still back in Cyprus attending to business, but he came from the same breed of men. His job today was to serve at the tables and to play the Bouzouki after the meal, tasks which he would normally have performed with his shirt sleeves rolled up, but today his jacket stayed on and the loaded pistol sat neatly in one of the pockets.

Andreas had spared no expense, and the tables in the normally functional fish and chip shop had been laid out to restaurant standards.

The four men present shook hands – no warmth, just enough pretence to avoid difficult looks from the women and children. Not one to miss an opportunity, Andreas kissed Jenny and Sandra warmly on both cheeks.

Andreas sat at the head of one table, with Joe and Quinn either side of him. Eleni busied herself with Marios in serving, before taking her place alongside Sandra and Jenny at the other end of the table.

Hope and Sean sat at a separate table with Savvakis and Maria, who were completely oblivious to the thunderbolt that had struck Sean on first meeting with Hope. He simply could not take his gaze from her and had to work hard to avoid it becoming embarrassing. This was not going to be a good afternoon – it was going to be a great afternoon, as the warmth of the late afternoon sunshine burst through the blinds.

Andreas poured wine for the adults and raising his glass to all present announced, "Welcome, - Stin yeia mas – to our health," and five minutes later followed it through with, "Stin yeia sou – to your health."

As Joe and Quinn maintained an unhealthy silence across the table the food was served – it was in the form of a traditional meze and the food just kept coming – and coming.

For starters small plates of scrambled eggs with tomatoes, chopped fried mushrooms with onions, haloumi on the grill, lounza on the grill, and fried sausage cut in pieces, appeared on small plates and Hope and Sean giggled as Savvakis and Maria tried to teach them some Greek words. In the background taped Greek music from Spyros Zagoreos, and Vasilis Tsitsanis filled the small room.

After this Marios brought the main course out with pork chops on the grill, sieftalia, kebab, kleftiko with potatoes, and stuffed vine leaves.

As the wine flowed, and the food came, Joe and Quinn worked hard to keep their heads clear but they were not in control at this stage and as the alcohol took its course they almost relaxed for a short while, with the smell of the food and the infectious music filling their nostrils and ears.

The sweets came – mbaklava, kateifi, galatopourekko with cream, and glikatou koutaliou in syrup – the children's eyed bulged with the sight of so much syrup, sugar and cream.

"Ladies and young people. Marios has some entertainment for you now whilst the men have some business to attend to upstairs. Enjoy yourselves. We won't be long."

Andreas removed a bottle of Zivania from the freezer, and opened a couple of beers before motioning to Joe and Quinn to follow him.

They followed him into the back room and then through a door which led to some narrow stairs and up into a room which contained a bed, a couple of armchairs, and a coffee table. A useful addition for Andreas' extra-nocturnal activities.

Andreas placed the drinks on the table and announced "Gentlemen, you have business to sort out which I do not need to be aware of. I would ask you to respect the hospitality extended to you today and not to engage in any childish fisticuffs. It would not be professional and I do not want to be disrespected. Take as long as you need and I will be downstairs when you have finished."

Joe and Quinn viewed each other with pure hatred in their eyes – they had both lost members of their 'families' at the hands of each other. They were already both murderers for whom negotiation and compromise were a difficult concept.

Andreas left them and went back to the party.

As Marios played the Bouzouki expertly, Andreas launched himself into the dance of Zeipekkiko. As Maria knelt down to clap him on, the children did likewise, and Sean found himself next to Hope feeling the warmth of her body and the beauty of her smile. They exchanged glances and felt the mutual attraction.

As Andreas finished his dance Maria took his place, and for a few minutes she was back home in a happier place and away from this bastard who gave her nothing but pain. Her children looked on admiring their mother and then took her place as she stepped back. The music enveloped them all.

Then it was Jenny and Sandra's turn to click their fingers and sway to the music. The wine had removed their inhibitions as they moved in much the way that puppets without strings do. The room was full of laughter and noise as mothers and children poked fun at each other. At one point Sean found himself lightly touching Hope's waist, and it was a moment that seemed to last for an age.

Upstairs two angry men talked.

"Okay now it's time for 'Zorbas Dance,'" announced Andreas "We are going to teach you sirtaki."

Andreas lined the four children up in the room with Sean and Hope in the middle between Savvakis and Maria. He straightened their arms and placed Sean's hand gently onto Hopes shoulder. They smiled as Andreas delivered his instructions and the two Cypriot children sought to guide the feet of their newfound English friends.

Marios played the tune slowly and they moved slowly, struggling to get the footwork right whilst they all remained joined at the shoulders. Gradually the music got faster as Andreas added Jenny and Sandra into the line – and the music got faster.

Finally Maria took to the head of the line as the music reached its peak and after three more circuits of the room it came to an abrupt end and they all collapsed, heaving for breath and laughing uncontrollably.

Upstairs two angry men talked.

Sandra and Jenny insisted on joining Maria in the back room to clear up the mound of dishes. They chattered together as women do, lost in the moment, and happy in the moment, and the joy of also seeing their children happy. They had no comprehension whatsoever of the catastrophic events that were to follow. All they knew was that they had plenty in common, and completely unforeseen, liked each other.

Andreas sat in a corner drinking coffee with Marios – Cypriot men did not wash up.

The youngsters sat chatting about music, school, ambitions, and clothes. Sean chose his moment carefully and on one of the discarded serviettes wrote his home number down and passed it to Hope who received it without question. He had merely done what she had hoped for.

Upstairs two angry men concluded their business. This was never meant to be a day for agreements, more of an understanding of each other's positions and an opportunity to place some 'markers' down. Neither wanted to compromise, but neither wanted to risk their business interests either, and both knew that they would destroy each other if a war broke out.

The only thing that they did agree on was that further killing would prove fruitless and that the 'blood feud' would come to an end. Joe agreed not to move into Quinn's area of business, and likewise Quinn agreed to keep the Black Souls away from Joe's operation.

There were no handshakes, and as they stood up at the end of the meeting to leave the room they both subconsciously measured each other up - the type of thing that two gladiators would do before entering into mortal combat. Both returned downstairs vowing that the other was a dead man when the time was right.

The Cypriots would act as go-betweens in any further communications or negotiations.

Maria kissed Jenny, Sandra and the children goodbye, and wished them good luck. She squeezed Hope and kissed her on the forehead – she loved girls.

Joe, Sandra, and Hope turned left out of the front door and Quinn, Jenny, and Sean turned to the right.

Sean looked back and saw Hope holding Sandra's hand as they walked together, Joe out in front already focused on the business. Then they were lost from sight as they turned a corner. In the next two weeks they were to exchange frequent phone calls in secret. Something told them never to reveal their relationship to their parents.

Quinn drove home in silence with Jenny and Sean. He was thinking, *'Can't wait to get this fucking shirt off'*.

On Monday morning Andreas sat having a coffee in the upstairs room. The shop was not yet open and there was only him and one other person on the premises. He sat sipping his coffee in silence as Rob Docker listened intently to the cassette tape that whirred away with the sounds of two angry men in the background.

Chapter Forty: 'Waterloo'

(Abba)

1974

On the 5 November 1974, the Conservative Party Headquarters in Edmund Street was bombed and an incendiary device was found in Constitution Hill. On the 14 November 1974 another incendiary device was found in Ladywood, just a ten-minute drive from the city-centre.

Within twenty-four hours, James McDade, aged twenty-eight years, a Provisional Irish Republican Army volunteer, was killed by his own bomb in Coventry as he attempted to plant it at a telephone exchange and postal sorting office.

***

On the 21 November 1974, PC Stuart Edgar sat in the empty Fire Station at Elmdon Airport along with hundreds of other officers. All of them bored silly, collars undone with black ties skewed to one side, they passed the time playing endless rounds of 'niggle' cards on upturned boxes. This was 'organized chaos' at its best – even the Superintendent in charge had no clue as to how long they were expected to stay there for. Normally this man was one of the organ-grinders but today it seemed like he was just one of the monkeys as well.

As a young PC, Stuart Edgar was well down the food chain

so he knew he would be one of the last to be told what was going on. He'd had a kip, ate his packed lunch which included a chocolate bar, crisps and a curly cheese sandwich. Now he just wanted to go home. The saying was that they were, *'mushrooms, kept in the dark and fed shit'*.

In essence they were guarding the coffin containing the body of a man, or at least what was left of it, after a failed bomb attack in Coventry went disastrously wrong for the bomber and the device exploded prematurely. The PIRA had promised to honour his death, and the police were determined to prevent any 'military' displays, with thirteen hundred officers drafted into Birmingham, before McDade's coffin was eventually flown to Dublin Airport.

Stuart sat back and watched the scene unfold, *'What a fucking crazy world we live in,'* he mused. Suddenly someone approached the Superintendent with a look of urgency and whispered into his ear – it was all happening in Birmingham City Centre. The sounds of scraping chairs, hurried adjustments to uniforms, and barked instructions started to fill the room as the temperature rose palpably.

***

Sean had arranged to meet Hope on the concourse of New Street Station, as she was travelling into Birmingham on one of the local trains. He got there early and started to pace up and down, whilst all the time keeping his eye on the ticket barrier. He was to put it mildly 'a bag of nerves' and was desperate for things to go well.

Sean had been with a couple of girls, but had never felt like he did with Hope. He knew that he was pushing it, after all he was eighteen today and she was only fourteen, but she did look a lot older, having inherited her father's size, and genes, that tended to endow girls generously at an early age.

He was only too aware of some of the extremes of the Black Souls' lifestyle but the teenage rebel in him had inverted the normal rejection of society values by turning away from the Angel's life and towards more staid ambitions. He intended to study, get a degree, and make a proper life for himself.

His father was a closed book as far as his business was concerned, but Sean was no fool, and he saw only too clearly the pressures and necessities of running a criminal empire and wanted none of it. Like many teenagers Sean hadn't yet dared appraise his father of the rejection of all he stood for.

He also had a sensitive side to him and even for one of such a young age Hope represented his future – he was in love.

Hope was late, but when she finally emerged from the station overbridge, and made her way through the barrier towards him, his heart skipped a beat. She was beautiful, but in a simple way, and although the carefully crafted make-up had the desired effect of aging her by several years it had not been over-done.

Sean greeted her with a light kiss on the cheek and as they moved off he held her hand awkwardly, "I was starting to think that you weren't coming," he ventured.

"I nearly got myself in a bit of a pickle. Dad was out at work but I had to convince mum that I was going to visit friends for a few hours. I mustn't be late. She's gonna pick me up from the station," she responded as she squeezed his hand.

They made their way to the rear entrance of the station and a three-minute walk took them to the 'Mulberry Bush' pub. It was Sean's eighteenth birthday and he had promised to take her to her first pub to celebrate.

"When we go inside you go and find a seat away from the bar and I'll get a couple of drinks," said Sean reassuringly.

Sean collected the drinks and sat down next to Hope, "Cheers – to us," he raised his glass, "I have something for you that I want you to have."

Sean reached into his pocket and pulled out the gold signet ring bearing the letters 'BS' and reached out for Hope's hand, "There aren't many of these rings about. They're special – like you."

Sean found a finger on her left hand that was a reasonable fit and gently eased the ring onto it.

Hope beamed and leaned forward to kiss him.

Suddenly, their exclusive moment was savagely interrupted, "Nigger lover! The split–second of bliss was shattered.

At the table next to them sat an unkempt white male, clearly the worse for drink, and ready for a fight, "Look at the coon, look at the coon" he mimicked the sound of a pigeon cooing.

Sean sprang out of his seat to confront him, whilst Hope sat frozen by the sudden and unexpected onslaught. She had experienced racism at school before but had escaped the worst due to the lightness of her skin. This however was different – it was from two feet away and the perpetrator was an adult.

"Who the fuck do you think you are!" Sean exploded, and squared up to their tormentor.

"Alright young man hold it there. We don't entertain fighting in here," came a shout from the bar as the licensee quickly moved in to defuse the situation.

Well experienced in handling truculent individuals, he didn't 'mince his words. "Gerry, fuck off and don't come back tonight or you'll feel the end of my fist."

Gerry had felt that fist before and didn't need telling twice. With a sneer at the couple he raised his hands, palms outwards, and said, "No problem boss, I'm going," and staggered towards the exit. Little did he know it then but his decision to act like a racist bigot, but not to stand his ground, saved his miserable life.

Sean started to relax, "And you young man, take your underage girlfriend out of here as well." As Sean began to protest, feeling a sense of injustice, he felt a tug at his arm as Hope motioned for them to leave.

As they paused at the doorway the fresh evening air caught them, "I'm sorry Hope. I really am."

"It ain't your fault Sean, and I can't change the colour of me skin. There's bound to be another pub a bit further down."

Sean took her arm and they strolled round the corner and along New Street, the short distance to the 'Tavern in the Town'.

At the doorway Sean said, "We don't have to go in, if you preferred we could get some chips, or some chestnuts, and have a walk up towards the Town Hall.

"I feel a bit cold Sean, – let's go inside just for half an hour," Hope responded.

As they walked down the stairs Sean squeezed her hand again before they found a quiet corner to sit in. For the next thirty minutes they talked about music and clothes as Hope giggled and Sean smiled like the cat that got the cream, happy that they had found each other. Hope pulled him a little closer.

***

Joe had sorted some paperwork out at the club and decided to visit a couple of the city-centre pubs before things got busy. He provided doormen for a number of them now, and one or two of the independent ones – independent of his gangster peers in the city, were now complaining about the price and threatening to bring their own people in. This was not something that Joe wanted to see happen and he needed to have a chat or two as to what the consequences might be.

One of them was the 'Tavern in the Town,' and whilst in years to come it would become the preserve, on some nights, of members of the 'Zulu Warriors', Birmingham City's football hooligan element, for now it was just the usual drunken behavior that the door staff needed to moderate.

Joe was feeling unusually calm. Business was good, and Sandra and Hope filled his home with the love that he craved. The Quinn problem had been put on ice for a while and his brother being on Special Branch meant that his manipulative attentions were temporarily turned towards the Irish. *'Yes, a nice period of calm would do me good'* he thought.

He walked briskly along New Street and was just about to enter 'The Tavern in The Town' when he heard a shout behind him, "Mr. Docker!"

Joe turned, instinctively tensing, ready for the unexpected, then saw Colin rapidly approaching him, "I was trying to catch up with you Mr. Docker but you do walk so fast. I've only got little legs!"

Colin was an eighteen-year-old 'rent-boy' whose 'patch' centred around New Street Station. He made a living by selling himself to older men for sex.

"How you doing Colin, how's business?" Joe said, now relaxed again.

"Well you know how it is Mr. Docker – people 'come' and then they go," Colin laughed at his own joke, "I'm no butter fingers Mr. Docker – you know me I always hold onto everything tight!" he laughed again.

Joe wasn't keen on spending too long in the public gaze speaking to Colin. "I've got some business to do here Colin perhaps I'll see you around later."

"I'm off to a party later with a few of the 'old queens' but I'm free now Mr. Docker. You know you can rely on me," Colin winked and brushed his hand against Joes.

Joe hovered at the top of the steps of the pub not knowing that his daughter was in deep conversation less than fifty feet away from him, living, breathing, and happy.

Joe's brain told him to get a grip and to get on with his work but his dick told him otherwise, and like always it won the argument.

Joe gave in, like he always did on this one issue, "I've got fifteen minutes Colin, so it's going to have to be rough-and-ready. Let's find somewhere by Station Street." They walked off.

Twenty-five minutes later he was back in his office, not particularly proud of himself, but needs must. This was part of his life that Sandra knew nothing about and never would. He had decided to make a couple of phone calls before doing the rounds of the pubs.

Minutes later he heard the sound of an explosion.

Joe spoke to his staff to reassure them and then phoned Sandra, "Summat's going on near here. I'm just phoning to say I'm okay so no need to worry bab. When I know the score I'll give you another call."

Sandra blurted out, "Hope is in Birmingham Joe. I dropped her at the train station to visit friends. What if summat has happened to her?"

"Don't worry bab I'll find her." Joe soothed her fears before replacing the handset.

Joe stepped out into the street and all he could hear was a discordant orchestra of police sirens. The world was going mad.

***

Graham stood quietly in his usual position at the end of the bar, nearest to the stairs, and pondered on the slowly decreasing contents of his pint glass. He was a solitary figure and that's the way that he liked it.

He watched with minimal interest as the young couple came down the stairs, a white youth, and a 'half-caste' girl. They were holding hands and clearly nervous – strangers who didn't quite fit. She made her way to a corner whilst he got some drinks before joining her.

'Young Love,' he reflected bitterly – a situation he was most surely not going to experience during the rest of his life unless he paid for it.

He went back to his drink and after a few minutes heard what sounded like a 'muffled thump' coming from the street above. Graham was well accustomed to the sound of noises in Birmingham City Centre and thought nothing of it until a police officer walked in and spoke to the staff behind the bar before hurriedly leaving again.

"Fuck me, it's like New Street Station in here tonight," he muttered to himself as the bar staff huddled together in hushed conversation.

Graham was a Special Branch informant for his sins and had been tasked with getting around his usual haunts in the city-centre. *'Eyes and Ears'* his handler had said, which meant absolutely fuck all to Graham and so far all that had attracted his attention was love's young dream over there.

At that moment the bomb exploded.

Graham was blown against a wall by the force of the explosion and, as he lay stunned, his brain registered the screams of a young female. As the ceiling collapsed around him and the room descended into darkness he staggered dazed and aimlessly amongst the rubble.

He felt the warm trickle of blood from a head wound, blood that entered his mouth and added to a sense of asphyxiation and panic. As he stumbled towards where he thought the stairs were he found that most of the stairway had been destroyed. There was no other way out. He was trapped and at this point one of his legs gave way as the fractured bones refused to support him any further.

Graham lay there listening to the screams around him and was hit by the overwhelming smell of burning flesh, as exposed electric cables sparked here and there.

For a short period Graham found peace, as he hovered in and out of consciousness, and in those moments his brain took him back to his childhood and happier times. The screams were no longer so intense but the pain of the injured remained all around him. For a moment in the dusty haze he imagined that he could see the young lad still holding onto the hand of the girl. She was quiet now.

Next to him lay a severed limb, but the meaning of it refused to fight its way through the constant pain in his head.

After what seemed an age he saw figures emerge through the haze from the destroyed steps and watched as they picked their way carefully through the devastation, torches sending out small rays of light, small rays of hope. He could hear the shouts of a young man screaming for help.

Eventually he was lifted onto the top of a broken table and four rescuers struggled to get him to the surface. Sweating profusely, and with blood and dust on their hands and clothing, they finally placed him on the ground in the street outside. He prayed for the first time in years that he would live.

Yards away from him, the remnants of a destroyed West Midlands bus added to the sense of complete carnage.

They carried him to a nearby hotel where eventually a couple of ambulance- men placed him on a stretcher, and released him from his pain with a morphine injection.

***

A bright light filled the room and everything went into slow motion. Sean's ears were filled with sudden pressure and although Hope was screaming in front of him he could hear nothing as both eardrums perforated. As she clung to him a layer of white dust enveloped them and Sean was struck in the face, at which point he entered a world of darkness.

Sean managed not to let go of the hand that still gripped his but the only sense left to him was that of smell – the smell of death as the ceiling collapsed around them. At that moment Hope's hold on life hung in the balance.

***

The Mulberry Bush pub was situated on the lower two floors of the twenty-five storey Rotunda office block. At 2017 hours a bomb planted in a bag exploded in the premises killing ten people. A section of the roof collapsed and a large hole was blown in the floor by the force of the explosion.

The Tavern in the Town pub was a basement-pub in New Street directly beneath the Tax Office. At 2027 hours a bomb planted in a bag exploded in the premises killing nine people at the time, with a further two people subsequently succumbing to their injuries.

With twenty-one deaths, and one hundred and eighty two people injured, many of them seriously; the people of Birmingham faced a terrorist outrage of huge proportions. One man lost both legs, whilst another woman was blinded by shrapnel. The majority of the casualties were aged between seventeen years to thirty years. One couple were on their first date.

***

Adrian Nelson had been a Police Constable with the British Transport Police for some years and working at New Street Station he was very familiar with the ebb and flow of crowds of people as they passed, in the main anonymously, through the railway station. He was a large man, fearless in a fight, but he also had a serious and sensitive side to him. He was a 'coppers copper' and proud to wear the uniform that his father before him had also worn.

On Thursday 21 November 1974 the BTP Police Office at New Street was busy, as a training course was being run to improve the chances of officers who were trying to get through promotion examinations. With just one window in the whole of the office the place was like working in a claustrophobic underground bunker but on this night it was a safe place to be.

Adrian went down to the station booking office, to sign for some papers, and on the way back stopped to speak to one of his shift colleagues PC Don Raw, an ex- serviceman who stood ramrod-straight on the station concourse, observing the comings-and-goings of people arriving in town for a night out, and the office workers who had taken an extended pub-break before wending their way home.

On occasions they used to play calming music over the station tannoy system. In the mornings they used to play marching music so that people would put their best foot forward and leave the station quickly.

It was almost 8.20pm.

Adrian and Don were enjoying their general chat about the latest rumour that the 'railway police' were going to be taken over by Home Office forces. There were as many rumours as there were types of raincoat worn by the officers but it made for good 'canteen gossip'.

In that instant the Mulberry Bush bomb blew up.

Adrian and Don had already been exposed to the effects of the recent IRA campaign and on one occasion Don had suffered a 'near miss', having been blown off his feet as he struggled to maintain a safe area around the signal box as a bomb went off.

They turned and ran through the glass doors onto the front car park as a plume of dust, and smoke, rumbled towards them and up the side of the Rotunda building, rising floor by floor as broken glass spewed from windows onto the ground below.

The two officers instinctively ran towards the scene and were met by a swirling mass of chaos as the walking wounded were helped from the remnants of the building, bleeding and concussed, into taxis that had driven from the rank on the station to help.

Working with local officers, some casualties had to be carried, and before long both of them were sweating heavily, covered in blood and grime. As 'brothers' would they stuck closely to each other as instructions were shouted here and there from rescue workers. The fire service arrived and started to erect a tarpaulin in an effort to provide some dignity to the dead, and to shield customers evacuating from the Odeon Cinema from the shock of seeing torn limbs.

There was another explosion a short distance away and it was obvious that the target was the 'Tavern in the Town' pub.

"Come on Don," Adrian shouted, as the adrenalin pushed them on and they ran down the street towards the chaos. They had long since lost their helmets and both were tieless and disheveled.

As they reached the entrance there was barely anything left

of the steps down into the pub and they hesitated momentarily before plunging into the darkness and hell. Other people were equally bent on rescue as the screams of the living and the silence of the dead mixed together.

Don had a small torch with him, and Adrian clung onto his tunic belt as they moved cautiously through the wreckage. Twisted metal, broken furniture, collapsed ceilings and shattered glass. A broken, 'Happy Hour,' sign produced a touch of irony. They moved slowly and cautiously as other rescuers moved amongst the casualties.

Adrian heard muffled sounds coming from one of the far corners of the building and he guided Don towards the noise of pain and anguish.

They reached the corner and in the darkness found the remnants of an upturned table beneath which two people were trapped. One a young mixed-race female held her hand up feebly towards Don who instinctively held it gently as the signet ring inscribed with the letters 'BS' rubbed gently on the inside of his hand.

"Please help me. I want me mum," she wept as he tried to support her. In that instant she closed her eyes and died. There was no hope, as Don bowed his head for a moment overwhelmed by the futility of it all.

Adrian turned his attention to the young white male next to her, whose left arm lay trapped under a heavy steel girder. He was barely conscious and had serious cuts across his face and his eyes, but he was alive. "Don't worry son we 'll get you out. We won't leave you,"

Sean screamed in pain before shouting, "Hope please - speak to me!" He struggled vainly to free his crushed arm as the intensity of the pain gripped his crippled body.

Adrian cradled the young man, who would never be the same again, in his arms. It was the only comfort he could provide until an ambulance-man arrived, followed eventually by a doctor.

Sean lost consciousness as the fire-service battled to free his shattered arm before he was carried gently to the surface. Hope was carried alongside him still joined in death but soon to be parted. Sean could not see her – but then he couldn't see anything even without the heavy bandages encasing his head and eyes. He never would see again, and despite a battle to save his arm it was a battle lost.

In New Street, notebook in hand, the collar of her coat pulled up against the cold, Jane Smith stood with a photographer on the other side of the police tape. She tried to engage the officers who held the cordon in conversation but they were in no mood for polite conversation, leastways not with a reporter. It mattered not, she would get the inside story from Rob in the coming days. She always got her story.

Adrian and Don made their way back to the police office, searching amongst the rubble for their helmets along the way. Not many words passed between them during the five-minute walk, and the climb up the metal-edged staircase to reach the front door, which although normally kept locked had been wedged open.

Fred the tall 'skipper' with grey hair, but going bald, met them at the entrance, "Come with me lads." He coaxed them gently into the Sergeants Office, sat them down, and shut the door. Reaching down into his bottom drawer he took out three white teacups and a bottle of whisky. Three large measures were poured, as they looked at each other in shocked silence, "Take a drink – you can't do anymore for anyone tonight."

At that moment Don and Adrian no longer cared whether they were going to be amalgamated with another police force or not. In the safety of that small room they were not afraid to shed tears as adrenaline turned to shock, and hands shook as they gripped the white cups.

Many of the casualties never recovered from the trauma of the night and as the people of Birmingham rallied round, the Mayor set up a fund for victims and some were later sent to Spain to try to recuperate. It was a solid gesture but one which for many failed to remove the tortured dreams, and the fear of being in enclosed spaces.

Many miles away that night British Transport Police Officers would have a busy shift at Heysham Harbour as men were taken into custody.

In the weeks to come there would be a severe backlash against the Irish population in Birmingham, including beatings on factory floors, windows broken and petrol through letterboxes. Over the water questions began to be asked about who had scored the 'own goal' and why no warnings had been telephoned in.

***

Earlier, there had been a sense of anticipation in the Special Branch operations room. They knew that the IRA was going to target the city-centre but did not know the intended targets. The informant had been able to say the when, but not the where.

Rob had people out on the ground, and all over the city extra uniform patrols were deployed, but there was only so much that they could do without placing the informant in mortal danger.

Some of the city-centre pubs were unusually quiet and there was a palpable sense of fear in the air – as the saying went *'the police had to get it right every time whilst the terrorists only needed to get it right once'*.

Rob sat at his desk fiddling with his pen as he watched colleagues answering phones, poring over files, and updating logs. There was something about SB officers that he didn't much take to, they were a different breed to 'normal' detectives, and he was always careful around them.

He hated waiting for anything – the word was just not in his vocabulary. The minutes passed by and he knew that police officers had been posted to static points outside the city-centre to stop the IRA paying any form of tribute to their fallen comrade, prior to his flight in a coffin.

What they didn't know was that someone in the IRA had decided on a 'spectacular' instead.

They all heard the muffled 'thump' of the explosions from their office. There was no mistaking what it was and suddenly everyone went into 'adrenalin mode' and the phones started to ring frantically.

Two pubs in the city-centre hit – glass and debris everywhere, people in shock covered in dust, people injured, people dead – chaos.

Rob felt the urge to leave the office and make towards that terrible sound but that was not his role tonight – the uniforms would see to that.

The TV in the operations room came to life with the news as the sound of sirens from ambulances, fire engines, and police cars clamoured in unison.

It had been a bloodbath.

***

Quinn sat listening intently on the telephone at Defford to a familiar voice with a broad Northern Irish accent. Something had gone badly wrong in Birmingham and he was given specific instructions to keep all 'operational activity' to a minimum for the time being and to keep a low profile.

Quinn was furious but just about managed to contain himself. This had not been in the plan, and his friends 'across the water' had played fast and loose with him about what their real intentions were.

He put the handset down and went looking for Jenny.

"I could do with a drink," he said when he found her, "Where's Sean tonight. I haven't seen him for a few hours."

"He went to Birmingham in the car," she said, as Quinn froze.

Within minutes he was on the road to Birmingham with two other members of the Black Souls. Speed limits were ignored, as were the pleas of a lone PC who tried to stop them at a police cordon on the outskirts of the city. They simply rode round him, but when they got to Broad Street they could get no further.

Quinn found a phone box and called Jenny – there was no news and she was beside herself as every television screen in the UK, and half the world, filled with vivid images of the explosions.

Quinn gave instructions to his escort and they split up to check the hospitals.

***

Rob remained at his desk for several hours, calm and collected, as people scurried around him – an oasis of serenity in the desert of madness that engulfed the office. He made sure that 'All Ports Warnings' were sent out and that his colleagues in London, in the police, and security services, were kept up to date with developments. A convoy of interested parties was already making its way north up the M1.

He was provided with a list of the known casualties sent through by officers working liaison at the Accident and General Hospitals. He flicked through looking for obvious Irish names just in case they had scored another own goal, and suddenly two names caught his attention – 'Hope Docker' and 'Sean Baker'.

Rob managed to get a driver to take him to the Accident Hospital and kept a low profile as he wandered through the main reception area, and on into the adjoining corridors. He was a Special Branch officer there to see, but not to be seen.

Uniformed officers were everywhere, taking details from injured people, and loved ones – groups clustered here and there, hugging each other for comfort, tears and anguish in profusion.

It wasn't too difficult to find a black face amongst the throng of people, and even less to spot a man sporting a biker's leather jacket.

This was the first time that Robert Docker, Joseph Docker, and Patrick Quinn had found themselves all together in the same place.

Rob approached his brother first, "Is there anything I can do?" he asked Joe who responded flatly, "Unless you know how to bring someone back from the dead – No," and motioned towards a curtained off cubicle.

Rob stepped inside and saw the bloodstained sheet covering the body of his niece. Ordinarily she would have been in the mortuary by now, but they had just been too busy. He held her lifeless hand for a fleeting moment and memories of Rose flooded back to him.

He felt a hard object pressing into his palm and when he looked he was surprised to see a ring with 'BS' inscribed on it, a ring he recognised immediately. He didn't know why, but he felt a need to slip the ring from Hope's finger and into his pocket. An ordinary man would have shed a tear but Rob had always resisted the urge to be ordinary, especially where emotion was concerned.

Stepping back outside, Rob said to Joe without any trace of emotion, "I'm sorry for your loss but I need to go back to work. Call me when you're ready." Joe stared back blankly unable to comprehend reality.

Even through his grief Quinn registered the fact that there was some sort of relationship between the two men.

Rob turned his attention to Quinn who was stood some ten yards away, outside another curtained off cubicle, from which came cries of pain. Joe looked on with disinterest. He was already well aware of Rob's relationship with this man but now was not the time.

"How is he Pat?" Rob enquired – almost matter of fact, and Quinn responded in the same manner, "They're trying to stabilize him before operating. He's probably lost his sight and most likely one of his arms."

Ignoring the impact of Quinn's personal grief Docker said flatly, "It looks like you well and truly fucked up on this one Pat. This was the big one we needed to know about and we could have stopped it. Who is worse Pat, your friends or us? Killing women and babbies, what's left to do next?"

Quinn clenched his fists and felt the urge to punch Docker in the face but he needed to be with his son, and with so many coppers around he stood no chance. Even worse, he knew that Docker was right and he felt sick, knowing in his heart that the Black Souls had no doubt transported the bomb parts that had maimed his son. That trail led way back to Derry all those years ago, and a youth in a pub with 'One -Eyed Jimmy'. *'Tomorrow I'm going to think this through, the time to settle all scores and end it has come'*, he thought.

Rob detected the change, and it worried him. A Quinn with nothing to lose was a big problem. He too needed time to think, "I'll be in touch – I have to go – sorry." He put his hand in his pocket and the ring tumbled against it. He took it out and proffered it to Quinn, " This was on the girl's finger. Only one person could have put it there. I'm getting a bit sick of giving you this fucking ring back all the time - its nothing but bad luck."

Rob turned and walked away, not wishing to be seen talking to this man for too long in public. He never realized how close to death he had come a moment previously.

It was most unusual for Rob to be sorry about anything and those few words to the two men were the most that he could offer. He had no plans to take on the grief of others – he had more than enough of his own to live with every day.

Rob went back to the office, continued working until the early hours, and then went home to snatch four hours sleep before returning to work. Typically, he found Lilian sound asleep with not a clue in the world about what was going on around her. He didn't feel inclined to wake her and was out of the house again before she was inhaling her first cigarette of the day. In truth he detested this empty woman and resented the happiness that Joe had found with Sandra, the woman who should have been his.

***

PC Stuart Edgar was travelling on the top deck of a Midland Red bus back from Elmdon into Birmingham City Centre, as the bus-load of anxious officers around him worried about loved ones who might have been out on the town in Birmingham. Stuart had no-one to worry about in this regard but harboured the same resentment for the Irish men, and women, who had brought carnage to their streets. As the bus passed Digbeth Police Station he observed a column of row after row of police officers marching up towards the Rotunda in the half-light. It was like a scene from the 'blitz'.

To his surprise Stuart was stood down to return for an early shift next day, whilst others were posted for hours on static cordon lines, surveying the sheer scale of death and destruction with disbelief. He didn't want to go home; he wanted to do his job and to be there to do his duty.

Stuart left some of his kit and uniform in his locker before picking up a catapult and some steel ball bearings he had confiscated from a young tear-away a few days previously. The contents of his locker would have been of interest to the Complaints and Discipline Department but PC Edgar was a careful individual.

Driving home in the early hours in the darkness, he knew well the locations of some of the Irish pubs and he chose his targets carefully. A few more broken windows to add to the list in the next twenty-four-hours would make no difference as the backlash against the one hundred thousand strong Birmingham Irish community started to take hold.

Six people, who later became known as the 'Birmingham Six' had been arrested.

A week later the Prevention of Terrorism Act was passed in Parliament. And the lives of three men were about to unravel.

Chapter Forty One: 'Takin Care Of Business'

(Bachman-Turner Overdrive)

1974

Rob sat next to Lilian at Hope's funeral. Whilst only six inches separated them it could just as easily have been six miles. The church was full of sobbing, distraught youngsters, there to grieve and say goodbye to their friend.

Rob felt cold and shivered, *'some fucker's just walked over me grave,'* he thought.

Joe caught Rob's eye at the end of the service and they had a few moments face-to-face at the rear of the empty church.

Joe was in no mood for pleasantries, "I want to see you and it won't wait so don't fuck me about. It won't be in your interests to ignore me any longer, so I suggest that we agree a time and a place – and just you and me, none of your tricks."

Two days later they sat uncomfortably, side by side on a bench in the middle of Cannon Hill Park, next to the lake. Set in an area covering some two hundred and fifty acres, and the most popular park in Birmingham, there were plenty of places to put some distance between them and prying eyes, and ears.

"I've got ten minutes Joe – say what you need to say," Rob tried to take control.

Joe looked at his brother with pure contempt, "For years I tried to protect your sorry ass and you turned away from me because of a girl, and the colour of me skin. You're pathetic."

Rob recoiled – this was a new Joe.

"I won't allow the bastards who killed me daughter to get away with it. They'll pay and you are going to help me," demanded Joe.

Rob gathered himself, "I can't help you Joe, it's out of me league."

Joe parried, "Don't try and fucking soft soap me you cunt. I'm not here for a debate. You'll help me, not cause you're me brother, which should be the reason if you had a shred of decency and honour, but because you're a survivor. It's something we both share." Joe slid a folded A4 envelope from within his jacket and pressed it into Rob's hands.

Joe spoke calmly, "Have a look Rob. In fact keep it. It's only a copy; it's just a taster of what I can bring down around your ears if you refuse. I should think that you would be looking at about a twenty-stretch easy. How long do you think that you would last in prison Rob? Deny me and I'll take you all the way to the fucking cleaners."

As Rob opened the envelope Joe reflected on how that fat bastard Malcolm Reid had really come good in the end.

Rob Docker remained outwardly calm as he digested the contents but inside his stomach was churning like a washing machine, and he felt physically sick. It wouldn't do to start gagging in front of his brother though – he needed to fight the feeling.

Joe was now firmly in the driver's seat, "Rob. I ain't asking you to think about it. You'll get me the names of the IRA people involved in this. I don't care how you do it and I don't give a shit what part they played. They're all going to pay. The original papers I have are where you can't get at them, in a bank box. He shook his keys. You can have them when the job's finished."

Joe continued talking – ranting, as Rob listened impassively, mind racing. He wasn't holding any cards, and for now accepted defeat. The way Joe was talking worried him. His twin was clearly capable of anything right now, including carrying out his threat.

Joe concluded, "I know the circles you move in and some of the bastards you have in tow. You're gonna help me to get rid of the people who killed me daughter. It's not finished until I say it's finished."

They walked off in different directions but with one purpose.

***

Rob had not made much progress with his twin's request, and the fear of exposure was beginning to dominate his waking moments, when, at the beginning of January 1975, an opportunity presented itself. It came from an unexpected quarter, and Rob was to make the most of it.

One of his senior officers was a dour individual who smiled only when he had 'wind' and looked down on most 'normal' police officers as being lesser beings. He was vetted to the highest level and had access to state secrets. He was a powerful man and he intended to remain so, hence his propensity for a little too much alcohol had been successfully hidden from the people in London who would have taken action to address the risk.

As an inspector, Rob was required to take his turn at staffing the Special Branch operations room at Headquarters, but as all the staff had been working flat-out after the bombings he was operating with just a skeleton team. His boss had reluctantly allowed officers with families to take some time-off over Christmas, and New Year, but they would soon be back to twelve-hour days.

The senior officer had been in a briefing in his secure office all afternoon, together with other senior officers from the Force, and some other 'faceless' individuals whom Rob did not know. After the latter had left, the former had their own intimate 'debrief' where the contents of two bottles of good malt whisky were consumed. A celebration; the usual sign of a good result.

One by one the gang of cronies that ran things left the office until finally the man was on his own with just his thoughts, and another half bottle that needed to be finished. Just one more hour and he would be off home. He didn't have far to drive and was well able to function with a good drink inside him – in fact in his opinion he was a better driver for it.

Having assessed his condition, his staff knew better, and being loyal, two officers took him and his vehicle home They would receive their thanks in due course once the date for their personal career reviews came round. In any event this was not the first time that they had played the part of taxi-drivers for senior officers, and they knew the score. What happened in the office stayed in the office.

The remaining officer was duty-bound to stay in the operations room, to answer any hotline calls, so Rob was alone in the general office. He went for a piss, and as he passed the senior officers room he noticed that the door was slightly ajar, it hadn't been pulled properly closed and swung open at his touch. Never one to miss an opportunity, Rob went inside.

It was his lucky day; the safe in which secret papers were stored was open. The two officers had failed to notice when they had half-carried their charge from the office and the man himself wouldn't remember.

Rob looked inside and was gratified to see a number of folders marked 'Secret'. They could only relate to one thing, it was the only job in town after all.

Memorising the position of each set of papers carefully, he flicked through them to confirm his luck, and then set about photocopying the contents of the three folders. He put the copies into his briefcase and returned the originals to the safe.

He closed the door and spun the dial. *'Now we have the fuckers, and I'm safe.' He thought'*.

The next afternoon when he came back on duty he was invited into his boss's office, He felt a moment of tension – had his boss noticed something?

The man was clearly still suffering from the effects of a good hangover "I just wanted to say how well you are doing Rob - very well."

Rob nodded and smiled warmly "That's very kind of you sir – thank you. I appreciate your support. Can I get you a coffee or anything?" He stood there preening like butter wouldn't melt in his mouth.

In Rob's experience it was often what was implied, as opposed to what was actually said which was most important. He breathed a sigh of relief. The fool clearly thought that Rob had arranged the lift home.

Another favour in the bag, Rob was already busy getting ready for his next meeting with Joe – it was an important one.

Rob had scrutinized the copies he had made in the safety of his home.

He now had the names of the three bomb-placers and they weren't included in the six currently under arrest. He couldn't work out what was going on but he knew that where the faceless men from London were involved, wheels moved within wheels. This time however, once Joe got to work, their schemes were liable to come unstuck.

***

Rob met Joe in the park again. This time it was his turn to proffer a brown envelope and Joe studied the contents intently. Rob waited and watched the swans swimming gracefully on the lake, *'Serene on top but paddling like fuck underneath'* he reflected. He definitely was.

Finally Joe looked up, "I do sometimes wonder what your precious police force would think if they knew what a bent and corrupt bastard you are," he mused.

Rob countered, "I ain't got all day. I've done me part. Now what?"

Joe smiled, "Not so fast brother – there's the small matter of three people to deal with and then you're done."

For once Rob was confused, "I gave you three names...."

Joe was still in the driving seat, "You're in too far Rob – no going back now. Doing the job on one of these fuckers will have your name on it. You gonna become a murderer Rob – get used to the idea. Payback time you shithole."

There was a distant rumble and Joe felt a few spots of rain. "Hark at that Rob, a bit of thunder and lightning coming. I think we're going to have a storm."

Joe proceeded to outline his thoughts in relation to the bomb placers – three Irish women all living locally. He made it clear that capital punishment was on his mind and that Rob would not be excused from 'doing his duty' – the alternative was exposure and prison.

Joe went on as he thumbed through the papers, "We need to deal with these pretty much at once so none of them get wind of it and fuck off back to Ireland where we cant get to them. They're our starter for ten to get the others involved so we mustn't fuck it up.

Leave this woman Maureen to me. You can deal with this cow Bridgett. I may have to get help to do the third one. I'll have a think and get back to you tomorrow. By the way, these ain't enough to save your skin yet brother, one of these three needs to give us names, or you'll be up stream without a fucking paddle, and well and truly bollocksed."

It took Rob twenty minutes to persuade Joe that the answer to the third problem could be resolved with the support of Quinn. He was a killer, he had a motive - revenge, he had the Irish connections, most of all Rob had him, and Rob might need a card to play in respect of Mister Quinn. Involving him in murder seemed like a good start.

Joe finally relented, "It's done then. Speak to Quinn and get the ball rolling. I don't wanna talk to the bastard but I don't doubt he'll do the business. You'll find it easier to top someone than you think Rob, and knowing you I don't suppose that your sleep will be disturbed by it that much. By the way how is that bird Jane Smith that you were fucking, told Lilian about her yet?"

Joe was enjoying the sight of Rob squirming – he had him on the ropes and knew it. He could wait for the killer punch for now.

Meeting over, they parted.

Chapter Forty Two: 'Only Women Bleed'

(Alice Cooper)

1975

Rob's relationship with Liam had long since passed the point of being that of a police officer handling an informant, to one of mutual interest and survival. They had routinely embarked on criminal conspiracies that would see them both serving lengthy prison sentences if detected, and now they were about to embark on murder. There was no shred of humanity left in either of them – no saving graces to look for.

Liam was a Protestant and although not in the slightest bit religious he remained true to his origins and despised what the IRA stood for. He was part of Great Britain and proud of it.

"Her name's Bridgett and she lives in Sparkhill in a ground-floor flat on her own." Rob briefed Liam on the plan. In the early days of their relationship he had balked at some of the things he had been tasked with doing but now he understood that Rob had no limits and preferred to stay on his right side – besides he was going to get paid as well as receiving some side-benefits.

Rob arranged to attend a big two-day conference in Manchester on, 'the future of policing,' and informed Lilian that he would be away and not contactable. He never told her much and she didn't ask. She was past caring and as far as she was concerned it would be yet another excuse for him to go on a piss up.

He drove to the venue the night before, booked into his hotel room and then made a bit of a fuss about the size of it with the reception staff before accepting another one with good grace. He wanted them to remember him, and following half an hour in the bar introducing himself to some of the delegates, he made his excuses for an early night. *'Fucking boring bastards,'* he reflected, as he made sure that he had been ticked off the delegates list and provided with a delegates pack.

Rob remained in his suit, left the hotel and returned by car to Birmingham where he picked up Liam, who had clearly already had a couple of drinks for 'Dutch courage'. Later on Liam's intention was to get as pissed as a parrot. Rob frowned but kept the peace. This was a moment for calm.

"When we get there, leave all the talking to me." Docker instructed.

They drove in silence to the address - they had already changed the number plates on the car and time was of the essence for the plan to work.

Bridgett had not been expecting visitors, indeed she was something of a solitary figure, but the knock at the door was measured, with no sign of urgency, and she felt obliged to answer.

She found herself face-to-face with the two people who would be the last to see her alive. One of them had the appearance of authority, whilst the second looked oddly out of place.

Docker calmly introduced the pair after casually flipping his warrant card in front of her face and went for the shock approach;

"We're here to arrest you on suspicion of being involved in a conspiracy to cause explosions. You are not obliged to say anything unless you wish to do so, but anything you do say will be put into writing and may be given in evidence. Do you understand?" Bridgett kept her mouth shut and nodded.

At 5' 4" tall Bridgett was not about to struggle – she was a placer, not a street-fighter. She complied with Rob's instructions as the handcuffs were applied behind her back. She knew that she had been very forensically careful and was confident that they had nothing that would stick.

After this though, she would most certainly be on the first flight back home to Belfast.

Bridgett was placed into the rear of the vehicle, in the left hand passenger seat, and Liam sat next to her. "You don't look like a police officer," Bridgett remarked to him. She smiled weakly, not convinced that the 'all sweetness and light approach' would work on this occasion. She was right.

"You don't look like a Provo so shut the fuck up," Liam responded.

They drove into the darkness and Bridgett took the advice – her confidence began to ebb away.

Thirty minutes later they pulled onto a building site on an industrial estate in Wolverhampton and came to a halt.

Bridgett panicked, "What's going on? Why are we here?"

Rob Docker looked back at her and replied simply, "You can cut the crap, bitch. We know what you did, and we want some answers, but before that you need to understand that we're serious and that the rules don't apply here. Liam here is going to give you lesson number one."

"Jesus, Mother of Mary - what the fuck," Bridgett tried to scream as Liam forced a gag into her mouth and tied it tightly at the back.

Liam opened the rear door and dragged her by her legs onto the floor outside where he flipped her over onto her stomach. Before she could find the strength to kick out he was astride her. With one hand he forced her face into the dust and tarmac, whilst with the other he ripped her underwear away from her body.

Putting the whole weight of his body on her small frame he whispered into her right ear, "I've always wanted to fuck a good Catholic girl. Enjoy."

Liam was well versed in the art of buggery having been on the receiving end of it many times in prison. His animal instincts took over and within minutes he lay spent on top of her.

Rob Docker had looked on impassively. This was part of the plan and he needed to walk away from this with a name. It was a matter of survival.

Together they dragged the disheveled figure back into the back of the car. Bridgett was already bleeding in several places. Her eyes were wild – her spirit already broken. She had already lost the love of her life to duty, and now she had been unbelievably violated.

Rob tried to sound compassionate "I just need the name of the bomb-maker and we'll throw you out of the car somewhere. As long as you give us a name and fuck-off back to Ireland I don't care what happens. Think carefully Bridgett, are you going to give us the name?"

Liam and Rob stared at Bridgett as she shook her head vigorously.

The bag went on effortlessly as Bridgett shook violently and within seconds was fighting for breath.

The bag came off, "A name Bridgett – then it all stops"She shook her head.Three times the process was completed until Rob judged the moment "The name Bridgett – just a name. That's all we want."After what seemed an eternity Bridgett nodded – defeated.

Rob had been here before. He had a sixth-sense for that moment when suspects were ready to give up their secrets. "We're gonna remove the gag Bridgett. If you scream I got a gun in me pocket and I'll shoot you. Do you understand?" She nodded.

Bridgett was both physically and mentally exhausted. She wanted desperately to live and once the words started coming she could not control the content. She confirmed that the bombers had worked in a team of three, all women. Two placed the bombs and one kept lookout. Their instructions had been to phone a warning to the Birmingham Post offices as had been done previously, but the first two phone boxes they tried had been vandalized and then it was too late, the first bomb went off.

A man by the name of Dominic Joyce was the bomb-maker.

She had worked within the same cell and made the cardinal mistake of having an affair with him. In fact she loved him, but as with all men she had known he had ultimately let her down. The relationship had been cooling on his side but the bombings had finished it off.

They had been ordered to lay low and he had taken money on offer to move from Birmingham, leaving her behind. She had broken the rules again by trying to re- kindle the relationship but he had moved on, allegedly pursuing his true first love, fishing.

She thought that he was simply scared to death that he would be killed to keep his mouth shut and used the fishing as an excuse. He was the only link to those who had ordered the bombings. He briefed her, and she briefed the others, so they had never met him. The affair had been a major breach of the rules and he had been worried that they would be punished for the potential security breach. Now she was alone. She would not trust another man again.

She was right not to.

Liam slammed the strong clear plastic bag over her head again and drew the drawstrings tightly around her neck. The sounds of her screams were muffled inside the bag as she struggled to get her breath. Bridgett was not going to give up easily but with her hands behind her back, and secured, Liam only needed to maintain his grip and pile in on top of her to restrict her body movements. Rob looked on.

It was not a pretty death, and not a quick one, as Bridgett had the life sucked from her and her face contorted with the agony of gasping for any small breath that she could steal. Liam clung on for a long time – he had to be sure before releasing his grip.

Liam had done the groundwork, and they quickly found the open excavations that awaited next morning's delivery of concrete. Rob got out of the car and put a pair of overalls on over his suit before swapping his shoes for wellingtons.

Bridgett was about to become part of the foundations of a two-storey commercial unit as she was wrapped into black plastic sheeting and carefully placed in situ. Liam did the donkey - work and Rob watched as the body was covered with a good layer of soil. She would not be the first person to end her life in a concrete grave.

They changed the number plates, and after reverting back to his suit, Rob dropped Liam off at Wolverhampton railway station before heading north again.

Rob issued Liam with a timely reminder, "Keep your gob shut Liam. This ain't something where you'll just get your face re-arranged if the Irish find out. You'll be dead fucking meat."

On the way back he stopped the car in a quiet lane and vomited for several minutes. In truth Rob was disgusted with himself – he had reached the very bottom of the cesspit that enveloped him. He was drowning in violence and pain. Bridgett's face and her last moments stayed with him as he drove on into the night. He would never have got involved in this but for Joe blackmailing him – if it took every last breath in his fucking body he would sort the bastard out once and for all.

He arrived back at the hotel in the early hours and was

careful to access the hotel by one of the doors leading onto the rear gardens. In the quiet of his room he vomited again, showered and lay awake on the bed until his alarm signalled the time to move.

Breakfast was not something that he wanted to contemplate, but he needed to be seen and he was not the only pale face in the restaurant as a number of delegates nursed sore heads from the after effects of alcohol abuse the night before. Some of the twats were already looking forward to a liquid lunch after the morning session.

Rob had made sure that he had put himself down for one of the workshops, and played the part of a thoughtful police officer interested in management change, the formation of business plans, and strategic awareness.

These clowns were convinced that they were the next class of the ruling elite who would be able to make 'a difference' in society – he mused. Most of them looked as if they had never seen an angry man in their lives or felt someone's collar. It was pure torture for him, but not of the type that just hours before he had just inflicted, and he wanted to go home – even if it meant seeing Lilian.

He met Joe that evening and relayed the information. His twin expressed satisfaction, "That was a bit of luck, picking her first, it makes it easier with the others, don't need to get them to talk now."

Rob drove home in silence, fuming, and with revenge uppermost in his mind. His head was full of hate

***

Joe sat in the back room of the Fish and Chip shop sipping a Greek coffee from a small white cup, a glass of water at the side to accompany it. He waited patiently for Andreas to consider his proposal and to reach a decision. There was nothing moralistic about his offer – it purely came down to the brown envelope that sat on the table between them and the wad of cash contained within it.

"I need a clean skin for this Andreas, and I want someone who knows what they're doing. I know you can make it happen," said Joe to break the silence. As Andreas pondered the envelope on the table he looked at Joe and said, "You know Joe, death and money sometimes go together."

Joe looked at him puzzled.

"We have a story in Cyprus about three brothers who go to see the coffin of their dead father who is awaiting burial. The lid is opened for them to say their goodbyes. The first son is very rich and places one thousand Cyprus pounds into the coffin so that if his father needs anything in the place that he is going to he will have some money. The second son is not so well off but when he sees the money he feels obliged to follow suit and reluctantly places another thousand pounds inside the coffin."

Joe looked on stone-faced, "Don't start getting on me wick Andreas. What the fuck are you talking about?"

Andreas smiled, held up the palms of his hands and said, "Patience my friend. The third brother went to the coffin and saw the money inside. He wrote a cheque out for three thousand pounds and placed it inside the coffin before removing the cash. He said to his dead father, "Dad if they have money where you are going they must also have cheques so you will find this more useful."

Andreas burst out laughing at his own joke, "The moral of the story Joe is that the envelope will need to contain three thousand pounds – and no cheques."

Joe remained unamused, he didn't have time for this but he needed the man.

Andreas brokered the deal, "You English have a saying I believe Joe – 'let the dog see the rabbit.' Let us see if the envelope contains the right price shall we?"

Once the deal was done Andreas placed a bottle of Zivania with two glasses on the table, poured a hefty measure for both of them, and saluted him with his glass, "Joe I think that you have a bit of Cyprus blood in you my friend. You just don't give up do you?" The black olives and bread would come next.

Joe drank the measure in one and proffered his glass for a second. The weight was slowly starting to lift from his shoulders. The guilt that he felt because he had put his own desires first that night at the doorway of The Tavern in The Town, when he might have saved Hope, would stay with him forever. At least he could now see a plan developing which would lead to the destruction of the people who had caused her death. He would have his revenge, on everyone. Including his twin brother. That was all that mattered now.

"I want a clean job doing. When we've finished with the Irish bastards I'll double the payment for the next job." Joe felt the warmth of the Zivania in his stomach.

Andreas looked at him – he asked the question knowing what the answer would be already, it was, after all, just what any Cypriot father would do, "Who?"

"Quinn. Patrick Quinn. One way or another I want Quinn dead after we top the Irishmen. If it wasn't for that cunt, and his runt of a son, my daughter would still be alive today. After this is done I am going to fuck me brother up so good he'll be lucky not to get a life-stretch. I'm paying all debts this time. Are you in or out?"

Andreas almost purred, "Ma Fisika Ime o tapinos o sas doulos! – But of course I am your humble servant." He poured a third measure and already the bottle was half-empty.

Andreas was a man with a finger in many pies and they weren't all made of meat and pastry.

***

Costas was a meticulous planner and for two weeks adopted the profile of a Birmingham city-centre office worker. Travelling daily by train from Coventry railway station into Birmingham New Street Station each morning, and then returning back, during the rush-hours, he was to all intents and purposes nothing more than one more commuter, albeit one that apparently had only one arm.

Travelling on the same trains, morning and night, was his intended target, a slim woman in her mid-twenties, with long black hair and pale features. Unbeknown to her work colleagues in the Tax Office, Colleen was a fanatical Republican and had done her duty for 'The Cause' without any compunction or regrets. Her soft Irish accent, and Birmingham origins, belied the fact that she had blood on her hands just as surely as if she herself had detonated the bomb that she had helped to carry into Birmingham. In war there were always casualties and people suffered – it was inevitable.

Since then Colleen had been stood down by the higher command, and was now just another 'sleeper' within the city.

Costas wore a suit and a long black raincoat with the right sleeve pinned halfway up to signify the loss of a limb. To complete his appearance he wore a trilby hat, black-rimmed spectacles, and carried a seemingly heavy briefcase. It wasn't the most comfortable of disguises but he wanted to convince his fellow travellers that he was a man with a disability and was very careful to keep his right hand out of sight beneath the coat.

Each morning Costas stood on a windswept platform at Coventry station waiting for the train. There had been a station in the area since 1838 to provide workers with a means of accessing Birmingham's better job prospects, but Costas found the experience mind numbing.

His assessment of Birmingham New Street railway station and the daily commute was no better. In the 1960s the station had been completely rebuilt, much of it enclosed with buildings over most of its span. Passenger numbers were double that for which it was designed and it creaked, and strained, on a daily basis to deal with the volume; indeed in the early Seventies, marching music playing over the station tannoy system would encourage early morning commuters to leave the station briskly.

It was a great place to get lost in as its twelve working

platforms struggled to cope with the traffic, travelling both north and south, through the tunnels at each end of the station.

Costas had never seen so many miserable-looking people in his life, and it was at times like this that he missed the blue skies and warmth of his home country. All he saw was a sea of washed-out, and washed-up people grinding out a daily routine. In the mornings those that could get a seat in the grime-ridden carriages either stared rigidly out of the windows, or pulled their newspapers ever closer to their faces. This was an environment where people minded their own business.

By the start of the second week Costas was happy. Colleen was a creature of habit and stuck to her routine. No longer on active service, she was relaxed and showed no signs of being surveillance conscious. By Friday it was time for Costas to act.

Colleen caught her usual train in the morning and Costas carefully made a mental note of her clothing for the day. As she disappeared into the throng of people on arrival at Birmingham, and headed towards New Street, Costas made his way to one of the public phone boxes on the concourse and made some calls. It was going to be a long day.

At 4.30pm Costas waited patiently at the bottom of Corporation Street and soon saw his target moving up the ramp towards the station. He followed her from a distance across the shopping area, down the escalators onto the concourse, through the ticket barriers, onto the over-bridge, and down the steps and onto the platform.

Colleen occupied her usual position at the edge of the platform and Costas took up his position behind her.

He knew that it would all be about timing, coupled with an element of luck, but Costas remained calm. This was his job and he was good at it.

The seconds ticked by, but for Costas time stood still as he remained totally focused. The platform was filling up around him as people jostled for position. Those that travelled every day like Colleen knew the routine – they knew where the train would stop and where the doors would open. It gave them access to those precious seats.

On time the train approached to their right from the northern tunnel and headed down the platform towards the waiting passengers. People jostled ever closer for position.

Costas already had the middle-button of his raincoat open and timing it perfectly as the engine approached he raised his briefcase to shield him from view on one side, stepped deftly on Colleen's left foot, and with his unseen right hand pushed her sharply in the small of the back into space.

She screamed as she landed between the rails, and struggled vainly to get to her feet. As the train hit her Costas heard the impact of her lowered head striking the front of the engine and exploding like a broken coconut shell, before she disappeared underneath, the sound of squealing brakes filling the air.

People around him went into shock and hysterics as the reality of what they had just witnessed hit home. No-one was focused on the one-armed man who stepped back, also seemingly in shock, then wandered slowly down the platform.

Two minutes later Costas was occupying a cubicle in the toilets on the station over-bridge, home to the activities of many a 'rent-boy' in their time. He swiftly removed a rolled up nylon holdall from the briefcase and inserted the briefcase, his raincoat, hat and glasses into it. Knowing that the Coventry lines would now be blocked, his plan was to head north for Wolverhampton where he would stay with friends for a few days. The truth was that more Cypriots lived outside Cyprus than lived in it, and Costas was never short of a place to rest his head. No-one would ever turn a freedom fighter away.

As Costas weaved his way down the steps to catch the local train he spotted the British Transport Police officers on the track, and heard the sound of approaching sirens, as the emergency services responded to a report of a person trapped underneath a train.

The following morning he woke early, a little the worse for wear after one too many glasses of Zivania. Produced in Cyprus since the Republic of Venice ruled the Island around the end of the 15th century, it was his favourite tipple and had become a good friend during his EOKA days hiding in villages in the Troodos Mountains. As a remedy for dealing with the cold as well as being used to treat wounds, he always carried a bottle with him.

At the newsagents next door to where he was staying he picked up a copy of the Wolverhampton Express and Star.

'British Transport Police are investigating the death of an as

yet unnamed female who appears to have fallen underneath a train at Birmingham New Street Station last night. Police are appealing for witnesses but at this stage they are describing it as a 'tragic accident.'

During the course of the day Rob read a similar story in the Birmingham Evening Mail. It appeared that someone had done a decent job – a clean one.

***

Caitlin was sometimes called the 'Countess' by her family in honour of the heroine of W.B. Yeats play in 1899 inspired by an Irish folktale. The story goes that in a time of famine the Devil offers food to the starving poor in exchange for their souls, but Caitlin convinces Satan to take her soul instead. When she dies the Devil comes to collect her soul but God intervenes and carries Caitlin to heaven saying *'such a sacrificial act cannot justly lead to evil consequences.'*

Caitlin had already sold her soul to the devil but was not expecting redemption in any form. She had worked tirelessly for 'The Cause' and prayed for the day that British boots would be removed from the necks of her people and Ireland was united again. God did not enter into the equation for her.

It had been complex but not impossible for Rob to get Caitlin picked up based on 'intelligence' provided by a prolific informant whilst covering his role in the matter. He did not want his bosses in Special Branch connecting him in any way to what was about to happen.

Despite her protestations of innocence, she found herself lodged in a cell in the Central Lock-Up in Birmingham. Special Branch picked up on the arrest and there was another meeting in the boss's office to review the situation. Something was going on with their three suspects. Within twenty-four hours one was dead, one arrested, and one disappeared. Elsewhere, six men were awaiting trial.

It was complicated and the decision was made to monitor Caitlin's arrest whilst an attempt was made to ascertain what was going on and decide what, if anything to do about it. Rob sat in on the decision-making process – an observer watching his more experienced colleagues plan their next moves – something of a cuckoo in the nest, except it was he who disliked them in the main. It was past time for his generation to take over.

Built next door to Steelhouse Lane Police Station in the 1890s, the cell-block in the Central Lock-Up could cater for up to fifty prisoners, and its Victorian features created an oppressive atmosphere that pervaded around the whole of the building. The constant noise of keys turning, doors banging, and footsteps echoing on the wrought-iron staircases connecting three stories of open galleried landings, added to the sense of drama. The shouts of the 'damned' across the mesh-covered spaces completed the picture.

Female prisoners were kept in a separate wing overseen by women officers who ensured that they were fed and watered. For hours Caitlin sat alone on the wooden bench in her cell completely mystified as to why she was there. She was certainly guilty of something but not what they had arrested her for. Apart from being scrutinized now and again, through the cell hatch, and receiving an evening meal in a tin foil container, she was left to her own devices.

Her training had taught her what to do. She remained totally silent during an interview where she was questioned at length about some piffling theft offences she knew nothing about. Her silence clearly frustrated the two CID men questioning her, and she was not at all surprised to find an unsigned 'confession' had subsequently appeared in one of their pocketbooks. The bastards had well and truly stitched her up.

Caitlin was charged shortly afterwards, and remanded in custody to appear at Birmingham's Victoria Law Courts later that day, where police objected to bail on the basis that she might abscond. It was no co-incidence that she appeared before Joe's friendly magistrate.

HM Prison Drake Hall was located in Staffordshire and was formerly used as a residence for female munitions workers during World War II. In the Sixties it became a male open prison, but in 1974 was designated as a women's prison.

Caitlin had been remanded in custody for seven days, and was confident that they would not be able to hold her longer when she next appeared on remand. The evidence against her was clearly false, but she had kept her mouth shut as trained to do in case it was part of a plot by the English security services. She was not too impressed by the two large cellmates who dwarfed her, and who seemed to be enamoured of each other, but she endeavored to keep her head down, as well as her heavy Irish accent.

Two days into the remand Caitlin took her place in the

bottom bunk after lights-out in the evening, and prayed for the next day to come round quickly. It never did.

At 4am a prisoner officer doing the rounds looked through the cell-hatch and saw two of the occupants sleeping soundly in each other's arms in the single bed across from the bunks – seemingly dead to the world. Both were heavily tattooed, the letters 'BS' figured prominently on the neck of one of them.

Caitlin's body hung from the girder that stretched the full length of the cell. Attached to the girder at one end was a torn bed sheet. The other end was wrapped tightly around her neck and a chair lay sideways on the floor underneath the body. With a gag in her mouth it had taken the combined strength of the two to suppress her, and with the noose in place one of them had put her entire body weight on her legs until Caitlin had lost consciousness.

All hell broke loose in the prison – Caitlin had gone to meet her devil.

Back in Special Branch there was another meeting after which three files were no longer in the safe. Somebody, somewhere had been all over this like a herd of elephants – were our friends across the water protecting their own backs?

***'

A lucky man indeed,' he thought to himself as he watched the rod tips illuminated by his torch beam. It was a clear evening and the sky was heavy with bright stars. A full moon was coming up, bestowing a silvery sheen to St Catherine's Chapel on the hill behind him and bringing the Dragon's Teeth into sharper relief. It was the best fishing place, by the old tank-traps, but a long walk from the car park.

He exhaled and watched as the steam of his breath, illuminated by the paraffin lamp hanging on his home made shelter, whipped away in the wind. He loved it here, alone with his thoughts, the waves crashing in - the chance of a cod or two. He was untroubled by conscience. He had been a soldier. God and a just cause sanctified those things that he had done.

Now he had been rewarded for his years of loyalty. A tidy little sum to buy a cottage in Abbotsbury, a new name, and a regular income to ensure he disappeared and kept his mouth shut. He had been required to make just one more sacrifice - they didn't know about Bridgett and would have considered it an unacceptable risk.

Relationships on active service were frowned upon and he had feared for both their futures if it continued after the pubs went up. It had all gone wrong with that job. There were a lot of recriminations going on higher up, lot of nerves, and nerves made for itchy trigger-fingers in his experience.

No, he had done the right thing, told her it must finish. There had been tears, then anger, and they had not parted well. That had been the first and last time that she had visited him in his retirement. He shrugged the memory off, and thanked God for what he had.

He had chosen the Dorset village for two reasons, firstly it was the back of beyond, almost as good as leaving the country, and secondly the proximity to Chesil Beach. The strand of shingle ran for eighteen miles ending at Portland, and was a mecca for an obsessive fisherman.

Dominic Joyce was more than obsessive. He had learnt to fish in the sea as a lad in Ireland and never lost his love for it. He had to make do with lakes and rivers in The Midlands but always knew he would return to the saltwater. Fishing was his love and no woman could ever take its place in his heart. So here he was, alone, and, weather permitting, he intended to fish every day until he died.

Joyce was swaddled and muffled against the cold. He wore rubber waders, an oilskin smock and a woolly hat. He knew that he shouldn't wear waders here. The beach was steep and the undertow ferocious when the wind blew from the South like tonight. He would be okay though, he had no intention of getting them wet, and they were simply the warmest and driest option.

If you went in too deep though, waders could either fill with water and drag you down, or trap air and turn you upside down. Either way - curtains. He was a careful man and had set up well above the tide line. There were freak waves here that could take you away and there had been many times that fishing gear had been discovered on Chesil unattended, and a body found washed up miles away, days later.

It was a perfect evening for it. The day after a blow was always prime time for cod, high tide coincided with darkness tonight and he didn't even have to stay up until the small hours like in the summer. No, he would fish until ten then go for a pint before closing time.

He was surprised he was alone, but it was a work night, a

long walk and the wind was still fearsome, so it must have put people off. Joyce felt lucky again, *'no more work for me to worry about'*.

His stomach rumbled. He checked his watch, seven-thirty, well past teatime. He opened his sandwiches and was halfway through the first slice when he heard the crunch of footsteps on the shingle. He squinted into the gloom, and then shone his torch. There were sometimes some strange people on the beach at night but he had a sharp knife and could handle himself.

"It's Sean, Dom. Thought I recognized the set-up," came a voice as the beam caught the figure of a man.

Joyce relaxed. "Lovely evening it is. What's this another walk?"

"Yes, getting my head clear now," came the reply as the man drew closer, hands firmly thrust into his pockets. *'No threat here,'* Joyce thought.

Joyce had chatted to the man a number of times over the last couple of weeks. He was staying at a Bed-and-Breakfast in the village. They had shared a table in the pub and Joyce had been pleased to discover that they had a communal view of the world. He hadn't met many Paddies since moving down and had felt it necessary to keep his opinions to himself. Sean was a kindred spirit. Although from the North, Derry originally, he was a proper Catholic and hated the English and the Protties.

Sean had explained that he was having family trouble and had come away to clear his head and sort out his problems. Joyce had waxed lyrical about fishing and the beach and Sean had taken to evening walks and a chat on the shingle. He had even half-expected to see the man tonight after explaining to him in the pub the night before where the Dragons Teeth were, and how peaceful it was out there.

He gestured for Sean to join him behind the shelter."Any luck yet?" said his new friend.Joyce shook his head. "No but I'm hopeful, the conditions are right." They chatted as Joyce consumed his sandwiches. He screwed up the bread wrapper that had packaged them and knelt down, rummaging in his bag, "Do you fancy a coffee, or a nip of something? I've got a flask and a hip-flask in me bag," he asked.

Suddenly he was face down, the shingle digging into his cheek. He couldn't seem to move and his first thought was that he had had a stroke or something. He could see Sean's boots by his side and couldn't understand why he wasn't helping him.

Then Sean's face appeared as the man knelt, "Bit of a shock that wasn't it – a bit unexpected?" He spoke quietly but with an edge that Joyce had not detected before.

Sean disappeared from view then more weight came crashing down on Joyce's back. He felt his arms being cuffed, and then his legs were bent up - hog-tied. Joyce's brain went into over-drive, *'Was it the Cops, or worse had the bosses decided to shut him up for good'?* Then his wader's buckles were undone and they, and his pants, were pulled down past his bent knees further constricting his movement.

Joyce started trembling with a combination of the cold and fear *'Not cops then – was this Sean some sort of pervert?"*

The weight left his back and he was flipped over. Joyce registered that Sean was far stronger than he looked. A boot crashed into his stomach, winding him.

"Now we're going to have a little chat, and if you tell me the truth I'll let you live. Bridgett sends her regards by the way."

The words chilled Joyce. *'No pervert, no cop, his own side or the Orangemen then. Perhaps it was a test of whether he could keep his mouth shut'.*

"Fuck you," he spat out.

Sean responded evenly – this was a man in total control. He might even be enjoying himself, "I was hoping you might say something like that so I've thought up some suitable encouragement that I thought might appeal to a keen fisherman." He paused for effect, "Personally I don't think that you could fight your way out of a fucking paper bag but I've got a little treat for you. I've been shopping at the tackle shop in the village and got me some really strong line." He held up a spool, "150lb, can take a shark they said. I've also got me some matching hooks."

Sean walked off a couple of paces and returned with the paraffin lamp. He placed it close to Joyce so that it cast a pool of illumination over him. He bent down and proffered a wicked looking barbed hook, "See, like a fucking meat-hook. They even showed me how to do a strong knot; I'll show you." he attached one end of the line to the hook, "We can test it in a minute."

Sean went on, "All I want from you is one little name. I'll get it one way or another so this is your last chance before I give you a taster of what the fish feel like. I want the name of the bastard that ordered the hit on the Birmingham pubs and you walk away."

Joyce was mute, shaking his head.

"Ok then..." Sean moved closer holding the hook up and Joyce attempted to scrabble backwards, but he was too slow and Sean pinned him down by dropping onto his chest with one knee, winding him again. Once more he was pinioned to the ground.

Sean persisted, "I know you made the bombs because Bridgett told us. She also told us that you were the only one who dealt with the big man who ordered the job. You know what - we believed her."

Joyce tried to struggle but then felt excruciating pain from his groin.

Sean was relentless, "I've found me a worm to fish with. Now let's see about that knot." He stood up and walked towards the rod-rest, keeping the line taut. Joyce had to follow, inching his way forward like a human crab, wracked with pain as the hook ripped into his penis. The line was kept at just the right tension to inflict maximum pain without ripping the member completely.

"Have you got that name on your lips yet? No? Hang on, let's add some more encouragement." The line was looped over one of the rod-rests then Sean pulled down, raising Joyce's pelvis off the ground, suspended on the hook. Joyce hung there for what seemed like an eternity then the tension was released. The cessation of pain almost caused him to pass out.

Sean slapped his face, "Wake up dozy." Joyce's eyes focused once more on his tormentor, "Tell me. I'll hang you up there as many times as it takes and I've got more hooks and line. The next one goes through your balls."

Joyce cracked and blurted out hysterically, "I don't know the name, only a nickname. Everyone calls him 'The General'. He's a high-up, silver hair; I only ever met him once."

"There's a good lad. Not so hard now was it. Mind you I don't think you'll be getting hard again in a hurry." Sean stood over him and dropped with both knees onto Joyce's chest, crushing the air from him. Some life was beginning to come back into his limbs, but too slowly, and his arms were still trapped and cuffed beneath him. He couldn't move.

Joyce was gasping for breath due to the compression on his chest and he opened his mouth wide, consumed by terror.

"It's a bit messy this way, but the satisfaction is worth the risk. By the way I lied, you're going to die." Quinn spoke the words in an almost matter of fact way as he began stuffing Joyce's mouth full of shingle whilst at the same time pinching Joyce's nostrils shut, "I bet this is how they felt in The Tavern, gasping for breath, pinned down, dying slowly. You might be thinking what's my reason for doing this? My son was in there you bastard."

Joyce had to breathe, had to pitch the man off, but his legs had no strength, his head was gripped between the man's knees, he had no air, and was choking. This was not to be a soldier's death....

No-one missed Joyce that night. The next morning in the half-light a local fisherman discovered the unattended rods. One had a bend in it and the fisherman reeled in a decent codling. He looked around thinking that the owner had gone for a piss, or perhaps he had missed him sleeping behind the shingle ridge.

Three weeks later a dog-walker saw a bright yellow object on the beach at Chesil Cove, where Portland starts. He was making a seascape display in his garden and washed-up buoys were particularly effective so he set off to recover it.

The locals shook their heads and adopted wise-looks 'Newcomer, didn't respect the sea, the beach. Fancy wearing waders! Death trap, he would have had no chance.'

The local paper covered the story - yet another tragic accident. There was no enquiry, the crabs had been at the body, and Quinn had removed the hook. Anyway, everyone knew how it was on that beach.

Quinn had moved on – his mind already focused on other priorities.

Chapter Forty Three: 'Pick Up The Pieces'

(Average White Band)

1975

For once Rob sat patiently and listened. His mind was racing as he tried to work out how on God's Earth he had come to this point. How had he come to be in this car, listening to Quinn, a man he detested, being drawn into a murder, and finding himself engaged in a personal crusade against the most dangerous organization he knew?

It was the sort of stuff that you read about in crime fiction novels but this wasn't fiction – it was a fucking nightmare and he was living it.

Now he had to speak to his brother again - a task he didn't relish.

***

Devlin had maintained his contact with 'The General' all the long years, a double- agent feeding misinformation about the Black Souls whilst picking up scraps about McCann's operations where he could. Now he was making what he hoped would be his final call.

***

McCann entered the room head held high, projecting his usual confidence and arrogance. Inside he was worried. He had been the blue-eyed boy, chosen to run the mainland campaign due to the contacts and infrastructure he had built - Quinn and the Black Souls being a key cog in that machine. He had repaid that faith by waging a brutal and deadly campaign with no compassion for innocent people.

The Council had been divided from the start between those who considered themselves soldiers in a war, wanting to focus on military and establishment targets, and those, like himself, who considered terrorism the means to their political end.

Tension had ebbed and flowed with the mainland campaign but the bombings of the two pubs, with no obvious enemy targets and twenty-one civilians dead, many of them youngsters, had proved to be a step too far.

Due to the fact that Sean had been registered under Jenny's surname at birth Quinn was able to keep the awful reality of his son's disabilities, following the bombings, away from the IRA.

There had been a huge backlash against the Irish in Birmingham and major damage to the image the IRA liked to portray of freedom fighters in a war. It had been too much for the ruling minds to stomach. As a result the proponents of indiscriminate terror had lost the reins of power and McCann had become uncomfortably aware that questions were being asked – he was under scrutiny.

He had made enemies through an uncompromising stance during his rise to the governing Council, and those he had trodden on were always waiting for a chance to get even. Too much attention would spell trouble for him. He had some little business enterprises on the side that needed to be kept out of the spotlight. An investigation could cause him some embarrassment and result in a bullet in the head one night, followed by a one-way trip to the peat bogs.

The Council had decreed that all active-service personnel in the Midlands were to be stood down and tracks covered. There were to be no more 'spectaculars'. McCann knew which way the wind was blowing and conveyed an air of apologetic humility. He was assiduous in volunteering to lead on damage limitation. He would *'sort his own mess out,'* he said. That way he would keep prying eyes away.

Then his people had begun to disappear. At first he suspected the Security Services, then the Police, or Army, but his usually reliable intelligence operatives on the ground were keeping their heads down and the few that sniffed around found nothing.

When Joyce had been found washed up on the shore of a beach dead, he knew someone was hunting, someone with contacts and ability, and that he would be the biggest game. He could almost sense the net closing. Such a threat required an extreme answer, and he was the man to provide it.

When Devlin told him that they had found the killer and that Quinn could lure this darkie gangster to a meeting he had thanked God. Thus, he entered the Council meeting intent on being tasked to deal with the situation himself and found no difficulty in persuading the others to agree.

So it was that McCann, together with his cousin and trusted deputy, Brendan Muldoon, alighted from the Holyhead ferry and headed for Defford. He could trust no-one else to accompany him.

At the farm they met Quinn, Seamus and Devlin. He saw a flash of recognition cross Quinn's face when he was introduced to Brendan and mused, *'you don't forget do you? Even after twenty years. Too clever by far you are. It might be time to tie up your loose end too.'*

Quinn had last seen McCann's bull-necked cousin across the table in Eire on the occasion when the deal was struck to grant Seamus the farm - and Tony Romano's death warrant was signed.

For now though, all was bonhomie and they shared a scotch, Irish of course, before Quinn handed over two semi-automatic pistols. Security at the ferry terminals had been intensified following the Birmingham blasts and they had felt unable to risk carrying.

The Black Souls had plenty of hardware, after all it was a staple of the commodities they were importing and transporting, so it had been no problem to request that guns should be waiting for them.

"You'll be wanting to test these, get the feel. We might need to use them in a hurry." said Quinn smiling confidently, "We've got a range at the Clubhouse now – and I can show you around." McCann was initially suspicious, this was the first time he had entered the biker's sanctum, but he relaxed as Quinn conducted a guided tour, finishing at the twenty-five-yard firing range.

Devlin issued a clip for each gun. "Empty these, we've got

more."

***

Devlin drove. It was a Transit van fitted with seats in the back. McCann insisted on sitting in the front with Devlin. This was a high-risk day and he wasn't about to sit in the back of any vans. It was noisy and there was no conversation as they travelled to Birmingham. There was nothing to say. They all knew what was about to happen, they just had different plans for the outcome.

McCann knew all about Joe Docker now, except why he had decided to track down and murder the bombers, Quinn had deliberately kept that back. McCann intended to find out why, and whether anyone else needed dealing with. He planned a slow and painful death for Mister Docker.

Sat on the bench-seats in the back, Quinn and Muldoon faced each other in silence. They definitely had nothing to say to each other.

The meeting had been set for ten in the morning when the chip shop would be closed. They arrived at nine-thirty. McCann had insisted on arriving early. He wanted to assess the battlefield and choose the best ground. There was a reason that he was known as 'The General', he planned meticulously.

Andreas opened the door and ushered them inside, and to the back upstairs room, where Costas waited to fix the drinks, and to provide an element of reassurance to the meeting.

Quinn had successfully pitched the use of the Cypriots, and

the chip shop, as being a neutral spot. He had met Joseph Docker here once before, he had explained, and the man would be less suspicious of the venue.

The IRA had links to EOKA and were comfortable that there was no interest in the Irish struggle from that quarter; in fact they were more likely to be sympathetic having a history of fighting British rule. Quinn knew otherwise.

Joe was thinking similar thoughts as he cruised towards the venue in his new Granada Ghia. Neither his brother, nor Quinn, knew of his history of confrontation, then close collaboration with the Cypriots – or so he thought.

Joe was alone in the vehicle, having already arranged everything with Andreas and Costas. Today was going to be a good one. His hatred of Quinn had been channelled into an obsessive belief that Hope would still be alive but for the biker President. He knew that the Black Souls worked for the Irish, and that they must have been involved in the bombings somehow.

If he and Quinn had not required that truce meeting, Hope and that bastard son of his would never have met and carried on their secret romance. It was the son who had taken her to her death. She should never have been in The Tavern that night. No, Quinn was as equally responsible as was this 'General'. Quinn was going to pay as well – he had to.

Andreas met him outside the door and shook his hand firmly, "They're here Joe. There's two Irishmen, and Quinn. Costas is upstairs with them. He will be ready. There is another biker sat in the

Transit van across the road. He may have to be dealt with too." Joe shrugged. "We'll get him inside afterwards. It's just one more body to get rid of."

In an unusual display of warmth Andreas clasped his shoulders and whispered, "O Theos na se prosechi Joe – may God protect you."

Joe took the chance to order his thoughts – this was the moment.

He followed Andreas upstairs. As had been agreed Andreas returned to the front door to make sure that there were no unexpected guests and Joe entered the room alone. He had rehearsed Rob's plan in his mind repeatedly. It was complicated but should work - especially as Quinn had arranged a little insurance.

McCann had been told that Docker was expecting to talk, and that Quinn and the Cypriots guaranteed safety. He had swallowed the story, having been told about the long-standing truce between the biker and the black.

In reality, Joe, Quinn, and Costas would be on the same side. Joe reluctantly admired Rob's cunning brain, however Rob didn't know everything. Joe had arranged his own little extra twist in the tail for Quinn.

Joe had no illusions that the Irish intended to interrogate and murder him. He was the cheese in the trap. They had gambled correctly that McCann would want to find out his motive and whether there were any others involved.

As Docker entered the room McCann reviewed the plan. It would be four against one, Quinn having bought off the Cypriots on his behalf with a wad of cash from Eire. McCann always tried to stack the odds in his favour - it was how he had lasted so long. He had the buying power to outbid any other suitor for the Cypriot's services, including body disposal afterwards.

Costas would execute Docker before he could draw any weapon.

McCann had also been pleased that Quinn was part of the plan. He still had doubts about the man, even after all these years. Some primeval instinct told him that Quinn posed a danger, he had just never been able to pin the feeling down to anything concrete that would persuade The Council to allow him to take action. Today would bind Quinn even closer, another murder, another hold on him.

After this he intended to get his people to focus on Quinn and if McCann didn't like what they found the Black Souls would need a new President.

Quinn was sat at the head of the table. McCann and Muldoon were sat together to his right.

Quinn motioned Joe to a seat on his left. Costas moved subtly to stand between Joe and Quinn and slightly behind the pair of them. *'The Cypriot is perfectly placed to put a bullet in Quinn'* noted Joe as he settled back in his seat. McCann had the same thought regarding Costas shooting Joe, who observed that everyone seated had their hands in open view on the table so he did the same.

Joe allowed himself a moment to reflect upon the bizarreness of the situation. No doubt everyone in the room had a weapon concealed, and murder in their minds, and everyone knew that Costas would be armed, but with differing views as to whom he was about to shoot. Joe adopted his best poker-face, hiding the fact that he had several trump cards stashed away.

There was no space for ceremony, "Which one of you two Irish bastards is 'The General'?" he snapped.

"That would be me," said the silver-haired man as he leaned forward searching for something in Joe's eyes – some hint of his intent. "You've been killing my people for some reason that I don't understand. We have no quarrel with you or your kind."

Joe suppressed the desire to physically pull the bastard apart, "It's quite simple really. You think you're in an army, fighting a war, but really you're a murdering bastard, killing women and babbies."

'The General' shrugged and was deliberately provocative, "In every war innocents always die. The end justifies the means. What is that to you, nigger-boy?"

The silver-haired man's face cracked into a fatal smile.

Joe could suppress the anger no longer, "Because me daughter was in The Tavern in the Town," he shouted, and drew his gun, as he upturned the table and scattered chairs.

The two Irishmen were anticipating the move and drew at the same time as Quinn did. McCann had seen Costas ease his weapon from a shoulder-holster moments before and was confident that the Cypriot would put a bullet into Docker's head before he could pull the trigger.

Joe knew better.

He shot McCann between the eyes, as a second hole blossomed red an inch from the one he made. Quinn had made doubly sure.

Costas pumped two bullets into the other Irishman. The place was starting to look like a scene from a Mafia movie. Rob Docker's plan had come to bloody fruition. McCann and Muldoon both fired before they died but Devlin had given them replacement clips filled with blanks after they had emptied the real ammo into the range targets. A simple ruse and a gamble, but the odds of success were good given McCann's trust in Devlin, and belief that Quinn had stacked the odds in his favour by buying-off the Cypriots.

The Irishmen were both dead. Quinn and Joe both surveyed the carnage with satisfaction for different reasons.

"That went like clockwork," said Quinn. He knew it wasn't over.

Joe swung his arm around until the gun muzzle pointed at the biker, "Drop your gun onto the floor. Do it now!" he raged

Quinn locked his ice-blue eyes on Joe for a third and final time. Joe saw no fear in them, even at this moment of death - and was impressed despite his hatred for the man.

Joe felt suddenly tired, very tired, "The truce is over Quinn. It finished the day it was agreed only we didn't know it. That was the day Hope and your son met."

The shot rang out.

***

Costas received his orders, "You've got some tidying up to do, you've been paid three times for it so you'd better do a good job," he said indicating the bodies of the Irish, and then turned to the other body. "But first give me a hand to the car with him."

Costas called down the stairs and Andreas came up to the room, initially cautious until he realised that there was no longer any danger. He had seen blood many times before and he was impervious to the sight of the three bodies.

"Get Devlin to pull the van up at the back of the shop with the back doors open then get him up here." Andreas was not used to taking orders but responded without question.

Both men returned within a couple of minutes, "Jesus, it's like a fucking abattoir in here," exclaimed Devlin as he surveyed the blood spattered walls, floor and table.

"Give the van keys to Andreas. You and me are going to take our friend here for a ride in his car," said Quinn, indicating Joe's lifeless body.

Costas had shot him once through the right side of the head at close range.

Blood, God, nor money had been able to protect Joe.

***

Two weeks previously Robert Docker had done something that was alien to him – he had cried.

As the tears flowed he had been unable to hold back and had sobbed uncontrollably.

It had been only the second time in his life that he had found himself in that situation; the first following the untimely death of his precious daughter Rose, this time as he had reluctantly taken the final steps in preparing to complete the 'death warrant' for his twin-brother Joseph Docker.

Rob had allowed himself to admit that despite everything he still retained that bond which twins have from birth. He had reflected on how hard Mary had fought for both of them, how she and Joe had protected him from the bastard Richard, and how their lives had become entwined and estranged over the years, but finally none of it had made any difference to his decision.

Rob had been presented with a dilemma by Joe's decision to pursue Quinn to destruction. The last time he had met his twin the change in attitude, the aggression had been apparent. Once Andreas had informed him of Joe's intentions he had known that his twin had crossed a line and intended to settle all scores at once, including the many he held against Rob. Either choice incurred an unacceptable result, but one would have to be accepted, a classic 'Hobson's Choice'.

If he carried out his plan his brother would die. If he didn't, Quinn would die, which didn't bother him at all, but Rob would be exposed and spend the rest of his days in prison. He had no illusions how short and unpleasant those days would prove to be. He had put a lot of good villains away over the years – there would be scores to settle.

Above all else Rob put himself first, and the notion of sacrificing himself had not entered his mind. The tears had only come once.

He had crafted the Informant Profile extremely carefully, making sure that Joe's details portrayed a history of useful service, initially to the police, and more latterly to the security services, via his 'handler' in the police. Joe was a man who was portrayed as an extremely useful asset in the fight against the Provisional Irish Republican Army.

Rob had used all of his experience to age the profile, inserting real intelligence logs, and simply redacting details of the informant, or inserting Joe's pseudonym and informant number where practical. He had used different pens and inserted realistic spelling mistakes that were initialed using the names of different Controllers over the years.

The profile had also contained the payment record and signatures from Joe for payments received. They were signed using a pseudonym so it mattered not whether it bore any similarity to his real signature.

Towards the front of the profile a new intelligence log graded as A1 had revealed some important information.

'There is evidence to suggest that a number of key figures

within PIRA have been personally benefitting for several years from the activities of the Black Souls in relation to the movement of contraband and arms between Northern Ireland, the USA and the UK mainland. The main beneficiaries in the process of 'creaming off profits' are believed to be Dermot McCann aka 'The General' and his self-styled Deputy, his cousin Brendan Muldoon. It is further suggested that the money is kept in substantial bank accounts in the Birmingham area over which the informant exerts an element of management. The two communicate via a trusted intermediary (identity unknown), and never meet in person.'

By the time Rob had finished with his artwork the informant profile had become a substantial document that would withstand scrutiny.

Before passing the profile to Quinn he had decided to lay one more false trail for the IRA to follow. A known sympathiser worked as a cleaner at one of the main-line railway stations in the city and Rob had tasked an officer with conducting enquiries in relation to a briefcase purported to have been lost in the toilets on the station. The briefcase apparently contained important documents and Rob directed the officer to make sure that all of the cleaners were interviewed.

The fact that the briefcase did not in fact exist mattered not as the officer, eager to please his boss, did his job with some vigour. The cleaner reported back to his senior contacts in due course, as to the unusual level of police interest in a piece of lost property that apparently contained some important papers. A legend to support the loss of the fake profile had been created.

Rob had passed the profile to Quinn with the observation; "It's over to you now. I can't do any more – make it work otherwise you're gonna to finish up in a coffin, and I'll be in a cell."

It had been a simple matter for Devlin to contact his father and to hand over not only the profile, but also real evidence of theft from the IRA that Jenny had been compiling for years. McCann and his cousin had been siphoning money off. This truth cloaked the false profile. Both were laid before the IRA Council by Devlin senior.

Quinn had of course offered his services in resolving the situation. The rest was history. Quinn put Rob's plan into effect.

Andreas had been Rob's informant for years, and Rob had enough to put both Andreas and Costas away for life. Andreas' betrayal of Joe was made sweeter by the fact that he was paid for his, and the service of Costas, three times; by McCann to kill Joe, by Joe to kill McCann and Quinn, and by Rob to kill Joe. It had also allowed him to settle that old score with Joe – Cypriots never forget.

Quinn's back was covered. He emerged as a loyal soldier for 'The Cause', having terminated both the traitors and the man responsible for murdering the bombers. The IRA thought it was Quinn's plot coming to such neat fruition and had no idea that it had been Rob's plan of plans, his crowning glory.

***

The bodies of McCann and his cousin were never found, and nobody asked any questions about them. The Cypriots had taken them in Devlin's van to the farm where the pigs were well fed.

Joe was found in his car later that day in a wooded area near Cofton Park, the gun used by Costas in his right hand. The verdict was suicide. The police view was 'good riddance,' and a cursory investigation found plenty to suggest that Joe's balance of mind could have been disturbed by the untimely death of his daughter, and the potential risk that his sexual double-life was about to be exposed to the public. Even now, Rob's links to the newspapers were still coming in handy,

"Jane, I've got some bad news that will give you a good news story," he had asserted.

Rob's one act of contrition was to arrange for Joe to be buried in the Docker family plot next to their mother. No one missed the safety deposit box key Quinn had removed from Joe's keyring. Quinn had been tempted to use the file, but he knew that Rob would take Quinn down too, so gave the papers up once he had them.

Quinn had of course chosen the location of Joe's penultimate resting place in memory of Joey. He thought he could hear his friend laughing. The Angel's code had been followed.

Epilogue

A few weeks after the end of the killing spree, Rob made a phone call to Quinn, "I need you to tie up just one more loose-end to cover both our backs then we're done and I'll keep me promise."

***

Liam was feeling pretty happy with life. He had a nice little sideline going in selling counterfeit goods and was well off the radar of the local 'pigs'. These days he kept away from the temptation of drugs, apart from the occasional joint, and was getting his shit together.

His contact with Rob had reduced dramatically, and at last, after so many years of feeling like a puppet on the end of a string, he felt free. There were some things that still disturbed his sleep at night but his new girlfriend had just given birth to their first child and he was looking forward to being a dad. She had accepted him for what he was, and knew everything about his past. Liam was never going to be the perfect family man but he had started to outgrow the rotten life that had consumed his earlier years.

Liam had enjoyed wetting the baby's head in his local pub, and emerged at closing time somewhat the worse for wear. It was a chilly night and he tugged at the zip on his tracksuit top and pulled the hood up. He failed to see the car ease slowly out of the car park behind him and come to a stop in the roadway, engine running.

It had been some years since the driver had last seen Liam, but he hadn't changed that much except for a bit of a fake 'nigger-walk'.

Liam had just a ten-minute walk to reach home and he made steady, if not erratic progress, humming softly to himself as he went. At the nearby junction he stood for a moment to light a cigarette, inhaled deeply whilst looking up at the stars, and stepped into the road.

Liam heard the noise of the car's engine revving behind him and turned just in time to see the two headlamps blazing like the eyes of a demon in the darkness. He made an involuntary move to shield his eyes from the glare then bounced across the bonnet and hit the windscreen before rolling off and hitting the ground.

The car stopped and the driver looked in his rear view mirror, *'He's still alive,'* he thought as one of Liam's arms waved crazily like a bird with a broken wing.

Quinn put the car into reverse gear and picked up speed as he ran over Liam's flailing body again. For good measure he engaged first gear, moved forward and hit him again before driving off.

One hour later a vehicle was discovered by a police patrol in Worcester burnt out. It had been stolen earlier that day. Elsewhere police officers in the West Midlands were investigating the death of a man as a result of a 'hit and run' incident. These were not the days of expensive computers, and clever analysis, and the two incidents in different force areas would never be connected.

***

Rob Docker sat at home with a glass of whisky in his hand, Lilian had long since departed for bed. He knew that he was a disgrace to the uniform that he had once proudly worn, and to the many thousands of his police colleagues who battled every day to protect the innocent.

He had put some good villains away but it all counted for nothing. He recalled the definition that some clever graduate had put forward at the police conference he had attended in Manchester,

'Noble cause corruption is corruption committed in the name of good ends, corruption that happens in order to get the bad guys off the streets - the corruption of police power when officers do bad things because they believe that the outcomes will be good. Planting or fabricating evidence, lying in reports or in court, and abusing authority to make charges stick.'

Rob had played all of those games but what might have started out in his head as something 'noble' had stretched far beyond recognition – Rob was just as much a villain as Quinn was, and Joe had been, and all three of them had the blood of the dead on their hands. He asked himself whether it had all been worth it?

***

Rob stared from the fifth floor window of Force Headquarters and watched the traffic below. Hundreds of cars and people moving relentlessly like bees looking for their hive; going somewhere and probably going nowhere. His mood nowadays was routinely pessimistic – he saw nothing positive around him and was empty inside. He looked at the clock waiting for 'happy hour' to come for some temporary relief.

He kept his door shut these days, no more open door policy for him. He occupied the floor with a bunch of 'yesterday's men' and knew only too well that there was a queue of 'today's men and women' waiting in the wings to occupy their offices.

They were a different breed, these people of the Nineties, full of management principles, strategies, diversity and ethics. He didn't think that they were that different to him at heart though, most of them would walk over their own grandmothers to get on, they just didn't shed real blood. Each day as he passed the framed portraits in the corridor, of chief officers past and present, he was well aware that his picture would not be appearing there.

Docker's outside line rang and he answered with a single curt, "Yes". A voice he didn't want to hear responded. "I need help," said Quinn curtly. The conversation was brief and as Rob eased his Crombie coat on to stem the cold, he made a call to Special Branch and collected a trusted detective sergeant who had previously worked with him.

They drove in silence. Rob was not great company these days, and the DS knew that he was there just to make the numbers up, and to provide some semblance of authenticity.

Outside the house sat a panda car, together with two unmarked police vehicles and an undertakers van, the occupants of which sat munching on their sandwiches as they waited for permission to remove the body. The Ambulance medics had already left – they only dealt with the living.

A uniform PC wrote their details on a paper log as they

entered. Rob came face-to-face with the man he was not particularly keen on seeing again – Patrick Quinn.

This was a different Quinn to the ruthless man that he had known, visibly shaken, and almost normal. Quinn went to rise from his seat but Rob waved him down and said, "I want to see the body first. I didn't know he lived in Birmingham."

Quinn replied, " He never forgave me, came here to get away, looked after himself."

Docker made his way into the kitchen, and through an interior doorway into the attached garage.

Sean's body had already been lowered to the floor, the rope cut from the wooden beam overhead but with the noose still attached firmly to his neck, imbedded deeply into the purple skin. The blind eyes bulging, tongue blackened, Sean had not died quickly. The artificial arm had become detached and lay some feet away where it had fallen.

There was nothing pretty about asphyxiation and those dying moments would have lasted minutes, rather than seconds, as his body danced crazily at the end of the rope.

Docker recalled being on his Junior CID Course many years previously as a young detective, when some idiot in the class had reflected on how quickly someone would die from a lack of oxygen. No more than three minutes, the young detective had confidently asserted, and all over very quickly. Rob had persuaded him to try to hold his breath for one hundred and eighty seconds to see how it felt, whilst someone loosely held their hands around his neck. He didn't make it past halfway before starting to panic, and to gasp for breath.

Standing alongside the body was a local detective, and in the background a scenes of crimes officer busied himself taking photographs.

"Looks like a straightforward suicide sir," the local officer ventured cautiously. He was not used to seeing a detective chief inspector at this type of sudden death, and definitely not a Special Branch officer, who had probably not seen the sharp end of a body for several years.

Rob looked at him, wanting to strike a reassuring tone, "Any note?"

"As a matter of fact there is something," the officer passed a grubby sealed envelope to Rob which was contained in a clear polythene exhibit bag.

Rob paused for effect, "You seem to have done a good job and covered all the bases. I'm more than happy. I'll need to keep the note for the time being. Let's just say that there's a sensitive side to this enquiry. National interests that sort of thing. Just make a note on your report that I have it."

Rob turned on his heels, not waiting for a reply, and went back into the living room with the exhibit bag in his hand. Quinn looked up, "Come with me," Docker beckoned as he instructed the DS to remain.

Rob took Quinn to an upstairs bedroom where they spoke in muffled tones for several minutes after which Rob concluded, "This is the last time that we'll meet as far as I'm concerned. I'm close to me thirty years and I'll be glad to be out of it. Don't phone me again. Enjoy your freedom and keep away." Quinn just looked at him for a while, then nodded.

Back in the office Rob stared at the torn envelope on his desk and the single sheet of paper that lay on top of it.

Scribbled in hardly legible writing were the words, *'My father is an IRA killer. Look at the pub bombings.'*

Rob reached for the shredder button – the truth was best left buried with those who were not coming back. If anyone asked what the note had said he could easily make up something innocuous. In the event no-one did, suicide was the verdict. Case closed.

Quinn was out of his life for good, a problem that no longer needed resolving in blood.

Robs thoughts turned, as they did with ever increasing frequency, to the daughter that he had lost, and the daughter that he might have had with Sandra, but had also lost. He looked up at the clock – 'happy hour' thank God.

***

In 1992, Robert Docker officially retired from the police service having achieved the rank of detective superintendent. He went through the usual charade of attending a leaving do and listening to the platitudes of senior officers who knew absolutely nothing about the real Rob Docker and wouldn't know how to catch a cold let alone a criminal.

The supreme irony came when the clearly disinterested Chief Officer produced the Police Oath and insisted on reading it out. Rob wondered briefly if he was taking the piss, but decided that the man had done it just to fill up some space in a speech he didn't really want to make. He listened to the words that he had sworn in front of a Magistrate thirty years previously and couldn't help but measure himself against them, coming up with a verdict of failure apart from having locked up a load of bastards who deserved it, evidence or not.

'I solemnly and sincerely declare and affirm that I will well and truly serve Our Sovereign Lady the Queen in the office of constable, without favour or affection, mal- ice or ill-will, and I will to the best of my power cause the peace to be kept and pre- served and prevent all offences against the person and properties of Her Majesty's subjects, and that while I continue to hold the said office I will to the best of my skill and knowledge discharge all the duties thereof faithfully and according to law.'

He then suffered in silence as Lilian received her bouquet of flowers – the loyal wife beside her successful husband. She of course knew nothing of his years of infidelity – or did she?

If Docker had only taken a moment in his sorry life to notice, he would have seen quickly that she wasn't as thick as she made out to be. He might have been able to detect the moment that prisoners were ready to confess but he had never been able to see the look of real cunning in her flat, empty eyes. Lilian had managed to sponge off him for years and enjoy every minute of it, even more so after that first slap.

Life changed that day for good, as the emptiness that work

had held at bay reached into his inner-soul like frost spreading across the windscreen of a car. Rob worked as an advisor for a while but he held the business world in more contempt than he did some of his former colleagues. Nothing felt right and it wasn't long before his services were no longer required.

Once a month he met some of the 'chosen-few' in a pub on the outskirts of the city, well away from all the usual haunts. They put the world to rights and achieved nothing but to convince themselves that they knew best and that the means had justified the ends. In time they even managed to believe that all the, 'bungs and back- handers,' were a figment of other people's imaginations and that their crusade against crime had been a noble and just cause.

They started off as a group of ten, initially standing tall and straight, wearing suits for the occasion. Gradually, as time passed, numbers dwindled as the grim reaper took his toll and Rob started on the merry-go-round of funerals and wakes. It was the only time that his black Crombie coat and clip-on black tie came out as he lined up to pay respects with other men from the past.

***

Robert Docker woke up as normal at 6am. He had never been able to get out of the habit of rising early and had long since retreated to his own bedroom so as not to disturb Lilian, but more importantly to be left alone to his thoughts. A picture of his daughter sat on the dressing table.

He switched the BBC news on and listened to the usual stories of death, desolation, and destruction, driven by nature, religion or politics. It was the same everyday – there was simply nothing to be happy about, never any good fucking news.

Rob opened one of the curtains to survey the walled garden beneath a clear blue sky that was promising a good day to come. His collection of roses was in full bloom, *'about the only thing I ever grew,'* he thought.

He looked in the mirror, at the face of the man who had previously exercised such power. The face looked back at him impassively and then contorted as the tingling sensation in his fingers spread slowly through his arms, his chest, and his jaw.

Lilian Docker found her husband dead on the floor two hours later, already cold, the life had passed from him at the age of sixty-one years, as much a thief and a criminal as those he had hunted. She happily consigned him to the Docker family plot to rejoin his twin and mother for eternity, oblivious to the fact that if there was an afterlife there would be no resting in peace between the brothers buried there.

***

Assistant Chief Constable Mark Leary's next meeting, after the unwelcome duty of speaking the eulogy at the funeral of Robert Docker, was in fact with the operational head of 'Operation Hunter.'

Detective Chief Superintendent Graham Howard was a short, dour man, who lived with his team of undercover investigators in a world set apart from normal policing. Their offices were on an industrial estate in Staffordshire and to all intents and purposes they were running a recruitment agency.

"Well Graham, the bastard is definitely dead. I've stood next to his fucking coffin this morning, so unless he's Houdini he's now under six feet of soil."

"Where does that leave us then?" Howard asked, even though he already knew the answer.

"We're done I think Graham. We can't put dead men on trial and for the good of the Force I think that we should let sleeping dogs lie. It wouldn't do for Joe Public to think that we're all a bunch of bent bastards would it? Liam's missus won't be happy when we tell her that she won't have her day in court but that's the way it is. It took her years to pluck up the courage up to tell us what she knew, but this enquiry has already cost a fortune and chasing shadows won't help anyone. We may have been cheated from getting a result with Docker but at least we've seen a few others off along the way."

Howard reflected on the warrant they had executed at Malcolm Reid's home. The silly pratt had kept all sorts of stolen documentation in his garage, including a couple of scrap metal registers that had gone missing and had resulted in a case collapsing at court. For good measure he had also kept a diary of payments received from Joe Docker. The man had gone as white as a sheet when arrested for corruption and conspiracy to pervert the course of justice, and now spent his days mopping floors in the hospital wing at Winson Green Prison, trying to stay out of the way of vengeful 'old lags' who would be happy to rip the bent copper apart.

Then there was the bank manager Arthur Mason who literally shit himself and wet his pants, as the modern day version of Elliot Ness's men and women took his door off at 6am one morning. His wife was none too pleased to discover the facts about his money laundering exploits and the extra marital visits to saunas had tipped her over the edge. Arthur was unlikely now to be the beneficiary of her estate but in any event he would have had nothing to spend it on whilst serving his five-year stretch in an open prison, where he gave lessons on accountancy to pass the time away.

Joe's empire had certainly taken a battering as, one by one, the saunas and porn bookshops were closed down by teams from outside forces who had no local affinity and were simply 'untouchable'. Sandra had sold what she could immediately after Joe's death and retired to Spain on the proceeds. Charlie Docker had continued as licensee of the club and Joe's old friend Lloyd had taken over the business side. In the Nineties the Hole in The Wall had closed its doors and had been demolished to make way for a supermarket.

Leary picked up the phone, "Ask Steve to come in will you please?" and replaced the receiver.

A few minutes later there was a knock at the door and PC Stephen Long entered the room. To his friends and colleagues he was just 'Steve' but to the Black Souls during the last three years he had been the friendly licensee at The Star Inn in Pershore, still their local. The task of bugging the table used by the inner circle of the Black Souls had been relatively easy.

Leary pointed to a chair, "Steve you've done a fantastic job for which we're all very grateful. I'll be arranging for you to meet with the Chief Constable personally, so that he can express his thanks, but I wanted to tell you myself that we think the time is right now for you to come out completely."

Steve was not about to argue. Years of working as a long-term undercover operative had already cost him one marriage, and he knew that he was beyond reintegration into the police service in the normal sense of the word. He had witnessed the activities of the Black Souls first hand, at their worst, and when he felt that they had hit a level of violence which could not be exceeded, they somehow found the ability to hurt someone else even more. He was sick of it and desperately wanted to feel normal again.

Steve's supreme moment of satisfaction had come when a bulldozer on loan to the 'Operation Hunter' team had smashed through the walls of the clubhouse and scattered the men of violence to four corners of the room. He had reveled silently in that moment of success.

It was true that the Black Souls had survived the onslaught, but without their iconic leader, who was God knew where, and had been for so long he had become almost a legend to the bikers, an ageing council, and with a good number of men serving prison sentences, they were no longer a dominant force, and years of previous slow decline were hastened. Their funding and commodity sources had dried up, as the Northern Ireland Peace Process led to the, for them unwelcome news, that on Wednesday 31 August 1994, the Provisional IRA had announced a 'cessation of military operations'.

The links to California had been ruptured by a series of US Drugs Enforcement Agency operations, and a number of the key Madmen were languishing in jail. The Black Souls were fast becoming, 'small-time'. Jenny had departed a year previously and was last reported to be living the life of a recluse somewhere in the wilds of Cornwall, although the truth was, no-one was exactly sure where she was. Some thought she might have gone to find Quinn, but no-one knew for certain.

The three officers spent some time discussing the exit strategy for Steve after which he shook hands with the two men and left.

Leary stood up and looked at Howard "Steve will need a lot of support Graham. Once you've been on the other side you know how hard it is to get back. He's one of the good guys. We shouldn't forget that."

It was time for his next meeting.***

(Michael Layton & Stephen Burrows 2016)

Co-Author's Note This work of fiction has been eighteen months in the making. In seeking to create a fictional storyline, which would be credible, the authors made a conscious decision to include a number of factual incidents, covering a period of more than fifty years, which have been replicated in part. Whilst all of the incidents referred to have a historical context, some of them relate to natural tragedies, and others to acts of violence, and more specifically acts of terrorism carried out at the hands of human beings. The 'so-called' Birmingham Pub Bombings of 1974 are a specific point in question, and whilst the characters and story line are fictional, the authors are nevertheless conscious that this particular incident remains an unhealed scar on the face of Birmingham. It is also an ongoing personal tragedy for the families of the victims, who still seek justice and the truth to this day. Lest we, or future generations, forget, a memorial plaque to the twenty-one people that died in this atrocity can be found in the churchyard of Saint Philip's Cathedral in Birmingham City Centre. The inscription on the plaque reads *'The people of Birmingham remember them and those who suffered.' Michael Layton & Steve Burrows (2016)*

Acknowledgements

Our grateful thanks go to our three 'critical readers', Carol Dickinson, Bill Rogerson MBE, and Maggie Doyle, who volunteered to test the plot, characters and credibility of the story, and delivered their verdicts within a demanding deadline. Also thanks to Sign Local Ltd of Bromsgrove for creating the cover artwork.

PLEA FROM THE AUTHORS

Hello dear reader. Thank you for reading to the end of the book, we hope that means that you enjoyed it. Whether or not you did, we would just like to thank you for buying it, and giving us your valuable time to try and entertain you.

If you would like to find out more about our other fiction and non-fiction books then please search on our names on Amazon. We also have a Facebook Page, 'Bostin Books' and Linkedin and Twitter accounts.

If you enjoyed this book we would be extremely grateful if you would consider leaving a review on Amazon.co uk, (or the Amazon site for your country). To do this, find the book page online, scroll down, and use the 'review button'.

The most important part of a book's success is how many positive reviews it has, so if you leave one then you are directly helping and encouraging us to continue on our journey as authors. Thank you in advance to anyone who does.

Printed in Great Britain
by Amazon